D1483606

JAVA 2
CERTIFICATION EXAM GUIDE
FOR PROGRAMMERS AND DEVELOPERS

Java 2 Certification Exam Guide for Programmers and Developers

by Barry Boone
and Willam R. Stanek

McGraw-Hill
New York • San Francisco • Washington, D.C.
Auckland • Bogotá • Caracas • Lisbon • London
Madrid • Mexico City • Milan • Montreal • New Delhi
San Juan • Singapore • Sydney • Tokyo • Toronto

McGraw-Hill

A Division of The McGraw-Hill Companies

P/N 0-07-006887-9
PART OF ISBN 0-07-913740-7

The sponsoring editor for this book was Michael Sprague and the production supervisor was Clare Stanley. It was set in Century Schoolbook by D&G Limited, LLC.

Printed and bound by RR Donnelley / Crawfordsville.

CONTENTS

Contents

Contents

Contents

Contents

ACKNOWLEDGMENTS

Writing Java 2 Certification Exam Guide for Programmers and Developers was a lot of fun—and a lot of work. It is gratifying to be able to put many years of programming experience into this book so that others may benefit and become certified Java Programmers and Developers. But no man is an island and this book couldn't have been written without help from some very special people.

First of all, I would like to offer a huge thank you to Mike Kaufman. Mike is a Software Engineer living in Seattle, WA. He spent many long hours reviewing the code for this book, ensuring every bit of code is fully compliant with Java 2. Bravo, Mike for doing a wonderful job!

I would also like to thank the editorial staff at McGraw-Hill. It was challenging to get this project rolling and stay on track. We went through a lot of twists and turns but I think the result is a first-class book. Jennifer, Regina, and Frannie were a big help. Beth Brown from D&G Limited, LLC helped put the book in final form for the printers.

I would also like to thank Studio B Literary Agency and my agents David Rogelberg and Neil Salkind. Thanks also to Sherry who managed to straighten out last minute contractural issues.

Hopefully, I haven't forgotten anyone but if I have, it was an oversight. Honest.

Introduction

What This Book Is All About

To distinguish yourself from the growing crowd of Java programmers and developers, you should become Sun-certified. To prepare for the certifications exams, you should read this book.

What Does It Mean to Become Sun Certified in Java?

Sun offers certification in the Java language at three levels:

- As a programmer, which tests for a basic understanding of the language and your ability to code given a set of specifications.
- As a developer, which tests for advanced Java knowledge in putting together real-world applications using Java.
- As an architect, which tests skills for building and deploying enterprise applications and for the ability to resolve application design issues.
- When you are Sun-certified as a Java programmer and Java developer, your employers, peers, and friends know that you can walk the walk and talk the talk. It's not just you saying so; it's Sun, the inventor of the Java language.
- As you know, the Java programming market is red-hot. Companies are paying huge sums to programmers who can demonstrate expertise in Java. Consulting and contracting firms specializing in personnel placement cannot get knowledgeable Java programmers fast enough.
- As the Java market heats up even more, programmers will need a way to distinguish themselves as Java experts in an increasingly crowded field. Certification is your means of separating yourself from those less knowledgeable.

Why Use "Java Certification for Programmers and Developers" to Prepare for the Exams?

The exams are not free, and they are not easy. We know of a number of Java instructors who failed the test on their first try because they did not study!

It's best to have a clear idea of what you need to know before you plunk down your money and walk into the exam. After all, you don't want to fail, and you don't want to waste your time and money when you can pass the first time with a little preparation.

KEY CONCEPT: "Java Certification for Programmers and Developers" *helps programmers with a basic understanding of Java pass the Java certification exams with flying colors.*

Java Certification for Programmers and Developers is written as a study guide. This book explains the specific concepts and coding assignments found in the certification exams. It carefully separates what is and is not on the test. This book also contains complete practice tests and programming assignments similar to the ones on the exams, all with detailed answers, so that when you walk into the test, you'll know you'll pass.

KEY CONCEPT: *This book aims to make you a Java expert.*

In addition to helping programmers pass these exams, this book can help Java programmers become experts in their field. We cover important Java features not on the test at the end of each chapter. That way, even when the test does not explicitly require you to know a particular topic, you'll still learn about the topic in detail. After all, as a certified programmer, you'll be expected to be a Java expert.

The CD that comes with this book contains all the source code presented in this book, the sample questions, and many other resources to help programmers study for these tests.

Where Else Can You Go to Prepare for the Test?

A number of Internet and Web-based resources can serve as supplements to what appears in this book. McGraw-Hill maintains a wonderful Web site for this book at `http://www.pbg.mcgraw-hill.com/computing/`. Sun posts information regarding the certification exams at `http://suned.sun.com/usa/cert_test.html`. You can find the most up-to-date numbers to call to sign up for the exam and all the test locations throughout the U.S. and the world at this Web site.

Sun also offers instructor-led courses you can attend through Sun Educational Services. You can find these courses by following the Internet link in the previous paragraph.

And finally, William's company, Web@Work Studio Ltd., offers products and services to help you learn Java. Drop by William's Web page at `http://www.tvpress.com` to learn more.

What Should You Know Before You Start Studying?

We assume you already know something about programming in Java. This book does not teach Java programming from scratch; many great books are available on that topic. Just peruse the bookshelves at your local bookstore or visit one of the excellent Web-based bookstores, such as Amazon.com or cbooks.com, and search for "Java programming."

We expect that you know how to do things like write a simple "Hello, world" program and how to define a class with instance variables and instance methods. You don't need to be an expert to begin studying for the exams, but you should have done some Java programming before. If you're not sure you know enough to begin studying for the exams, try this simple exercise.

Exercise 0.1

For example, you should be able to invoke your program from the command-line by typing:

```
java Hello William
```

and, in the standard output, the program should display.

(We know that some development environments, such as Metrowerks CodeWarrior, ask you to enter command-line parameters in a separate window. Follow the procedures for your particular development environment when working through the instructions in this book.)

You might not realize it at first glance, but if you can write this program, you know how to do many basic things in Java, including

- Define a class
- Write a `static` method
- Work with an array
- Invoke a method
- Access a class variable
- Work with Java's String class
- Write a String to the standard output

Even though this list appears fairly long, the program itself can be written in four or five lines of code. The answer to this exercise appears at the end of this introduction.

The majority of test questions for both exams are quite a bit more complicated and trickier than this exercise, but the point is that you should already know something about Java before you begin to study for the exam. If you feel comfortable writing this simple program, you're ready to use this book to start preparing to become a Sun-certified Java programmer and Java developer, and win the accolades and respect that goes with these titles.

What Is Barry's Background?

If we're going to be spending some time together, you might as well know a bit about us.

Barry is a Sun-certified Java programmer and Java developer. He'll share his experiences in taking these tests in these pages. Barry lives in Seattle, but he travels all around the country teaching. He loves teaching. The thrill of working with students when they "get it" and understand a concept is always an exciting moment. Books are a natural extension of his love of learning and teaching, and he hopes this fun comes across while you're studying.

He is the author of two previous books on Java, *Java Essentials for C and C++* Programmers and *Learn Java on the Macintosh*, with Dave Mark. He's had some great conversations with readers since these books were first published. He has taught classes in Java and object-oriented programming throughout the U.S. In doing so, he's discovered what confuses students learning Java and what they need to know to get through the tougher concepts.

He's consulted and worked for Fortune 500 companies on object-oriented design and development for the past 11 years, writing many real-world applications that play a role in this book.

What Is William's Background?

William has over 15 years of business and technology experience. He is a leading network technology expert and an award-winning author. Over the years, his practical advice has helped programmers, developers, and network engineers all over the world. He is also a regular contributor to leading publications like *PC Magazine*, where you'll often find his work in the "Solutions" section. He has written, co-authored, or contributed to over 20 computer books, which are sold all over the world and have been translated in many languages. Current or upcoming books include Windows 2000 Administrator's Pocket Consultant, SQL Server 7.0 Administrator's Pocket Consultant, and Exchange 6.0 Administrator's Pocket Consultant.

Back in the early days of Java, William wrote *Peter Norton's Guide to Java Programming* and has been writing about Java ever since. One of his most intense programming projects was writing the *Netscape Mozilla Source Code Guide*. During the project, William had to swim through a maze of 10 million lines of code (and that was before all the wonderful documentation was available at `mozilla.org`). Two years later, his book *Netscape Mozilla Source Code Guide* was published by IDG Books.

William has been involved in the commercial Internet community since 1991. His core business and technology experience comes from over 11 years of military service. He has experience in developing server technology, encryption, Internet development, and a strong understanding of e-commerce technology and its deployment. In 1994, he founded and was CEO of Virtual Press, an Internet consulting, design, and publishing firm. During 1998 and 1999, he worked as a senior member of the technical staff at Intel Corporation's IDS New Business Unit at iCat.

He has an MS in Information Systems with distinction and a BS Computer Science degree magna cum laude. He is proud to have served in the Persian Gulf War as a combat crew member on an electronic warfare aircraft. He flew on numerous combat missions into Iraq and was awarded nine medals for his wartime service, including one of the U.S.'s highest flying honors, the Air Force Distinguished Flying Cross. He currently resides in the Pacific Northwest with his wife and four children.

How Is This Book Organized?

This book is structured like a self-study course. Each chapter contains sections describing

- objectives for that chapter
- the concepts for that chapter
- examples of how to use Java to implement these concepts
- exercises you can work through to ensure you have learned the objectives
- review questions
- the complete answers to the exercises and review questions to make sure you've learned what you need to learn

Java certification for programmers and developers is divided into three sections:

- The first section helps make sure you can figure out how an existing program works and that you can program in Java, given a set of specifications. These skills are at the heart of the programmer exam.
- The second section ensures you can use Java to solve problems, design a solution, and write your own code. These abilities are the crux of the developer exam.
- The third section contains sample tests and programming assignments you can use to prepare for the exams. These practice exams are modeled on the actual exams and are of the same degree of difficulty that you'll find in the real tests.

Java certification for programmers and developers covers in depth those topics that are on the test. However, if we only covered the material on the test questions, this would not be a complete Java review. In addition to becoming an expert, sometimes you just want to know about the other stuff, so we try to provide additional information where possible and will let you know that this information isn't on the test. This will help round out your knowledge of

Java and might even provide you with some insight into things that are on the test.

To help you reconcile the divergent paths of studying as quickly as possible and studying as thoroughly as possible, we've used a variety of call-outs to make sure you can easily distinguish between what you need to know to pass the exam, what is good background information, and what you'll be expected to know by your peers as you enter the world as a certified programmer and developer.

PREREQUISITES: *This book is a review of Java for those who have already programmed in Java, at least a little. We'll list what you should know at the start of each chapter.*

OBJECTIVES: *We'll list the objectives at the beginning of each chapter, and we'll repeat each objective as we cover it in the sections within the chapter.*

KEY CONCEPT: *We'll make sure the key concepts in each chapter are easy to spot so that you can quickly review a chapter and be certain you've gotten the important information.*

TIP: *Tips, advice, shortcuts, and tricks have this icon.*

WARNING: *We've given anything that can get you into trouble this icon.*

BACKGROUND: *We've also marked general background information, such as design issues and concepts, so that you can see more easily what you need to study and the background explanations that can help you understand why a feature is designed the way it is.*

What Do You Do Once You're Ready to Take the Test?

Once you've studied and feel comfortable that you know what you need to know, you can sign up for the test. To become a Sun-certified Java programmer, you need to take and pass exam 310–025 for Java 2. This test is administered through Sylvan PrometricTM. You can schedule an exam by calling Sun Educational Services or an Authorized Prometric Test Center. Part III of this book provides phone numbers to call to schedule your exam.

To become a Sun-certified Java developer, you need to first be a Sun-certified Java programmer. Then you must successfully complete a programming assignment and pass exam 310–027. These exams are also administered through Sylvan Prometric.

No matter where you are, don't worry. Test centers are located throughout the U.S. and around the world, so you'll find a place you can go to get certified.

Onward!

You're ready to prepare for the test. Good luck and have fun as you become a certified expert in the Java programming language.

Answers to the Exercises

Exercise 0.1

Here's a version that fulfills the requirements of the exercise:

```
class hello {
 public static void main(String[] args) {
   System.out.println("Hello, " 1 args[0]);
 }
}
```

This version is fine, but we can improve it by checking whether the user has supplied a command-line argument so we don't get an ArrayIndexOutOfBoundsException if a name is not supplied:

```
class hello {
 public static void main(String[] args) {
   if (args.length > 0) //safety feature
     System.out.println("Hello, " + args[0]);
   else
     System.out.println("Hello, someone");
 }
}
```

Whether you wrote the exact program that we've written is not important. What is important is that you should feel familiar with defining a class, writing a main() method, accessing an element in an array, and writing to the standard output. If you can do these things, you probably know enough Java to tackle this book. If you know much more than this, that's fine, too. Either way, we'll help you focus on what the test will cover so that you'll pass on your very first try.

PART 1

Studying for the Programmer's Exam

1

Taking the Programmer Exam

In this chapter, we'll introduce the topics covered in the Sun-certified programmer exam for Java 2 Platform (Exam number 310–025). As you study the chapters in Part I, you can refer to the exam roadmap to check on specific exam objectives. The chapter also provides tips for taking the Programmer exam.

What Is the Programmer Exam Like?

The exam contains about 60 questions and on average you'll have two minutes to answer each question. The questions consist mostly of analyzing programming snippets and identifying true and false statements about the way the language works, and supplying short class definitions and method calls.

For the programming snippets, you'll be asked a variety of questions. Do they produce the expected results? What do they write to the standard output? Do they even compile in the first place? There are three types of questions:

1. Multiple choice, where you select as many valid answers as are listed.
2. Single choice, where there is only one right answer from a list.
3. Short answer, where you'll be asked to enter a single line of code or sometimes just a single word, such as a specific class name or keyword.

The programmer test focuses on all the basics of Java, including classes, objects, methods, exceptions, threads, user interfaces, applets, and some of Java's core classes, such as String and Math.

What's on the Exam

Previous versions of the programmer exam had a wide list of objectives. For the Java 2 exam, this list of objectives has been narrowed to 30 objectives. Fewer objectives doesn't mean the exam is easier; it isn't. In fact, in many ways, the latest exam is more difficult. The Sun-certified programmer exam for Java 2 focuses on the core programming language and core API packages. The specific exam objectives are organized by topic. The topics and objectives supplied by Sun follow.

Declarations and Access Control

- Write code that declares, constructs, and initializes arrays of any base type using any of the permitted forms both for declaration and for initialization.

- Declare classes, inner classes, methods, instance variables, static variables, and automatic (method local) variables, making appropriate use of all permitted modifiers (such as public, final, static, abstract, and so forth). State the significance of each of these modifiers both singly and in combination, and state the effect of package relationships on declared items qualified by these modifiers.

- For a given class, determine if a default constructor will be created and if so state the prototype of that constructor.

- State the legal return types for any method, given the declarations of all related methods in this or parent classes.

Flow Control and Exception Handling

- Write code using if and switch statements and identify legal argument types for these statements.

- Write code using all forms of loops, including labeled and unlabeled use of break and continue, and state the values taken by loop control variables during and after loop execution.

- Write code that makes proper use of exceptions and exception-handling clauses (try, catch, finally) and that declares methods and overriding methods that throw exceptions.

Garbage Collection

■ State the behavior that is guaranteed by the garbage collection system and write code that explicitly makes objects eligible for collection.

Language Fundamentals

■ Identify correctly constructed source files, package declarations, import statements, class declarations of all forms (including inner classes), interface declarations and implementations (for java.lang.Runnable or other interfaces described in the test), method declarations (including the main method that is used to start execution of a class), variable declarations, and identifiers.

■ State the correspondence between index values in the argument array passed to a main method and command line arguments.

■ Identify all Java programming language keywords and correctly constructed identifiers.

■ State the effect of using a variable or array element of any kind when no explicit assignment has been made to it.

■ State the range of all primitive data types and declare literal values for String and all the primitive types using all permitted formats, bases, and representations.

■ Write code to implement listener classes and methods, and in listener methods, extract information from the event to determine the affected component, mouse position, nature, and time of the event. State the event classname for any specified event listener interface in the java.awt.event package.

Operators and Assignments

■ Determine the result of applying any operator, including assignment operators and instanceof, to operands of any type, class, scope, or accessibility, or any combination of these.

- Determine the result of applying the boolean equals(Object) method to objects of any combination of the classes java.lang.String, java.lang.Boolean, and java.lang.Object.
- In an expression involving the operators &, |, &&, ||, and variables of known values, state which operands are evaluated and the value of the expression.
- Determine the effect upon objects and primitive values of passing variables into methods and performing assignments or other modifying operations in that method.

Overloading, Overriding Runtime Type, and Object Orientation

- State the benefits of encapsulation in object-oriented design and write code that implements tightly encapsulated classes and the relationships "is a" and "has a."
- Write code to invoke overridden or overloaded methods and parental or overloaded constructors, and describe the effect of invoking these methods.
- Write code to construct instances of any concrete class including normal top level classes, inner classes, static inner classes, and anonymous inner classes.

Threads

- Write code to define, instantiate, and start new threads using both java.lang.Thread and java.lang.Runnable.
- Recognize conditions that might prevent a thread from executing.
- Write code using synchronized, wait, notify, and notifyAll to protect against concurrent access problems and to communicate between threads. Define the interaction between threads and between threads and object locks when executing synchronized wait notify or notifyAll.

The java.awt Package—Layout

■ Write code using component, container, and layout manager classes of the java.awt package in order to present a GUI with specified appearance and resize behavior, and distinguish the responsibilities of layout managers from those of containers.

The java.lang Package

■ Write code using the following methods of the java.lang.Math class: abs, ceil, floor, max, min, random, round, sin, cos, tan, and sqrt.
■ Describe the significance of the immutability of String objects.

The java.util Package

■ Make an appropriate selection of collection classes/interfaces to suit specified behavior requirements.

How Does the Text Map to the Programmer's Exam Objectives?

Chapters 1 through 19 cover all the objectives on the programmer exam. Like the exam itself, the chapters do not go through the exam objectives sequentially. Instead, the chapters examine specific subjects, such as control flow, exceptions, and layout managers. The chapters also cover subjects that don't have specific objectives. For example, the exam doesn't have specific objectives that cover java.io, yet there is a chapter on input and output. The reason for this is that you'll need a working knowledge of java.io to answer some of the exam questions.

How the Test Is Administered

The programmer exam is a given as a computer-based test. The exam questions appear on the computer screen one at a time. You can answer the question at that time or skip the question and come back to it later. You can also move forward and backward through the exam questions at any time.

The programmer test is administered by a company called Sylvan Prometric. They have test centers all over the U.S. and the world. When you show up, you sign in, identify yourself by showing two forms of ID (one with a picture, and both with signatures), and then you take the test at your scheduled time.

You can't bring any paper into or out of the testing room. They don't want you taking a crib sheet in with you or writing out test questions during the test. (Of course, once you leave the testing area, you can try to recall as many questions as possible. However, be aware that the tests are copyrighted, so you can't turn around, make copies of them, and publish the questions.)

You also can't bring in any pagers or cellular phones. After all, in this day and age, it would be a simple matter to have your local Java guru talk you through the test.

Even though you can't take any paper in with you, the people at Sylvan Prometric do give you either some scratch paper or a small marker board and a marker to help you work out answers.

How to Sign Up and Take the Exams

You must call Sun and buy a voucher (or get a voucher from your company, who has in turn purchased a voucher through Sun). The idea behind the voucher system is that your company may offer vouchers for free or at a discount to the regular price of the test if they are encouraging you to become certified.

The main number for Sun Educational Services in the U.S. is 1–800–422–8020. Listen to the options from the phone menu and make sure you tell them what test you want to sign up for. Outside the U.S., check out the Web site at `http://suned.sun.com/suned/` for additional phone numbers.

The good people at Sun will ask for a credit card to pay for the voucher. You've got to then wait for the voucher to arrive before you can sign up for the test. They send the vouchers by FedEx, so you'll get any vouchers you purchase by the next business day. Once you get it, don't misplace it—it's like money. You can't replace them and if you drop it on the street, that's that. Some random person can pick it up and go take a Java test.

The voucher is supposed to be good for up to one year after you purchase it. However, Barry's came with an expiration date set to seven months after the purchase. Voucher expiration dates cannot be extended, but here's the loophole. After you sign up for a testing appointment, you can extend the appointment for up to one year.

Once have your voucher, you're still not done yet. You've still got to register for the test. You can do this by calling Sylvan Prometric. Their number is 1–800–795–EXAM. (I know, I hate dialing by letters, too. The number is 1–800–795–3926.)

You'll have to give them your social security number for identification, and they'll ask you some questions, such as which company you're with, your phone number, and your address. Then they'll schedule you for a test.

When they schedule you, they'll find a time that's convenient for you to visit one of their testing centers. You need to be there on time, because you can't stay past your stop time; the computer will shut you off! What they do is distribute the test electronically to the test center where you'll be. According to a person I spoke with at Sylvan, you need to be there when the test is ready to go.

If they can fit you in the next day and that's what you want, they'll do their best to accommodate you. The only possible problem might be that a space is not available at the test center closest to you.

Just so that your friendly neighborhood Java expert doesn't show up in your place as a ringer, you need to bring two forms of ID, one of which must be a photo ID.

If you want to postpone for some reason, if you're panicking, or you just can't make it, you can do so up until the day before the test.

You'll find out immediately whether or not you've passed the exam, because the software that administers the test prints out your results. You need to get at least 70 percent of the questions right to pass. You can always restudy and take it again if you do fail, and since it's a difficult test, many people go this route.

Test-Taking Tips for the Programmer Exam

When you first sit down at the computer, you'll be asked to type in your test-taking ID, which is most likely your social security number (Sylvan Prometric will tell you). The test software will then ask whether or not you're familiar with the application. If you'd like, you can take a short tutorial. The test does not begin until you look at the first question, so looking over the tutorial doesn't take away from your testing time. If you're ready, then go ahead and start the exam.

What the Test Looks Like

The font is large and easy to read. Buttons on the bottom of the screen enable you to go to the next or a previous question. The program that administers the test is very friendly. There's a clock in the top right of the screen that counts down, showing you the remaining time. You can double-click this clock to see what time you started, the maximum time allowed for the exam you're taking, and the current time.

You can go through most of the test just by clicking. The multiple choice questions come in two types: exclusive and non-exclusive. The non-exclusive questions enable you to pick as many answers as are valid. The exclusive answer questions have round radio buttons. The multiple answer questions have square check boxes. In addition, a small message at the bottom of the question indicates whether you should select just one right answer or all the valid answers.

The questions that require you to type in a response have a single-line text field, indicating that all your typed responses should be short—no full class definitions, no algorithms. All you'll need to do is invoke a method or specify a class name. You should click in the text field to begin typing.

At the end of the test, after you've answered the last question, you'll see a list of all the questions and your responses. You can double-click on a question/answer in this list to jump to it and review it. There's also a little check box in the top left that says "mark." If you click this, then when you review your questions at the end, you'll see a little yellow square with the letter "m" beside your question in the question/answer list. This little yellow square can remind you that you had a question about something and wanted to go back to review your answer. If you have any incomplete answers, you'll see this in the review screen at the end as well. Incomplete answers have a red square with an "I" to indicate their incomplete status. A help button provides a good overview of what you're seeing on the screen. If there's a real problem, there's always someone you can call into the room.

Be Careful!

Sometimes a question is too long to fit on one screen. This is usually the case when the question contains a code snippet or a full program for you to analyze. If you want to scroll down, you might inadvertently click in the answer area instead of over the scroll bar. If that happens, check your answers. If you click over the same row as an answer, even if it's all the way over to the right, the test application recognizes that click and will mark the answer in that row.

Take Your Time and Answer the Easy Ones First

You have close to two minutes per question. Believe me, unless you fall asleep, you won't run out of time; you'll have plenty of time to read over each question and think about it.

Not all questions take the same amount of time. Some questions you'll answer right off the bat. Some are so easy you'll read them over a second time, thinking you missed some trick. Most take about a minute to answer.

If you get impatient with a long question involving a big class definition, feel free to skip it and go back to it later. You can answer all the easy ones first and then return to the more difficult or long questions later. All questions are worth the same number of points, so you might as well. Sometimes this strategy works particularly well, because a later question might contain the answer to something you were pondering earlier.

You might remember from your days in high school or graduate school that one of the tricks in taking the SAT or GRE is to eliminate the wrong answers first to increase your odds. That's a great technique for this test as well. You'll find some answers that are obviously wrong (trust me, you will). When you do, you'll be that much closer to picking the right one.

It's also better to answer a question than to not answer it at all. You're only marked for right answers; there's no penalty for a wrong answer, so you should always at least guess, rather than leaving something blank.

Beware of Tricks

Sometimes the test questions try to trick you. For example, a particular question might present answers where you should pick all the valid ones. For example, you might see a question like this

Which identifiers are valid in Java?

a) `max_num`

b) `max-num`

c) `3DogNight`

d) `star*power`

e) `(train)`

Since this question enables more than one correct answer, you might think that there must be more than one correct answer, but that's not so. In fact, only one of these is a valid Java identifier:

a) `max_num`

The rest are not valid at all.

Another trick is to present some irrelevant information in a question. For example, check out the following # trick.

Given the following preliminary specification for a class that will be shared by different packages, write the beginning of a class definition that indicates the new class' access control keywords (if any) and what the new class inherits from.

"A Satellite is a SpaceCraft. It maintains information for its orbital information, which is an array of six double values."

This might lead you to think your answer should look something like this

```
public class Satellite extends SpaceCraft {
double[] orbitalInfo 5 new double[6];
}
```

However, the question only asks that you indicate the access control for the class and the class from which it inherits. What's more, you can only enter one line anyway for short answer questions. So, the answer it's really looking for is simply

```
public class Satellite extends SpaceCraft
```

Both types of trick questions arise because the test is assembled semi-randomly from components in a question database. (The assembly of questions is not completely random, because the program that assembles the questions makes sure that there is not a concentration of questions on any particular area.) Sometimes there will be multiple answers for a question that allows multiple answers, but sometimes there won't be. And sometimes more information will appear in a question than you need to answer that question. Don't be fooled. Think about the question and give the best answer you can, not what you think the question requires for an answer.

Understand Why the Question Is on the Test

One great way to feel good about an answer to a question is to understand why it is on the test. For example, imagine the following question, given the following code:

```
class ClassA {
 public static void main(String[] args) {
  ClassA a = new ClassA();
  ClassB b = new ClassB();
  ClassA a2 = b;
  System.out.println("test() for a is: " + a.test());
  System.out.println("test() for a2 is: " + a2.test());
 }
 String test() {
  return "ClassA";
 }
}
class ClassB extends ClassA {
 String test() {
  return "ClassB";
 }
}
If you invoke main() for ClassA, what messages appear
in the standard output?
a)
test() for a is: ClassA
test() for a2 is: ClassA
b)
test() for a is: ClassA
test() for a2 is: ClassB
c)
test() for a is: ClassB
test() for a2 is: ClassA
a)
test() for a is: ClassB
test() for a2 is: ClassB
```

You probably have this narrowed down to either a or b. The answer is b. The reason is that the method that is invoked depends on the actual object type referenced by the variable, not on the declared type of the variable. Once you realize this, it's obvious why this question would appear on the test: it's making sure you understand this concept.

Know Your Test Center

It's helpful to show up early to get the feel for what the test center is like, and it can eliminate problems. I showed up about 20 minutes early and was told that my name wasn't on the list of test takers for that day. The people at the test center had to call Sylvan Prometric's "Hot Line" and ask them to download the test right then, which took some time. By the time this was accomplished, it was time to take the test.

Not all test centers are created equal. Some have 14-inch monitors and some have 17-inch monitors; some have Pentiums and some don't. If you're lucky enough to have a choice of test centers, call ahead and ask what their screen size is and what kind of computers they use. I'd say your first priority is a big screen, followed by a fast processor as a close second. Some questions (in fact, most questions) take up more screen real estate than a 14-inch monitor can supply. Long code snippets are particularly annoying to look at when you have to keep scrolling up and down. It's not tragic if you have a 14-inch screen; I had one and it wasn't debilitating, but having said that, the bigger the screen, the better it is. And the faster the computer is, the better. Remember, your test is being administered by a computer. The last thing you want to do is wait around for the question to pop up on your screen.

What Happens When You're Done?

When you tell the computer you're done, it will grade your exam right there on the spot. It then displays the percentage of questions you got right and whether you passed or not. You need 70 percent to pass. With 59 questions, this means you need to get 42 right (of course, this also means you can get up to 17 wrong).

If you pass, the computer will print a certificate, which the people at your Sylvan test center will then emboss, stamp, and hand to you for your safe-keeping. At that point, it's official. You're a Sun-certified Java programmer!

Sun's Take on Certification

In talking with a number of people at Sun Educational Services, including those responsible for creating the certification program, we have come to a good understanding of how they view the certification process. Here's a summary of their thoughts, many of which will be discussed throughout this book.

Java certification is a way for individuals to differentiate and promote their skills and for employers and clients to know that a programmer is credible. Sun needed to implement a certification program because Java is so new. It's simply not possible for a programmer to claim he has several years of experience with Java. Thus, it's a challenge to employees to demonstrate they know what they say they know. Becoming certified in Java is a recognized way of validating your skills.

If you'd like to get up to speed as quickly as possible, Sun Educational Services offers courses that cover many of the topics that are part of Java certification. Other courses (both live and on the Web) cover these topics as well, as do books, seminars, and lectures. There is also no substitute for real-world experience. Regardless of how you learned Java in the first place, remember to study for the test. You can't know too much going into the exams!

As you prepare, you should also give some thought as to what your goals are for becoming certified. Are you studying just to pass the exams or are you truly trying to become an expert?

You are certified according to a particular Java release. Therefore, you are Java certified in 1.0.2, 1.1, or 1.2, depending on when you took the certification exam. If you would like to be certified in a new version of the language, you must take the certification exams again (which means paying the testing fees once more).

When you become certified, Sun sends you some material in the mail. This includes a logo that you can place on your business cards to tell the world you're Sun-certified, a certificate, and a lapel pin (so others can see you're certified without even glancing at your business card).

How Sun Manages the Certification Process

Sun Educational Services sends the questions to Sylvan Prometric with all the right answers. The programmer exam takes into account that there can be more than one right answer for a question. For example, the difference between a comma and a semicolon could be that one's right and one's wrong, but the question, "What if I put spaces around my parameters in a parameter list?" has a different answer. They're both right, and the test will mark both answers as correct.

Sun is constantly monitoring the feedback they receive from test takers to make sure they did not miss anything. Sun does not publish numbers of how many people take the test and how many people pass. Sun does not want this to be the kind of test where you can just walk in, sign your name, and pass. This is not simply certification on paper. Passing really means you know your stuff.

Where Certification Is Heading

Sun certification is becoming the standard in the industry. As the inventors of the Java language, other companies are looking to Sun to verify their skills. For example, IBM's own certification program will include Sun's Java certification exams.

Java certification is part of the 100 percent pure Java initiative. JavaSoft administers the applications and systems side of this initiative; Java certification represents the people side. Java certification answers the question "Do you have the capability to develop 100 percent pure Java programs?"

Java certification is also becoming important in corporate education. For example, when an employee is trained in Java, how does a company know if the training hit the mark? Java certification is a standardized way to make sure that employees learn what they need to know.

CHAPTER 2

Java
Programming
Essentials

In this chapter, we'll look at Java's features that relate to object-oriented programming. In particular, we'll create class hierarchies and use keywords that limit access to classes and class members.

MARGIN NOTE: *Before tackling this chapter, you should already be familiar with object-oriented concepts including classes, objects, instance methods, class methods, instance variables, class variables, and inheritance. You should know how to define a class in Java, and you should be able to implement methods and define variables.*

Objectives for This Chapter

- Create object-oriented hierarchies using "is a" and "has a" relationships.
- Define classes, including member variables and member methods.
- Define and use packages, using the `package` and `import` keywords.
- Use the class modifiers `public`, `abstract`, and `final` appropriately.
- Distinguish legal and illegal orderings of top-level Java source file elements, including `package` declarations, `import` statements, `public` class declarations, and non-`public` class declarations.
- Declare variables and methods using the `private`, `protected`, `public`, `static`, `final`, `native`, or `abstract` modifiers.
- Identify when variables and methods can be accessed based on access control keywords.

Object-Oriented Relationships Using "Is a" and "Has a"

Here's an example of the kind of thing you've got to understand for the test (and putting aside the test for moment, you've got to understand this problem and its solution to be an effective Java programmer). How would you define a class hierarchy with these classes?

1. An employee class that maintains an employee number.

2. A full-time employee class that

    a. maintains an employee number,
    b. maintains the number of hours worked that week, and
    c. calculates its own pay using its own salary() method.

3. A retired employee class that

    a. maintains an employee number,
    b. maintains the number of years worked, and
    c. calculates pay using its own salary() method.

Then, using these classes and the resulting class hierarchy, create an object for a full-time employee named Ralph Cramden. Think about this for a moment, then read on. Perhaps you're thinking of something like Figure 2-1 for the class hierarchy.

At first blush, this seems to work. We have employee at the top level, defining an instance variable, and an `abstract` method that both full-time and retired employees inherit. We could create a new instance of the full-time employee class for Ralph. Figure 2-1 cer-

Figure 2-1
A hierarchy that works in theory

tainly fits the classes into a class hierarchy. So what's the problem? Here's an example of where the design in Figure 1-1 falls apart.

Ralph Cramden is hired as a bus driver when he's 25. At that time, the program creates a new full-time instance for him. Over the years, the application accumulates references to this object throughout the system, because Ralph's on various lists for medical benefits, employee phone numbers, and so on. The application runs fine for years. But after 20 years he decides to retire to spend more time with his wife. Now we want to represent Ralph as an instance of the retired class. Does this mean we create a new object for him, that we try to find all the references to the old object and replace it with the new object? And what happens if he takes time off in the middle of his career? What happens if he works in a temporary position in which his salary is calculated differently from other employees? Do we constantly create new objects to represent our employee named Ralph Cramden?

We only want to create one object for Ralph. Clearly then, something's wrong with the design. What's wrong is that we did not fully grasp the difference between "is a" and "has a" for our particular domain.

EXAM POINTER: *The phrase "is a" defines a direct relationship between a superclass and a subclass; a subclass is a type of a superclass. The phrase "has a" describes a relationship between part of an object and another object, usually of a different type; an object has a part that is another object.*

Sure, a full-time employee or a retired employee "is an" employee. However, we would be much better off saying that the employee class "has a" part that "is a" status, and that an employee's status is either full-time or retired. Now our hierarchy looks like Figure 2-2.

With this arrangement, we can keep the same employee object forever and simply change its status when needed. We can add to our status hierarchy as the needs of the application change. If Ralph takes a leave of absence at the birth of his son, we can define a class to represent that new type of status and use a new instance of this class as Ralph's current status. If Ralph works part-time for

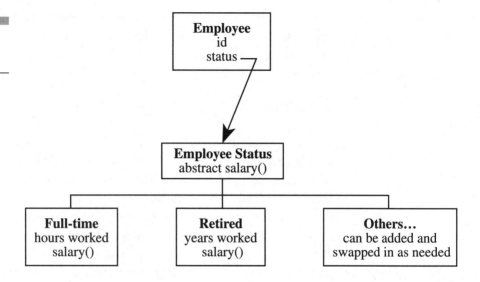

Figure 2-2
A hierarchy that
works in practice

a while as he pursues a bowling career, an instance of a class called part-time could be swapped in as his new status. Our hierarchy works smoothly because we have used "has a" and "is a" correctly for our domain. An employee "has a" status; part-time, full-time, or retired "is a" status.

TIP: *This example shows why creating class hierarchies falls somewhere between engineering and craft. You use your skills to make trade-offs until you find something that works in practice. The primary skills you use are your ability to discern between "is a" and "has a" relationships for the domain you're working in and your ability to imagine scenarios that test your design.*

Our next step is to start implementing the classes and class hierarchies you design.

Exercise 2-1

Create classes for 2DShape, Circle, Square, and Point. Points have an (x, y) location. Circles have an (x, y) location as well as a radius.

Squares have an (x, y) location as well as a length. Which are the superclasses and which are the subclasses? Are any classes related by a "has a" relationship?

Exercise 2-2

Define a class hierarchy to represent a shipment of coffee beans. The beans may have different characteristics in an inventory system, depending on whether they are *untested* or whether they have been tested and found to be *stale* or *fresh*. A shipment of beans is first entered into the inventory system before it is tested. What classes might you need? How are these classes related in "is a" and "has a" relationships? Which kind of class should you create an instance for when the shipment first arrives before it is tested? What should you do after the shipment is tested?

Review: Classes, Variables, and Methods

For the exam, you should be able to define classes, including member variables and member methods. We assume you can already create classes and define member variables and methods. Here's a quick review.

Classes

A class definition has some or all of these components:

```
[keywords] class MyClass [extends Superclass] [implements
Interface] {
//class variables
//static initializers
//instance variables
//constructors
//class methods
//instance methods
}
```

Member Variables

Here is an example of a class that inherits from class Object and defines three instance variables:

```
class Movie {
  String name;
  int runningTime;
  boolean thumpsUp;
}
```

The first instance variable is an object reference to an instance of class String. The next two are primitive data types. These instance variables enable Movie objects to store their own unique values.

A `static` variable belongs to the class, not to the objects.

```
class Movie {
  static int id;
  String name;
  int runningTime;
  boolean thumpsUp;
}
```

The `id` variable can be accessed from any class that can access Movie, starting from when Movie is first loaded into the *Java Virtual Machine* (JVM). Because it is declared as static, the `id` variable exists exactly once, no matter how many objects are created and even if no objects are created. In addition to `static`, we'll get into the other keywords for member variables (`public`, `protected`, `private`, and `final`) later in this chapter.

Member Methods

To define a method, simply declare the method within the class it belongs to, stating the method's keywords, return type, name, parameters, and any exceptions it might throw. In this chapter, we're concerned with the object-oriented design aspects of methods—where they fit into a class hierarchy and which classes can access them. How you define a return type, specify parameters, define any exceptions a method might throw, override and overload methods, and define `native` and `synchronized` methods is discussed in Chapter 8, "Exceptions." In addition to `native` and `synchronized`, method definitions can be modified by the keywords `public`, `protected`, `private`, `final`, and `abstract`. These last five keywords all relate to object-oriented design, so we'll look at them later in this chapter. You can also define a `static` method to assign it to the class.

Here's an example of defining a method for our Movie class (we'll use access control keywords in the next section):

```
class Movie {
  static int id;
  String name;
  int runningTime;
  boolean thumpsUp;
  boolean letsSeeIt() {
  return thumbsUp && (runningTime < 130);
  }
}
```

The `letsSeeIt()` method says that we'll see movies that have been given a thumbs-up by the reviewer and that have a running time of less than two hours and 10 minutes. Let's move on from this review and organize the classes we create into packages.

Packages

For the exam, you need to know how to define and use packages using package declarations and import statements. To help you work more easily with a bunch of classes at once, Java enables you to group classes into packages. Packages help you associate classes with a particular function. For example, the Abstract Window Toolkit package (`java.awt`) is used for building user interfaces. As another example, the Input/Output package (`java.io`) is used for reading from and writing to streams. The classes in a package may or may not be related in a class hierarchy. They are, however, related in purpose.

Packages have three effects on your object-oriented design:

1. Packages enable you to define stricter access control.
2. They make it easier to reuse common names.
3. They collect classes so that they can be shared more easily between applications.

We'll look briefly at each of these three aspects; then we'll fill in the details.

Access Control

By default, all of your classes can reference other classes in the same package, and all methods can invoke other methods and access variables in the same package. (If you do not explicitly define a package, all of your classes are placed within the same default package.) The keywords `public` and `protected` do not affect access between classes and members in the same package. The keyword `private`, however, restricts access to the class that defines the `private` member.

Table 2-1 shows what happens when a class within the same package as a `public` and default class tries to access members of the `public` and default classes. These members are defined with different access control keywords. Figure 2-3 helps you visualize what we mean here.

In the table, the entry "yes" indicates that a class can access the member in the class type named for that column; the entry "no" indicates that a class cannot access the member. Also, a default class is a class defined without any access control keywords and a default member is a member defined the same way.

Table 2-1		Public class	Default class
Access for a class within the same package as a Public and Default class	`public` member	yes	yes
	`protected` member	yes	yes
	`private` member	no	no
	Default member	yes	yes

Figure 2-3
A class accessing
members of other
classes within the
same package

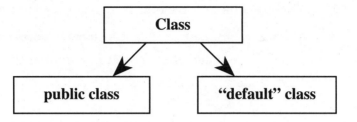

Table 2-2

Access for a class
outside a package
defining a Public
and Default class

	Public class	Default class
`public` member	yes	no
`protected` member	yes*	no
`private` member	no	no
Default member	no	no

*If the accessing class is a subclass of this class; otherwise, no.

EXAM POINTER: *Classes in the same package can access each others' variables and methods, except for private members. Classes outside of the package can only see classes that are defined as public and can only access methods and variables defined using the* `public` *or* `protected` *keyword. What's more, only subclasses of classes with protected members can access those protected members outside a package.*

Table 2-2 shows a method in a class outside the same package as a `public` and default class trying to access members with different access control keywords. Figure 2-4 shows this using images.

TIP: *Notice that access is much more restrictive than when the accessing class is in the same package as the* `public` *and default class. Packages enable you to fine-tune how and when others can make use of your classes.*

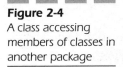

Figure 2-4
A class accessing members of classes in another package

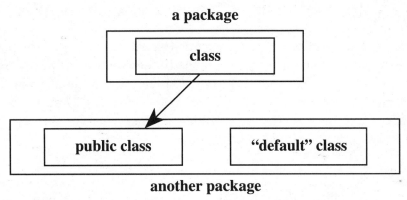

Reuse Names

With a package, you can fully qualify a class name so that Java knows where to look for it. This enables you to use the same class name as one defined in another package. That is, fully qualifying a class name enables you to reuse common class names, since you can specify where Java should look to find where these classes are defined.

For example, perhaps you've decided to use the class names `Point` and `Rectangle` in your own package `COM.Bluehorse.shapes`. However, you also want to use the `java.awt` classes called `Point` and `Rectangle`. One way to proceed is to import the AWT classes, using the `import` statement at the top of your file:

```
import java.awt.Point;
import java.awt.Rectangle;
```

Whenever you want to refer to Java's `Point` or `Rectangle` class, you can do so directly, as in

```
new Point(10, 10);
```

You can reference your own classes by fully qualifying them. For example, you could create a new instance of your own `Point` class like this:

```
new COM.Bluehorse.shapes.Point(10, 10);
```

Sharing Classes Between Applications

Since classes within the same package are placed in their own directory, you can easily refer to the entire collection of classes and use them in another application without worrying about whether you are importing extra baggage that belongs to application-specific classes. For example, you can import all the classes in a package named shapes by writing

```
import COM.Bluehorse.shapes.*;
```

When you do this, you know that you are only getting the *shapes* classes, as opposed to, say, the shapes classes plus some application-specific classes. Only those classes in the shapes package are in the shapes directory.

TIP: *When placing a collection of classes into its own package, you should strip out the application-dependent aspects of these classes. In a good design, a package will contain application-independent classes that you can reuse in any number of applications.*

Creating a Package

A simple example of creating a package is

```
package shapes;
//class definitions
```

The package keyword tells the Java compiler to assign the classes in that file to the named package, in this case, shapes.

EXAM POINTER: *To create a package, name the package at the top of the source file containing the package classes. Use the keyword* package, *followed by the name of the package.*

TIP: _You can have more than one file whose classes belong in the same package._

Package names determine a directory structure for compiled classes. For example, let's say we have two source files, Draw.java and Shapes.java. Draw.java contains an Applet subclass named Draw. Shapes.java defines two classes, Square and Circle. We assign the Square and Circle classes to the shapes package by using the package keyword. Figure 2-5 shows how Java would require the classes to be organized.

 TIP: _You can specify more levels of organization in your package by using subdirectories._

You specify each subdirectory using a dot (.), as in

```
package Bluehorse.shapes;
```

If used with the classes we just discussed, this would require the directory structure shown in Figure 2-6.

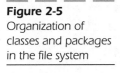

Figure 2-5
Organization of classes and packages in the file system

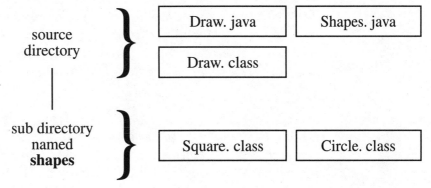

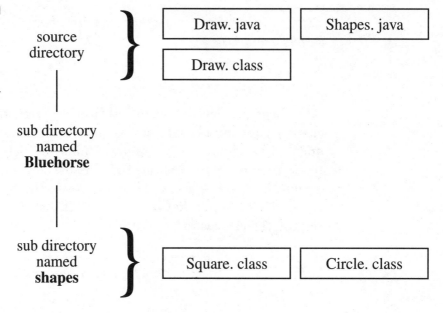

This enables us to collect other packages under the top-level directory Bluehorse. For example, the Bluehorse directory could have the subdirectories brushes, pens, and papers, in addition to shapes. The Java class libraries are organized using subdirectories, with the lang, util, io, and other packages organized under the java directory.

TIP: The Sun Java Development Kit and other environments contain options to automatically place your package classes into the correct directories and subdirectories when they are compiled. With the JDK, you can use the -d option when you compile.

EXAM POINTER: To use a class in a package other than the one in which it is defined, you must first import that class. You can import a class using the import statement, specifying the package the class is placed in.

To import a class named `Circle` named `Bluehorse.shapes`, you can write

```
import Bluehorse.shapes.Circle;
```

You can also import all of the classes in a package by using wild-card notation. Here's an example of importing all the classes in `Bluehorse.shapes`:

```
import Bluehorse.shapes.*;
```

And as you saw, you can also fully qualify the class name, so that Java knows where to find it when you reference it:

```
class SpecialCircle extends Bluehorse.shapes.Circle {
}
```

If you do not define a package for a source file, you can consider the classes in that file to be in the same default package.

Exercise 2-3

Suppose you had a `Circle` class defined like this:

```
class Circle {
  double radius
  double area() {
  return radius * radius * Math.PI;
  }
}
```

Place this class into a separate package. Add the appropriate access control keywords so that you can access this class from your default package, create a new `Circle` instance, assign your new instance a radius value, and display its area.

Exercise 2-4

Given a package named `COM.Company.Utilities`, how would you import a class in this package named `Calculator`? What would the structure be for the directories and subdirectories that contained the `Calculator` class?

Class Keywords

Classes can be modified from their default state using any of three keywords: `public`, `abstract`, and `final`. As you've seen, the `public` keyword relates to access control; you'll see in a moment how the `abstract` and `final` keywords relate to your design.

public

If you import a package, you can only access those package classes that are declared to be `public`. All of the classes you see in the Java APIs are declared `public`. Since each of these classes is defined in a different package from your application, declaring them `public` is the only way you can get at them.

abstract

An `abstract` method consists of a method declaration without a body. That is, you define the keywords, return type, name, parameters, and the exceptions the method throws, but no instructions between a set of curly braces. Here's an example:

```
public abstract double area(double radius)
throws IllegalGeometryException;
```

Since there is no code supplied for the `area()` method, the class itself cannot be instantiated. If it could be, then there is nothing stopping some other code from instantiating the class and invoking its `area()` method, but there are no instructions yet for `area()`. This flies in the face of Java's philosophy of doing its best to keep the programmer from making mistakes involving how the pieces fit together.

If you have defined any methods as abstract, you must define your class to be abstract as well. You can declare a class to be abstract even if no methods are declared as abstract. Subclasses are automatically concrete. Two examples of this are Java's own Container and Component classes, defined in java.awt. Again, declaring the class as abstract forces programmers to instantiate subclasses of these classes. So, instead of allowing a programmer to instantiate Component, a programmer must instantiate Button, Choice, Checkbox, or some other subclass. However, an object reference of type Component can refer to any of these.

BACKGROUND: *Why declare a method to be* abstract? *Can there possibly be a good reason for not providing any behavior at all and insisting that the class itself be* abstract?

The reason has to do with design. Declaring a class to be abstract *organizes your class hierarchy a certain way and forces a programmer using this class hierarchy to do things according to your understanding of the domain. For example, the* java.lang *package defines a class called* Number. *This class is* abstract. *This class defines the* abstract *methods* intValue(), longValue(), floatValue(), *and* doubleValue(). *The role of the* Number *class is to organize and unite a variety of "wrapper" classes into the same branch in the class hierarchy and to specify what their interface will be. Concrete subclasses of* Number *are* Integer, Long, Double, *and* Float. *These subclasses implement the behavior for the* abstract *methods they inherit and make this behavior mean something specific to their class type.*

The reason these methods are declared to be abstract *(rather than, for example, defining a method that returns a default value such as 0) is because the* Number *class is never intended to be instantiated. According to the design, it makes no sense to instantiate* Number. *The purpose of the subclasses is to put an object-oriented wrapper around a primitive data type that corresponds to the class* name—int, long, double, *or* float. *However, there is no generic number type, so making a* Number *object has no meaning.*

Making Number abstract *forces programmers to instantiate the classes that were intended to be instantiated. You can do the same thing in your design, so that programmers use your classes as you intended.*

One of the benefits of this type of design, that is, of uniting the wrapper types under the same branch in the class hierarchy, even if you cannot instantiate the superclass, is that you can define an object reference to be the superclass type. Then this object reference can refer to any subclass of that type. For example, you can write something like this:

```
Number n;
s = getInput();
if (isInteger(s))
n = new Integer(s);
else if (isFloatingPoint(s))
n = new Double(s);
```

The variable n *can be used to invoke methods that are defined in* Number, *including* Number's *abstract methods that are implemented in the subclasses. Since* Number *defines* intValue(), longValue(), floatValue(), *and* doubleValue(), *we can invoke any of these methods using the variable* n.

final

A final class makes all of its methods final as well, since a final class cannot be extended. As an example of a final class, the classes Integer, Long, Float, and Double are declared as final, so all of their methods are final as well. None of these wrapper classes can be subclassed. If you would like to make your own type of wrapper, you must extend the class Number. Another commonly used class that's declared as final is String.

EXAM POINTER: *If you want to stop programmers from ever making a subclass of a particular class, you can declare that class to be* final.

BACKGROUND: *The* final *keyword optimizes your code and makes your design more secure. First, let's look at optimization. When a variable is declared to be* final, *Java knows its value is a constant. A* final *variable must be initialized when it is declared, because it can never be changed later. Since this value is a constant, the compiler could feel free to optimize by replacing references to that variable with its constant value, eliminating the need to look up its value when it is referenced. As an example, the variables* PI *and* E *in the Math class in* java.lang *are defined as* final.

When a method is declared to be final, *Java knows that the method can never be overridden. A* final *method must be fully defined when it is declared; you cannot have an* abstract final *method, for example. Since Java knows the method can never be overridden by subclasses, the Java compiler can replace the call to the method with inline code if it wants. This eliminates all sorts of class look-ups to find the method in the class hierarchy and makes the method invocation much faster.*

How about security? Declaring a method to be final *is one way to guarantee that its contract, its published API, will never be violated. For example, the method* getClass() *in class* Object *is declared as* final. *No subclass can override this method so that it violates its contract and returns some other class type to hide its identity.*

Exercise 2-5

Given the following class definition,

```
abstract class Shape {
  abstract double perimeter();
}
```

create a subclass of Shape named TwoDShape, and a subclass of TwoDShape named Square. Like Shape, TwoDShape should also be an abstract class, but Square should be concrete and should know how to calculate its perimeter. Define whatever instance variables you need for Square.

Exercise 2-6

Modify the classes you created above so that programmers cannot make subclasses of your `Square` class.

Ordering of a Java Source File

You need to be able to distinguish legal and illegal orderings of top-level Java source file elements, including package declarations, import statements, public class declarations, and non-public class declarations. Three basic entries can be placed within a Java source file:

1. A package definition

2. Any number of import statements

3. Any public and non-public classes and interfaces

If you include a package declaration, this must be the first thing to appear in a source file. Any `import` statements come next; you can have as many `import` statements as you'd like. After the `package` and `import` statements, you can define any classes and interfaces that you'd like.

TIP: *In Sun's JDK, you can only define one* `public` *class. What's more, if you do define a* `public` *class, the source file must be named after the class. For example, if you are defining a* `public` *class named* `Earth`, *then the source file it is defined in must be named* `Earth.java`.

Other Java development environments do not have this restriction of one `public` class per source file.

Exercise 2-7

What's wrong with this class file?

```
import java.util.*;
import java.awt.*;
package myUtils;
public class Util {
 public double avg(double a, double b) {
 return (a + b)/2;
 }
}
```

Try compiling this file if you can't find the answer.

Variable and Method Keywords

You should be able to declare variables and methods using modifiers. First, we'll present keywords that are used with variables and methods. Then we'll summarize the access control keywords mentioned earlier in this chapter.

static

As we mentioned earlier, a static member belongs with the class. A static variable always exists exactly once for a class, no matter how many instances are created. A static method belongs with the class. Since a static method is not associated with a particular object, you cannot use this or refer to an instance member by name, as you would from a non-static method.

abstract

An abstract method defines the method's signature, return value, and the exceptions it might throw, but it does not define the code that implements the method. If you define an abstract method, you must make that class abstract as well.

final

A final member cannot be changed after it is defined. This means that a final variable is a constant, and a final method cannot be overridden by subclasses. As we mentioned when describing what it means to declare an entire class to be final, the two benefits of a final method or variable are with security (enforcement of the API) and optimization (placing code inline). A final member provides these benefits on a member-by-member basis, rather than for the class as a whole.

synchronized

A synchronized method can only be invoked by one thread at a time. A synchronized method can belong to an object or a class. If a thread enters a synchronized instance method, no other thread can invoke any other synchronized instance method for that object. If a thread enters a synchronized static method, no other thread can invoke any other synchronized static method for that class. There's much more information on synchronized methods in Chapter 11, "Input/Output."

native

A native method is defined in a platform-dependent language, or at least some language other than Java. We'll return to the topic of native methods in the second section of this book, because native methods appear mostly in the Developer exam.

transient

A transient variable is not stored as part of an object's persistent state. It indicates that a variable may not be serialized and is used to protect sensitive data from being written to a stream. For example, if you want to protect sensitive data regarding a customer's account number, you could designate it as transient. In this way, the account number wouldn't be written to a stream outside the JVM. Transient variables cannot be declared as final or static.

volatile

The `volatile` modifier indicates that a variable can be modified asynchronously in a multiprocessor environment. Although this modifier isn't covered in the exam, it is a good idea to use this modifier whenever a variable can be accessed by two or more threads without synchronization.

Exercise 2-8

What is wrong with this class definition? Fix it so that it works when you invoke `main()`.

```
class Avg {
 public static void main(String[] args) {
 double a = 5.1;
 double b = 20.32;
 double c = 32.921;
 System.out.println(findAvg(a, b, c));
 }
 double findAvg(double a, double b, double c) {
 return (a + b + c) / 3.0;
 }
}
```

Access Control Keywords

For the exam, you'll need to be able to identify when variables and methods can be accessed based on access control keywords. You've already seen a couple of tables regarding access control for class members. Here's a quick summary of these keywords. We'll follow this summary with a number of exercises involving access control.

If no access control keywords are on a class, then only those classes defined in the same package can attempt to access members of that class. If no access control keywords are on a member, then only those classes in the same package can access that member.

public

A public member can be accessed by any class that can access the member's class. If a class in package number 1 wants to access the member of a class defined in package number 2, the class in package number 2 must be declared public so that the first class can get to it. Then the first class can access any members that are declared as public.

private

You can restrict all access to a specific member from all classes except the one in which it is defined by using the keyword private on the member.

protected

A protected member can only be accessed by classes within the same package or by subclasses in the same package or in different packages from the member's class.

Exercises

The following exercises deal with keywords that you can place on classes and class members.

Exercise 2-9

Imagine this hierarchy:

```
Tree (defines a protected instance variable named age)
Deciduous extends Tree
Evergreen extends Tree
Pine extends Evergreen
Forest
```

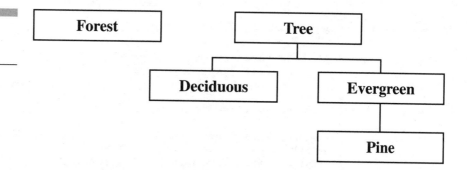

Figure 2-7
A hierarchy of
tree classes

This hierarchy is shown in Figure 2-7.
Now create the following objects:

```
Deciduous d = new Deciduous();
Evergreen e = new Evergreen();
Pine p1 = new Pine();
Pine p2 = new Pine();
Forest f = new Forest();
```

Which objects can access the protected field in class Tree if all of these classes are defined as part of the same package? Which objects cannot access this protected field?

Exercise 2-10

What if each class in Exercise 2.9, Forest, Tree, Evergreen, Deciduous, and Pine, as defined in different packages? Which objects could then access the Tree's protected field?

Exercise 2-11

What will happen when you first compile the file named Tree. java and then compile the file named Forest.java, as presented below? If there is a problem, fix the code.

```
File Tree.java

package Flora;
public class Tree {
 protected int age;
}
File Forest.java

import Flora.Tree;
public class Forest {
public static void main(String[] args) {
 Tree t = new Tree();
 System.out.println("The tree's age is " + t.age);
 }
}
```

Exercise 2-12

What will happen when you first compile the file named `Tree.java` and then compile the file named `Forest.java`, as presented below? If there is a problem, fix the code.

```
File Tree.java

package Flora;
public class Tree {
 protected int age;
}
File Forest.java

public class Forest {
 public static void main(String[] args) {
 Tree t = new Tree():
 System.out.println("The tree's age is " + t.age);
 }
}
```

Exercise 2-13

Tie together the `Violin` and `Guitar` classes presented below with a superclass, and make the `Violin` class unable to be subclassed. Use Java's `abstract` and `final` keywords where appropriate.

```
class Violin {
 int numStrings;
 void play() {
 System.out.println("mmm")
 }
}
class Guitar {
 int numStrings;
 void play() {
 System.out.println("twang")
 }
}
```

Exercise 2-14

Change the following class definition for Employee. Restrict access to the Employee id to be read-only. (You can use a combination of a keyword on this variable and a new method to achieve this.) In addition, outside of this package, id should be able to be accessed by only the Employee class and Employee subclasses.

Maintain an id counter internally in the class. Start the id counter at 1 for the first employee, and for each new employee, add 1. Any class should be able to create a new employee, even classes in other packages. Use the keywords private, protected, public, and static, as necessary.

```
class Employee {
 int id;
 Employee(int id) {
 this.id = id;
 }
}
```

Exercise 2-15

Here is a small application to draw a square wherever the user clicks the mouse. When the user clicks in the applet, the applet detects this event and creates a new Square object, adding it to a Vector object. In the applet's paint() method, we enumerate through the Squares in the Vector and draw each one.

If you're not familiar with graphical applications yet, don't worry too much about this exercise. If you feel comfortable with them, however, look over the code and see if you can answer the questions that follow.

File Shape.Java

```
package COM.Bluehorse.Shapes;

import java.awt.*;
public abstract class Shape {
 Point loc;
 public abstract void draw(Graphics g);
}
```

File Square.java

```
package COM.Bluehorse.Shapes;

import java.awt.*;
public class Square extends Shape {
 public Square(int x, int y) {
 loc = new Point(x, y);
 }
 public void draw(Graphics g) {
 g.drawRect(loc.x, loc.y, 20, 20);
 }
}
```

File DrawApplet.java

```
import java.awt.*;
import java.awt.event.*;
import java.applet.Applet;
import COM.Bluehorse.Shapes.*;
import java.util.*;
public class DrawApplet extends Applet {
 Vector shapes = new Vector();
 public void init() {
 addMouseListener(new MouseHandler(this));
 }
 public void paint(Graphics g) {
```

```
    Square s;
    for (Enumeration e = shapes.elements();
    e.hasMoreElements(); )
    {
    s = (Square)e.nextElement();
    s.draw(this.getGraphics());
    }
    }
}
class MouseHandler extends MouseAdapter {
 DrawApplet applet;
 public MouseHandler(DrawApplet a) {
 applet = a;
 }
 public void mouseReleased(MouseEvent e) {
 applet.shapes.addElement(new Square(e.getX(), e.getY()));
 applet.repaint();
 }
}
```

Here are some questions regarding access between classes:

1. Is it possible for the mouseUp( ) method in DrawApplet to access the Square's loc field?

2. Is it possible for mouseUp( ) to access the Square's draw( ) method?

Exercise 2-16

Here are a few questions and thought experiments about combinations of keywords. If you're not sure of the answers, write some code and try to compile it.

1. Can an abstract method be final?

2. Can an abstract method be static?

3. Can you define a public-protected field?

Casting Classes

You can cast one object type to another type. If you cast down the hierarchy, you must cast the class type. If you cast up the hierarchy, you can assign an object to a superclass reference without casting. For example, imagine these three simple classes:

```
class Parent {
 public static void main(String[] args) {
 Derived1 d1 = new Derived1();
 Derived2 d2 = new Derived2();
 Parent p = new Parent();
 // we'll add code here . . .
 }
}
class Derived1 extends Parent{}
class Derived1 extends Parent{}
```

Let's replace the comment we'll add code here with some actual code. If we want to set d1 to p, that's no problem. All we need to do is write

```
p = d1;
```

This is because we've cast up the hierarchy. All Derived1 objects are also of type Parent, so this assignment is perfectly legal.

TIP: *Interestingly, this does not change the object type as far as invoking a method. The actual object type referenced by* p *is still of type* Derived1. *So, if* Derived1 *overrides a method in* Parent, *invoking that method using* p *(now pointing to a* Derived1 *object) still invokes the version of that method in* Derived1.

If, instead of

```
p = d1;
```

we wrote

```
d1 = p;
```

the code would not compile. This kind of cast is somewhat similar to trying to assign a float value to an int. You are attempting to assign a value with more detail to a type that knows less detail. If we were dealing with float and int, we could cast the float to an `int` to make the compiler and runtime know that everything is okay and that we're aware of what we're doing. The same is true with classes; we can cast `Parent` to `Derived1` and the code will compile.

```
d1= (Derived1)p;
```

However, just because the compiler allows for the possibility that this is a legal cast, that does not mean that it actually is. Whether or not this is legal depends on what the object's type is at runtime. According to the code we've written, the object reference p refers to an instance of class `Parent`. `Parent` does not inherit from `Derived1`, so, at runtime, this code would throw a `ClassCastException`.

If we created a new object instead and assigned it to p, like this

```
Parent p = new Derived1();
```

then this code

```
d1= (Derived1)p;
```

would both compile and run successfully.

You can only cast up and down the hierarchy. For example, you cannot cast between two classes that are siblings. To illustrate this warning, you could not write

```
d1 = d2;
```

or even

```
d1= (Derived1)d2;
```

because d1 and d2 are not in the same branch of the class hierarchy. The compiler would complain that this is an invalid cast.

Interfaces

An interface defines a set of `abstract` methods and class constants. In other words, as its name implies, an interface defines an interface, not an implementation. The implementation of an interface, that is, the behavior for the methods, is left to the class implementing the interface.

BACKGROUND: *The need for an interface arises because Java only has single inheritance of implementation. This means that every class has exactly one superclass. If you want to inherit behavior from two classes, you just can't do it.*

The reason for this restriction is purely one of eliminating complications. For example, imagine this class situation, shown in Figure 2-8, that arises in languages that enable multiple inheritance. If we invoke d's test() *method, and* test() *invokes* super.test(), *which method gets executed next?* c's *or* b's? *Maybe each gets executed once? What if each of these* test() *methods invokes its* super.test() *method? Would that mean that* a's test() *method gets executed twice?*

In Java, this confusion is not possible, since a class can only have one superclass. Even though multiple inheritance of implementation is not allowed, a design based on multiple inheritance can be very useful. Imagine you are designing a forms package. You would like the user to drag and drop TextField, Checkbox, and Choice objects onto a form. You would like to identify your subclasses of these java.awt classes as being FormElements. In a multiple inheritance environment, you could design your classes like those in Figure 2-9.

In this design, your own form objects inherit behavior from FormElement. In Java, even though you cannot pass an imple-

Figure 2-8
The multiple
inheritance diamond

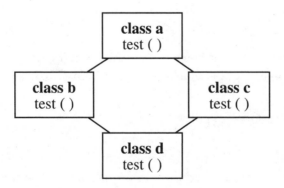

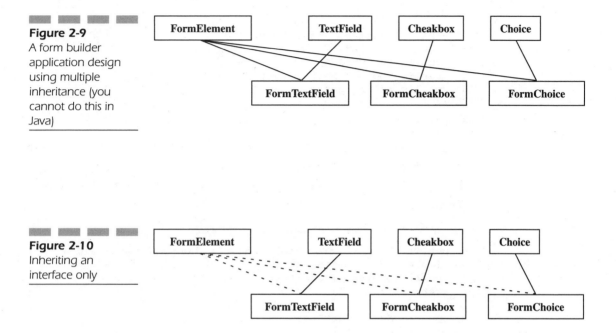

Figure 2-9
A form builder
application design
using multiple
inheritance (you
cannot do this in
Java)

Figure 2-10
Inheriting an
interface only

mentation to a subclass of another class, you can still pass an implementation to that class. The way you do that is by defining `FormElement` to be an interface. `FormElement` can still define a method, but instead of the `java.awt` subclasses inheriting an implementation, they only inherit a method signature. It is up to these subclasses to provide their own behavior for any methods defined by the interface. Figure 2-10 gives a sense of this relationship.

You define an interface similar to a class that defines only abstract methods and class constants. However, you do not have to use the `abstract` and `final static` keywords to define these things, since an interface assigns these keywords by default. Here's an example of a `FormElement` interface:

```
public interface FormElement {
  public int TEXT = 1;
  public int CHOICE = 2;
  public boolean mustAnswer();
  public String getResponse();
}
```

This interface defines two class constants, TEXT and CHOICE and two abstract methods, mustAnswer() and getResponse(). Here is how you might implement an interface in the Form-TextField class:

```
public class FormTextField extends java.awt.TextField
  implements FormElement {
  public boolean mustAnswer() {
  return true;
  }
  public String getResponse() {
  return getText();
  }
}
```

How to Clone Objects

Operators do not enable you to make a direct copy of an object in memory. Instead, to make a copy of an object, you must invoke its clone() method. Not all classes enable their objects to be cloned. Only those that implement the Cloneable interface can be cloned.

An interesting thing about the Cloneable interface is that it does not define any methods that must be implemented. So why define an interface at all? Because defining your class as implementing an interface marks objects of that class as an instance of that interface. Thus, we can use an interface as a kind of indicator of desired behavior. Before the Java runtime clones an object, it checks to see if the object's class implements the Cloneable interface. If so, then the clone() method returns a clone of the object. Otherwise, the clone() method throws a CloneNotSupportedException.

TIP: *The JVM does not call an object's constructor when you clone the object.*

Static Initializers

A static initializer is defined using the keyword `static`, followed by a set of curly braces in which you can place code, as in

```
static {
  System.out.println("The class is loading");
}
```

The JVM executes all static initializers for a class when the class is first loaded. The JVM initializes any static variables and executes any static initializers in the order they are listed in the class.

TECHNICAL TRAP: *Be careful to avoid dependencies between static initializers in different classes. There might be a dependency, for example, if a member variable or static initializer refers to variables or methods in another class. When the JVM comes across a reference to a class it has not yet loaded, the JVM stops loading the first class and attempts to load the second class. If that second class in turn refers back to the first, the member variables not yet initialized would have only their default values, instead of the values assigned in their initialization statements. This might make your class behave in ways you had not expected.*

Exercise 2-17

Use a `static initialize` to set a static array of three floating-point numbers to three random numbers between 0.0 and 1.0. You can acquire a random number of type double between 0.0 and 1.0 by writing

```
Math.random();
```

We'll cover arrays in depth in Chapter 4, "Memory and Garbage Collection."

Answers to the Exercises

Exercise 2-1

This is a classic example of knowing when to use "is a" and "has a." The confusion comes into play with the fact that points, circles, and squares all have a position on the screen. Here is one way to do the hierarchy, where it looks as though you have pushed as much information up the hierarchy as possible.

The problem here is not that 2-D shapes such as circles and squares don't have a screen position; they do. The problem is that 2-D shapes are not special kinds of points. In other words, points are not well represented as circles with a zero radius. This does not feel right or represent the situation as you think of it in the real world. Instead, it might make more sense to have the 2DShape class refer to a Point instance. In other words, a 2DShape "has a" point, a position on the screen, but a 2DShape "is not a" point.

Figure 2-11
An awkward class hierarchy, don't you agree?

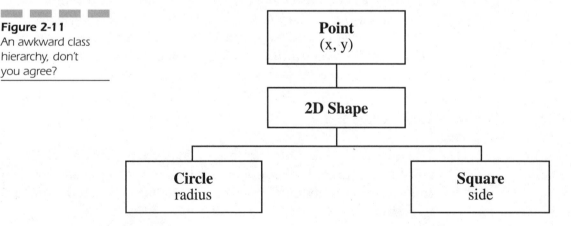

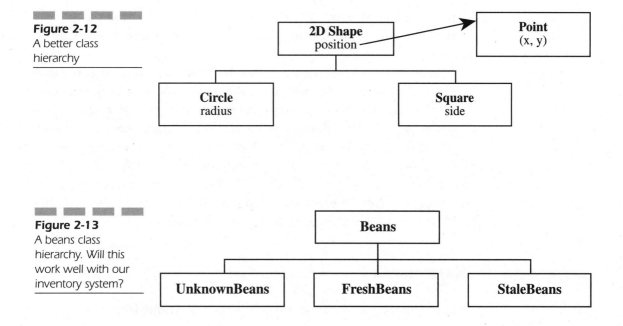

Figure 2-12
A better class hierarchy

Figure 2-13
A beans class hierarchy. Will this work well with our inventory system?

Exercise 2-2

This question has many possible answers. One possible class hierarchy for coffee beans is shown in Figure 2-13.

Before this discussion, you might have been tempted to say the shipment can be represented by an instance of class Beans. But when it is determined to be stale or fresh, what class would you use then? The instructions to this exercise state that the beans have some different characteristics and behavior, depending on whether they're untested, fresh, or stale. You could simply keep a flag in the class itself that indicates state, but then you'd have to write an if-else or switch-case statement in the class to perform the correct behavior, depending on whether the beans have been tested or not, and if they have been, what the outcome was. Using control flow to determine something that can be done using subclasses is a strong indication that you're not taking full advantage of object-oriented programming and that it's time for some reworking of your class hierarchy.

The hierarchy presented above will work fine, but in conjunction with another class. One way to make this work is to define a class named Shipment. The Shipment class can delegate its responses to the method calls that depend on its state as a Beans object reference. At first, the shipment is assigned an object of type UnknownBeans. Once the Shipment is tested, its Beans object reference can be assigned a new object, of type FreshBeans or StaleBeans, as appropriate. Now the relationship is that Shipment "has a" taste, and that taste is either unknown, fresh, or stale.

Exercise 2-3

You can modify Circle to place it into a package, like this:

```
package shapes;

public class Circle {
 public double radius;
public double area() {
 return radius * radius * Math.PI;
 }
}
```

With everything public, classes outside of the package that Circle is defined in can now use the Circle class as before. Using Sun's JDK, if this is defined in a file named Circle.java, you can compile this by writing:

```
java -d . Circle.java
```

Here's how you can define a class to create a new Circle object:

```
import shapes.*;

class CircleTester {
 public static void main(String[] args) {
 Circle c = new Circle();
```

```
c.radius = 10;
System.out.println("area with radius = 10 is
" + c.area());
}
}
```

Exercise 2-4

You can import the class like this:

```
import COM.Company.utilities.Calculator;
```

The directory structure starts with COM at the top level, with Company as its subdirectory. A subdirectory of Company is utilities. In the utilities directory, you'll find the Calculator class.

Exercise 2-5

```
File Shape.java
abstract class Shape {
 abstract double perimeter();
}
File Square.java
abstract class TwoDShape extends Shape {
}
class Square extends TwoDShape {
 double side;
 double perimeter() {
 return 4 * side;
 }
}
```

Exercise 2-6

All you have to do to stop programmers from making subclasses of a class is to declare it using the final keyword. For the Square class, you could write

```
final class Square extends TwoDShape {

  double side;
  double perimeter() {
  return 4 * side;
  }
}
```

Exercise 2-7

A `package` declaration must come first in a source file before any `import` statements or class definitions. The code presented in the exercise would cause a compile-time error.

Exercise 2-8

What's wrong here is that the `static` method attempts to invoke the non-`static` method named `findAvg()`. Since there is no instance of `Avg` to use to invoke `findAvg()`, this is a compile-time error. To fix this, we could either make `findAvg() static` or create an instance of `Avg` and use that when invoking `findAvg()`.

Exercise 2-9

The `protected` keyword is commonly defined as restricting access of a member of the same class or of a subclass of that class. However, `protected` is not as straightforward as that. Actually, within a package, any class can access any other class's `protected` field. So, all objects in this example, `d`, `e`, `p1`, `p2`, and `f`, can access any `protected` fields in `Tree`.

Exercise 2-10

Outside of the package a class is defined in, only subclasses can access a superclass's `protected` field. Thus, `d`, `e`, `p1`, and `p2` can access the `protected` field, while `f` cannot.

If you have an object reference, say, to object e, can the object
p1 access e's protected field as defined in Tree? The answer is
yes. However, could e access p1's protected field defined in Tree?
Here, the answer is no. The reason is that the object accessing the
protected field must be of the same type of object reference. p1,
a Pine, is of type e, an Evergreen, so it can access e's protected
field. However, the reverse is not true. An Evergreen is not
(always) a Pine, so e cannot access p1's protected field. Similarly, p1 cannot access d's protected field, since Pine does not
inherit from Deciduous.

Exercise 2-11

The first file will compile fine, but when you try to compile Forest,
the compiler will display a message indicating that Forest cannot
access the protected field defined in Tree. A simple way to fix
this problem is to make the age field public. Another way is to
define a public method that accesses the age field and returns its
value. The Forest class can then invoke this public method from
main().

Exercise 2-12

Both files will compile fine and you can execute Forest's main()
method without a hitch. It will access Tree's age field, even though
it's protected, because Forest and Tree are in the same
(default) package.

Exercise 2-13

```
abstract class StringedInstrument {
int numStrings;
abstract void play();
}
final class Violin extends StringedInstrument {
void play() {
System.out.println("mmm");
```

```
  }
 }
class Guitar extends StringedInstrument {
 void play() {
 System.out.println("twang");
  }
 }
```

Exercise 2-14

Here is one possible answer to this exercise:

```
public class Employee {
private static int next_id = 1;
private int id;
public Employee() {
id = next_id++;
  }
 protected int getId() {
 return id;
  }
 }
```

Exercise 2-15

1. Is it possible for the mouseUp( ) method in DrawApplet to access the Square's loc field? No. Since loc is not defined with a public keyword, only those classes in the same package as the class defining loc can access this field.

2. Is it possible for mouseUp( ) to access the Square's draw( ) method? Absolutely. Both Square and draw( ) are defined with the public keyword, so any class in any package can invoke draw( ).

3. Could a subclass of DrawApplet, whose source is in the file DrawApplet.java, access DrawApplet's shapes field? No, shapes is private, so only DrawApplet itself can access this field.

Exercise 2-16

1. Can an `abstract` method be `final`? No. An `abstract` method must be overridden by a subclass, but `final` methods cannot be overridden.

2. Can an `abstract` method be static? No. You cannot override a `static` method (think about it—there is no `this` or `super`, since there is no current object responding to a `static` method, so there's no way to invoke the superclass's behavior). Since you cannot override a `static` method, a `static` method cannot be abstract.

3. Can you define a `public protected` field? No. Only one access control keyword can be used at a time. (There is an oversight in earlier versions of Java where `protected private` was allowed, but it no longer is.)

By the way, you cannot define an `abstract` method to be `native`, either.

Exercise 2-17

Since `Object` is defined in a different package other than your own (`Object` is defined in `java.lang`), declaring `clone()` to be `protected` puts some restrictions on which objects can request a `clone()` of which other objects. An object can only request a clone of another object whose class is the same type or subclass of the object being cloned. The idea is to only enable a method to request a clone of an object whose class is in the same branch of the class hierarchy as itself.

First of all, all objects can clone themselves. Beyond that, as indicated in the class hierarchy in Figure 2-14, some references to other object types that are allowed are as follows:

- `Pine` objects can clone `Evergreen` or `Tree` objects.
- `Evergreen` objects can clone `Tree` objects.
- `Deciduous` objects can clone `Tree` objects.

Figure 2-14
Restricting cloning to
the same branch of a
class hierarchy

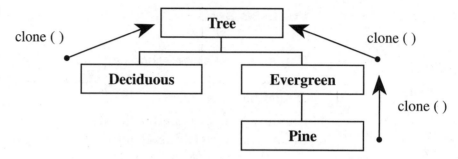

This stops arbitrary objects that have no relationship to each other from cloning each other. For example, Deciduous objects cannot clone Evergreen objects, and no Tree object can clone a Forest object.

Exercise 2-18

The compiler issues an error because Maple is not in the same branch of the class hierarchy as Pine, clone() is protected, and class Object, which defines clone(), comes from a different package.

Exercise 2-19

Here is one way to define the array and static initializer (we've put them into a class called Example):

```
public class Example {
 public static double[] d = new double[3];
 static {
 for (int index = 0; index < d.length; index++)
 d[index] = Math.random();
 }
}
```

Review Questions

1. What happens if you try to compile code that looks like this:

```
class MyString extends String {
}
```

   a. The code compiles successfully.
   b. The code does not compile because you have not defined a main( ) method.
   c. The code does not compile because String is abstract.
   d. The code does not compile because String is final.

2. If you have this class definition

```
abstra ct class Shape{
 abstract void draw();
}
```

   What happens if you try to compile the following class definition?

```
class Square extends Shape{
}
```

   a. Everything compiles successfully.
   b. Shape compiles, but Square does not.
   c. Square compiles, but Shape does not.
   d. Neither Shape nor Square compiles.

3. What happens if you try to compile the Shape and Square class from Question 2 if the Shape class is declared like this:

```
abstract class Shape {
}
```

   a. Everything compiles fine.
   b. Shape compiles, but Square does not.
   c. Square compiles, but Shape does not.
   d. Neither Shape nor Square compiles.

4. The following class definitions

```
class Bridge {
 Road road;
}
class Road {
 String name;
}
```

   represent

    a. an "is a" relationship

    b. a "has a" relationship

    c. both

    d. neither

5. Specifying this line at the top of your source file

```
package awt;
```

    a. results in a compile-time error because Java already defines an awt package.

    b. specifies that all of your classes in this file should go into Java's awt package.

    c. specifies that all of your classes in this file should go into your own awt package.

    d. imports all of the classes in your own awt package.

6. Given these two source files

```
File FormQuestion.java
package forms;
public class FormQuestion {
  int type;
}
File Form.java
package forms;
class Form {
  int getType(FormQuestion question) {
  return question.type;
  }
}
```

What is the outcome of compiling FormQuestion.java and then Form.java?

    a. Both compile successfully.

    b. Neither compile successfully.

    c. Only FormQuestion.java compiles.

    d. Only Form.java compiles.

7. What keyword can you give a class so that classes outside of the package that this class is defined in cannot access the class?

    a. Don't give the class a keyword at all.

    b. private

    c. final

    d. protected

8. To restrict access to a static member to the class itself,

   a. use the `final` keyword.
   b. use the `private` keyword.
   c. do not use a keyword at all for the member.
   d. a `static` member cannot be restricted in this way.

9. Which of the following statements is false?

   a. An instance method can be both `protected` and `abstract`.
   b. A `static` variable can also be `final`.
   c. A `static` method can also be `protected`.
   d. A `static` method can also be `abstract`.

10. By default—that is, without keywords—all classes can access all members except for those defined

   a. using the `final` keyword.
   b. using the `abstract` keyword.
   c. in another package.
   d. in the same package.

Answers to the Review Questions

1. d. `String` is defined using the keyword `final`. Therefore, it cannot be subclassed, and the compiler will tell you that extending `String` is not allowed.

2. b. `Square` will not compile because it should either be declared as `abstract`, or it should implement the `draw()` method.

3. a. A subclass of an `abstract` class that does not declare any `abstract` methods is not `abstract` by default.

4. b. A bridge "has a" road, represented by the instance variable `road` inside `bridge`. Neither class extends another class (except for class `Object`, so in that sense, it does represent an "is a" relationship).

5. c. The `package` keyword defines your own package for the classes in that file.

6. a. Both files compile successfully and are placed into the same package. Therefore, both classes can access each other and each others' members (as long as the accessed member is not `private`).

7. a. The default access control for a class—that is, defining a class without a keyword—restricts other classes in other packages from accessing the class.

8. b. You can restrict access to a member by using the `private` keyword, regardless of whether that member is `static` or `non-static`.

9. d. A `static` method cannot be overridden. Therefore, it cannot be `abstract`.

10. c. All classes can access all members by default, except for those defined in another package. To access classes and members in another package, those classes must be declared using the `public` keyword, and the members must also be declared `public` (or `protected` if the accessing class is a subclass of the class defining the `protected` member).

CHAPTER 3

Keywords and Constructors

Keywords are reserved words. You cannot use a reserved word as the name of a class, variable, or method. You've no doubt seen all the keywords in Java in your travels through the language, or have you? This chapter makes sure you're familiar with Java's keywords by listing them all by category (under headings such as exceptions, access control, and so on) and by providing examples of how to use each of them.

We'll look at constructors as well. Constructors are somewhat similar to methods. Instead of directly calling a constructor, however, Java executes a constructor for you just after Java allocates the memory for your object and after it has set the object's instance variables to their initialization values. As with methods (which are discussed in depth in Chapter 9, "Methods"), you can override and overload constructors. Java invokes the constructor that corresponds to the parameters supplied with the new statement.

Objectives for This Chapter

- Identify all Java keywords.
- State what each Java keyword is used for.
- Describe the default constructor.
- Identify situations when the default constructor is created for you and when it is not.
- Overload and override constructors.
- Use `this()` and `super()` to invoke constructors in the current or parent class.

An Alphabetical List of the Keywords

The Java language specifies 50 keywords. These keywords cannot be used as identifiers for variables, methods, classes, or labels. Two keywords are reserved but currently unused in Java 1.2.2. These keywords are const and goto.

Here is the complete list of Java keywords:

abstract	default	goto	null	synchronized
boolean	do	if	package	this
break	double	implements	private	throw
byte	else	import	protected	throws
case	extends	instanceof	public	transient
catch	false	int	return	true
char	final	interface	short	try
class	finally	long	static	void
const	float	native	super	volatile
continue	for	new	switch	while

For the rest of this chapter, we've divided the keywords into their logical categories and provided explanations for each one. Feel free to skim over these sections if this is mostly a review for you. You can reference this chapter later if you want to quickly look up a keyword or find an example of how to apply it.

Organizing Classes

`package` specifies that classes in a particular source file should belong to the named package. You use the `package` keyword at the top of a source file, followed by the name of the package.

```
package shapes;
```

`import` requests the named class or classes be imported into the current application. Any number of `import` keywords can follow the `package` keyword. Each `import` statement specifies the name of a package to import.

```
import shapes.*;
```

Defining Classes

`class` defines a class, a collection of related data and behaviors that can also inherit data and behaviors from a superclass. Define a class by writing the word `class` followed by the class name. The class definition follows within a set of curly braces.

```
class Circle
```

`extends` indicates which class to subclass. Write the keyword `extends` after the class name if you would like to extend a class other than class Object.

```
class Circle extends Shape
```

`interface` defines class constants and abstract methods that can be implemented by classes. Interfaces can extend other interfaces. Specify an interface by writing the keyword `interface` followed by the interface name. The interface definition follows within a set of curly braces.

```
interface Editable
```

`implements` indicates the interface for which a new class will supply methods. The `implements` keyword appears after the name of the superclass you are extending or after the name of the class you are defining if you are simply extending a class object.

```
class Circle implements Editable
class Circle extends Shape implements Editable
```

Keywords for Classes and Members

`public` means that the class, method, or variable can be accessed from classes outside of the package in which they're defined. Place the `public` keyword in front of the class or member.

```
public Circle
public double radius;
public double area()
```

`private` means only the class defining the method or variable can access it (classes cannot be private). Place the `private` keyword in front of the member.

```
private double radius;
private double area()
```

`protected` means that when a class inside a package defines a member as protected, the only classes outside the package that can access the protected member are subclasses (classes cannot be protected). Place the `protected` keyword in front of the member.

```
protected double radius;
protected double area()
```

`abstract` specifies the class cannot be instantiated directly. You must declare a class as `abstract` if

- any of its methods are `abstract`
- it inherits information from a class that defines `abstract` methods and does not implement these methods
- it extends an interface but does not implement its methods

Optionally, you can also decide that you do not want other programmers instantiating your class and can declare your class to be `abstract`, even if your class does not contain any `abstract` methods. The `abstract` keyword is placed in front of the class definition if the class is `abstract`, and in front of a method definition if the method is `abstract`.

```
abstract class Shape
abstract void draw()
```

`static` indicates that a member belongs with the class. Place the `static` keyword in front of the member.

```
static double radius;
public static double area()
```

TIP: *By convention, access control keywords are placed first.*

`synchronized` indicates only one thread can access the synchronized methods for a particular object or class at a time. You can define a `synchronized` method by placing this keyword in front of the method.

```
synchronized void initCircle()
```

You can also define a `synchronized` block of code by writing the keyword `synchronized`, followed by an object or class that will be used to obtain the monitor or lock (more information on threads and synchronization will be covered in Chapter 13, "Threads").

```
synchronized (this) { }
```

`volatile` tells the compiler that a variable may change asynchronously due to threads. Declaring a variable to be `volatile` makes the compiler forego optimizations that might turn the variable into a constant and eliminate the possibility of it changing asynchronously.

```
volatile int numCircles;
```

final means that this variable or method cannot be changed by subclasses. A final member can be optimized by the compiler and turned into a constant if it is a variable or turned into an inline code if it is a method. A final method keeps programmers from changing the method's contract, its agreed-upon behavior.

```
public static final int RADIUS = 20;
final double area()
```

native indicates a method is implemented using native, platform-dependent code (such as C code). The native keyword indicates the method is not written in Java, but in some platform-dependent language.

```
native double area()
```

Simple Data Types

We'll discuss Java's data types in Chapter 5, "Data Types and Values." Here's a quick list of all the primitive data types:

long is a 64-bit signed integer value.

int is a 32-bit signed integer value.

short is a 16-bit signed integer value.

byte is an 8-bit signed integer value.

double is a 64-bit floating-point value.

float is a 32-bit floating-point value.

char is a 16-bit Unicode character.

boolean is a true or false value.

Values and Variables

true and false are Boolean values. this refers to the current instance in an instance method. The keyword this is really a "magic" object reference that refers to the object responding to a method. With this, you can pass the current object to another method or refer to an instance variable when a local variable might hide the instance variable.

```
addToList(this);
this.length = length;
```

super refers to the immediate superclass in an instance method. The keyword super is really a "magic" object reference that refers to an object responding to a method whose type is the superclass of the responding object. With super, you can pass a method to call up the class hierarchy.

```
super.draw();
```

null represents a nonexistent instance. void indicates that a method does not return a value. You can use void instead as the return type of a method to indicate the method does not return a value.

```
void draw()
void writeToScreen(String s)
```

Exception Handling

throw signals that an exception has occurred. You must write a throwable object following this keyword. Typically, a new instance of an Exception class is created on the spot. Exception implements the throwable interface. Further explanation concerning these keywords is covered in Chapter 8, "Exceptions," which covers exception handling.

```
throw new IOException();
```

try marks the stack so that if an exception is thrown, it unwinds to this point. The above explanation for try is a cryptic way of saying that you try to execute a block of code, and following the try block, you catch any exceptions that the methods you invoked might have thrown. You can also execute a `finally` block following the `try` block (see below).

```
try { }
// followed by exception handling and/or a finally block
```

`catch` handles an exception. A `catch` block follows a `try` block. After the `catch` keyword, write the type of exception that your `catch` block will handle. This exception type is written in parentheses, similar to a method parameter.

```
//a try block precedes a catch block
catch (IOException x) { }
```

`finally` says "execute this block of code, regardless of control flow statements." A `finally` block can follow a `try` block or a try/catch block.

```
// following a try or try/catch block
finally { }
```

`throws` indicates the types of exceptions a method is allowed to throw. Methods that might throw a checked exception must indicate the exception type with a `throws` clause in the method declaration.

TIP: *Methods can optionally indicate that they throw unchecked exceptions. Unchecked exceptions inherit from* `RuntimeException` *or* `Error`.

```
void pauseGame(int seconds) throws InterruptedException { }
double area(String area) throws NumberFormatException { }
```

Instance Creation and Testing

`new` creates new instances. Following a `new` keyword, specify the class name you'd like to create an instance of, and supply the appropriate parameters for the constructor you want to invoke. The new keyword returns an object reference to the new object.

```
Circle c = new Circle();
Circle c = new Circle(40, Color.blue);
```

instanceof tests whether an instance derives from a particular class or interface. This keyword is really an operator that tests an object reference to see what it derives from. The instanceof operator will respond true if the object reference refers to an object that is an instance of the class being tested, if it is an instance of a subclass of that class, or if it is an instance of a class that implements the interface specified with this operator.

```
if (objRef instanceof Cloneable)
if (objRef instanceof Shape)
```

Control Flow

Java's control flow statements are similar to the control flow statements in other languages, such as C. switch tests a variable, while case executes a particular block of code according to the value tested in switch. default means the default block of code executes if no matching case statement is found. break jumps out of the block of code in which it is defined.

The switch-case construct is a convenient way to pick from a variety of possible values for an expression and take a different action for each of them, rather than writing lots of nested if-else statements.

```
String nobelWinner = null;
switch (year) {
case (1938):
nobelWinner = new String("Enrico Firmi");
break;
case (1921):
nobelWinner = new String("Albert Einstein");
break;
case (1903):
```

```
nobelWinner = new String("Marie Curie");
break;
default:
nobelWinner = new String("unknown");
}
```

for signifies iteration. A for statement contains three parts: initialization of the loop index, a test for halting the loop, and modification of the loop index, all of which are separated by semicolons. You can place more than one expression in any of these three parts by separating them with a comma.

continue continues with the next iteration of a loop. The continue statement can be a convenient way to skip over code and go on to the next loop iteration.

```
for (int index = 0; index < limit; index++) {
if ((result = calculate(index)) == 0)
continue; // loop back to the for loop
//more code in this loop . . .
}
```

You can also use labels with a continue or break statement. Then instead of continuing with the next loop iteration in the block where the continue is used, or instead of breaking out of the block the break is defined in, you can continue or break to the block defined by the label. Examples of this are included in Chapter 7, "Control Flow."

return returns from a method, optionally passing back a value. if tests for a condition and performs some action if true. else performs some action if an if test is false.

```
String nobelWinner = null;
if (year == 1938)
nobelWinner = new String("Enrico Firmi");
else if (year == 1921)
nobelWinner = new String("Albert Einstein");
else if (year == 1903)
nobelWinner = new String("Marie Curie");
else
nobelWinner = new String("unknown");
}
```

do performs some statement or set of statements. while performs some action while a condition is true. To perform a block of code conditionally, you can use while without do, as in

```
while (condition == true) {
doThis();
}
```

To perform a block of code at least once, and thereafter conditionally, you can use while in conjunction with do:

```
do {
doThis();
} while (condition == true);
```

Exercises

Exercise 3-1

Sort the following list into reserved and non-reserved words.

```
for
do_while
Integer
int
implements
equals
Object
java
switch
break
test
code
goto
```

Exercise 3-2

List all the keywords that can be used to define control flow statements.

Exercise 3-3

List the keywords reserved by Java but not used in Java 1.2.

The Default Constructor

For a given class, you'll need to be able to describe the default constructor. You'll also need to be able to identify situations when the default constructor is created for you and when it is not. Basically, if you do not define a constructor explicitly, Java defines one for you. This *default* constructor takes no arguments and invokes its superclass no-args constructor.

Here's a simple example for a class named Queue. This class is a subclass of Vector. (A queue stores values using a first-in, first-out strategy.)

```
import java.util.Vector;
class Queue extends Vector {
void enqueue(Object obj) {
addElement(obj);
}
Object dequeue() {
Object obj = firstElement();
boolean success = removeElement(obj);
return obj;
}
}
```

Given this class definition, you can create Queue objects by writing code like this

```
Queue q = new Queue();
```

You can add() objects to and get() objects from this Queue object by invoking Queue's methods.

Defining, Overloading, and Overriding a Constructor

Now that you've reviewed default constructors, let's look at defining, overloading, and overriding constructors. The Queue class created in the previous example works fine except for one thing: it does not support other constructors defined by Vector. These constructors are defined in the documentation within java.util (where Vector is defined) as

```
public Vector(int initialCapacity);
public Vector(int initialCapacity, int capacityIncrement);
public Vector(Collection c);
```

As with methods, the *Java Virtual Machine* (JVM) determines which constructor to execute by the arguments you supply when creating a new object. These additional constructors overload the default Vector constructor. If you do not override one of these overloaded constructors in the Queue class and try to create a Queue object like this

```
Queue q = new Queue(100);
```

and you think that this would invoke the correct Vector constructor to set the initial capacity of this Queue/Vector, think again. The only constructor Java provides for you is the no-args constructor. So the above line won't work with the code we've written so far; Java will say there is no constructor for Queue that takes an int as a parameter. To make this work, you've got to write the appropriate constructor in the Queue class.

You can define a constructor for a class by writing any access control keywords, the class name, a set of arguments in parentheses, any exceptions the constructor might throw, and then the body of the constructor, just as you would for a method, except that you do not define a return value. Constructors *never* return a value. If you specify a return value, Java will interpret your intended constructor as a method.

The constructor we need for Queue could take an int and invoke the corresponding constructor defined in Vector by using super():

```
Queue(int capacity) {
super(capacity);
}
```

Now the line of code

```
Queue q = new Queue(100);
```

runs without a hitch. We could also write a constructor for `Queue` to handle the second `Vector` constructor, the one that takes two `int` parameters, an initial capacity, and an increment.

This `Queue` class now works fine, except we can no longer create a `Queue` object the way we did before by writing

```
Queue q = new Queue();
```

What gives? We've fixed one problem and created another. The problem is that Java only supplies the default no-args constructor if you do not define any other constructor. Since we have now supplied a constructor that takes an int, Java does not define a no-args constructor for us. The way around this problem is to supply a no-args constructor ourselves. Here is a complete definition for our new Queue class:

```
import java.util.Vector;
class Queue extends Vector {
Queue() {
super();
}
Queue(int capacity) {
super(capacity);
}
Queue(int capacity, int increment) {
super(capacity, increment);
}
void enqueue(Object obj) {
addElement(obj);
}
Object dequeue() {
Object obj = firstElement();
boolean success = removeElement(obj);
return obj;
}
}
```

Invoking Another Constructor

You can invoke one of the overloaded constructors by supplying the appropriate parameters in super(). Placing a call to super() in any line other than the first one results in a compiler error. If you do not invoke a superclass constructor yourself, Java will attempt to invoke the no-args constructor in your superclass. If the superclass does not have a no-args constructor, the Java compiler will detect this situation if it can and issue a compiler error. Otherwise, if the compiler doesn't detect this situation (because of classes loaded dynamically at runtime), Java will throw a runtime exception when it encounters trouble.

You can use this() and super() to invoke constructors in the current or parent class. If you invoke another constructor directly, make that direct call as the first line of your constructor. For example, let's say you want to define a constructor for Queue that takes an array of objects to place into the Queue, and you want to set the initial capacity of that Queue to the length of the array. You can write such a constructor like this

```
Queue(Object[] objs) {
this(objs.length);
for (int index = 0; index < objs.length; index++)
addElement(objs[index]);
}
```

This constructor invokes a constructor in the same class that takes an int value (the constructor that takes the int value defines the initial capacity). The constructor then performs some additional processing to add the objects in the array to the Queue.

Exercise 3-4

Create a subclass of class Frame called MyFrame. Define MyFrame so that you can create a new MyFrame object with a title. The Frame class defines a constructor that takes a title as a String as in

```
Frame (String s);
```

The Frame class is a real Java class defined in java.awt.

Exercise 3-5

Here is a class named Bridge:

```
class Bridge {
int length;
Bridge(int length) {
this.length = length;
}
}
```

Modify this class definition to construct a new Bridge instance without explicitly supplying the Bridge's length, like this

```
Bridge b = new Bridge();
```

Exercise 3-6

Given this class definition

```
class Railroad {
String name;
Railroad() {
System.out.println("I've been working on the railroad");
}
Railroad(String name) {
this.name = name;
}
}
```

How could you adjust the second constructor (the one that takes the String) most efficiently so that it also displays the message I've been working on the railroad when it is invoked?

Answers to the Exercises

Exercise 3-1

Don't mistake class names for reserved words:

- `for`
- `int`
- `implements`
- `switch`
- `break`
- `goto`

non-reserved words

- `do_while`
- `Integer`
- `equals`
- `Object`
- `java`
- `test`
- `code`

Exercise 3-2

The keywords used with control flow statements are `do`, `while`, `if`, `else`, `for`, `break`, `continue`, `case`, `switch`, `default`, and `return`.

Exercise 3-3

The two unused keywords are `const` and `goto`.

Exercise 3-4

To create a class called MyFrame that defines a title, you've got to override the Frame's constructor that takes a String and pass that String object up to the Frame's constructor, like this

```
import java.awt.Frame;
class MyFrame extends Frame {
MyFrame(String s) {
super(s);
}
}
```

Exercise 3-5

The no-args constructor is only supplied for you if you have not defined another constructor. In this case, since there is already another constructor, you've got to write the no-args constructor explicitly:

```
class Bridge {
int length;
Bridge(int length) {
this.length = length;
}
Bridge() {
}
}
```

You do not have to supply any code for this no-args constructor. The JVM will invoke your superclass' no-args constructor for you, and since length is already set to 0 as its default value, you do not need to initialize length in the constructor itself.

Exercise 3-6

You can invoke the no-args constructor in the Railroad class using
`this()`, as in

```
class Railroad {
String name;
Railroad() {
System.out.println("I've been working on the railroad");
}
Railroad(String name) {
this();
this.name = name;
}
}
```

Review Questions

1. Which word is not a Java keyword?

   a) integer
   b) double
   c) float
   d) default

2. Which keyword is not used to control access to a class member?

   a) public
   b) protected
   c) private
   d) default

3. Identify the keywords from this list:

abstract	class	object	reference
double	character	Boolean	this

   a) abstract, class, object, double, this
   b) class, object, this
   c) abstract, class, double, this
   d) abstract, class, object, double, character, this

4. What is the result of attempting to compile and run the
following code?

```
class Ex {
public static void main(String[] args) {
Fx f = new Fx();
}
Ex(int i) {
}
}
class Fx extends Ex {
}
```

a) The code does not compile because the Ex class does not define a
no-args constructor.
b) The code does not compile because the Fx class does not define a
no-args constructor.
c) The code does not compile because there is no code in the Ex(int i)
constructor.
d) The code compiles and runs successfully.

5. What is the result of attempting to compile and run the
following code?

```
class Ex {
public static void main(String[] args) {
Fx f = new Fx(5);
}
Ex() {
System.out.println("Ex, no-args");
}
Ex(int i) {
System.out.println("Ex, int");
}
}
class Fx extends Ex {
Fx() {
super();
System.out.println("Fx, no-args");
}
Fx(int i) {
super(i);
this();
System.out.println("Fx, int");
}
}
```

a) The messages Ex, int, Fx, no-args, and Fx, int appear in the standard output.
b) The messages Ex, no-args, Ex, int, Fx, no-args, and Fx, int appear in the standard output.
c) The code does not compile because the Fx(int i) constructor is not defined legally.
d) The code does not compile because the Fx( ) constructor is not defined legally.

6. What is the result of attempting to compile and run the following code?

```
class Ex {
public static void main(String[] args) {
Fx f = new Fx(5);
}
Ex() {
System.out.println("Ex, no-args");
}
Ex(int i) {
System.out.println("Ex, int");
}
}
class Fx extends Ex {
Fx() {
super();
System.out.println("Fx, no-args");
}
Fx(int i) {
this();
System.out.println("Fx, int");
}
}
```

a) The messages Ex, int, Fx, no-args, and Fx, int appear in the standard output.
b) The messages Ex, no-args, Fx, no-args, and Fx, int appear in the standard output.
c) The code does not compile because the Fx(int i) constructor is not defined legally.
d) The code does not compile because the Fx( ) constructor is not defined legally.

Answers to Review Questions

1. a. The integer data types are int, long, byte, and short, but there is no integer type. (Integer, with a capital I, is a class name.)

2. d. The default keyword is used with switch-case statements.

3. c. The others (object, reference, character, and Boolean) are not keywords.

4. a. The default constructor in Fx will attempt to invoke a no-args constructor in Ex. Since Ex already defines a constructor, Java does not supply a no-args constructor by default. The compiler will catch this problem and complain.

5. c. The Fx(int i) constructor is defined like this

```
Fx(int i) {
super(i);
this();
System.out.println("Fx, int");
}
```

However, a direct call to a constructor must appear as the first thing in a constructor. Although super(i) is first, this( ) is second, and this( ) is also a direct call to a constructor. This is illegal.

6. b. First, Java invokes the constructor Fx(int i). This calls Fx ( ), which invokes the no-args superclass constructor Ex(). This writes Ex, no-args to the standard output. Then the Fx() no-args constructor continues, which writes Fx, no-args to the standard output. Then the Fx(int i) constructor continues, which writes Fx, int to the standard output.

CHAPTER 4

Memory and Garbage Collection

Java manages your program's memory. This eliminates all manner of bugs that creep into programs built with languages where you must access and manage memory directly. Java's role in managing memory eliminates bugs involving

- Freeing memory too soon (resulting in a dangling pointer)
- Not freeing memory soon enough or at all (resulting in a memory leak)
- Accessing memory beyond the bounds of the allocated memory (resulting in using uninitialized values)

When you want to define a new data type, you define a new class. You allocate an instance of a class by using the new keyword which returns an object reference. This object reference is essentially a pointer to the object in memory, except in Java you cannot manipulate this object reference like a number. You cannot perform pointer arithmetic.

Objects are allocated from a garbage collected heap. You cannot directly alter the memory in this heap. You can only get at the objects in this heap by using object references. Since Java manages the heap, and since you cannot manipulate object references, you must trust the *Java Virtual Machine* (JVM) to do what's right: free memory when it should, allocate the correct amount of memory when needed, and so on. But don't worry, the JVM is very good at its job, much better than any of us error-prone humans.

Objectives for This Chapter

- Identify when an object referred to by a local variable becomes eligible to be garbage collected (in the absence of compiler optimization).
- Describe how finalization works and what behavior Java guarantees regarding finalization.
- Distinguish between modifying variables containing primitive data types and object references and modifying the objects themselves.

■ Identify the results of Java's "pass by value" approach when passing parameters to methods.

Garbage Collection

For the exam, you'll need to be able to identify when an object referred to by a local variable becomes eligible to be garbage collected (in the absence of compiler optimization). Since Java manages the garbage collected heap, which is where all your objects live, you've got to trust Java to manage the memory for you. This includes believing that the JVM really will free memory you no longer need when it runs low.

When Does an Object Become Eligible for Garbage Collection?

An object becomes a candidate for garbage collection when your program can no longer reference it. Here is an example. Say you allocate an object and only assign it to a method variable. When that method returns, there is no way for you to ever refer to that method variable again. Therefore, the object is lost forever. That means that when the method returns, the object is a candidate for garbage collection.

As another example, you might create an object, assign this object to an object reference, and then set this object reference to `null`. As soon as you lose the reference to the object, that object becomes a candidate for garbage collection.

Just because your program might lose a reference to an object does not mean that the JVM will reclaim that object's memory right away, or even at all. The JVM will only perform garbage collection if it needs more memory to continue executing. For almost all simple programs, including the ones you've seen so far, the JVM doesn't even come close to running out of memory.

Technical Trap: *The reason the garbage collector does not reclaim memory as soon as it is available is that garbage collection takes time. If the garbage collector continuously expunges allocated memory you could no longer access, it would seriously slow your program's execution. There is no guarantee as to the order in which the garbage collector reclaims objects. This enables the garbage collector to run as efficiently as possible.*

Even though there is a `new` keyword, notice that you do not explicitly indicate how much memory to set aside. The JVM determines this for itself. The JVM determines the memory your object requires based on two factors:

1. The amount of memory needed to maintain instance variables for the object

2. A standard overhead required by all objects

What's more, even though Java supplies the keyword `new`, there is no corresponding `delete` or any other way to directly free memory. The way you indicate you are through with an object is to set its object reference to `null` or to some other object. Or, as mentioned, when a method returns, its method variables will no longer be valid, so the garbage collector also knows any objects referenced by method variables are candidates for garbage collection.

Invoking the Garbage Collector

Even though you cannot free objects explicitly, you *can* directly invoke the garbage collector. This will activate the garbage collector, which will reclaim candidates for garbage collection.

Running the garbage collector is done in two steps:

1. Get an object that represents the current runtime.

2. Invoke that object's gc( ) method.

Here is a snippet that does this:

```
Runtime rt 5 Runtime.getRuntime();
rt.gc();
```

Exercise 4–2 asks you to work through an example of this.

Finalization

For the exam, you'll need to know when finalization takes place. In most situations, you'll never know when garbage collection has occurred. Java runs the garbage collecting process as a low-priority background thread. The garbage collector runs whenever memory gets low, but you can also manually run it. If you want to perform some task when your object is about to go away, you can override a method called `finalize()`. Java will invoke the `finalize()` method exactly once for every object in your program. `finalize()` is declared as protected, does not return a value, and throws a throwable object.

Java invokes the `finalize()` method just before an object is about to be garbage collected. You might take advantage of this notification to clean up any resources that have been allocated outside this object. A classic example is a file that an object has opened that might still be open. The object can check to see if the file has been closed in `finalize()`, and if not, it closes the file.

Technical Trap: *Although you can try and catch blocks in* `finalize()`, *uncaught exceptions are ignored. The official documentation says that* `finalize()` *will be run for all objects when the program exits. However, on some platforms and in earlier versions of Java, this was not always the case. Sometimes* `finalize()` *simply did not run unless the JVM ran out of memory or, if it did not, you explicitly invoked the garbage collector.*

You can also invoke your own object's `finalize()` method. Typically, you would not invoke `finalize()` yourself, but would allow the JVM to do this for you. If you do invoke `finalize()`, remember that `finalize()` is declared as throwing a throwable and that it is declared as `protected`, so only objects with the proper access can invoke this method.

It's easy to forget that `finalize()` can be implemented in a superclass. Be certain to invoke your superclass' `finalize()` method so that you don't break the code that you're inheriting from. Since Java only invokes `finalize()` once per object, you should not resurrect an object in `finalize()`. If you did and the object is finalized again, its `finalize()` method will not get called. Instead, you should create a clone of the object if you really need to bring the object back to life.

TIP: *Always invoke your superclass's* `finalize()` *method if you override* `finalize()`.

Exercise 4-1

Write a class called Test whose objects write the message `We're in finalize` to the standard output when their `finalize()` methods are run.

Exercise 4-2

Given the following code for a class called GC, create a new Test object in GC's `test()` method and then make that object a candidate for garbage collection. Do this before the call to `fullGC()` in `test()`.

When this code is working, running GC with the Test class you wrote should cause the message `We're in finalize` to appear in the standard output automatically, without you explicitly invoking `finalize()`.

```
class GC {
 public static void main(String[] args) {
  GC gc = new GC();
  gc.test();
 }
 void test() {
  fullGC();
 }
```

```
void fullGC() {
 Runtime rt = Runtime.getRuntime();
 long isFree = rt.freeMemory();
 long wasFree;
 do {
  wasFree = isFree;
  rt.gc();
  isFree = rt.freeMemory();
 } while (isFree > wasFree);
 rt.runFinalization();
 }
}
```

Accessing Members

You should be able to distinguish between modifying variables containing primitive data types and object references and modifying the objects themselves. Given an object reference, which variable you access and which method you invoke depend on different things. The type of the *object reference* determines which variable you access. The type of the *underlying object* determines which method you invoke.

As an example, consider the following code:

```
class Acc {
 public static void main(String[] args) {
  First s = new Second();
  System.out.println(s.var);
  System.out.println(s.method());
 }
}
class First {
 int var = 1;
 int method() {
  return var;
 }
}
class Second extends First {
 int var = 2;
 int method() {
  return var;
 }
}
```

What do you expect this program to display in the standard output? Notice that the variable s in `main()` is defined as an object reference for the First type, but we've actually allocated a new object of type Second, a subclass of First.

When we use s to access a variable, the type of s, which in this case is First, is used to grab the variable. So, we access `var` from First, which is 1. Thus, in the first `println()` statement, 1 appears in the standard output.

When we use s to invoke a method, the type of the object referenced by s, which in this case is Second, is used to invoke the method. So, we invoke `method()` in Second, which accesses its local variable named `var`. This makes the second `println()` statement display 2 in the standard output.

What would happen if we change the class definition of Second so that it no longer overrides `method()`? In this case, even though `s.method()` will look first in the Second class to access `method()`, the call will get passed up the class hierarchy. The `method()` that's defined in First will execute and will access its local `var` variable, which is 1, so the second `println()` statement would display 1.

Exercise 4-3

When you invoke a method given an object reference, is there a way to force the JVM to invoke the overridden method that's defined in that object's superclass, instead of invoking the method in the class type of the object itself? For example, given the classes First and Second defined in the previous section, is it possible to invoke `method()` defined in First, rather than `method()` defined in Second, given an object reference of type Second?

Passing Parameters to a Method

For the exam, you'll need to be able to identify the results of Java's "pass by value" approach when passing parameters to methods. When Java passes method parameters *by value*, Java makes a copy of the parameter and passes this copy to the method.

For a primitive data type, such as int, float, boolean, or char, the result of passing by value should be clear: anything that happens to that value inside the method does not affect the original value in the calling code.

Here's an example:

```
public class ch0401 {
 public static void main(String[] args) {
  double pi = 3.1415;
  System.out.println("before: pi is " 1 pi);
  zero(pi);
  System.out.println("after: pi is " 1 pi);
 }
 static void zero(double arg) {
  System.out.println("top of zero: arg is " + arg);
  arg = 0.0;
  System.out.println("bottom of zero: arg is " + arg);
 }
}
```

First, we set a value for a variable named pi, and then we pass this value to a method that sets this value to 0. The value of pi gets to the method named zero() just fine, and zero() does its job of setting the value it receives to 0. However, zero() has received a copy. The original value of pi in main() is not affected. The output from this program is

before: pi is 3.1415

top of zero: arg is 3.1415

bottom of zero: arg is 0

after: pi is 3.1415

Although the same call by the value rule is in place when the argument is an object reference, rather than a primitive data type, unraveling what's really going on involves some careful thinking.

Let's redo the previous program, this time making the variable pi an object reference that refers to an instance of a class we'll create called Pi. This class will have one instance variable and will look like the following program.

```
class Pi {
 double value = 3.1415;
 public String toString() {
  Double d = new Double(value);
  return d.toString();
 }
}
```

TIP: *By overriding the method* toString(), *we provide a way to place the object reference directly in a* println() *statement to display its value. You can use this trick in your own programs to help make your code easier to read and your objects easier to work with.*

Let's rework the original program to use an instance of the Pi class, instead of passing the value of pi directly as a double.

```
public class ch0402 {
 public static void main(String[] args) {
  Pi pi = new Pi();
  System.out.println("before: pi is " + pi);
  zero(pi);
  System.out.println("after: pi is " + pi);
 }
 static void zero(Pi arg) {
  System.out.println("top of zero: arg is " + arg);
  arg.value = 0.0;
  System.out.println("middle of zero: arg is " + arg);
  arg = null;
  System.out.println("bottom of zero: arg is " + arg);
 }
}
```

What do you expect the outcome of this program to be? To answer this question correctly, you need to have a picture in mind of what's going on in memory. In main(), after creating the instance of Pi and assigning it to an object reference called pi, we have something like Figure 4-1.

Figure 4-1
An object reference
accessing an object
in the garbage
collected heap.

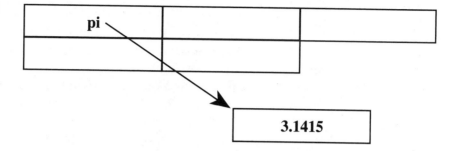

Figure 4-2
Two object
references pointing
to the same object in
the garbage
collected heap.

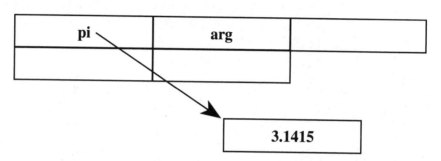

There's a chunk of memory somewhere that we refer to by the name pi. This chunk of memory (which is four bytes long, to be exact) points to an object that's somewhere else in memory. Notice that an object reference like pi is a pointer, even though there is no way in Java to manipulate pi as if it is a pointer, as you can in C or C++. The object referenced by pi has an instance variable set to 3.1415, so that's how we've depicted it in the diagram.

As soon as weinvoke the method named zero(), Java needs to keep track of another object reference: the method parameter (that is, the variable) we've named arg. The variable arg is completely separate from the variable pi, because parameters are passed by value, and so Java makes a copy of the variable. However, as with the double values in the previous example, the contents of each variable are the same. Hence, arg also points to the same object as pi. See figure 4-2.

Now if we use the variable arg to change the object, we change the object directly. The code, for example, sets arg.value to 0. See figure 4-3.

The final section of code in the method `zero()` sets the value of `arg` to `null`. This does nothing to the object itself or to any other object references; setting `arg` to `null` only changes the object reference named `arg`. See figure 4-4.

The variable `arg` loses its reference to the object, but the object itself is still intact. Also intact are any other references to the object. If `arg` is the only object reference to the underlying Pi object, then the object would become a candidate for garbage collection. However, `arg` is just a parameter, and there is another reference to the underlying object, the reference in the calling code. The output of this code, then, looks like this

before: pi is 3.1415

top of zero: arg is 3.1415

middle of zero: arg is 0

bottom of zero: arg is null

after: pi is 0

Figure 4-3
Changing the same object by using the second object reference

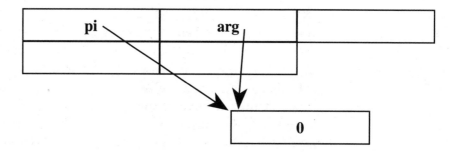

Figure 4-4
Setting one of the object references to null, but the object is untouched

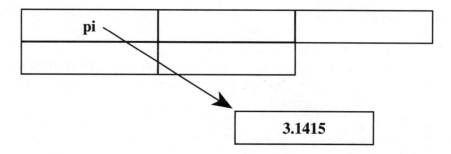

Exercise 4-4

Find a way to change the following code so that you can pass the values a, b, and c in test() to calc(). Then have calc() update these values and return them to test(). As the values are currently defined, there is no way to pass them to calc() and then return them to test(). The reason for this is that the values are defined as primitive data types. Perhaps there is another data type that you can pass to calc() so that this will work?

```
class A {
 public static void main(String[] args) {
  A a = new A();
  a.test();
 }
 void test() {
  int a = 10;
  int b = 13;
  int c = 24;
  System.out.println("before: a = " 1 a);
  System.out.println("before: b = " 1 b);
  System.out.println("before: c = " + c);
  calc(a, b, c);
  System.out.println("after: a = " + a);
  System.out.println("after: b = " + b);
  System.out.println("after: c = " + c);
 }
 void calc(int a, int b, int c) {
  a *= 2;
  b *= 3;
  c *= 4;
 }
}
```

What's Not on the Test—Forcing Garbage Collection

Exercise 4-2 contained some code that used a Runtime object to force garbage collection. This is not something that is on the test, but it's useful to know how to do this. Four methods are defined by

Runtime that you can use to help keep track of and interact with the garbage collector:

- `gc()` By the time this method returns, the JVM has performed garbage collection.

- `runFinalization()` By the time this method returns, the JVM has run the `finalize()` method for all objects awaiting garbage collection whose `finalize()` methods have not yet been run.

- `totalMemory()` This method returns an `int` containing the total amount of memory available in the JVM for allocating objects.

- `freeMemory()` This method returns an `int` containing the total amount of free memory in bytes. Free memory is the amount of memory available for allocating objects. This amount will always be less than the value returned by `totalMemory()`.

Answers to the Exercises

Exercise 4-1

You can write a Test class that overrides `finalize()` like this

```
class Test {
 protected void finalize() throws Throwable {
   super.finalize();
   System.out.println("We're in finalize");
 }
}
```

Remember, `finalize()` is declared as `protected` and throws a throwable.

Exercise 4-2

Your test method in GC should now look like this

```
void test() {
  Test t = new Test();
  t = null;
  fullGC();
}
```

Exercise 4-3

No, you can invoke super() from a method, but you cannot invoke a method defined in a superclass given only an object reference.

Exercise 4-4

One way to solve this problem is to create a new class that has three int values for a, b, and c, pass an instance of this class to calc(), and have calc() operate on the instance variables of this object.

Another way is to create an array of int values and to pass the array to calc(). Remember, an array is an object, so you can pass the array to a method and if the method modifies the elements of the array, these changes will appear in the calling method's array as well. Here is an example.

```
class B {
  public static void main(String[] args) {
    B b = new B();
    b.test();
  }
  void test() {
    int[] arr = {10, 13, 24};
    for (int i = 0; i < arr.length; i11)
```

```
    System.out.println("before: a" 1 i 1 " = " 1 arr[i]);
   calc(arr);
   for (int i = 0; i < arr.length; i11)
    System.out.println("after: a" 1 i 1 " = " 1 arr[i]);
 }
 void calc(int[] arr) {
  arr[0] *= 2;
  arr[1] *= 3;
  arr[2] *= 4;
 }
}
```

QUESTIONS

1. What would the result be in the standard output if you executed the class named Acc2, listed below?

```
class Acc2 {
 public static void main(String[] args) {
  First s = new Second();
  Second s2 = (Second)s;
  System.out.println(s2.var);
  System.out.println(s2.method());
 }
}
class First {
 int var = 1;
 int method() {
  return var;
 }
}
class Second extends First {
 int var = 2;
 int method() {
  return var;
 }
}
```

    a. 2
       2
    b. 2
       1
    c. 1
       2
    d. 1
       1

2. How many objects are candidates for garbage collection by the end of the following code snippet?

```
String s = "kanga";
s = "kanga" + "roo";
int[] arr = {1, 4, 9, 25};
arr[3] = 16;
arr = new int[4];
s = null;
```

    a. 1
    b. 2
    c. 3
    d. 4

3. Which answer defines a legal finalize( ) method?

    a.

```
protected void finalize() {
 super.finalize();
 System.out.println("finalize");
}
```

    b.

```
private void finalize() throws Throwable {
 super.finalize();
 System.out.println("finalize");
}
```

    c.

```
protected void finalize() throws Throwable {
 super.finalize();
 System.out.println("finalize");
}
```

d.

```
void finalize() {
 super.finalize();
 System.out.println("finalize");
}
```

4. What happens if you attempt to compile and run this code:

```
class Clean {
 public static void main(String[] args) {
  Dirty d = new Dirty();
  d.finalize();
  d = null;
  Runtime r = Runtime.getRuntime();
  r.gc();
  r.runFinalization();
 }
}
class Dirty {
 protected void finalize() throws Throwable {
  System.out.println("Dirty finalization");
 }
}
```

   a.   The code will not compile because of a problem invoking finalize( ).
   b.   The code will compile but will display nothing.
   c.   The code will compile and will display Dirty finalization once.
   d.   The code will compile and will display Dirty finalization twice.

ANSWERS

1. **a.** Since we cast the object reference s from type First to type
   Second, we then access Second's var and method.

2. **c.** Let's take this line by line:

```
String s = "kanga";
s = "kanga" + "roo";
```

At this point, we have created two objects. The first `String` object contained the characters `kanga`. The second contained the characters `kangaroo`. Since we can no longer reference the first `String` object, we have reused the `s` object reference; this is the first object now available for garbage collection.

```
int[] arr = {1, 4, 9, 25};
arr[3] = 16;
```

At this point, we have created a new int array and accessed one of its elements.

```
arr = new int[4];
```

Now we create a new `int` array and assign it to the object reference `arr`. Therefore, we lost track of the first array that contained 1, 4, 9, and 25. This is the second object that is now available for garbage collection.

```
s = null;
```

Setting `s` to null makes us lose the reference to the String containing kangaroo. This object is now available for garbage collection as well.

3. c. The `finalize()` method is protected and throws an object of type throwable.

4. a. The problem with invoking `finalize()` is that it is declared as throwing an object of class Throwable. That means the direct call to `finalize()` must be placed within a `try-catch` block. There's a full explanation of exception handling in Chapter 9, "Methods."

CHAPTER 5

Data Types and
Values

This chapter provides a review of Java's data types, how to use them, and what their default values are. We also look at declaring, constructing, and initializing arrays.

Objectives for this Chapter

- Define the range of values for all primitive data types.
- Construct literal `char` values using both quoted formats and Unicode escape sequences.
- Identify the default values of instance and `static` variables.
- Define arrays.
- Determine the default values for elements in an array.
- Use curly braces { } as part of an array declaration to initialize an array.

Data Types

For the exam, you'll need to be able to define the range of values for `byte`, `short`, `int`, `long`, and `char`. Java has eight primitive data types as shown in Table 5-1.

Table 5-1	**Data Type**	**Size in Bits**
Primitive Data Types	byte	Signed 8-bit integer
	short	Signed 16-bit integer
	int	Signed 32-bit integer
	long	Signed 64-bit integer
	float	Signed 32-bit floating-point
	double	Signed 64-bit floating-point
	char	16-bit Unicode character
	boolean	Either true or false (special values built-in Java)

For the exam, you'll need to be able to state the range for all primitive data types. The ranges are listed in Table 5-2.

Data Type	Range
byte	22^7 to 2^7 - 1 (2128 to 127)
short	22^15 to 2^15 - 1 (232,768 to 32,767)
int	22^31 to 2^31 - 1 (22,147,483,648 to 2,147,483,647)
long	22^63 to 2^63 - 1
float	Float.MIN_VALUE to Float.MAX_VALUE, Float.NaN, Float.NEGATIVE_INFINITY, Float.POSITIVE_INFINITY
double	Double.MIN_VALUE to Double.MAX_VALUE, Double.NaN, Double.NEGATIVE_INFINITY, Double.POSITIVE_INFINITY
char	0 to 2^16 - 1 (0 to 65,535)
boolean	Either true or false (special values built into Java)

Table 5-2

Ranges for primitive data types

Default Values

If you do not supply a default value for member variables, they use a standard default value. These default values are as follows:

Type	Default Value
boolean	false
byte	0
char	\u0000
short	0
int	0
long	01
float	0.0f
double	0.0d

Table 5-3

Default values for primitive data types

Not defining a default value for a local variable results in a compile-time error.

Literals and String Literals

You can specify integer values in three bases: decimal, octal, and hexadecimal. To specify a decimal number (a number in base 10), just write the number in the usual way (for example, 123 and −403 represent integer numbers in base 10).

To specify an octal number (a number in base 8), put a leading 0 in front of it. To specify a hexadecimal number (a number in base 16), place a leading 0x in front of it. For example, in base 10, the following values

```
10
010
0x10
```

are equal to 10, 8, and 16, respectively.

By default, integer values are of type `int` and floating-point values are of type `double`. You can force an integer value to be a long, however, by placing an `L` after it. You can also force a floating-point value to be a float by placing an `F` after it.

Java also supports String literals. String literals are not primitive data types. Instead, they are a kind of shorthand notation used to represent String objects. Strings consist of characters enclosed in double quotes (`" "`). You can use any of the available escape codes to represent special characters in a string. Some of the most used escape codes are shown in Table 5-4.

Character Values

A `char` variable can contain any Unicode character. You can use the escape sequence \udddd to represent any Unicode character, where d is a hexadecimal digit. The ASCII characters are all found in the range \u0000 to \u00ff. The default value for any class variable or instance variable declared as a char is \u0000.

Escape Sequence	Meaning	Unicode representation
\b	Backspace	\u0008
\f	Form feed	\u000C
\t	Tab	\u0009
\n	Linefeed	\u000A
\r	Carriage return	\u000D
\"	Double quote	\u0022
\'	Single quote	\u0027
\\	Backslash	\u005C
\ddd	An octal char (each d is between 0 and 7)	
\udddd	A Unicode char (each d is between 0 and 9, and A and F)	

Table 5-4

Escape sequences

TECHNICAL TRAP: Don't confuse \u0000 *with a space character, which is* \u0020.

Floating-Point Arithmetic

Unlike integer data types, floating-point data types never throw an exception if some ill-defined state arises when performing arithmetic. For example, if you divide by 0 using integers, Java will throw an ArithmeticException. However, if you divide by 0 using floating-point types, Java assigns the value to infinity (of the appropriate sign matching the numerator). The class "wrapper" types double and float even define the class constants called POSITIVE_INFINITY and NEGATIVE_INFINITY that you can use to acquire these values.

In fact, arithmetic with floating-point values will never throw an exception. If the result is not a number at all, the result is NaN. Table 5-5 shows various outcomes with 0, finite values, and infinity.

The sign of infinity depends on the signs involved in the arithmetic expression. Any arithmetic expression involving NaN yields NaN.

Casting

You cannot implicitly coerce a data type with greater accuracy into a data type with less accuracy. In fact, trying to do so results in a compile-time error. This means, for example, that you cannot write code that looks like

```
int i = 5;
byte b = i;
```

because an int holds larger numbers than a byte. An int is more accurate. The Java compiler will complain that these are incompatible types for the = operator and that you need an explicit cast to convert the int into a byte. The way to do this is to write

```
int i = 5;
byte b = (byte)i;
```

The same is true with floating-point values. You cannot assign a double to a float, because a double is more accurate than a float,

Table 5-5

Arithmetic with floating point values

Value		Result	
x	y	x/y	x%y
finite	0.0	infinity	NaN
finite	infinity	0.0	x
0.0	0.0	infinity	NaN
infinity	finite	infinity	NaN
infinity	infinity	NaN	NaN

so you must explicitly cast it. Similarly, you cannot assign any kind of floating-point number to an integer type without an explicit cast.

Exercises

Exercise 5-1

What is the smallest integer data types you could use to hold

- the number of letters in the alphabet?
- the net worth of Bill Gates in U.S. dollars?
- the number of pages in this book?
- the number of people in the U.S.?

Exercise 5-2

Write a program that displays the default values for each integer type.

Exercise 5-3

What is wrong with the following program? How would you fix this code?

```
class Test {
 public static void main(String[] args) {
  int index;
  boolean found;
  for (index = 0; index < 10 && !found; index++) {
   if (index > Math.PI) {
    System.out.println(index + " is greater than Pi");
    found = true;
   }
  }
 }
}
```

Arrays

For the exam, you'll need to be able to declare, construct, and initialize arrays. Arrays of data types can be declared by writing square brackets after the data type, as in

```
int[] myIntArray;
```

or

```
MyClass[] myClassArray;
```

These two array declarations create variables whose types are an array of integers and an array of objects, respectively. Also, note that arrays are objects. Use new to create the array and allocate the array to the appropriate size. For example,

```
MyClass[] myClassArray = new MyClass[5];
```

allocates an array large enough to hold five elements. In this case, we have allocated an array of object references. The first element in an array is element 0. The last element is element length –1.

You'll also need to determine the default values for elements in an array. Java sets each element in an array to its default value when the array is created. For myClassArray, defined previously as an array of objects, each element is set to null when the array is first allocated. For an array of int values, each element would be set to 0.

TIP: *Something interesting about arrays in Java is since they are objects allocated at runtime, you can use a variable to set their length, which is something you cannot do in C/C++ when you must lay out the memory for an array at compile time.*

Rephrasing the tip above, an array's length can be determined at runtime. For example, you can write

```
String[] attendees = new String(numAttendees);
```

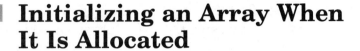

Initializing an Array When It Is Allocated

You don't have to use new explicitly to allocate and initialize an array. Instead, you can use curly braces to set its size and default values in one fell swoop. For example, you can create and initialize an array like this:

```
String[] movies = { "The Red Shoes", "Jeremiah Johnson",
"Ninotchka" }
```

The example allocates the movies array to three elements and initializes each element with a new String instance. This works just as well with object references in place of string literals. For example, you can write

```
String s1 = "The Red Shoes";
String s2 = "Jeremiah Johnson";
String s3 = "Ninotchka";
String[] movies = {s1, s2, s3};
```

This type of array initialization also works for primitive data types. For example, you can write

```
int[] arr = {1, 2, 3};
```

to declare and allocate an array of three integers whose elements are 1, 2, and 3.

By the way, the array declaration

```
String movies[]
```

works just like

```
String[] movies
```

TIP: *Although the first version uses the same syntax as* C/C++, *the second version is preferred, because* String[], *not* String, *is the data type of the variable* movies.

You can find the length of an array, or how many elements it is allocated to, by using the special array variable `length`, as in

```
int numMovies = movies.length;
```

TECHNICAL TRAP: *The curly braces used to initialize an array can only be used when the array is declared. That is, the curly braces can only be used as an* initializer.

To illustrate the previous caution, you cannot write something like this

```
int[] arr = new int[5];
arr = {1, 2, 3, 4, 5}; //will not compile!
```

To correct the problem, you would need to rewrite the code as follows:

```
int[] arr = {1, 2, 3, 4, 5}; //this compiles!
```

Exercise 5-4

Write a program that calculates the first 10 squares (1, 4, 9, 16, and so on) and places each entry in an array of integers. Then create a new array and use curly braces to initialize the new array to the values in the old array. At the end of the program, write out all the entries in the second array to verify that the program worked. Be sure your array has 10 elements and that your values range from 1 to 100.

Arrays of Arrays

You can define an array of arrays by using multiple sets of square brackets. For example, a two-dimensional array could be declared like this

```
int[][] chessBoard = int[8][8];
```

You can also use curly braces when declaring and initializing an array of arrays, as in

```
double[][] identityMatrix = {
  { 1.0, 0.0, 0.0 }
  { 0.0, 1.0, 0.0 }
  { 0.0, 0.0, 1.0 }
};
```

So that this doesn't trip you up, take note: you can place a comma in the last line of a multi-array initialization. There's no comma in the third line in the above array initialization, but there is a comma in the third line of the initialization in the snippet below:

```
double[][] identityMatrix = {
  { 1.0, 0.0, 0.0 },
  { 0.0, 1.0, 0.0 },
  { 0.0, 0.0, 1.0 },
};
```

Either version will compile successfully.

Just as you might expect, you can find the length of each array within the array. For a two-dimensional array, you might think of the first entry as the row number and the second as a column. To find the number of columns for row 0 in a two-dimensional matrix called `catalog`, you can write the following:

```
catalog[0].length;
```

You can also allocate the length of each column one at a time. You can start by allocating the number of rows in an array. Let's say our catalog array is an array of string arrays:

```
String[][] catalog = new String[100][];
```

Notice that the number of columns is left undefined at first. This enables us to work with one column at a time, and each column in our array of arrays can be a different length.

```
catalog[0] = new String[5];
catalog[1] = new String[10];
```

and so on. Then we can refer to each element in the array by specifying its row and column. For example, the first element is

```
catalog[0][0]
```

and we can set this to a String object, as follows

```
catalog[0][0] = new String("shirt");
```

We can refer to other rows and columns as we'd like to.

Where Arrays Fit into the Class Hierarchy

If arrays are objects, what's their class type and where do these classes fit into the class hierarchy? Arrays follow a parallel hierarchy of the class types they hold. Let's look at an example of a class hierarchy involving Vehicle, Car, and SportsCar that looks like Figure 5-1.

Then the hierarchy of arrays looks like Figure 5-2.

In other words, Vehicle[] is a sibling of Vehicle, Car[] is a sibling of Car, and SportsCar[] is a sibling of SportsCar. And, as the figure shows, Vehicle[] inherits directly from Object[], just as Vehicle inherits from Object. Of course, all arrays are objects, so Object[] in turn inherits from Object.

Figure 5-1
A hierarchy involving
three classes

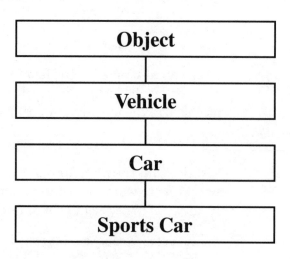

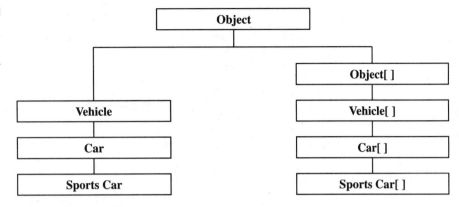

Figure 5-2
The parallel hierarchy
of arrays

Answers to the Exercises

Exercise 5-1

A byte holds values up to 127. It could hold the number of letters
in the alphabet (26). An int is not large enough to hold the net
worth of Bill Gates (what is it now, around 16 billion dollars?). A
long holds values up to 9,223,372,036,854,775,807. (However, if
Microsoft stock splits a few more times . . .)

A short can hold values up to 32,767. This is large enough to
hold the number of pages in this book. A byte would be too small,
while an int can hold up to around two billion, which is enough to
keep track of the number of people in the U.S. for some time to
come. A short would be too small.

Exercise 5-2

Here is one possible solution to this exercise:

```
class Def {
  byte b;
  short s;
  int i;
```

```
long 1;
public static void main(String[] args) {
  Def d = new Def();
  d.defaults();
}
 void defaults() {
  System.out.println("default values:");
  System.out.println(b);
  System.out.println(s);
  System.out.println(i);
  System.out.println(l);
 }
}
```

Exercise 5-3

The method variable named `found` is not initialized before being used, which results in a compile-time error. You must set this variable to `false` for this program to compile and work as intended.

```
class Test {
 public static void main(String[] args) {
  int index;
  boolean found = false;
  for (index = 0; index < 10 && !found; index++) {
   if (index > Math.PI) {
    System.out.println(index + " is greater than Pi");
    found = true;
   }
  }
 }
}
```

The variable `index` is initialized in the `for` loop before it is referenced.

Exercise 5-4

One possible solution is as follows:

```
class Squares {
 public static void main(String[] args) {
  int[] first = new int[10];
  for (int i = 1; i <= 10; i++)
   first[i-1] = i * i;
  int[] second = {first[0], first[1], first[2], first[3],
   first[4], first[5], first[6], first[7], first[8],
   first[9]};
  for (int i = 1; i <= 10; i++)
   System.out.println("entry " + i + " is " + second[i-1]);
 }
}
```

Review Questions

1. The range of values for the integer data types is

   a. $-2^{\wedge}15$ to $2^{\wedge}15 - 1$
   b. $-2^{\wedge}$(number of bits $- 1$) to $2^{\wedge}$(number of bits $- 1$)
   c. $-2^{\wedge}31$ to $2^{\wedge}31 - 1$
   d. $-2^{\wedge}$(number of bits $- 1$) to $2^{\wedge}$(number of bits $- 1$) $- 1$

2. What are two ways to set a char variable named c to a blank space?

   a. c = " " and c = ' '
   b. c = " " and c = '\u0000'
   c. c = ' ' and c = '\u0020'
   d. c = " " and c = '\u0020'

3. What is the result of trying to compile and run this program?

```
class Q3 {
 int instVar1 = 1;
 int instVar2;
 public static void main(String[] args) {
  int localVar = 3;
  Q3 q3 = new Q3();
  System.out.println(q3.instVar1 + q3.instVar2 + localVar);
 }
}
```

    a. 4

    b. 0

    c. The code does not compile because `localVar` is not initialized correctly.

    d. The code does not compile because `instVar2` is not initialized at all.

4. How can you initialize an array of three Boolean values to all true?

    a. `boolean[ ] b = new boolean[3];`

    b. `boolean[ ] b = {true, true, true};`

    c. `boolean[3] b = {true, true, true};`

    d. `boolean[ ] b = new boolean[3]; b = {true, true, true};`

Answers to the Review Questions

1. **d.** The range of values for an integer data type depends on the number of bits. For an `int`, which holds 32 bits, the range goes from -231 to $231 - 1$. The number of bits is 8 for a byte, 16 for a short, 32 for an `int`, and 64 for a long.

2. **c.** A char value can be set using single quotes or the format `\udddd`. The value `\u0020` is a blank space.

3. **a.** This code compiles and runs successfully. An instance variable, such as `instVar2`, is set to 0 if it is not explicitly initialized.

4. **b.** This example shows how to use curly braces in an initializer to set the values for an array. (Since the default value for a `boolean` is `false`, answer a will not work).

CHAPTER 6

Operators

Java has lots of operatorsl; most of them are quite simple. Some of these operators include the standard arithmetic operators of +, -, *, /, and %, but there are also some others that you might feel a little less familiar with. Guess what? Those are the ones on the test! We'll cover them thoroughly in this chapter.

The test covers the bitwise operators. If you're like most programmers, you probably don't use these operators much on a day-to-day basis. The bitwise operators include

1. Right shift (>>)
2. Left shift (<<)
3. Right shift, don't keep the sign bit (>>>)

Other bitwise operators will be covered in this chapter.

The test also makes sure you know how the operators used with objects and object references work. These include the +, ==, and instanceof operators. You should know the difference between == and equals() and which classes respond differently to equals() than the class Object.

Objectives for This Chapter

■ Determine the result of applying any operator, including assignment operators and instanceof, to operands of any type, class, scope, or accessibility, or any combination of these.

■ In an expression involving the operators &, |, &&, ||, and variables of known values, state which operands are evaluated and the value of the expression.

■ Use the instanceof operator correctly.

■ State the difference between the == operator and equals().

■ Determine the result of applying the == comparison operator and the equals() method to instances of class String, Boolean, and Object.

■ Determine the effect of passing variables into methods and performing assignments or other modifying operations in that method upon objects and primitive values.

Operators

In this section, you'll find summaries of all the operators. Java has many different operators. These operators originate from C and C++ but don't necessarily have the same behavior as the same operators in C/C++.

Arithmetic Operators

Table 6-1 summarizes arithmetic operators. Study the examples and be sure you understand how the results are achieved.

MARGIN NOTE: Note that the string concatenation operator (+) really isn't an arithmetic operator, but it doesn't fit into any of the other tables. Thus, I've added it here rather than have a separate table with one element.

Table 6-1

Arithmetic operators

Operator	Operation	Example	Result
+	Positive	+4	4
–	Negation	a=2;-a	-2
+	Addition	2 + 2	4
–	Subtraction	2-1	1
*	Multiplication	2 * 3	4
/	Division	3 / 3	1
%	Modulus	5 % 5	0
++ (Prefix)	Increment	a=2;b=++a	a=3;b=3;
++ (Postfix)	Increment	a=2;b=a++	a=2;b=3;
–– (Prefix)	Decrement	a=2;b=-a	a=1;b=1;
–– (Postfix)	Decrement	a=2;b=a-	a=2;b=1;
+ (String)	Concatenation	"y" + "ou"	"you"

The most difficult to understand arithmetic operator is modulus. Modulus returns the remainder from a division operation. If you divide 5 into 12, the remainder is 2 and thus a modulus operation returns 2.

Other difficult concepts to understand are prefix and postfix notations. When you use a prefix notation, you perform the operation on the original value and assign the result to the original value. Thus, a=3 and b=++a results in both a and b being equal to 4. When you use a postfix notation, you perform the operation without affecting the original value. Thus, a=3 and b=a++ results in both a being equal to 3 and b being equal to 4.

Assignment Operators

Table 6-2 summarizes the assignment operators and their usage. For these examples, the value of a is 4 and the value of b is 2 initially. The most difficult to understand assignment operator is modulus. Modulus returns the remainder from a division operation. If you divide 5 into 12, the remainder is 2 and thus modulus returns 2.

Comparison Operators

Table 6-3 shows Java comparison operators. These operators always return true or false. We'll discuss the instanceof operator in greater detail later.

	Operator	Operation	Example	Result
Table 6-2				
Assignment operators	=	Assign value	a = 4	a=4;b=2
	+=	Add to current variable	a += b	a=6;b=2
	-=	Subtract from current	a -= b	a=2;b=2
	*=	Multiply current	a *= b	a=8;b=2
	/=	Divide current	a /= b	a=2;b=2
	%=	Modulus current	a %= b	a=0;b=2

Table 6-3

Comparison operators

Operator	Operation	Example	Result
==	Equal	3 == 2	false
!=	Not equal	3 != 2	true
<	Less than	3 < 2	false
>	Greater than	3 > 2	true
<=	Less than or equal	3 <= 2	false
>=	Greater than or equal	3 >= 2	true
instanceof	Check for class instance	"hello" instanceof String	true

Table 6-4

Logical operators

Operator	Operation	Example	Result
&	logical AND	true & false	false
|	logical OR	true | false	true
^	logical XOR	true ^ false	true
!	Not	!false	true
&&	short-circuit AND	false && true	false
||	short-circuit OR	false || true	true
?:	conditional (ternary)	false ? 5 : 8	8

Logical Operators

Table 6-4 shows the logical operators for Java. Generally, these operations result in true or false. The exception is the conditional operation that returns a value based on whether the first operand evaluates to true or false. If the first operation results in true, the value of the second operand is returned. If the first operation results in false, the value of the third operand is returned.

MARGIN NOTE: *Note that the conditional operator (?:) really isn't a logical operator, but it doesn't fit into any of the other tables, so I've added it here so I can discuss it in terms of logical operations.*

The easiest way to consider logical AND, OR, and XOR is to use true tables. Table 6-5 shows the result of logical AND operations given the forms shown.

Two types of logical operators give programmers the most problems: conditional and short-circuit. Conditional or ternary operators have the basic syntax of

```
operand1 ? operand2 : operand3
```

With ternary operators, `operand1` must be a boolean type. When the operation is performed, the value of `operand1` is evaluated. If the value is true, the operation returns the value or `operand2`. Otherwise, the operation returns the value of `operand3`. Consider the following example:

```
class Ter {
 public static void main(String args[]) {
   for(int i=0;i<10;++i)
     System.out.print((i%2==0)?("" + i) : " ");
 }
}
```

If you run this example, the result you'll get is

```
0 2 4 6 8
```

Table 6-5	**a**	**b**	**a & b**	**a	b**	**a ^ b**

a	b	a & b	a | b	a ^ b
false	false	false	false	false
false	true	false	true	true
true	false	false	true	true
true	true	true	true	false

Table 6-5

Truth table for logical AND, OR, and XOR operations

Short-circuit operators can also give you problems if you aren't paying attention. The && and || operators are called short-circuit operators because they don't always evaluate the second operand before returning a result. When the first operand is false and you use the && operator, false is returned without checking the second operand. Otherwise, the second operand is evaluated and its result of true or false is returned. When the first operand is true and you use the || operator, true is returned without checking the second operand. Otherwise, the second operand is evaluated and its result of true or false is returned.

Bitwise Operators

Table 6-6 summarizes the Java bitwise operators. These operators are the most challenging operators to understand and key operators are covered in the sections that follow.

Table 6-6

Java bitwise operators

Operator	Operation	Binary Example	Binary Result
&	Bitwise AND	10011011 & 11010101	10010001
|	Bitwise OR	00001010 | 00001000	00001010
^	Bitwise XOR	00001010 ^ 00001000	00001000
<<	Left shift	00000010 << 00000001	00000100
>>	Right shift	00101011 >> 00000010	00001010
>>>	Zero-fill right shift	00101011 >>> 00000010	00001010
<<=	Left-shift assignment	00000001 <<= 00000101	00100000
>>=	Right-shift assignment	00000001 <<= 00000101	00000000
>>>=	Zero-fill right-shift assignment	00000001 >>>= 00000101	00100000
		Decimal Example	Decimal Result
~	Bitwise complement	~3	−4

The >> Operator

The >> operator shifts the bits a specified number of places to the right. For example, if you run the following program

```
class Bit {
 public static void main(String[] args) {
    int i = 0x00000010;
    int ans;
    System.out.println("before: " + i);
    ans = i >> 1;
   System.out.println("after: " + i);
 }
}
```

The result will be

```
before: 16
after: 8
```

because the hex number 0x00000010 is 16 in base 10. The 32 bits representing this number are

```
0000 0000 0000 0000 0000 0000 0001 0000
```

Shifting the bits once to the right yields the bit pattern

```
0000 0000 0000 0000 0000 0000 0000 1000
```

which is the hex number 0x00000008, or 8 in base 10.

Negative numbers might yield results you did not expect, because the sign bit is moved to the right, even though the number stays negative. Here's the simplest example. Running this program

```
class Neg {
 public static void main(String[] args) {
    int i = 0x80000000;
    int ans;
    System.out.println("before: " + i);
    ans = i >> 1;
   System.out.println("after: " + i);
 }
}
```

yields the following result

```
before: -2147483648
after: -1073741824
```

The variable i is assigned the hex value 0x80000000, which, as a bit pattern, is

```
1000 0000 0000 0000 0000 0000 0000 0000
```

Now in Java 2's complement notation, this is a negative number, the most negative an int can be in Java. You can see this in the result for i in the "before" printout; −2147483648 matches the value in java.lang.Integer.MIN_VALUE. Then, moving this bit one to the right, but keeping the sign, yields the bit pattern

```
1100 0000 0000 0000 0000 0000 0000 0000
```

which is the same as the base 10 number in the "after" printout.

The >>> Operator

To get around this strange "the sign bit both stays and moves to the right" syndrome, you can use the >>> operator instead. For example,

```
class Neg1 {
 public static void main(String[] args) {
   int i = 0x80000000;
   int ans;
   System.out.println("before: " + i);
   ans = i >>> 1;
   System.out.println("after: " + i);
 }
}
```

yields the result

```
before: -2147483648
after: 1073741824
```

In other words, the bit pattern went from

1000 0000 0000 0000 0000 0000 0000 0000

to

0100 0000 0000 0000 0000 0000 0000 0000

TIP: *The >>> and >> operators yield the same results when the number is positive.*

The << Operator

There is one more similar operator, the << operator, which moves all the bits to the left the indicated number of places. The result of applying this operator is straightforward, but you might wonder what happens when the bit pattern moves from

0100 0000 0000 0000 0000 0000 0000 0000

one step to the left, as in this program:

```
class Back {
 public static void main(String[] args) {
   int i = 0x40000000;
   int ans;
   System.out.println("before: " + i);
   ans = i >> 1;
  System.out.println("after: " + i);
 }
}
```

Does the number change sign? Yes, indeed. The printout reads:

```
before: 1073741824
after: -2147483648
```

What about moving the bit pattern

```
1000 0000 0000 0000 0000 0000 0000 0001
```

one to the left using the << operator? Does the number stay negative or become positive? It becomes positive! The bit that indicates the sign gets shifted out completely. The result is

```
before: -2147483647
after: 2
```

The &, | and ^ Operators

With binary operations, the operators &, |, and ^ mean "bitwise and," "bitwise or," and "bitwise xor" respectively. These operators work on integers and yield integer results, not Boolean results. The & operator turns the bits on if both bits are on, and off if either or both bits are off. The | operator turns bits on if either or both bits are on, and off if both bits are off. The ^ operator turns bits on only when one of the bits is on and off when both bits are on or off.

It's easier to look at a simple example than it is to comprehend these operators by reading about them. If you perform this operation

```
3 & 2
```

the result is 2. You can see this clearly if you look at the bit patterns (we'll only look at the last four bits to make this easier to read):

```
0011 &
0010
--- -
0010
```

If you perform the operation

```
3 | 2
```

the result is 3. Here are the bits:

```
0011 |
0010
--- -
0011
```

However, if you perform the operation

```
3 ^ 2
```

the result is 13. Here are the bits:

```
0011 |
0010
--- -
0001
```

As with logical AND, OR, and XOR, a truth table can help you understand bitwise AND, OR, and XOR. With this in mind, take a moment to study Table 6-7.

Exercises

Exercise 6-1

Write a class that stores two short integers in a single `int` variable. Then write methods called `putVar1()`, `putVar2()`, `getVar1()`, and `getVar2()` to save and retrieve this value into the upper or lower

Table 6-7	a	b	a & b	a | b	a ^ b
Truth table for logical AND, OR, and XOR operations	0	0	0	0	0
	0	1	0	1	1
	1	0	0	1	1
	1	1	1	1	0

half of an `int`. You'll probably have to use the `>>` and `<<` operators to make this work as well as `&` and `|` to mask the bits when you set the `int`'s value.

Testing for an Object's Class Type

For the exam, you'll need to know how to use the `instanceof` operator correctly. The operator tests to see whether a particular object is an instance of a class or a subclass of that class. It can also test whether an object's class or subclass implements an interface.

Here are some examples. Let's say you have the following code:

```
class Fruit { }
class Apple extends Fruit {
 public static void main(String[] args) {
  Apple a = new Apple();
  if (a instanceof Apple)
   System.out.println("A is for Apple");
 if (a instanceof Fruit)
   System.out.println("A is a Fruit");
 if (a instanceof Object)
   System.out.println("A is an Object");
 }
}
```

Running this code writes `A is for Apple`, `A is a Fruit`, and `A is an Object` to the standard output, because the `instanceof` operator returns true for each test.

Here's another example that deals with interfaces:

```
interface Fruit { }
interface Apple extends Fruit { }
class GrannySmith implements Apple {
 public static void main(String[] args) {
  GrannySmith gs = new GrannySmith();
  if (gs instanceof Apple)
   System.out.println("gs inherits from Apple");
 if (gs instanceof Fruit)
   System.out.println("gs inherits from Fruit");
 }
}
```

The strings `gs inherits from Apple` and `gs inherits from Fruit` appear in the standard output when you run this program.

TECHNICAL TRAP: *Some compilers, such as Sun's JDK, will not allow code to compile if they can determine with the available classes that a particular object cannot possibly inherit from a class specified in* `instanceof`.

Exercise 6-2

Use the Apple and Fruit classes shown in the previous section (you can replace `main()` with your own code). Write a program that shows that an Apple array inherits from a Fruit array, that a Fruit array inherits from an Object array, and that an Object array inherits from Object.

Equals( ) and ==

For the exam, you'll need to know the difference between the == operator and `equals()` and be able to determine the result of applying the == comparison operator and the `equals()` method to instances of class `String`, `Boolean`, and `Object`.

The `equals()` method is used to test the value of an object. For example, do two object references refer to objects whose fields contain similar values? The == operator is used to test the object references themselves. For example, are two object references the same?

Identical object references can be in different variables. By default, `equals()` returns true only if the objects reside in the same memory location, that is, if the object references are equal. So, by default, `equals()` and == do the same things. This will be the case for all classes that do not override `equals()`.

The classes `String`, `BitSet`, `Boolean`, `Date`, `Calendar`, `File`, and `primitive wrappers` all override `equals()`. Each of these classes uses the data in its fields to determine whether the object represents the same thing:

- String objects are equal if they represent the same character strings.
- Boolean objects are equal if they have the same value.
- Wrapper objects including `Integer`, `Long`, `Float`, `Double`, `Character`, and `Boolean` are equal if they represent the same primitive data type.
- BitSet objects are equal if they represent the same sequence of bits.
- Date and Calendar objects are equal if they represent the same date and time.
- File objects are equal if they represent the same path, not if they refer to the same underlying file. (The danger here is that the path name might be a relative path name. In that case, they might easily represent two different files in the system.)

EXAM POINTER: *The exam objectives specifically state that you must know how to determine the result of applying the boolean* `equals()` *method to objects of any combination of the classes* `java.lang.String`, `java.lang.Boolean`, *and* `java.lang.Object`. *You don't have to know about the other classes that override* `equals()` *and there are a lot more than we've listed here. Still, it is helpful to understand how key classes are affected in comparisons.*

TIP: *You can override* `equals()` *for your own classes, just as the classes in the list above do, in order to perform whatever test for equality you feel is important.*

Exercise 6-3

Show that String objects and Date objects return true for `equals()` if they are created with the same data (the Date class is defined in `java.util`). What happens if you use the no-args constructor for Date and separate the creation of the Date objects by a few lines of code? Why aren't these Date objects equivalent, even though you supplied the same data-namely, no data at all-to the Date's constructor?

Exercise 6-4

Write your own `equals()` method for the following two classes:

```
class Employee {
  private String id;
  Employee (String id) {
   this.id = id;
  }
}
class Movie {
  String name;
  boolean thumbsUp;
  int year;
}
```

Operator Precedence and Evaluation Order

Java evaluates expressions from left to right. When multiple operators are used, the order of evaluation is determined by the precedence order, shown in Table 6-8. From the table, you can see that operators that are on the same line are evaluated using the normal left to right order. For example, if both an `a +` and a `-` operation occur in the same expression, Java will resolve the expression from left to right. However, if * and + are used, the multiplication takes place first because it has a higher precedence.

The separators [] and () change precedence. Everything within these separators is computed before Java looks outside them. Java evaluates the expression in separators using its regular rules of precedence, as in the following expression:

```
varA = (2 * 2 + 3) + (6 + 4 / 2);
```

The value of varA is 15. Multiplication is of a higher precedence than addition, so 2 * 2 is the first operation, which is then added to 3. In the next set of parentheses, division is of a higher precedence than addition, so 4 / 2 is the first operation, the result of which is then added to 6. The values from each set of parentheses, 7 and 8, are then added together and assigned to variable varA. See Table 6-8 for examples of operator precedence.

Table 6-8

Operator precedence, from high to low.

```
[]  ()

++ (Postfix)- (Postfix)

++ (Prefix)- (Prefix), + (Positive), - (Negative), !, ~

(Type)

*          /          %

+ (Addition)       - (Subtraction)

<<         >>         >>>

<          >          <=        >=        instanceof

==         !=

&

^

|

&&

||

?:

= += -= *= /= %= &= ^= |= >>= <<= >>>=
```

To get a better understanding of operator precedence, here's another example:

```
class checkExp {
 public static void main (String args [])
 {
  int IntA, IntB = 2;
  IntA = (IntB+=2) * (IntB+3);
  System.out.println("IntB = " + IntB);
  System.out.println("IntA = " + IntA);
 }
}
```

This is the output of this code:

```
IntB = 4
IntA = 28
```

In the previous example, variables IntA and IntB are declared to be type int and are initialized to 2. Then the value of variable IntB is incremented by 2, resulting in 4. The new value of IntB is increased by 3, resulting in 7. The result of the two values in parentheses, 4 and 7, is now multiplied. This value, 28, is then assigned to IntA.

Answers to the Exercises

Exercise 6-1

Here is a class called Half that stores two short values in one int variable:

```
class Half {
 int value;
 void putVar1(short s) {
  value &= 0xFFFF0000;
  value |= s;
 }
```

```
  void putVar2(short s) {
  value &= 0x0000FFFF;
  value |= (s << 16);
  }
 short getVar1() {
  return (short)(value);
  }
  short getVar2() {
  return (short)(value >> 16);
  }
 }
```

You can run a class such as Tester, listed below, to verify this class named Half is doing what it's supposed to do:

```
class Tester {
 public static void main(String[] args) {
  Half h = new Half();
  h.putVar1((short) 100);
  h.putVar2((short) -91);
  System.out.println(h.getVar1());
  System.out.println(h.getVar2());
 }
}
```

Exercise 6-2

```
class Fruit { }
class Apple extends Fruit {
  public static void main(String[] args) {
  Apple[] a = new Apple[1];
  Fruit[] f = new Fruit[1];
  Object[] o = new Object[1];
  if (a instanceof Fruit[])
  System.out.println("a inherits from Fruit[]");
  if (f instanceof Object[])
  System.out.println("f inherits from Object[]");
  if (o instanceof Object)
  System.out.println("o inherits from Object");
  }
}
```

Exercise 6-3

```
import java.util.Date;
import java.util.GregorianCalendar;
class Eq {
 public static void main(String[] args) {
  String s1 = new String("a");
  String s2 = new String("a");
  Date d1 = new Date();
  Date d2 = new GregorianCalendar(97, 2, 14).getTime();
  Date d3 = new GregorianCalendar(97, 2, 14).getTime();
  Date d4 = new Date();
  System.out.println(s1.equals(s2));
  System.out.println(d2.equals(d3));
  System.out.println(d1.equals(d4));
 }
}
```

This program displays true, true, false. The reason why the two Date objects d1 and d4 are not equal is that the no-args Date constructor initializes the Date objects to the current date and time to the nearest millisecond. Thus, their internal data are different.

Exercise 6-4

```
class Employee {
 private String id;
 Employee (String id) {
  this.id = id;
 }
 public boolean equals(Object obj) {
  if (obj instanceof Employee) {
   Employee e = (Employee)obj;
   if (e.id == id)
    return true;
  }
  return false;
 }
}
class Movie {
```

```
String name;
boolean thumbsUp;
int year;
public boolean equals(Object obj) {
  if (obj instanceof Movie) {
    Movie m = (Movie)obj;
    if (name.equals(m.name) && year == m.year && thumbsUp ==
m.thumbsUp)
      return true;
  }
  return false;
  }
}
```

Notice that we cast the object to the type being tested. Also, note especially the `equals()` test for Movie: the String object is tested using `equals()`, and the `thumbsUp` variable is not considered, since the movies might still be the same even if two different people rated them differently.

QUESTIONS

1. What will be the result of this expression:

```
5 & 2
```

a. 0
b. 2
c. 5
d. 7

2. What will be the result of this expression:

```
10 | 2
```

a. 0
b. 2
c. 10
d. 14

3. What will happen when you attempt to compile and run the following code?

```
class Tree { }
class Pine {
 public static void main(String[] args) {
  Pine[] p = new Pine[1];
  if (p instanceof Tree[])
    System.out.println("p inherits from Tree[]");
 }
}
```

   a. The compiler complains that Tree[ ] cannot inherit from Pine[ ].

   b. The compiler complains that Pine[ ] cannot inherit from Tree[ ].

   c. The program compiles and runs but does not display anything in the standard output.

   d. The program compiles and runs and displays p inherits from Tree[ ] in the standard output.

4. What is the result of invoking main( ) for classes A, B, and C?

```
class A {
 public static void main(String[] args) {
  Integer myInt = new Integer(5);
  Integer otherInt;
  otherInt = myInt;
  if (otherInt == myInt)
    System.out.println("equal");
  else
    System.out.println("not equal");
 }
}
class B {
 public static void main(String[] args) {
  Integer myInt = new Integer(5);
  Integer anotherInt = new Integer(5);
  if (anotherInt == myInt)
    System.out.println("equal");
  else
    System.out.println("not equal");
 }
}
class C {
 public static void main(String[] args) {
  MyClass mc1 = new MyClass(1);
  if (mc1.operatorEquals(mc1))
    System.out.println("equal");
```

```
    else
      System.out.println("not equal");
  }
}
class MyClass extends Object {
  int value;
  MyClass(int value) {
    this.value = value;
  }
  boolean operatorEquals(MyClass test) {
    return (this == test);
  }
}
```

   a. A: equal; B: equal: C: equal
   b. A: equal; B: not equal; C: equal
   c. A: not equal; B: not equal; C: equal
   d. A: not equal; B: not equal; C: not equal

5. What is the result of `0x800028FF >> 3`?

   a. `0x900005FF`
   b. `0x1000051F`
   c. `0x1000011F`
   d. `0x9000051F`

6. What is the result of trying to compile and run the following program?

```
class Phone implements Cloneable {
  public static void main(String[] args) {
    Phone p = new Phone();
    if (p instanceof Object)
      System.out.println("Object");
    if (p instanceof Cloneable)
      System.out.println("Cloneable");
  }
}
```

   a. The program does not compile.
   b. The program compiles and runs and writes Object to the standard output.
   c. The program compiles and runs and writes Cloneable to the standard output.
   d. The program compiles and runs and writes both Object and Cloneable to the standard output.

ANSWERS

1. a. It's clear if you look at the bits:

```
101 &
010
- - -
000
```

2. c. The bits are

```
1010 |
0010
- - -  -
1010
```

3. b. When the compiler figures out that an object cannot inherit from another object, it does not even compile the program. That's what Sun's JDK does in this case.

4. b. The only one that is not equal is class B, which checks for equivalence of object references. Since this check uses two different objects, the object references are different.

5. d. Translate the hexadecimal into a bit pattern to see this

```
0x800028FF is:
1000 0000 0000 0000 0010 1000 1111 1111
```

Shifting each bit three positions to the right and keeping the sign bit yields

```
1001 0000 0000 0000 0000 0101 0001 1111
```

or

```
0x9000051F
```

6. d. The object referenced by p will return true to the `instanceof` test with `Object` and `Cloneable`.

CHAPTER 7

Control Flow

The basic control flow elements of looping and branching are similar to those in other programming languages. In fact, Java uses all of the same keywords as C/C++, with some minor modifications. Most of this chapter reviews the basics of Java's control flow keywords. This chapter also covers the details (the differences between Java and C/C++) that might trip you up on the test. The test covers if and switch statements as well as all forms of loops. You'll need to know how to use labels to break out of nested loops, break statements, and continue statements as well.

Objectives for This Chapter

- Write loops and nested loops using a loop counter.
- Use the break and continue keywords with and without labels.
- Write nested if-else and switch constructs.
- Identify the legal argument expression type for if and switch.
- Use the operators && and || and determine their effects on control flow statements.
- Use other types of loops such as while do and do while.

Nested Loops

A for statement defines a loop. You can define a for loop like this:

```
for (initialization; termination; modification) { . . . }
```

Here is a common example:

```
for (index = 0; index < limit; index++) { . . . }
```

TIP: *In this case, index is assumed to be an integer, but it could also be a floating-point number, in which case the + + operator increments by 1.0, as you would expect.*

Each of the three parts of the `for` loop—initialization, termination, and modification—can be made of multiple expressions separated by commas. For example, you can write

```
for (row = 0, col = 0; row < numRows; row++, col++) {
. . . }
```

This loop could be used to look at the main diagonal in a square matrix, for example.

TIP: A `for` *loop without any expressions loops forever.*

This loop is an infinite loop:

```
for ( ; ; ) {  . . .  }
```

You can also define a loop variable within the initialization expression of a `for` loop. Java programmers do this all the time because it is so convenient. Here's an example:

```
for (int index = 0; index < limit; index++) {  . . .  }
```

TECHNICAL TRAP: *A loop index created on the fly, as in the previous code snippet, goes out of scope at the end of the loop.*

An example of the previous warning is the following, which is not legal:

```
for (int index = 0; index < limit; index++) {
  // do stuff here.
}
System.out.println("The final value for index is " + index);
  //the code won't compile!
```

Loops can be nested. To loop through an array of arrays, you could write

```
for (int row = 0; row < numRows; row++)
  for (int col = 0; col < numCols; col++)
    System.out.println(arr[row][col]);
```

Labels

You can assign a label to any code line. You can then break or continue to that label. A label is only useful with break and continue statements. Without a label, a continue statement continues with the next iteration of an inner loop, and a break statement stops its inner loop altogether.

Here's an example. We want to look over all the positions in a game board. If we see a mole, we want to hit it. After a swing of our mole bat, it's the next player's turn; we don't want to allow the user more than one swing of the mole bat per turn. In the example below, the break statement doesn't quite do what we want:

```
for (int row = 0; row < 8; row++) {
 for (int col = 0; col < 8; col++) {
  if (moleAt(row, col)) {
   bangIt(row,col);
   break;
  }
 }
}
```

Unfortunately, the `break` statement only breaks out of the inner loop. The outer loop—the one going through the rows—keeps going, allowing the user to bang at more moles. One way out of this predicament is to supply a label for the outer loop. We can then tie the `break` statement to the outer loop by using this label. Here's how we could update the code:

```
outer: for (int row = 0; row < 8; row++) {
  for (int col = 0; col < 8; col++) {
   if (moleAt(row, col)) {
    bangIt(row,col);
    break outer;
   }
  }
}
```

The appropriate, corresponding result would then occur with a `continue` statement. By naming the outer loop, the `continue` statement would continue with the next iteration of the outer loop, rather than with the next iteration of the inner loop.

Exercise 7-1

Rewrite the following code snippet so that it uses both a label and a `continue` statement:

```
boolean[] inCheck = new boolean[8];
for (int row = 0; row < 8; row++) {
  for (int col = 0; col < 8 && inCheck[row] == false; col++) {
   if (isKingInCheck(row, col))
    inCheck[row] = true;
  }
}
```

Nested if and else Statements

`if` statements can be nested inside other `if` statements, just as `for` loops can be nested inside other `for` loops. For example, you can write

```
if (expression)
  statement
else if (expression)
  statement
else if . . .
```

TECHNICAL TRAP: *There's a gotcha as far as nested* `if` *statements are concerned that can undermine the best laid plans: be sure that indentations of nested* `if-else` *statements don't cause you to mistake which* `else` *goes with which* `if`.

As an example of this warning, check out the following snippet:

```
if (result >= 0)
  if (result > 0)
    System.out.println("positive");
else
  System.out.println("negative"); //wait a minute  . . .
```

Yikes! Here's the same code written with a different indentation so you can see what's really going on:

```
if (result >= 0)
  if (result > 0)
    System.out.println("positive");
  else
    System.out.println("negative"); //wait a minute  . . .
```

So we'll get the message `"negative"` even if `result` is equal to 0. This is anything but good. To help avoid these situations, you can use curly braces to delimit your blocks of code. Thus, you can write

```
if (result >= 0) {
 if (result > 0)
  System.out.println("positive");
} else
  System.out.println("negative");
```

Legal Values for if Statements

The expression for an if and while statement must be a Boolean. This is simple enough to remember, unless you're coming from an entrenched background in C. Then you've got to write 10 times, so that you don't forget, "I will only use a Boolean in my if and while tests."

C programmers are familiar with using 0 and null to mean false, but in Java, you cannot coerce one to the other. Keep this in mind for the || and && operators as well. These operators combine Boolean arguments to achieve another Booleans.

Exercise 7-2

```
class Exp {
 public static void main(String[] args) {
  int i = 10;
  int j = 12;
  if ((i < j) || (i = 3)) {
   System.out.println("hello");
  }
  System.out.println(i);
 }
}
```

Fix this code so that it works as intended.

Switch and Case Statements

A `switch` statement can be used to test a variable or expression and jump to a corresponding case statement containing a constant equal to that expression. A `switch` statement takes the following form:

```
switch (expression) {
  case constant:
    statements
  case constant:
    statements
default:
    statements
}
```

A `default` statement is optional. If none of the constants in the `case` statements match the value of the variable in the `switch` statement, execution jumps to the `default` statement. If there is no `default` statement and none of the `case` statements match the `switch` expression, the switch block is, in effect, skipped altogether.

EXAM POINTER: *The expression in a* `switch` *statement must be of type* `int` *or* `char`. *The values in each case statement must be constants.*

A `case` block will fall through to the `case` block that follows it, unless the last statement in a `case` block is a `throw`, `return`, or `break`. Often, you will write code that follows the same approach as the following snippet:

```
switch (season) {
  case 0:
    System.out.println("Spring");
    break;
  case 1:
    System.out.println("Summer");
```

```
    break;
  case 2:
    System.out.println("Fall");
    break;
  case 3:
    System.out.println("Winter");
    break;
  default:
    throw new IllegalSeasonException();
}
```

The break statements at the end of each case takes control away from the switch to keep execution from flowing to the next unrelated case statement. If you want execution to flow from one case statement to the next, it is often a good idea to place a comment at the end of the case statement. That way, it is clear to others looking at the code that the lack of a break statement is intentional.

As with for loops and if statements, you can also nest switch statements inside each other by placing a second switch statement within one of the case statements. For example, you can follow this pattern:

```
switch (season) {
  case 0:
    System.out.println("Spring");
    switch month {
      case 3:
        System.out.println("March");
        break;
      case 4:
        System.out.println("April");
        break;
      case 5:
        System.out.println("May");
        break;
    }
    break;
  case 1:
    System.out.println("Summer");
      .
      .
      .
}
```

While and Do-While Statements

The while and do-while statements are not thoroughly covered on the test. The basic idea behind them is that the while statement takes a boolean expression. The block of code after while is executed only if the expression is true:

```
while (expression) {
   //do this only if expression is true
}
```

For example, you can write

```
while (b != -1); {
  b = in.read();
}
```

This code snippet checks the value of b before entering the loop. If b is already set to -1, the program would not be read from the input stream. If you want to always perform the block of code at least once, you can use a do-while statement, like this:

```
do {
   //do this at least once
} while (expression);
```

You would then write

```
do {
  b = in.read();
} while (b != -1);
```

This code snippet reads at least one byte from the input stream and stops reading when there are no more bytes.

Using && and ||

The operators && and || enable you to combine Boolean values for if and while conditions. The && operator means "logical-AND," and the || operator means "logical-OR." The expressions are evaluated in order from left to right. As soon as the condition of the `if` or `while` clause is resolved, no more expressions for that condition are evaluated. For example, in the `if` test

```
if (5 > 3 || 2 < 1)  . . .
```

the second expression, 2 < 1, is never evaluated. Since 5 > 3 is known to be true before 2 < 1 is evaluated, the *Java Virtual Machine* (JVM) already knows the entire if condition is true. If, however, the test is

```
if (5 > 3 && 2 < 1)  . . .
```

and if the first expression is true (which it is in this example), the second expression would be evaluated as well, because the entire `if` clause would only be true if both expressions are true. If the first expression is false, however, then the entire condition would be false; in that case, the second expression would not have to be evaluated.

Exercise 7-3

What will be the result of this program?

```
class Exp {
 public static void main(String[] args) {
   int i = 10;
   int j = 12;
   if ((i < j) || (i == 3)) {
    System.out.println("hello");
   }
   System.out.println(i);
 }
}
```

Run this code if it helps to see what's going on.

Answers to the Exercises

Exercise 7-1

```
boolean[] inCheck = new boolean[8];
 rows: for (int row = 0; row < 8; row++) {
   for (int col = 0; col < 8; col++) {
    if (isKingInCheck(row, col)) {
     inCheck[row] = true;
     continue rows;
    }
   }
  }
```

Exercise 7-2

The expression

```
i = 3
```

in the `if` test is the problem. Even though this expression will never be evaluated (since `i` is less than `j`), `i = 3` does not yield a Boolean. In fact, its result is an integer, the value of `i`, which is set to 3. Since an integer is not a legal argument for the || operator, this code will not compile.

Exercise 7-3

This program writes "`i is 10`". Since the first expression in the `if` test

```
(i < j)
```

is true, the second part of this test:

```
(i == 3)
```

is not evaluated. If it were, the value of i would be set to 3.

QUESTIONS

1. The legal expression for an if statement is
   a) an integer
   b) a. boolean
   c) a or b
   d) neither of these

2. Given the following code snippet

```
char c = 'a';
switch ( c ) {
  case 'a' :
    System.out.println("a");
    break;
  default:
    System.out.println("default");
}
```

what will happen if you attempt to compile and run the code that includes this snippet?

   a) The code will not compile because the switch statement does not have a legal expression.
   b) The code will compile and run, but nothing will be written to the standard output.
   c) The code will compile and run and the letter "a" will be written to the standard output.
   d) The code will compile and run and the word "default" will be written to the standard output.

3. Given the following code snippet

```
int myInt = 3;
if (myInt < 5)
 if (myInt < 3)
   System.out.println("< 3");
else
 if (myInt > 2)
   System.out.println("> 2");
else
 System.out.println("Other");
```

what will appear in the standard output?

a) `"< 3"`

b) `"> 2"`

c) `"Other"`

d) Nothing

4. What type of code line can have a label?

a) Any line of code

b) Only lines of code associated with a loop (just before, at the loop, or just after)

c) Only the line of code at the start of a loop

d) Only the line of code defining the most outer loop

ANSWERS

1. b. An `if` statement only works with a boolean.

2. c. This is perfectly valid code and the letter `"a"` will appear in the standard output.

3. b. To see this, a better way to indent this code would be the following:

```
int myInt = 3;
if ( myInt < 5 )
 if (myInt < 3)
   System.out.println("< 4");
else
```

```
if (myInt > 2)
  System.out.println("> 2");
else
  System.out.println("other");
```

4. a. Any line of code can be labeled.

CHAPTER 8

Exceptions

Java defines keywords and classes for exceptions, weaving exceptions right into the fabric of the language. You can throw exceptions to signal errors. By handling exceptions, you can separate the control flow involving error processing from the control flow that occurs when everything proceeds as expected. Exceptions are an extremely flexible way to report and respond to errors. We'll cover the basics as well as the advanced aspects of exceptions in this chapter as they relate to the test. For the exam, you'll need to be able to write code that makes proper use of exceptions and exception-handling clauses. You'll also need to be able to declare methods and override methods that throw exceptions

Objectives for This Chapter

- Determine the flow of control for `try`, `catch`, and `finally` constructions when execution proceeds normally, when an exception is thrown and caught, and when an exception is thrown but is not caught.
- Declare a method that might throw unhandled exceptions.
- Specify which exceptions a method can throw.
- Identify which exceptions can be legitimately thrown from an overriding method in a subclass.
- Write code to create and throw an exception.

Exception Basics

When you write a program, you need some way to report and handle errors. In a language such as C, the typical way to do this is with return codes. However, return codes have a number of down sides. First, you've got to remember to check them and know which "magic numbers" mean what. Second, checking return codes inevitably leads to mingling error processing with normal processing, making your code more difficult to read and understand. Third, methods must pass back return codes to report an error to their caller.

BACKGROUND: *Are exceptions more effort than they're worth? What problem do exceptions solve?*

All of this error-handling "protocol" must be managed and verified by the programmer. No formal mechanism is in place to make sure the programmer has checked return codes correctly. Java's exception reporting and handling gets away from these problems. First, the language itself requires that methods declare the methods they throw and that they catch the exceptions a called method might throw, thereby formalizing exception handling. Along with this, exceptions are *objects*, not *numbers*, so their class names and any data they contain, such as strings, explains what they're all about without resorting to "magic numbers." Second, exception handling separates error processing from normal processing. Normal processing goes into a try block; error processing goes into a catch block. Finally, exceptions can be passed on to their caller by declaring a method using the appropriate keywords; the language takes care of this chore for you.

Working with Exceptions

The idea in exception handling is that you *try* to execute a block of code, you *catch* any exceptions that were thrown, and you *finally* (always) do some cleanup. The template to follow when invoking a method that might throw an exception is

```
try {
 //do something here that might cause an exception
} catch (ExceptionType variable) {
 //handle the exception
} finally {
 //always do this
}
```

You can have multiple catch blocks, with each one specifying its own ExceptionType in an order that always progresses from the most specific exception you wish to catch to the superclasses for these exceptions that you wish to catch. Attempting to catch the superclasses first results in a compile-time error. For example, placing a catch block with type Exception before a catch block with type IOException results in a compile-time error.

BACKGROUND: *If you know C++, you might have always wondered what the big deal is with Java and exceptions; after all, there are exceptions in C++, too. The difference is that Java formalizes exceptions. In C++, exceptions are completely optional. In Java, you're forced to be very precise; methods must indicate which exceptions they throw in their declarations. Invoking methods that declare which exceptions they throw is not possible unless you catch these exception types. Java's insistence on a strict adherence to this protocol makes control flow for exceptions much more understandable and maintainable than when the exception policy is determined by individual programmers.*

A method that might throw an exception must state this possibility in its method declaration. Here's an example from a method defined by Java's Thread class named sleep():

```
public static void sleep(long millis) throws
InterruptedException
```

InterruptedException is a *checked* exception. Thus, any code invoking sleep() must be prepared to catch an InterruptedException. Checked exceptions must be caught (or rethrown—we'll get to that in a moment). Unchecked exceptions do not have to be caught. Whether a method is checked or unchecked depends on where the exception descends from in the class hierarchy. Here's a diagram to help you see where checked and unchecked exceptions fit into the class hierarchy.

TIP: *You should* never *throw an unchecked exception in your own code. All your exceptions should be checked.*

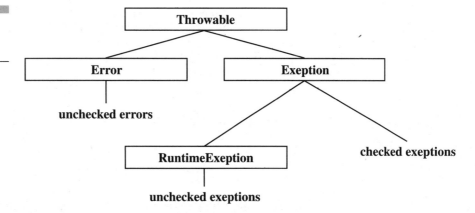

Figure 8-1
An exception
hierarchy

Exceptions and errors both inherit from class Throwable, which enables an object to be thrown using the throw keyword and caught using the catch keyword. However, instances of class Error are unchecked. There's also a subclass of Exception called RuntimeException. Instances of RuntimeException and its subclasses are also unchecked. All other exception classes—namely, all other subclasses of class Exception—are checked. See Figure 8-1.

You are not required to place calls to methods that throw unchecked exceptions in a try/catch block. However, it's often useful to do so anyway. For example, ArithmeticException is unchecked, but sometimes you will want to handle this exception if it arises.

Let's go back to the sleep() method whose definition I've provided above. If you want to invoke sleep(), you must place this call in a try/catch block, like so:

```
class A implements Runnable {
 Thread t;
 public static void main(String[] args) {
   A a = new A();
   a.go();
 }
 void go() {
   t = new Thread(this);
   t.start();
   try {
     System.out.println("try");
     t.sleep(1000);
```

```
    } catch(InterruptedException e) {
      System.out.println("catch");
    } finally {
      System.out.println("finally");
    }
  }
 public void run() {
   while(true) {
       //  . . .  infinite loop  . . .
     }
   }
 }
```

This example shows the `try/catch/finally` blocks in action. If everything works smoothly when we invoke `sleep()` and it does not throw an exception, then the messages `try` and `finally` will appear in the standard output. Otherwise, if `sleep()` does throw an `InterruptedException`, the messages `try`, `catch`, and `finally` appear. If `sleep()` does throw an unchecked exception, such as an `ArithmeticException`, the messages `try` and `finally` appear because there is no catch clause defined for an `ArithmeticException`.

TIP: *You always need a* `try` *block to use* `catch` *or* `finally`. *With a* `try`, *you can (and must) use* `catch`, *or* `finally`, *or both. You cannot use a* `try` *block on its own.*

Here's an example of using `try` and `finally` without a `catch` block at all:

```
try {

  if (result == 0) {
    doThis();
    return;
  } else {
    doThat();
    throw new MyException();
  }
} finally {
  alwaysDoThis();
}
```

The `finally` block is always executed when it's a matter of control flow. In other words, if you use a `return` statement or throw an exception, or if you try to use a `break` statement to branch around a `finally` block, your efforts to thwart the `finally` statement will be to no avail. (The exercises in this chapter ask you to identify a sure-fire way of avoiding `finally` by invoking a certain system method, but as long as the issue is one of control flow, `finally` cannot be avoided.)

Exercise 8-1

Rewrite this algorithm from a C method to use Java's exception handling. Then write the code, using an array as the return value.

Method name: Roots

Input: Double a, double b, double c, and a pointer to an array of two double values

Output: A Boolean indicating success or failure

Purpose: Implements the quadratic equation

1. Find the value of (b*b)–(4 * a * c).
2. If this result is negative, there are no roots. Return false.
3. If a is negative, also return false.
4. Otherwise, calculate (–b + this value) divided by 2 * a. Also calculate (–b–this value) divided by 2 * a. Place the results in the array reference by the pointer and return true.

Common Java Exceptions

It's useful to be familiar with the most common Java exceptions. These exception classes are defined in the package with which they are most associated. For example, IOException is defined in `java.io`; MalformedURLException is defined in `java.net`. Here are some exceptions that you might see from time to time.

Checked Exceptions

- IOException (*defined in* java.io)   Signals that an error occurred when reading from or writing to a file. You'll have to handle this kind of exception often when you use stream methods.

- FileNotFoundException (*defined in* java.io)   When you access a file, you must be prepared to handle this exception. Remember, just because you create a File object does not mean that the file exists.

- MalformedURLException (*defined in* java.net)   When you create a URL, you must be prepared to handle this exception in case the URL string supplied is not valid.

- InterruptedException (*defined in* java.lang)   When you put a thread to sleep or suspend a thread, you've got to be ready to handle this exception; a sleeping thread or a suspended thread could be interrupted before its sleeping time elapses or before someone invokes resume() for the thread, in which case it will throw this exception.

Unchecked Exceptions

- ArithmeticException (*defined in* java.lang)   Whenever an illegal math operation takes place, such as an integer divided by zero, the *Java Virtual Machine* (JVM) throws this exception.

- NullPointerException (*defined in* java.lang)   If you try to invoke a method using a null object reference, you'll see this exception. This exception can creep into your code when you least expect it. For example, you might have two method calls set up and expect methodOne() to return an object that you will use to invoke methodTwo(). If methodOne() returns null, however, attempting to invoke methodTwo() will throw a NullPointerException.

- NumberFormatException (*defined in* java.lang)   If you are converting a string to a number, you've got to be prepared to handle this exception in case the string does not really represent a number.

Of course, you'll probably come across many more exceptions in your travels as a Java programmer, but these give you a feel for what you'll find.

Using Methods Defined by Exception and Throwable

The most common way to use exceptions is to simply identify the exception that occurred by its class type. Most programmers only check whether the exception's class is `IOException`, `ArithmeticException`, and so on, and perform error handling in a `catch` clause appropriate for that class type. However, an exception is also a wealth of information. Exceptions can be created with a descriptive string that explains why the exception occurred. You can access this string using `getMessage()`, which is implemented in `Throwable`, the superclass of `Exception`.

You can also print the stack to the standard output or standard error. This can help with debugging so that you can see exactly where the exception was thrown. You can do this by invoking `printStackTrace()` for the exception.

Rethrowing an Exception

Let's look at the idea of rethrowing an exception. If you don't want to handle an exception yourself, you can let it go unhandled, meaning the exception will go up the call stack. Here's an example. Notice that the method called `doThis()` is declared as throwing `InterruptedException`:

```
class A implements Runnable {
    Thread t;
    public static void main(String[] args) {
        A a = new A();
        a.go();
    }
}
void go() {
```

```
      t = new Thread(this);
      t.start();
  }
  public void run() {
    try {
     doThis();
    } catch (InterruptedException e) {
      System.out.println("caught");
    }
  }
  void doThis() throws InterruptedException {
    t.sleep(2000);
  }
}
```

Even though `doThis()` does not handle `InterruptedException`, some method in the call stack above the call to `sleep()` must do so. Thus, the method run() handles this exception.

You can also declare the `doThis()` method, as in the following code, to achieve the same effect:

```
void doThis() throws InterruptedException {
   try {
      t.sleep(2000);
   } catch (InterruptedException e) {
      throw e;
   }
}
```

This version of `doThis()` explicitly rethrows the exception.

TIP: *You can list more than one exception in the throws clause if you separate them with commas.*

Exercise 8-2

Rewrite the following method so that instead of handling the exceptions itself, it rethrows the exceptions, putting responsibility on the caller to handle the exceptions.

```
int doDivision(InputStream in) {
  try {
    int c = in.read();
    return 100/c;
  } catch (IOException x) {
    return 0;
  } catch (ArithmeticException x) {
    return 0;
  }
}
```

Which Exceptions a Method Can Throw

A method can throw the exceptions listed in its throws clause or in the subclasses of those exceptions. A method can also throw any unchecked exception, even if it is not declared in its throws clause. Here's an example of throwing a subclass of an exception class specified in the throws clause:

```
import java.io.IOException;

class Throw {
    public static void main(String[] args) {
        Throw t = new Throw();
        try {
          t.test(4);
        } catch (Exception e) {
        }
    }
    void test(int i) throws Exception {
        if (i == 0)
            throw new IOException();
    }
}
```

The catch clauses must match the exceptions listed in the throws clause, but the test() method can throw any subclass of an exception listed in its throws clause.

Exceptions in an Overriding Method in a Subclass

For the exam, you'll need to identify which exceptions can be legitimately thrown from an overriding method in a subclass. Although there's more on overriding methods in the next chapter, we'll cover here how exceptions relate to overriding a method.

When you override a method, you must list those exceptions that the override code might throw. You can only list those exceptions, or subclasses of those exceptions, that are defined in the method definition from which you are inheriting. (A method can also throw any unchecked exception, even if it is not declared in its throws clause.)

When you override a method in a subclass, you cannot add new exception types to those you inherit. You can choose to throw a subset of those exceptions listed in the method's superclass, but a subclass farther down the hierarchy cannot then relist the exceptions dropped above it. For example, suppose you have the hierarchy shown in Figure 8-2.

Class A defines a method named test(). Class B is a subclass of class A and overrides test(). Class C is a subclass of class B and also overrides test(). If class A indicates in its test() method that it throws an IOException and class B does not, then class C cannot list IOException (or, in fact, any other exceptions if B does not also list any) in its throws clause.

Figure 8-2
A class hierarchy of a method throwing an exception in the superclass

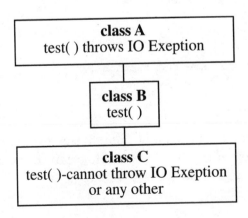

In this example, the code will not compile. Even though the super-class, class A, lists IOException in its throws clause, class B does not. Since we create an instance of class B in main(), it is class B's exceptions that must match the catch clauses listed after the try:

```java
import java.io.IOException;

class A {
 public static void main(String[] args) {
   B ref = new B();
   try {
     ref.test();
   } catch(IOException e) {
     // we can't catch something that's not thrown
   }
 }
   void test() throws IOException {
     throw new IOException();
   }
}
class B extends A {
   void test() {
   }
}
```

If we change main() so that it creates an instance of class A instead of class B, however, this will compile and run fine. This will also compile if the instance reference obj in main() is declared as type A. In that case, Java enables the possibility that this reference might really be of type A and the catch clause is fine.

If test() in class B invokes super.test(), then either test() in class B would have to indicate it throws an IOException, or the call to super.test() would have to be wrapped in a try/catch block.

Exercise 8-3

Take the above code and make the changes to it based on the possibilities listed above. First, try to compile the code as is. Then create an instance of class A and declare the variable as class A. Finally, try to invoke test() in class A from class B using super. If the compiler complains at first, do what you have to do to get this working.

Creating and Throwing an Exception

For the example, you'll need to be able to write code to create and throw an exception. You can define your own exceptions simply by extending class Exception. Typically, the class type is all you need to distinguish your exception from the others.

You can add behavior to your exception or take advantage of methods already defined in Exception and Throwable. You can also supply a string to the constructor when you create your new exception; this string can also contain text detailing why the error occurred. You can retrieve this string from the exception object using getMessage().

To throw an exception, you simply create a new instance of the exception you want to throw and write it after a throw keyword. For example, to throw an exception named IllegalValueException (presumably a subclass of Exception), you can simply write

```
throw new IllegalValueException();
```

As in the previous examples, the method that throws this exception must indicate it throws an exception of this type in its throws clause.

Exercise 8-4

Rewrite the quadratic equation exercise so that you throw your own exception type. Indicate the cause of the exception when you create it, and display this cause in an error message. You can use the answer for Exercise 8-1 as a starting point if you'd like.

■ ■ **Answers to the Exercises**

Exercise 8-1

Method name: Roots

Input: Double a, double b, double c

Output: An array of two double values (an object in Java)

Throws: ArithmeticException (could throw a new exception you defined yourself, called something like NoRootsException)

Purpose: Implements the quadratic equation

1. Find the value of b*b—4 * a* c.

2. If this result is negative, there are no roots. Throw the exception declared as part of this method.

3. If a is negative, throw the same exception.

4. Otherwise, calculate (–b + this value) divided by 2 * a. Also calculate (–b–this value) divided by 2 * a. Place these results in a new double array and return this array.

Here's what this code might look like. It contains a main() method so that you can run it and test the method:

```
class Quad {
   public static void main(String[] args) {
      Quad q = new Quad();
      try {
         double[] answer = q.roots(1.2, 3.2, -4.0);
         System.out.println("The roots are " +
            answer[0] + ", " + answer[1]);
```

```
        } catch (NoRootsException x) {
            System.out.println("No roots exist");
        }
    }
    double[] roots(double a, double b, double c) throws
    NoRootsException {
        double[] result = new double[2];
        double temp = (b * b)-( 4 * a * c);
        if (temp < 0)
            throw new NoRootsException();
        if (a < 0)
            throw new NoRootsException();
        temp = Math.sqrt(temp);
        result[0] = (- b + temp) / (2.0 * a);
        result[1] = (- b-temp) / (2.0 * a);
        return result;
    }
}
class NoRootsException extends Exception { }
```

If you threw something like ArithmeticException, that's fine for what you reviewed up to this point in the chapter. However, in general, you should not throw an unchecked exception (which is what ArithmeticException is). By creating your own exception type, as this chapter discusses towards the end, you can be specific about what error occurred and can make sure you throw a checked exception, an exception that must be handled.

Running the above Quad class' main() method yields this result:

```
The roots are 0.927443, -3.59411
```

To see an exception get thrown, try running with a equal to 0 or with b equal to 0 and a and c equal to something greater than 0.

Exercise 8-2

```
int doDivision(InputStream in) throws IOException,
    ArithmeticException {
    int c = in.read();
    return 100/c;
}
```

Exercise 8-3

Here is the original code, this time with line numbers:

```
 1: import java.io.IOException;
 2:
 3: class A {
 4:  public static void main(String[] args) {
 5:    B ref = new B();
 6:    try {
 7:      ref.test();
 8:    } catch(IOException e) {
 9:     // we can't catch something that's not thrown
10:    }
11:  }
12:  void test() throws IOException {
13:    throw new IOException();
14:  }
15: }
16:
17: class B extends A {
18:  void test() {
19:  }
20: }
```

First, compile the code as is. The JDK will complain about line 8 and will display the message

```
Exception java.io.IOException is never thrown in the body
of the corresponding try statement.
```

Then create an instance of class A instead of class B. To do that, change line 5 to read

```
A ref = new A();
```

Now the code will compile and run successfully when you run class A's main() method. Next try changing line 5 to read

```
A ref = new B();
```

The code will still compile and run successfully when you run class A's main() method. Then, after leaving the code defined as above and declaring the variable to be of class A, but creating an instance of class B, add after line 18:

```
super.test();
```

When you try to compile this, the compiler will complain about the line you just added (now line 19) and will say

```
Exception java.io.IOException must be caught, or it must be
declared in the throws clause of this method.
```

This problem can be fixed, however. The simplest way to proceed is to indicate that `test()` as defined in class B also throws a `java.io.IOException`, just like `test()` in class A. Thus, we can change line 18 to read

```
void test() throws IOException {
```

Now we can compile and run this code just fine.

Exercise 8-4

Notice in this answer how `NoRootsException` must provide a constructor that passes the string argument to its superclass. This enables the new exception to be initialized with a string containing an explanation of what went wrong. This string can later be retrieved using `getMessage()`.

```
class Quad {
    public static void main(String[] args) {
        Quad q = new Quad();
        try {
            // WORKS double[] answer = q.roots(1.2, 3.2, -4.0);
            double[] answer = q.roots(1.2, 0.0, 2.1); //
    Produces exception
            System.out.println("The roots are " +
                answer[0] + ", " + answer[1]);
        } catch (NoRootsException x) {
            System.out.println("No roots exist: " +
            x.getMessage());
        }
    }
    double[] roots(double a, double b, double c) throws
    NoRootsException {
        double[] result = new double[2];
        double temp = (b * b)-( 4 * a * c);
```

```
            if (temp < 0)
                throw new NoRootsException("negative square
                root");
            if (a < 0)
                throw new NoRootsException("divide by zero");
            temp = Math.sqrt(temp);
            result[0] = (- b + temp) / (2.0 * a);
            result[1] = (- b-temp) / (2.0 * a);
            return result;
        }
    }
    class NoRootsException extends Exception {
        NoRootsException(String s) {
            super(s);
        }
    }
```

QUESTIONS

1. Why is this code illegal?

```
class A {
    public static void main(String[] args) {
        try {
            System.out.println("hello");
        }
    }
}
```

a. You cannot have a try block without a catch and/or a finally.

b. Code that does not throw an exception cannot be in a try block.

c. The method main( ) must always throw something if the try block is used without a catch.

2. Analyze the following code and pick the best analysis from the ones presented below.

```
class A {
    public static void main(String[] args) {
        method();
```

```
    }
    static void method() throws Exception {
        try {
            System.out.println("hello");
        } finally {
            System.out.println("good-bye");
        }
    }
}
```

   a. This code will compile and display both "hello" and "good-bye".
   b. This code will do everything in choice a, but Java will then halt the program and report that Exception was thrown but not handled.
   c. This code will not compile.

3. What appears in the standard output if you run this program?

```
class A {
    public static void main(String[] args) {
        method();
    }
    static void method() {
        try {
            System.out.println("hello");
        } finally {
            System.out.println("good-bye");
        }
    }
}
```

   a. "hello"
   b. "good-bye"
   c. "hello" followed by "good-bye"

4. What appears in the standard output if you run this program?

```
class A {
    public static void main(String[] args) {
        method();
    }
    static void method() {
        try {
            System.out.println("hello");
            return;
```

```
      } finally {
         System.out.println("good-bye");
      }
   }
}
```

   a. "hello"
   b. "good-bye"
   c. "hello" followed by "good-bye"

5. What appears in the standard output if you run this program?

```
class A {
   public static void main(String[] args) {
      method();
   }
   static void method() {
      try {
         System.out.println("hello");
         System.exit(0);
      } finally {
         System.out.println("good-bye");
      }
   }
}
```

   a. "hello"
   b. "good-bye"
   c. "hello" followed by "good-bye"

6. What is the result of invoking class B first with no command-line argument and then with the command line argument "throw?"

```
class B {
   public static void main(String[] args) {
      B b = new B();
      b.test(args);
   }
   void test(String[] args) {
      String s;
      if (args.length == 0)
         s = new String("don't throw");
      else
         s = args[0];
```

```
    try {
        method(s);
        System.out.println("no exception");
    } catch (MyException e) {
        System.out.println("caught");
    }
}
void method(String s) throws MyException {
    if (s.equals("throw"))
        throw new MyException();
    else
        return;
}
}
class MyException extends Exception{}
```

a. The program prints "no exception" two times in a row.

b. First, the program prints "no exception". Then, the program prints "caught".

c. The program prints "caught" two times in a row.

7. This question builds on Question 6, which defined a class called B. Given that class, why is it illegal to write a subclass of B like this?

```
class C extends B {

    public static void main(String[] args) {
        C c = new C();
        c.test(args);
    }
    void method(String s) {
        if (s.equals("yes"))
            throw new MyException();
        else
            return;
    }
}
```

a. When you override a method, you must also indicate the exceptions the overridden method will throw.

b. The subclass C cannot invoke test( ) without overriding it.

c. A subclass cannot define main( ) if its superclass also defines main( ).

8. This question also builds on class B, defined in Question 6. Is it legal to write a subclass of B (and new subclass of Exception) like this?

```
class C extends B {

   public static void main(String[] args) {
      C c = new C();
      c.test(args);
   }
   void method(String s) throws AnotherException {
      if (s.equals("yes"))
         throw new AnotherException();
      else
         return;
   }
}
class AnotherException extends Exception {
}
```

  a. This code is legal.
  b. This code is illegal because AnotherException is not declared correctly.
  c. This code is illegal because the method you override cannot throw exceptions not declared by its ancestor's method.

9. This question also builds on class B, defined in Question 6. Is it legal to write a subclass of B (and a subclass of MyException) like this?

```
class C extends B {

   public static void main(String[] args) {
      C c = new C();
      c.test(args);
   }
   void method(String s) throws AnotherException {
      if (s.equals("yes"))
         throw new AnotherException();
      else
         return;
   }
}
class AnotherException extends MyException {
}
```

    a. This code is legal.

    b. This code is illegal because AnotherException is not declared correctly.

    c. This code is illegal because the method you override cannot throw exceptions not declared by its ancestor's method.

ANSWERS

1. a. Let's look at the two other choices.

- ▪ "Code that does not throw an exception cannot be in a try block." This is not true. You can have code that does not throw an exception within a `try` block. If you do, however, you need a `finally` block following it.

- ▪ "The method `main()` must always throw something if the `try` block is used without a `catch`." Again, this is not true because you can use a `try` block with a `finally` block. No exceptions have to be involved in that case.

2. c. This code will not compile. Exception must be handled in main( ) or main( ) must indicate that it throws an Exception.

3. c. Both "hello" and "good-bye" appear in the standard output.

4. c. Both "hello" and "good-bye" appear in the standard output. Even though the code in try issues a return statement, the finally block is still executed.

5. a. Only the word "hello" appears in the standard output. Why doesn't "good-bye" appear? Because this is not a control flow issue. We go from writing "hello" to invoking a method named exit( ) in the System class. The exit( ) method exits to the system. We never return to this method to reach the finally block. (Sneaky, I know.)

6. b. Run this to see the results in the standard output.

7. a. The overridden method in class C should be declared as follows:

```
void method(String s) throws MyException {
  if (s.equals("yes"))
    throw new MyException();
  else
    return;
}
```

8. c. The method you override can only throw exceptions that have been declared by the ancestor's method.

9. a. This is legal. A method you override can throw any exception declared by its ancestor's method or any subclass of one of these exceptions. In this case, AnotherException has been defined as a subclass of MyException, which class B's method named method() declares it is capable of throwing.

CHAPTER 9

Methods

Methods encode behavior. You can define `static` methods, which belong to the class, and `instance` methods, which belong to objects created from the class. Generally, `static` methods access static data, while `instance` methods access instance data.

Methods must be uniquely identified by name and signature; if there is more than one method with the same name, that method is said to be overloaded. Subclasses can override methods by defining their own method with the same name and signature as a method in any of their ancestors.

The programmer exam is big on overloading and overriding methods. Although the concept is fairly straightforward if you're familiar with object-oriented concepts, the details can be tricky. There are rules you should know about when overloading and overriding methods you inherit. These rules will help you move quickly through questions on the test, and we'll cover them in this chapter.

Objectives for This Chapter

- Distinguish between overloaded and overridden methods.
- Identify legal return types for overloaded and overridden methods.
- Write code for an overridden method that uses the special reference super.
- State what occurs when you invoke an overridden method in a base class and a derived class.

Defining a Method

Here's a quick review on defining a method. A method definition includes its access control keywords; keywords relating to its role in the class hierarchy; the type of its return value, name, and parameters; and any exceptions it throws. Access control keywords include `public`, `protected`, and `private`, which were discussed in

Chapter 1, "Taking the Programmer Exam." Other keywords (mostly relating to a method's place in the class hierarchy) include `abstract`, `final`, `native`, and `synchronized`. These are also discussed in Chapter 1. (The keyword `native` is discussed in the second part of this book when you'll prepare for the developer exam.)

The return type can be any class type, any primitive data type, or `void`. If the method throws any checked exceptions, these exception types must be listed in a `throws` clause after the method's signature. (You can also list any unchecked exceptions in the `throws` clause, if you wish.) Here is a simple method definition:

```
void test() { }
```

This method does not use any keywords, does not return a value, does not take any parameters, and does not throw any exceptions. Here is a complicated method definition:

```
public abstract synchronized Object test(String[] args,
    boolean b)
    throws IOException, MyOwnException;
```

This method can be accessed by any other method that can access the class defining it and is `abstract` (and so does not provide a method body). This method is `synchronized` so that only one thread at a time can execute this and other instance methods, it returns an instance of class Object, it takes two parameters, and it throws two exceptions (this definition packs quite a wallop).

Overloading a Method

You can overload a method by defining more than one method with the same name in the same class. If you define more than one method with the same name in the same class, Java must be able to determine which method to invoke based on the number and types of parameters defined for that method.

The return value does not contribute towards distinguishing one method from another; it does not affect which method Java invokes. The exceptions a method might throw also do not matter. All that matters is that the method is sufficiently different in its parameters that the *Java Virtual Machine* (JVM) can determine which method to invoke. Here's a simple example of overloading a method named test():

```
class Ex1 {
  public static void main(String[] args) {
    Ex1 e = new Ex1();
    e.test();
    e.test(1.0, 1);
  }
  void test() {
  }
  void test(double i, int j) {
  }
}
```

The JVM can easily determine which version of test() to invoke from main(). One version takes no parameters. The other takes a double and an int.

What if, instead of invoking the second version by writing

```
e.test(1.0, 1);
```

we wrote

```
e.test(1, 1);
```

In other words, we have two int values. In this case, there's still no confusion. The JVM can also determine which version to invoke. It's a simple matter to coerce an int to a double. This code will compile and run successfully.

Here's an example that doesn't work. In this case, the methods are not different enough for the JVM to determine which one to invoke:

```
//THIS WILL NOT COMPILE!
class Ex2 {
 public static void main(String[] args) {
  Ex2 e = new Ex2();
```

```
   e.test(1, 1); //CONFUSION!
 }
 void test(int i, long j) {
 }
 void test(long i, int j) {
  }
 }
```

This code won't even compile. The compiler will complain that the overloaded `test()` methods are too similar to each other to invoke using

```
e.test(1, 1);
```

However, there is nothing inherently wrong with the two `test()` methods. They are, in fact, different. If we change the line where we invoke `test()` to clear up which one to call, then this code compiles and runs fine. We can do so by writing

```
e.test(1L, 1);
```

Exercise 9-1

Write a class that defines two `static` methods. One should find the average for an `int` array, while the other should find the average for a double array.

Overriding a Method

Subclasses can override methods defined in their superclasses. To pass the method invocation up the class hierarchy (that is, to pass the method call to your superclass so that its version of the method is also invoked), you can use the special object reference `super`. This special object reference is an object whose type matches the superclass. Using `super`, an object can access the variables and methods defined by the superclass.

Here's a simple example of using `super`:

```
class Super {
 public static void main(String[] args) {
  Sub s = new Sub();
  s.test();
 }
 void test() {
  System.out.println("Superclass");
 }
}
class Sub extends Super {
 void test() {
  super.test();
  System.out.println("Subclass");
 }
}
```

This program writes `"Superclass"` followed by `"Subclass"` to the standard output. Here are some rules involving overriding methods:

Access Control

You cannot make a method in a subclass more private than it is defined in the superclass, although you can make it more public. For example, given the following method,

```
class Super {
 protected void test() {
 }
}
you cannot make the subclass look like this:
class Sub extends Super {
 private void test() {
  super.test();
 }
}
```

Other Keywords

A subclass may make an inherited method `synchronized`, or it may leave off the `synchronized` keyword so that its version is not `synchronized`. If a method in a subclass is not `synchronized` but the method in the superclass is, the thread obtains the monitor for the object when it enters the superclass's method. (There's more about threads in Chapter 12, "Passing Arguments to Programs.") You could also declare an inherited method to be `abstract`, but then there would be no way to get to the behavior in the hierarchy above the `abstract` declaration. Also, as covered in Chapter 1, you cannot override a `final` method.

BACKGROUND: *Why does an* `abstract` *method stop inheritance? Because you cannot invoke your superclass's behavior if your superclass defines the method to be* `abstract`, *since an* `abstract` *method does not define any behavior for the method. Hence, you cannot pass a method call up the class hierarchy beyond the* `abstract` *method declaration.*

Return Types

Return types must match the overridden method in the superclass exactly.

Parameter Types

The parameters of the overridden method must match those in the superclass exactly. Java does not coerce parameters, as it can with overloaded methods.

Exceptions

A method in a subclass cannot add exception types to the exceptions defined in the superclass. However, it can leave off exceptions. In the previous chapter, we covered exceptions in relation to overriding a method. The key concept from Chapter 8, "Exceptions," stated the rule explained in the following Exam Pointer.

EXAM POINTER: *When you override a method, you must list those exceptions that the override code might throw. You can only list those exceptions, or subclasses of those exceptions, that are defined in the method definition from which you are inheriting. (A method can also throw any unchecked exception, even if it is not declared in its throws clause.)*

Exercise 9-2

Create a subclass of Calculator called `FancyCalculator` that is able to provide all of Calculator's functions, plus sin, cos, and tan. Here is the class definition for Calculator:

```
class Calculator {
  private String[] functions = {"+", "-", "*", "/", "="};
  String getFunctions() {
    String s = functions[0];
    for (int i = 1; i < functions.length; i++)
      s += ", " + functions[i];
    return s;
  }
}
```

You can use the following code to test the Calculator class and your new class:

```
class Tester {
  public static void main(String[] args) {
    Calculator c = new Calculator();
    System.out.println(c.getFunctions());
```

```
      FancyCalculator f = new FancyCalculator();
      System.out.println(f.getFunctions());
    }
  }
```

The point of this exercise is to override a method and invoke the superclass' version of this method successfully.

Object References to Base and Derived Classes

For the exam, you'll need to be able to state what occurs when you invoke an overridden method in a base class and a derived class. A variable declared as an object reference for a certain class type can in fact hold an object reference for that class or an object reference for any subclass of that class. For example, suppose you have two classes. One is named Base, and it derives directly from class Object. The other is named Derived, and it extends class Base. You can create new classes and assign them to variables like this

```
Base b = new Base();
Derived d = new Derived();
```

As you can see, the class type defines the type of object reference. But you can also define a new object and assign its reference to a variable like this:

```
Base b_d = new Derived();
```

Even though b_d is defined as a type of class Base, this type includes subclasses of Base, such as class Derived. This has interesting effects when accessing data. For example, imagine we've defined the Base and Derived classes like this:

```
class Base {
  int i = 1;
}
class Derived extends Base {
  int i = 2;
}
```

It's perfectly legal to have two different instance variables with the same name if they are defined in two different classes where one inherits from the other. Which variable we access depends on the type of the object reference that the variable is declared to hold. For example, if we access and display the values for i like this

```
System.out.println(b.i);
System.out.println(d.i);
System.out.println(b_d.i);
```

what gets displayed depends on the object reference's declared type. The variable b is declared as a Base class, so b.i accesses i in the Base class and displays 1. The variable d is declared as a Derived class, so d.i accesses i in the Derived class and displays 2.

The variable b_d is trickier. We have created an instance of the Derived class and assigned it to this variable. However, as our rule says, the variable that gets accessed depends on the declared type of the object reference, which in this case is Base. So, b_d.i accesses i in the Base class, and displays 1.

In contrast to which variable gets accessed, the method that gets invoked depends on the underlying object. Imagine if our Base and Derived classes looked like this

```
class Base {
  int i = 1;
  String test() {
   return "Base";
  }
}
class Derived extends Base {
  int i = 2;
  String test() {
   return "Derived";
  }
}
```

As you can see, the Derived class overrides the method test() defined in the Base class. Now we create new instances as before:

```
Base b = new Base();
Derived d = new Derived();
Base b_d = new Derived();
```

This time what happens when we invoke the `test()` method for each object reference and print the results is as follows:

```
System.out.println(b.test());
System.out.println(d.test());
System.out.println(b_d.test());
```

The method that gets invoked depends on the actual type of the object itself, not on the declared type. So, `b.test()` invokes `test()` in the `Base` class, which displays `Base`. `d.test()` invokes `test()` in the `Derived` class, which displays `Derived`. Following our rule, `b_d.test()` invokes `test()` in the `Derived` class, since that is the actual object assigned to the variable `b_d`.

Declaring Native Methods

You may have to identify how you declare a `native` method in the Programmer test. Here's an example:

```
public native void method();
```

A `native` method does not have a body, not even an empty set of braces. Declaring a method to be `native` means that it is implemented in a language native to the platform you're running on. In other words, it is written in a language such as C and compiled for a particular platform.

TIP: *Some rules for native methods: a native method can throw exceptions; a native method cannot be abstract.*

Answers to the Exercises

Exercise 9-1

```java
class Avg {

  static double avg(double[] arr) {
   double sum = 0.0;
   if (arr.length > 0) {
    for (int i = 0; i < arr.length; i++)
     sum += arr[i];
    sum /= arr.length;
   }
   return sum;
  }
  static int avg(int[] arr) {
   int sum = 0;
   if (arr.length > 0) {
    for (int i = 0; i < arr.length; i++)
     sum += arr[i];
    sum /= arr.length;
   }
   return sum;
  }
  public static void main(String[] args) {
   // Test the methods.
   int[] intArray = {1, 2, 3, 4, 5};
   double[] doubleArray = {10, 20, 30, 40, 50};
   System.out.println(avg(intArray));
    System.out.println(avg(doubleArray));
  }
}
```

Exercise 9-2

Here is the new FancyCalculator class:

```java
class FancyCalculator extends Calculator {
 private String[] functions = {"sin", "cos", "tan"};
 String getFunctions() {
  String s;
  s = super.getFunctions();
```

```
        for (int i = 0; i < functions.length; i++)
          s += ", " + functions[i];
        return s;
      }
    }
```

Review Questions

1. What is the result of trying to compile and run this program?

```
class Example1 {
 public static void main(String[] args) {
   Example1 e = new Example1();
   e.test(5);
  }
  int test(int i) {
   System.out.println("int");
   return 1;
  }
  void test(long i) {
   System.out.println("long");
  }
}
```

    a. The program does not compile because the compiler cannot distin-guish between the two test( ) methods provided.

    b. The program compiles and runs, but nothing appears in the stan-dard output.

    c. The program compiles and runs and int appears in the standard output.

    d. The program compiles and runs and long appears in the standard output.

2. What is the result of trying to compile and run this program:

```
class Example1 {
 public static void main(String[] args) {
   Example1 e = new Example1();
   e.test(5, 5.0, 5L);
  }
```

```
void test(double a, double b, double c) {
  System.out.println("double, double, double");
}
void test(int a, float b, long c) {
  System.out.println("int, float, long");
}
}
```

   a. This code will not compile.
   b. The code will compile, run, and display double, double, double.
   c. The code will compile, run, and display int, float, long.

3. What is the result of attempting to compile and run this program?

```
class Over {
 public static void main(String[] args) {
  Under u = new Under();
  u.test();
 }
 int test() {
  System.out.println("Over");
  return 1;
 }
}
class Under extends Over {
 short test() {
  super.test();
  System.out.println("Under");
  return 1;
 }
}
```

   a. This code does not compile.
   b. This code compiles, runs, and displays Over followed by Under.
   c. This code compiles, runs, and displays Under followed by Over.

Answer to the Review Questions

1. c. The program compiles fine. When it runs, the word int appears in the standard output. Remember, the return type

is not part of the signature of a method. An overloaded method can have different return types and the code will still be legal. Also, the JVM can determine which version to invoke because literals such as 5 are `int` values.

2. b. The second parameter is 5.0. Floating-point numbers in Java are double by default. So, even though the first and second parameters are `int` and long and match the second definition of test(), the second parameter would have to be coerced to a float. Java invokes the first version of test( ), where no values have to be explicitly coerced.

3. a. The compiler complains because the method in the subclass `Under` returns a different type than the method in the superclass. Unlike an overloaded method, the return type for an overridden method must match the superclass's return type for that method.

CHAPTER 10

Essential java.lang and java.util

The `java.lang` and `java.util` packages are important parts of the Java language and, as you would expect, many exam questions pertain to these packages. This chapter focuses on the core aspects of `java.lang` and `java.util` that are identified with specific objectives in the exam, which includes wrapper classes for primitive data types, the `java.lang.Math` class, the `java.lang.String` class, and the `java.util` Collections API. You'll find separate chapters that cover other aspects of `java.lang`, such as exceptions, which are covered in Chapter 8, "Exceptions," and threads, which are covered in Chapter 13, "Threads." You'll also find a limited discussion of `java.util` classes in other chapters.

Objectives for This Chapter

- Use wrapper classes to represent primitive values as objects.
- Write code using the following methods of the `java.lang.Math` class: `abs()`, `ceil()`, `floor()`, `max()`, `min()`, `random()`, `round()`, `sin()`, `cos()`, `tan()`, and `sqrt()`.
- Identify legal operators for strings.
- Describe the significance of the immutability of String objects.
- Know the difference between the String and StringBuffer classes.
- Make an appropriate selection of collection classes/interfaces to suit specified behavior requirements.

Wrapper Classes

In Chapter 5, "Data Types and Values," we covered Java's primitive data types. Primitive data types are not objects and cannot be subclassed. Primitive data types cannot be created or accessed with methods either. If you want to create or manipulate a primitive data type, you may want to wrap the primitive type with its corresponding wrapper class. Wrapper classes provide methods for working with, converting, and using the wrapped data types. The constructors for wrapped classes allow objects to be created and converted from primitive values or strings.

Table 10-1 shows corresponding wrapper classes for each of the eight primitive data types. Each of the wrapper classes is examined briefly in the sections that follow.

The `Boolean` Class

The `Boolean` class is a wrapper for the `boolean` values. Key methods provided by the class are `booleanValue()`, `getBoolean()`, `hashCode()`, `toString()`, and `valueOf()`. These methods support type and class conversion. The class has two constructors:

```
public Boolean(boolean value)
public Boolean(String s)
```

Thus, you can construct the class using an actual `boolean` value, such as

```
boolean primitiveBool = false;
Boolean wrappedBool = new Boolean(primitiveBool);
```

Table 10-1	*Primitive Data Type*	*Wrapper Class*
Primitive data types and their corresponding wrapper classes	boolean	Boolean
	byte	Byte
	char	Character
	double	Double
	float	Float
	int	Integer
	long	Long
	short	Short

Or you can pass the constructor a string that represents the value to be wrapped, such as

```
Boolean wrappedBool = new Boolean("false");
```

The Character Class

The Character class is a wrapper for `char` values. The class provides many different methods for working with `char` values. You can use these methods to change case, determine the type of value, and perform class tests. The class has one constructor:

```
public Character(char value)
```

Following this, you must construct the class using an actual `char` value, such as

```
char primitiveChar = "A";
Character wrappedChar = new Character(primitiveChar);
```

The byte, short, integer, and long Classes

The `byte`, `short`, `int`, and `long` primitive data types all have different wrapper classes. These classes provide methods for working with, testing, and converting the values. They also provide the MIN_VALUE and MAX_VALUE constants.

These classes all have two constructors, one that expects to be passed a primitive value and another that expects to be passed a string. You could construct these classes using primitive values as follows:

```
byte primitiveByte = 18;
Byte wrappedByte = new Byte(primitiveByte);

short primitiveShort = 12345;
Short wrappedShort = new Short(primitiveShort);

int primitiveInt = 9876543;
Integer wrappedInt = new Integer(primitiveInt);

long primitiveLong = 9997654321L;
Long wrappedLong = new Long(primitiveLong);
```

If you wanted to construct the classes from strings, you could use

```
Byte wrappedByte = new Byte("18");

Short wrappedShort = new Short("12345");

Integer wrappedInt = new Integer("9876543");

Long wrappedLong = new Long("9997654321");
```

The float and double Classes

The `float` and `double` classes wrap the float and double primitive data types. These classes provide methods for working with, testing and converting the values. They also provide the MIN_VALUE, MAX_VALUE, POSITIVE_INFINITY, and NEGATIVE_INFINITY constants.

As with most other wrapper classes, the `float` and `double` classes have two constructors, one that expects to be passed a primitive value and another that expects to be passed a string. To construct these classes using primitive values, you could use

```
float primitiveFloat = 1.825F;
Float wrappedFloat = new Float(primitiveFloat);

double primitiveDouble = 1.825125125;
Double wrappedDouble = new Double(primitiveDouble);
```

To construct these classes using strings, you could use

```
Float wrappedFloat = new Float("1.825F");

Double wrappedDouble = new Double("1.825125125");
```

Using Wrapper Classes

Wrapper classes can be used in many different ways, so let's review some of the basics you'll need to know for the exam. When you use the string constructor for wrapper classes, all wrapper classes, with the exception of Boolean, will throw NumberFormatException if the string doesn't represent a valid value. Boolean doesn't throw this exception and instead only wraps a value as true when you pass in True or true.

After creating a wrapper class, you may need to extract the actual value. For example, if you create an `Integer` class and then need to perform a calculation on the Integer value, you would need to do this through the actual value. Each wrapper class has a method for performing this task. These methods are defined as follows:

```
public boolean booleanValue()
public byte byteValue()
public char charValue()
public double doubleValue()
public float floatValue()
public int intValue()
public long longValue()
public short shortValue()
```

The following code shows how you could wrap an `Integer` and then extract its actual value for use in a calculation:

```
Integer i = new Integer("590");
Integer j = new Integer("150");
int k = i.intValue()*j.intValue();
```

All the wrapper classes except `Character` have a `static` method called `valueOf()`, which parses a string, constructs a wrapper of the same class type, and then returns the wrapper. For example, `Integer.valueOf("405")` parses the value of the strings, constructs a wrapper of the `Integer` class, and then returns the wrapped value. You can also use the `equals()` method to check for equality of two wrappers. In the following example int1 and int2 are compared:

```
Integer int1 = new Integer("88995");
Integer int2 = new Integer("90110");
if (int1.equals(int2)) {
  System.out.println("The values are equal");
}
```

Exercise 10-1

Write a standalone program that sets values for a `byte`, `short`, `integer`, `long`, `float`, and `double`. These values should be represented as strings to the wrapper class constructors. You should catch `NumberFormatException` if it occurs and display the error `Incorrect number format`.

Working with the Math Class

For the exam, you'll need to be able to write code that uses the static methods defined in the Math class. These static methods include `abs()`, `ceil()`, `floor()`, `max()`, `min()`, `random()`, `round()`, `sin()`, `cos()`, `tan()`, `sqrt()`. Each of these methods is examined briefly in the sections that follow.

abs()

`abs()` returns the absolute value of a number. This method is overloaded with four versions; the argument can be a `float`, `double`, `long`, or `int`. The types `byte` and `short` are coerced to an `int` if they are used as arguments. This method returns the same type as the argument supplied.

ceil()

`ceil()` finds the next highest integer. The documentation says this method "returns the smallest (closest to negative infinity) double value that is not less than the argument and is equal to a mathematical integer." Let's unravel what this means with a simple example. Take a look at this program:

```
class M {
 public static void main(String[] args) {
  System.out.println(Math.ceil(9.01));
  System.out.println(Math.ceil(-0.1));
  System.out.println(Math.ceil(100));
  System.out.println(Math.ceil(Double.MIN_VALUE));
 }
}
```

When you run this, its output is

```
10.0
-0.0
100.0
1.0
```

The value `Double.MIN_VALUE` is the smallest possible positive number that a variable of type `double` can hold. The `ceil()` method went up to 1. If the number is an integer to begin with, it returns that integer. Otherwise, it goes to the closest integer, counting up.

floor()

`floor()` finds the next lowest integer. This method does the opposite of `ceil()`. Its documentation says that it "returns the largest (closest to positive infinity) `double` value that is not greater than the argument and is equal to a mathematical integer." Let's run the same program that we just ran, this time changing `ceil()` to `floor()`:

```
class M {
public static void main(String[] args) {
  System.out.println(Math.floor(9.01));
  System.out.println(Math.floor(-0.1));
  System.out.println(Math.floor(100));
  System.out.println(Math.floor(Double.MIN_VALUE));
 }
}
```

The output is

```
9.0
-1.0
100.0
0.0
```

max()

max() finds the maximum between two values. max() is overloaded with versions for int, long, double, and float. This method simply returns the larger of the two values supplied.

min()

min() finds the minimum between two values. min() is also overloaded with versions for int, long, double, and float. This method simply returns the smaller of the two values supplied.

random()

random() returns a random number, a double value, between 0.0 and 1.0. You don't have nearly as much control over this random number as you do when you use the Random class and can seed the random number generator. If you want to seed the number or retrieve random numbers in different ranges, use the Random class.

round()

This method finds the closest integer to a floating-point number. There are versions of round() for double and float (of course, integer values don't need to be rounded). For example, if you run this program

```
class Round {
 public static void main(String[] args) {
   System.out.println(Math.round(9.01));
   System.out.println(Math.round(9.5));
   System.out.println(Math.round(-9.5));
   System.out.println(Math.round(-0.1));
   System.out.println(Math.round(100.0));
   System.out.println(Math.round(Double.MIN_VALUE));
 }
}
```

you get these results:

```
9
10
-9
0
100
0
```

EXAM POINTER: *As you can see,* round() *went up at .5 or above, and down when it the number was less than .5. So, for 9.5, the number was rounded to 10. At −9.5, the number was rounded up to −9.*

sqrt()

sqrt() finds the square root of a number. If the argument is *not-a-number* (NaN) or less than zero, the result of sqrt() is NaN.

sin()

sin() finds the sine of a number given the angle in radians. If it's been a while and you don't remember, there are *2*pi* degrees in a circle. For example, *pi/2* radians equals 90 degrees.

`cos()`

`cos()` finds the cosine of a number given the angle in radians.

`tan()`

`tan()` finds the tangent of a number given the angle in radians.

Exercise 10-2

Using only the `Math` class, write a method that finds the maximum of two random numbers between 0 and pi. Then find the sine, cosine, and tangent of this number.

The String and StringBuffer Classes

For the exam, you'll need to be able to describe the significance of the immutability of strings. You'll also need to know how to declare strings and how to manipulate strings.

Java uses the `String` and `StringBuffer` classes to work with strings of characters. The `String` class supports immutable (or unchanging) strings. The `StringBuffer` class supports modifiable strings. Both strings and string buffers contain sequences of 16-bit Unicode characters.

String Operators

We'll get back to this notion of immutability in a moment. For now let's look at String operators. When used with Strings, the + operator creates a new String object that's a combination of the strings. For example,

```
String s = "hello," + " world";
```

results in the String s containing "hello, world". Strings also override the += operator, so that you can write

```
String s = "hello,";
s += " world";
```

The + and += operators also work as you would hope when used with a String object and some other primitive data types, such as a number, boolean, or char. For example, when used with a number in

```
String s = "Nine to " + 5;
```

the + operator results in s being set to the String "Nine to 5".

The Immutability of Strings

At the beginning of the chapter, we told you strings were unchangeable, yet as you've seen, you can indeed *change* strings. After all, you can change the value of strings using the + and += operators. If you want to add two strings together, you would concatenate them with the + operator, such as

```
String s1 = "Oh my";
s1 = s1 + " gosh";
```

The result of this operation is that s1 equals Oh my gosh, right? Well, yes and no, and this is where the whole notion of immutability comes into play. Strings created with the String class are read-only. When you add characters to a String object, say, using the + operator, the result is a new String object, not a modifification of the original String object. Although this behavior may seem a bit odd, there is a very good reason for handling strings in this manner.

In Java, every string literal, such as Oh my, is represented by an instance of a string. Java classes can have pools of strings. When a program containing a string literal is compiled, the compiler normally adds the string literal to an appropriate pool for the class. If the string literal already exists in the class, however, the compiler doesn't create a new copy and instead uses the existing literal from the pool. This is designed to save memory and cannot cause problems in the program because any time you modify a string, the result is a new string.

Several interesting quirks result from this behavior and you should note these for the exam. The first important behavior is that string literals are placed in a class-specific pool. If you create additional literals with the same value as an existing literal, the new literal strings will point to the existing literal. Considering the following example:

```
String s1 = "Monday";
String s2 = "Monday";
```

Here when you compile the program, the string literal "Monday" is placed into the pool of literal strings for the current class. When the compiler reads line 2, it checks the pool and finds an existing literal with this value and uses the existing value. So both s1 and s2 point to the same string literal in the class pool.

Another important behavior for strings occurs when you use the new String() constructor. If you've worked with strings, you know the String class has many constructors. The most basic constructor follows this format:

```
String stringName = "theString";
```

You can also construct a string explicitly by calling the constructor, such as

```
String s1 = new String("Monday");
```

When a program containing this line is compiled, the string literal "Monday" is placed into the literal pool for the current class. Then when the new String() statement is executed at runtime, a new instance of a string is constructed and returned. This new instance duplicates the string in the literal pool. Now you have two objects, one in the literal pool and another in the program's memory space. This uses memory unnecessarily.

Having two string objects with identical values can cause problems in your programs. To see how, consider the case where you are checking the equality of strings. If string s1 is a string literal stored in the literal pool and string s2 is a string created at run-time, say by user input, the equality operator (==) will not return true when comparing the s1 and s2:

```
s1 = "Monday";
//s2 created by user response
if (s1 == s1) {
  //execute these statements
}
```

The objects are not the same, and to successfully perform the comparison, you'd need to perform a comparison on the characters in the strings using the equals() method, such as

```
s1 = "Monday";
//s2 created by user response
if (s1.equals(s2)) {
  //execute these statements
}
```

TIP: *Because the* equals() *method must compare the actual characters in the strings, the method is slower than the equality operator (==). If a program performs lots of string comparisons using the* equals() *method, you may notice slow response times. To resolve this problem, you can use the* intern() *method of the* String *class to add a string to the literal pool. Once you do this, you can perform a comparison using the equality operator.*

Methods of the String Class

The String class defines many methods. You should be familiar with these methods:

charAt()   It returns the character at the index position passed to this method. The first character is at position 0. The last character is at position length() - 1. If you try to access a character that is outside the bounds of this string, this method will throw a

`StringIndexOutOfBoundsException`. This method returns type `char`.

concat() It concatenates a given string onto the end of the string object responding to this method. Of course, since strings are read-only, the string passed as an argument is not really appended to the original string. Instead, `concat()` returns a new string.

endsWith() It returns a `boolean` indicating whether the string passed as the parameter is at the end of the target string.

equals() It returns true if two string objects are the same lengths and contain the identical run of characters, taking case into account. String overrides the `equals()` method, which, by default, only returns true if the object references used with this method refer to the same underlying object. With a string, completely different objects can make `equals()` return true.

equalsIgnoreCase() It returns true if two string objects are the same lengths and contain the identical run of characters, not taking case into account. In other words, with this method, a pair of corresponding characters is considered equal if the `==` operator returns `true` as they are, if the `==` operator returns `true` after they have both been made upper case, or if the `==` operator returns `true` after they have both been made lower case. When this method runs, Java makes characters upper or lower case using a `static` character method called `toUppercase()` or `toLowercase()`.

indexOf() It finds the first occurrence of a character or substring. The method returns the value −1 if it cannot find the character or substring. Otherwise, the method returns the index where the character is.

lastIndexOf() It finds the last occurrence of a character or substring. The method returns the value −1 if it cannot find the character or substring. Otherwise, the method returns the index where the substring starts.

length() It returns an `int` of the number of characters in this string.

replace()   It returns a new string where all the occurrences of the first character passed as a parameter are replaced by the second parameter.

startsWith()   It returns a boolean indicating whether the string passed as the parameter is at the beginning of the target string. The startsWith() method is also overloaded to start at an optional offset into the string.

substring()   It returns a substring from the given string. There are two versions of this method.

toLowerCase()   It returns a new string object representing the lower-case equivalent of the string. If the lower-case equivalent is not different from the original string, toLowerCase() returns the original object.

toString()   It can be overridden in any class so that instances of that class return a string representation of themselves. This is useful when you want to place an object directly in an expression that calls for a string, such as an argument to System.out.println(). For a string, toString() returns itself, the same object reference (of course, pointing to the same object) that was used to invoke this method.

toUpperCase()   It returns a new string object representing the upper-case equivalent of the string. If the upper-case equivalent is not different from the original string, toUpperCase() returns the original string.

trim()   It returns a new string object that cuts off the leading and trailing whitespace for the string for which this was invoked. Java considers "whitespace" to be any character with a code less than or equal to \u0020. The character \u0020 is the whitespace character.

valueOf()   It is a static method that is overloaded for the basic primitive data types, character arrays, and class Object. It returns a string representing the value of the data type. For example, a boolean might be true or false and a float might be 3.14. Objects return their value for toString().

Exercise 10-3

Write a standalone program that takes any number of command-line parameters and displays the number of (naturally occurring) lowercase e's in all of them combined.

String Buffers

Java declares and manipulates objects of the StringBuffer class to handle most string operations. You can use the StringBuffer class directly as well with any of these constructors:

StringBuffer() It constructs an empty string buffer.

StringBuffer(int length) It constructs an empty string buffer with a specified initial buffer length.

StringBuffer(String initialString) It constructs a string buffer from a string object.

Normally, you'll construct StringBuffer objects from string objects, so the constructor you'll use the most is the third one. Whenever you want to manipulate the contents of a string, you probably want to use a StringBuffer object, instead of a string object. For example, if you want to read one character at a time from a source file or from the standard input and append the characters to what you've read so far, you would want to utilize a StringBuffer object, instead of a string, in most cases.

The append() and insert() methods of the StringBuffer class are overloaded to take every basic Java data type as well as character arrays and objects. This enables you to convert and append other objects and primitive data types to StringBuffer objects. In addition you can also do some interesting things to the characters in a StringBuffer, such as reversing the characters by invoking reverse(), or changing a particular character by using setCharAt().

StringBuffer does not inherit from String. If you want to use the string represented by a StringBuffer object as a parameter to a method (such as `println()`), you must obtain a string object from the `StringBuffer` object. You can do this by invoking `toString()`.

The following example shows how you could construct and manipulate a `StringBuffer` object:

```
public class StringBufferTest {
 public static void main(String args[]) {
  StringBuffer strBuf = new StringBuffer("ABCDEFG");
  strBuf.reverse(); //now strBuf is "GFEDCBA"
  strBuf.reverse(); //now strBuf is "ABCDEFG"
  strBuf.append(2, "-"); //now strBuf is "AB-CDEFG"
  strBuf.append(4, "-"); //now strBuf is "AB-CD-EFG"
  strBuf.append(6, "-"); //now strBuf is "AB-CD-EF-G"
  strBuf.setCharAt(3, "+"); //now strBuf is "AB+CD-EF-G"
  strBuf.setCharAt(6, "+"); //now strBuf is "AB+CD+EF-G"
  strBuf.setCharAt(9, "+"); //now strBuf is "AB+CD+EF+G"
  String str = strBuf.toString();
  System.out.println(s);
 }
}
```

Exercise 10-4

Both the `String` class and the `StringBuffer` class have `equals()` methods. Given what you know about the `equals()` method and these classes, what will be the output from the following snippet of code and why?

```
StringBuffer strBuf = new StringBuffer("12345");
String str = strBuf.toString();
if (str.equals(strBuf)) {
 System.out.println(str);
}
```

Rewrite the example to produce the output of "not equals" if there is no output.

Collections

The Collection classes and interfaces are an important part of the exam. For the exam, you will need to determine which collection classes/interfaces should be used in a given situation. These situations are based on meeting specific behavior requirements, such as the requirement for storing data elements that must not appear more than once in the data store or the requirement of having a set of key values to look up or index stored data.

The Collection classes and interfaces are often referred to as a framework. The reason they are called a framework is that each class is designed with a common behavior. Each implementation of a class is built on this framework and can optimize its own functionality as necessary. These functions include searching, synchronizing, and storing data.

Overview of the Collections API

Before taking a look at how you can use the Collections API, we'll provide a brief summary of the available classes and interfaces. Table 10-2 provides a summary of pre-JDK 1.2 collection classes and interfaces.

In JDK 1.2, maps are replacing dictionaries as a means to associate keys with values. Because of this, you should use map-related classes and interfaces instead of the `Dictionary`, `Hashtable`, and `Properties` classes.

Table 10-3 summarizes the new JDK 1.2 Collection interfaces. As you examine the table, note that four basic types of interfaces are defined: collections, lists, sets and maps.

Table 10-4 summarizes the Collection classes for JDK 1.2. These classes obtain their basic behavior from their related interface and the `AbstractCollection` class.

Table 10-2

Collection classes and interfaces

Type/Name	Description
Interface	
Enumeration	Provides methods for stepping through an ordered set of objects or values. This interface has been replaced by the Iterator interface in the JDK 1.2 Collection API.
Class	
BitSet	A growable set of bits. Each bit is represented by a boolean value and can be indexed like an array or vector.
Dictionary	This provides abstract functions used to store and retrieve objects using key-value pairs. Any object can be used as a key or value. This class is an abstract superclass of Hashtable.
Hashtable	Implements a hash table data structure that indexes and stores the objects in a dictionary using hash codes as the keys. This class does not allow the null value to be stored.
Properties	A subclass of Hashtable that can be read from and written to a stream. The class enables you specify default values to be used if a key is not found in the table.
Stack	Implements a *last-in, first-out* (LIFO) stack. Objects can be pushed onto the stack and popped off the stack. You can also peek at the last item on the stack without taking it off the stack.
Vector	An expandable array of objects with a clear order. You can add, delete, and insert elements into vectors. In JDK 1.2, this class implements the List interface and extends the AbstractList class.

Table 10-3

JDK 1.2 collection interfaces

Name	Description
Collection	Implements an unordered group of objects. Collections are sometimes referred to as bags because they enable duplicates and don't place constraints on the type or order of elements.
Comparator	Provides a basic mechanism for comparing the elements of a collection
Iterator	Provides a basic mechanism for iterating through the elements of a collection. It replaces Enumeration.
List	Extends the Collection interface to implement an ordered collection of objects. This ordered list can be indexed and can contain duplicate values.

Name	Description
`ListIterator`	Extends the `Iterator` interface to support the iteration of lists
`Map`	Provides basic functions to store and retrieve data using key values. The key values must be unique
`Map.Entry`	An inner interface of `Map` that specifies methods for working with a key-value pair
`SortedMap`	A `Map` whose elements are sorted in ascending order
`Set`	Extends the `Collection` interface to implement a finite set. Sets do not allow duplicate values, and simple sets do not have a specific order. Some sets allow the null value, but if they do, the value can only occur once
`SortedSest`	A set whose elements are sorted in ascending order

Table 10-4

JDK 1.2 collection classes

Name	Description
`Arrays`	Provides static methods for searching, sorting, and converting arrays to lists
`Collections`	Provides `static` methods for searching, sorting, and manipulating objects that implement the `Collection` interface
`AbstractCollection`	Provides a basic implementation of the `Collection` interface and is in turn extended by other classes
`AbstractList`	Extends `AbstractCollection` and provides the basic implementation of the `List` interface
`AbstractSequentialList`	Extends `AbstractList` and provides functionality for sequentially accessing a list (instead of randomly accessing the list)
`LinkedList`	Extends `AbstractSequentialList` and implements a doubly linked list. A linked list is a list in which each element references the next element. A doubly linked list is a list in which each element references the previous and the next element
`ArrayList`	Extends `AbstractList` and implements a resizable array

continues

Name	Description
AbstractSet	Extends AbstractCollection and provides the basic implementation of the Set interface
HashSet	Extends AbstractSet and implements a set of key-value pairs. The class uses hash tables for storage and doesn't allow duplicate values. You *can't* use the null value either
TreeSet	Extends AbstractSet and implements a sorted binary tree that supports the SortedSet interface. You can't have duplicate values in a TreeSet
AbstractMap	Extends AbstractCollection and provides the basic implementation of the Map interface
HashMap	Extends AbstractMap and implements a map of key-value pairs. The class uses hash tables for storage and doesn't allow duplicate values. You *can* use the null value
TreeMap	Extends AbstractMap and implements a sorted binary tree that supports the SortedMap interface
WeakHashMap	Extends AbstractMap and implements a map with weak keys. An entry in the hash table is automatically removed when its key is garbage-collected

Collection API Essentials

As you've seen, the Collection API provides an extensive set of classes and interfaces. For the exam, you don't need to memorize every facet of this API, but you do need to be able to select an appropriate collection class or interface to suit specified behavior. If you plot out the behavior of these classes and interfaces, you find four fundamental types:

- *Collections*   Simple collections can be unordered and don't have any restrictions. You can use any type of object and you can have multiple occurrences of an object. The Collection interface supports methods for adding, removing, counting, and checking items in a collection.

■ *Lists* Lists are ordered collections that enable multiple occurrences of an object. The order can be the natural order or the order in which the objects are added to the collection. Because the list is ordered, its objects can be indexed. The ListIterator interface provides methods for iterating through the elements of a list. Abstract lists can be accessed randomly, through an array, through a link list, or through doubly linked list.

■ *Sets* Sets are collections that do not enable duplicate values. Some sets allow the null value, but if they do, the value can only occur once. The AbstractSet and HashSet classes create sets that aren't ordered. The TreeSet class creates sets that are ordered through a binary tree.

■ *Maps* Maps are collections that use a set of values to look up or index stored data. With maps, you can search on a key field. Key fields values must be unique. In JDK 1.2, maps replace dictionaries as the preferred technique to associate keys with values. The AbstractMap, HashMap, and WeakHashMap classes create maps that aren't ordered. The TreeMap class creates maps that are ordered through a binary tree.

The way values are stored using the fundamental types is equally as important. If you examine the storage techniques used, you'll find values are stored using one of these techniques:

■ *Arrays* Arrays provide storage for ordered items with unique values. You can use arrays when you have a fixed number of elements with specific values. The array ordering makes it difficult to add and remove elements in the array. If an array is full, you'll need to create a new array and copy the contents of the current array before you can add elements. Arrays don't provide a special search mechanism.

■ *Linked lists* Linked lists provide storage for ordered items that don't need unique values. You can easily add and remove values from the linked list. The size of a linked list can grow dynamically because each element points to the next (and sometimes the previous) element. However, accessing linked lists is slower than accessing arrays. Linked lists also don't provide a special search mechanism.

- *Trees* Trees provide storage for items that are sorted in ascending order. With trees, you can easily add and remove elements as long as the order of the tree is maintained. Trees with elements distributed evenly can be searched more efficiently than linked lists and arrays.

- *Hash tables* In hash tables, each item is represented with a key-value pair. The key must be a unique identifier for the item being stored. Using the key, you can quickly and efficiently find items in the hash table. Using a hash table results in some additional overhead, which occurs when calculating hash values. Hash tables are best suited to large data sets.

Answers to the Exercises

Exercise 10-1

One possible solution for exercise 10-1 is as follows:

```
public class MyStrings {
public static void main(String args[]) {
  try {
    Byte wrappedByte = new Byte("18");
    Short wrappedShort = new Short("12345");
    Integer wrappedInt = new Integer("9876543");
    Long wrappedLong = new Long("9997654321");
    Float wrappedFloat = new Float("1.825F");
    Double wrappedDouble = new Double("1.825125125");
  }
  catch (NumberFormatException e) {
    System.out.println("Incorrect number format");
  }
 }
}
```

Exercise 10-2

```
void exercise() {

  double d1 = Math.random() * Math.PI;
  double d2 = Math.random() * Math.PI;
  double m = Math.max(d1, d2);
  System.out.println(Math.sin(m));
  System.out.println(Math.cos(m));
  System.out.println(Math.tan(m));
}
```

Exercise 10-3

```
class ECounter {
public static void main(String[] args) {
  String s;
 int index;
 int ecount = 0;
  for (int i = 0; i < args.length; i++) {
   s = args[i];
   index = 0;
   while ( (index = s.indexOf('e', index)) != -1) {
    index++;
    ecount++;
   }
  }
  System.out.println("There are " + ecount + " e's.");
 }
}
```

Exercise 10-4

The example in this exercise doesn't produce any output. Although the StringBuffer object and the String object have the same contents, they are different objects. You can compare a string to a string or a string buffer to a string buffer, but you cannot compare a string to a string buffer or vice versa.

Because the example produces no output, you should have rewritten the code snippet to produce the output "not equals". One possible solution is as follows:

```
StringBuffer strBuf = new StringBuffer("12345");
String str = strBuf.toString();
if (str.equals(strBuf)) {
System.out.println(str);
} else
  System.out.println("not equals");
```

QUESTIONS

1. What Math methods, invoked like this

   ```
   Math.method(x);
   ```

   would return the value −5 given the value of x to be −4.5?
   a. round( )
   b. ceil( )
   c. floor( )
   d. a, b, and c
   e. a and c

2. What is the possible output from invoking

   ```
   Math.random();
   ```

   a. 132.93
   b. 0.2154
   c. 29.32E10
   d. all of the above

3. To find the square root of a number, you can use the Math method
   a. srt( )
   b. sqrt( )
   c. squareRoot( )

4. Given this line of code,

   ```
   String s = "Penguin";
   ```

what will be assigned to c if you execute

```
char c = s.charAt(6);
```

a. 'n'
b. 'i'
c. Nothing will be assigned because charAt() will respond with a
   StringIndexOutOfBoundsException.

5. What do you expect the output to be for the following program?

```
class Str {
public static void main(String[] args) {
  String s = "Hi!";
  String t = "Hi!";

 if (s == t)
   System.out.println("equals");
   else
   System.out.println("not equals");
 }
}
```

a. "equals"
b. "not equals"

6. What do you expect the output to be for the following program?

```
class Str {
public static void main(String[] args) {
  String s = "Hi!";
  String t = new String(s1);
  if (s == t)
   System.out.println("equals");
   else
   System.out.println("not equals");
 }
}
```

a. "equals"
b. "not equals"

7. What do you expect the output to be for the following program?

```
class Str {
public static void main(String[] args) {
  String s = "HELLO";
  String t = s.toUpperCase();
  if (s == t)
    System.out.println("equals");
  else
    System.out.println("not equals");
 }
}
```

   a. "equals"
   b. "not equals"

8. Imagine the following lines of code:

```
String s = "Hello,";
String t = s;
s += " world";
if (s == t)
  System.out.println("equals");
else
  System.out.println("not equals");
```

What gets written to the standard output?

   a. "equals"
   b. "not equals"

9. In the following example primes provided, you create at instance of the `StringBuffer` class and then you call the `append()` method of the `StringBuffer`:

```
StringBuffer strBuf = new StringBuffer("12345");
strBuf.append("6789");
```

After executing line two, does `strBuf` still reference the same object instance?

10. If you need to store multiple data elements in a data store, which class/interface would you use if searching is a priority and you have a unique key field?

   a. List
   b. Set
   c. Map
   d. Vector
   e. Collection

11. If you need to store multiple data elements that must not appear more than once in the data store, which class/interface would you use if searching is *not* a priority?

   a. List
   b. Set
   c. Map
   d. Vector
   e. Collection

12. Which of the following can store duplicate elements?

   a. List
   b. Set
   c. Map
   d. Collection

13. When you want to associate keys with values and you are using JDK 1.2, which of the following classes are preferred?

   a. Dictionary
   b. HashTable
   c. Properties
   d. HashMap
   e. TreeMap

14. Can a null value be added to a set?

   a. Yes, but not with the HashSet class.
   b. Yes, but only with the AbstractSet class.
   c. Yes, but only with the TreeSet class.
   d. Yes
   e. No

ANSWERS

1. **c.** Only `floor()` will go to the next lower number. Both `round()` and `ceil()` go higher to −4.

2. **b.** Math.`random()` yields a result between 0.0 and 1.0.

3. **b.** I made up the other method names.

4. **a.** The first index position is 0, so `charAt(6)` results in the seventh character in the string, which is `"n"`.

5. **a.** The strings are equal. String `"Hi!"` is created as a string literal in the literal pool. Both String `s` and String `t` point to this string literal.

6. **b.** The strings are not equal. The first string is created as a string literal in the literal pool. At runtime, the second string is constructed as a new instance.

7. **a.** Surprised? The method `toUpperCase()` returns the original string if the parameter is already in upper case. Hence the `==` operator yields `true` in this example.

8. **b.** After these three lines of code execute, it might seem that we have modified the object reference `s`, and that `t` and `s` are still equivalent object references. However, this is not the case. The `+=` operator creates a new string object. The variables `t` and `s` now contain different references. The words "not equals" are written to the standard output.

9. Yes, the `StringBuffer` class is read-write. Because of this, the example modifies the existing `StringBuffer` object.

10. **c.** A map supports searching on a key field as long as the key values are unique.

11. **b.** A set rejects duplicate entries so if you want to ensure data elements only appear one this is the best choice. We could have used a map also. However, because searching isn't a priority, the best choice is b.

12. **a, d.** Only lists and collections can have duplicate elements.

13. **d, e.** Maps are replacing dictionaries as the preferred way to associate keys with values. Both `HashMap` and `TreeMap` are maps.

14. a. A null value can be added to most sets as long as the value only occurs once. With the HashSet class, however, null values are not allowed.

CHAPTER 11

Input/Output

Java defines a wide variety of classes and methods in its `java.io` package that you can use to read from and write to streams of data. What is a stream? A stream is an ordered sequence of bytes that have a source or destination, which can be a file or Internet resource, for example.

Different kinds of streams exist in Java. Some streams are associated with files and make it easy to read from or write to a file. Some streams can be chained together so that each type of stream adds its own processing to the bytes as they pass through the stream.

For the exam, no specific objectives cover File I/O and the questions do not directly address File I/O either. The material presented in this chapter, however, provides an essential background for concepts that are covered in the exam. With this in mind, review this chapter to ensure you know the essentials and then move on to focus on other chapters.

Objectives for This Chapter

- Construct "chains" of `InputStream` and `OutputStream` objects using the subclasses of `FilterInputStream` and `FilterOutputStream`.
- Identify valid constructor arguments for `FilterInputStream` and `FilterOutputStream` subclasses.
- Read, write, and update files using `FileInputStream`, `FileOutputStream`, and `RandomAccessFile` objects.
- Describe the permanent effects on the file system of constructing and using `FileInputStream`, `FileOutputStream`, and `RandomAccessFile` objects.
- Navigate the file system using the `File` class.

■ ■ The java.io Package

The top-level classes in the `java.io` package—`InputStream` and `OutputStream`, `FilterInputStream` and `FilterOutputStream`, `FileInputStream` and `FileOutputStream`, `File`, and `RandomAccessFile`—are all classes you should know about. Here's a quick review of these classes.

There are three pairs of classes and interfaces to understand. Once you grasp where these are in the class hierarchy for the I/O classes, the rest of the classes fall into place. These four pairs of classes and interfaces are

1. InputStream and OutputStream
2. FilterInputStream and FilterOutputStream
3. DataInput and DataOutput
4. Reader and Writer

InputStream and OutputStream

At the top level of the input/output hierarchy are the classes `InputStream` and `OutputStream`. These are abstract classes and define basic methods for working with streams of data, such as `read()`, `write()`, and `skip()`. They also declare a `close()` method to close the stream. Creating the object opens the stream.

These classes declare a few other methods as well. For example, `InputStream` declares a method called `available()` that tests to see whether any bytes are available to be read. `OutputStream` also declares a method called `flush()`, which writes any bytes in a buffer to the stream.

Individual subclasses of `InputStream` implement the `read()` method for reading one byte at a time. Individual subclasses of `OutputStream` implement the `write()` method for writing one byte at a time.

Figure 11-1
InputStream and
OutputStream are at
the top level.

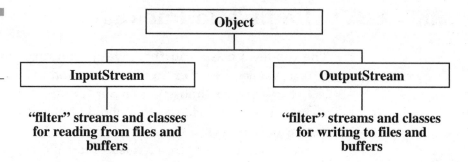

Subclasses of these top-level `abstract` classes include classes for reading and writing to files, buffers, byte arrays, and more. These are not on the test, so don't panic.

`FileInputStream` and `FileOutputStream` are used to read from and write to a file. `FileOutputStream` also creates the file you write to. We have supplied examples of using these classes later in this chapter.

In addition to `FilterInputStream` and `FilterOutputStream`, you can instantiate some direct subclasses of `InputStream` and `OutputStream`. The additional InputStream subclasses are

- `ByteArrayInputStream`, which enables you to use byte arrays, rather than a file, as an input stream.

- `ObjectInputStream`, which enables you to read data from an object.

- `PipedInputStream`, which enables you to associate an output file with an input file. Then you can read data from a `PipeInputStream` and write the data to a `PipedOutputStream`.

- `SequenceInputStream`, which enables you to read from a sequence of files. The class reads from the first file until it comes to the end, then it reads the second, and so on.

- `StringBufferInputStream`, which enables you to read from a `StringBuffer` as you would from a file.

The additional `InputStream` subclasses are as follows:

- `ByteArrayOutputStream` enables you to use byte arrays, rather than a file, as an output stream.

- ObjectOutputStream enables you to write data to an object.

- PipedOutputStream enables you to associate an input file with an input file. You can then write data to a PipeOutputStream and read the data from a PipedInputStream.

FilterInputStream and FilterOutputStream

Filter streams work with the bytes read from or written to another stream. The Filter stream classes are subclasses of InputStream and OutputStream. Although some subclasses of InputStream and OutputStream can be used by themselves, FilterInputStream, FilterOutputStream, and their subclasses are used with other stream objects.

When you create a Filter stream, you must specify the stream to which it will attach. This specification is done by passing an instance of InputStream or OutputStream as appropriate (depending on if you are creating a FilterInputStream or a FilterOutputStream) to the constructor. The Filter streams do not define a no-args constructor. This means they must be chained in some way; a Filter stream must reference either another Filter stream or an InputStream or OutputStream. (All Filter streams descend from either InputStream or OutputStream.)

A Filter stream processes a stream of bytes in some way. By "chaining" multiple Filter streams, you can add multiple filters to a stream of bytes. You can chain together as many Filter streams as you like. Each Filter stream in the chain continues adding processing to the bytes read from or written to a resource.

In Figure 11-2, you can see that the DataInputStream knows how to work with Java data types; the FileInputStream only knows how to read individual bytes. The figure shows where the File streams and the Filter streams fit into the I/O hierarchy we started earlier.

TIP: *The first Filter stream in a chain must be associated with some underlying file or other resource to be created in the first place. Once the first Filter stream is created, other Filter streams can attach to the first one.*

Figure 11-2
File streams and
Filter streams

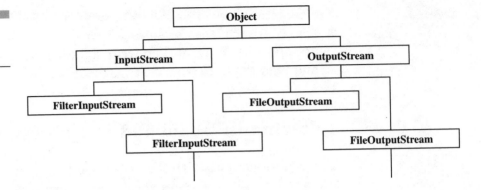

Both `FilterInputStream` and `FilterOutputStream` have several subclasses. The `FilterInputStream` subclasses are as follows:

- `BufferedInputStream` Invoking a read method for this subclass fills up the buffer and returns bytes from this buffer to the program doing the reading.

- `DataInputStream` This subclass expects a data input stream, which can be a file input stream, a pipe, or another type of input stream. You can pass in an input stream, read the data, and return an appropriate value.

- `LineNumberInputStream` This tracks which line number is currently being read.

- `PushbackInputStream`

The `FilterOutputStream` subclasses are as follows:

- `BufferedOutputStream` enables you to write bytes to a buffer. Once the buffer is filled, the contents are written to the designated output stream.

- `DataOutputStream` expects you to pass in an output stream. Then when you write data, it converts the output to bytes and writes them to the output stream.

- `PrintStream` provides `print()` and `println()` methods for the basic primitive data types as well as Object, String, and character arrays.

DataInput and DataOuput

DataInput and DataOutput are interfaces that declare methods for reading and writing Java's primitive data types: byte, short, int, long, float, double, char, and boolean. It is up to the classes that implement this interface to supply the specific methods that fulfill these contracts needed. Three classes implement the DataInput and DataOutput interfaces: DataInputStream, DataOutputStream, and RandomAccessFile. Figure 11-3 shows where these classes are in the I/O class hierarchy and their connection to the DataInput and DataOutput interfaces.

TIP: *Notice that* RandomAccessFile *implements both* DataInput *and* DataOutput *methods.* RandomAccessFile *objects can read from and* write *to files. That's why* RandomAccessFile *does not inherit from* FileInputStream *or* FileOutputStream; *it can do both (and remember Java does not allow multiple inheritance of implementation).*

With these three cornerstones of the I/O hierarchy (InputStream and OutputStream, the Filter streams, and the DataInput and DataOutput interfaces), you can begin to make sense of the other I/O classes.

Figure 11-3
Classes that implement the DataInput and DataOutput interfaces

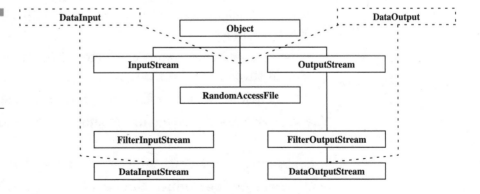

Reader and Writer

The `InputStream` and `OutStream` classes and their subclasses support 8-bit characters. With internationalization and localization initiatives, JDK 1.2 needs a way to read and write streams using 16-bit Unicode characters. The answer is the `Read` and `Writer` classes.

The `Reader` class is similar to the `InputStream` class. It is the root of an input class hierarchy and it includes subclasses for buffering and filtering input. Beyond this, the `Reader` class also supports pipes. Because the `Reader` class supports Unicode, it is preferred way to read files in JDK 1.2 and later.

The `Reader` class has six direct subclasses. These subclasses are

- `BufferedReader`, which supports buffered character input. Its `LineNumberReader` subclass keeps track of line numbers while reading buffered input.
- `CharArrayReader`, which enables Java to read a character input stream from a character buffer
- `FilterReader`, which is an abstract class that provides basic filtering for character input streams. Its `PushBackReader` subclass provides a filter that enables characters to be pushed back onto the input stream.
- `InputStreamReader`, which reads characters from an input stream, automatically converting between streams of bytes and sequences of Unicode characters. Its `FileReader` subclass provides basic functionality for reading a file given a file path or File handle.
- `PipedReader`, which reads characters from a pipe. Pipes are used in thread communication.
- `StringReader`, which reads characters from a string

The `Writer` class has seven direct subclasses. These subclasses are

- `BufferedWriter`, which supports buffered character output
- `CharArrayWriter`, which enables Java to write a character output stream from a character buffer

- `FilterWriter`, which is an abstract class that provides basic filtering for character output streams

- `OuputStreamReader`, which writes characters to an output stream, automatically converting between sequences of Unicode characters and streams of bytes. Its `FileWriter` subclass provides basic functionality for writing to a file given a file path or File handle.

- `PipedWriter`, which writes characters to pipes

- `PrintWriter`, which supports platform-independent character printing

- `StringWriter`, which writes characters to a string

The abstract `Reader` superclass provides a `read()` method that can be used to read character input. This method has three constructors:

- `int read() throws IOException` This reads a single character by returning the next char or ·1 if at the end of the input. The char is stored in the low-order 16 bits of the int return value.

- `int read(char cbuf) throws IOException` This reads an array of characters and returns the number of chars read or −1 if at the end of the input.

- `int read(char cbuf, int off, int len) throws IOException` This reads `len` characters using the given offset into the character buffer array and returns the number of chars read or −1 if at the end of the input.

The abstract `Writer` superclass provides a `write()` method that can be used to write character output. This method has five constructors:

- `int write(int c) throws IOException` writes a single character. The char is stored in the low-order 16 bits of c.

- `int write(String s) throws IOException` writes the String s.

- `int write(char cbuf) throws IOException` writes an array of characters.

■ `int write(char cbuf, int off, int len) throws IOException` writes `len` characters using the given offset into the character buffer array.

■ `int write(String s, int off, int len) throws IOException` writes `len` characters using the given offset into String `s`.

All readers and writers inherit from the `Reader` or `Writer` super-class so they also support the `read()` and `write()` methods shown here.

The File Class

With the `File` class, you can create, delete, and rename files. You can work with file names in a platform-independent way, test to see if a file exists, and find information about a file node. You can also create directories and temporary files. You can create a `File` object using one of three constructors. These constructors take

1. A string containing a path name
2. A string containing a path name and a string containing a file name
3. A file representing a path and a string containing a file name

The sections that follow examine the key methods of the `File` class.

TIP: *The* `File` *class defines a static variable named* `separatorChar` *that contains the platform-dependent path separator, which is either a backslash for Windows, a colon for the Mac, or a forward-slash for UNIX. You can use this character to write platform-independent code that navigates the file system.*

Testing to See if a File Exists

Just because you can create a `File` object, it doesn't mean the file or directory exists. To test to see if a `File` object refers to an existing file, you can invoke `exists()`, which returns `true` or `false`.

Finding Information about a File Node

The methods `canRead()` and `canWrite()` return `boolean` values that indicate whether the application can read from or write to the file. For example, a standalone application might be able to write to a file, while an applet, because of security restrictions, may not.

Another useful method is `lastModified()`. This method returns a platform-dependent value you can use to determine whether a particular file was created before or after another.

Deleting and Renaming Files

Although you cannot create files using the `File` class or a `File` object, you can use `File` methods to make a permanent change to the file system. For example, you can delete and rename files. Invoke `delete()` to delete a file. This method returns a `boolean` indicating success or failure. Invoke `rename()` to rename a file, and supply a `File` object that embodies the new name.

Creating Directories

You can also create directories using `File`. You can invoke the method `mkdir()` to create a directory specified by the `File` object. This method also returns a `boolean` indicating success or failure.

Navigating the File System

You can use the method `getParent()` to retrieve a string containing the name of the parent directory. The methods `getPath()` and `getName()` return the directory structure for this `File` object and the file's name, respectively. The method `getAbsolutePath()` returns the absolute path if this `File` object represents an absolute path.

TECHNICAL TRAP: *If you use* `getAbsolutePath()` *and the* `File` *object does not represent an absolute path, this method makes one up. It returns the name of the current user directory with the file name concatenated to it.*

Creating Files

To create a file using the `File` object, you create an instance of `File` and then invoke the `createNewFile()` method. This method returns `true` if the file can be created, or `false` if the file already exists. The following example creates a file called `A.txt` in the current directory:

```java
import java.io.*;
class A {
public static void main(String[] args) throws Exception {
File f = new File("A.txt");
 if (!f.createNewFile()) {
   System.out.println("A.txt already exists.");
 }
}
```

Files can also be created using `FileOutputStream` and `RandomAccessFile`. Here's a basic example of using a `FileOutputStream` to create a file, although this program does not do anything with the file it creates:

```
import java.io.*;
class A {
public static void main(String[] args) throws Exception {
  FileOutputStream out = new FileOutputStream("A.test");
  out.close();
 }
}
```

If you ran this program, you would see a file named A.test in the same directory as the program. Because you are working with a stream, you must close the stream when you are finished working with it. This is handled with the close() method.

Exercise 11-1

Write a standalone program that takes a command line parameter and, after ensuring the file does not exist, create a file with that name.

Creating Temporary Files

You can use the File object's createTempFile() method to create temporary files. The method has two constructors:

```
public static File createTempFile(String prefix, String
suffix)
public static File createTempFile(String prefix, String
suffix, File directory)
```

The first constructor creates a file with the file name given as the prefix and the file extension given as the suffix. With this constructor, the file is created in the current directory. The second constructor enables you to set the directory location as the third argument.

The following code snippet will create a file named ,MyAppn.tmp, where n is a number that is generated during the call to createTempFile():

```
void createTempFile() {
 try {
  File tempFile = File.createTempFile("~MyApp", ".tmp");
  tempFile.deleteOnExit();
 } catch (IOException ioe) {
  System.out.println("Error creating temporary file!");
 }
}
```

Note the use of the `deleteOnExit()` method of the `File` object. The call to `deleteOnExit()` will ensure the temporary file is deleted when the *Java Virtual Machine* (JVM) exits.

Writing to and Reading from Files

You can read, write, and update files using the objects `Reader`, `FileOutputStream`, and `RandomAccessFile` objects. Here's another program that does just that:

```
import java.io.*;
class A {
static String fileName = "A.test";
public static void main(String[] args) {
  try {
   FileOutputStream out = createFile();
   writeFile(out);
   readFile();
  } catch (IOException io) {
   System.out.println(io.getMessage());
  }
}
 static FileOutputStream createFile() throws IOException {
  File f = new File(fileName);
  FileOutputStream out = new FileOutputStream(f);
  return out;
 }
 static void writeFile(FileOutputStream out) throws
IOException {
  DataOutputStream ds = null;
  try {
   ds = new DataOutputStream(out);
   ds.writeBytes("hello!");
  } finally {
   if (ds != null)
```

```
    ds.close();
  }
}
static void readFile() throws IOException {
 BufferedReader br = null;
 try {
  File f = new File(fileName);
  FileReader in = new FileReader(f);
  br = new BufferedReader(in);
  String s = br.readLine();
  System.out.println(s);
 } finally {
  if (br != null)
   br.close();
 }
 }
}
```

This example consists of three static methods in addition to main(). The first, createFile(), creates a new file and returns a FileOutputStream object so that we can write to it. The second, writeFile(), attaches a type of Filter stream, a DataOutputStream, to the FileOutputStream object and uses the methods defined by DataOutputStream to write to our stream. The third, readFile(), creates a FileReader handle to the file, attaches a BufferedReader to it, and then uses the methods in BufferedReader to read from it.

Notice that we close the file deliberately by placing the close() call inside a finally block so that it is always executed, even if one of the methods in the try block throws an exception. We also check to make sure the Filter object is created (in fact, the compiler insists upon it) before invoking close().

TECHNICAL TRAP: *Creating a* FileOutputStream *object creates the appropriate file. What if the file already exists? In that case,* FileOutputStream *recreates the file and writes to it again. (That is,* FileOutputStream *replaces the existing file.)*

To append to a file instead of overwriting it, you need to use a RandomAccessFile object. RandomAccessFiles are described in the next section.

Exercise 11-2

Write a program that writes your phone number to a file. Don't write a string; write an `int` containing your seven-digit number.

RandomAccessFiles

`RandomAccessFile` objects do two things: they enable you to open a file as read-only or read/write, and they enable you to write to any location in the file, not just the beginning. The downside of using a `RandomAccessFile` is that it does not inherit from `InputStream` or `OutputStream`. This means that you cannot use them in a chain, for example, with the Filter stream classes.

A `RandomAccessFile` does at least implement the `DataInput` and `DataOutput` interfaces, so it supports all the methods for reading and writing Java's primitive data types. When you create the `RandomAccessFile`, you'll supply a mode as the second argument. This mode is a string that can be either `r` for read or `rw` for read/write. (The first argument is either a string containing the path and file name or a `File` object.)

You can determine where the file pointer currently is, in bytes, by invoking `getFilePointer()`. The 0th byte is the first position in the file. You can set the file pointer with `seek()`, passing this method the number of bytes to offset, and you can also determine the length of the file with `length()`.

Here's an example of appending to a file, rather than overwriting it, as would happen if we used `FileOutputStream` in place of `RandomAccessFile` in the program that follows:

```
import java.io.*;
class Ran {
 static String fileName = "Ran.test";
 public static void main(String[] args) {
  try {
    sayHello();
    appendHi();
    readGreeting();
```

```
    } catch (IOException x) {
     System.out.println(x.getMessage());
    }
  }
  public static void sayHello() throws IOException {
   DataOutputStream ds = null;
   try {
    File f = new File(fileName);
    FileOutputStream out = new FileOutputStream(f);
    ds = new DataOutputStream(out);
    ds.writeBytes("hello!");
   } finally {
    if (ds != null)
      ds.close();
   }
  }
  public static void appendHi() throws IOException {
   RandomAccessFile out = null;
    try {
     File f = new File(fileName);
     out = new RandomAccessFile(f, "rw");
     out.seek(out.length());
     out.writeBytes(" hi!");
    } finally {
     if (out != null)
       out.close();
    }
  }
  public static void readGreeting() throws IOException {
    RandomAccessFile in = null;
    try {
     File f = new File(fileName);
     in = new RandomAccessFile(f, "r");
     String s = in.readLine();
     System.out.println(s);
    } finally {
     if (in != null)
       in.close();
   }
  }
}
```

The output from this program is a file named Ran.test that contains the following:

`hello! hi!`

In addition, this program also writes these contents to the standard output.

If we used a `FileOutputStream` instead if a `RandomAccessFile` in the `sayHi()` method, the file would simply contain

hi!

because `hello!` would have been overwritten. We were able to append using a `RandomAccessFile` because `RandomAccessFile` objects don't recreate the file if it already exists, and we can set the file pointer exactly where we want it, which in this case is to the end of the file.

You can also see that the first time we wrote to the file we used a `FileOutputStream`. It was only when we wanted to append that we needed a `RandomAccessFile`. We created the `RandomAccessFile` object using `rw` the first time, because we wanted to write to it. The second time, in `readGreeting()`, we used `r`, because we only wanted to read from the file.

Also notice how we used `readLine()` to read from the file. This method is declared in the `DataInput` interface, which is implemented by `RandomAccessFile`.

NOTE: *As with the earlier example of working with files, we wrapped the* `close()` *call inside a* `finally` *block so that the file is always closed when we're done with it.*

File Descriptors

There is one more way to create a `FileOutputStream` object, and that's by using a constructor that takes a `FileDescriptor` object. A `FileDescriptor` represents an existing, open file. It is a handle to the open file, but it does not have any methods you can use, other than a method called `valid()` that returns true if the file it represents exists and is open.

You can get a `FileDescriptor` object by invoking a `FileOut-putStream`'s or `RandomAccessFile`'s `getFD()` method. It is sometimes necessary to use a `FileDescriptor` if you have an existing stream and want to create another stream object that references the same underlying file. However, streams do not supply a method that enables you to retrieve the name of the underlying file, nor do they supply a method that enables you to retrieve a `File` object for the underlying file. `FileOutputStream` and `RandomAccessFile`, however, do supply the magical `getFD()` method. If you do not know the `File` object or the file name the stream refers to, you must use the `FileDescriptor` object returned by `getFD()` to create your new stream. (You can also create a new `RandomAccessFile` using a `FileDescriptor`.)

Exercise 11-3

Finish this program to first write the numbers 1, 3, and 5 to a file, leaving gaps for the even numbers. Then on a second pass, write the numbers 2 and 4 in the proper places. Use the method declared by the `DataOutput` interface called `writeBytes()` to write out a String for 2 and 4 as appropriate.

```java
import java.io.*;
class Gaps {
 public static void main(String[] args) throws Exception {
  File f = new File("Gaps.test");
  RandomAccessFile out = new RandomAccessFile(f, "rw");
  out.writeBytes("1 3 5");
  System.out.println("len is " + out.length());
  // Supply the missing code here to write out "2" and "4"
  // in the gaps in the character "1 3 5" already written to
  // the file.
  out.close();
 }
}
```

Answers to the Exercises

Exercise 11-1

```java
import java.io.*;
class NewFile {
 public static void main(String[] args) {
   if (args.length != 1) {
     System.out.println("Supply a file name.");
     System.exit(1);
   }
   try {
     File f = new File(args[0]);
     if (!f.createNewFile())
       System.out.println(args[0] + " already exists.");
     } catch (IOException io) {
       System.out.println(io.getMessage());
   }
 }
}
```

Exercise 11-2

```java
import java.io.*;
class Phone {
 static String fileName = "Phone.test";
 public static void main(String[] args) {
   try {
     FileOutputStream out = createFile();
     writeFile(out);
   } catch (IOException io) {
     System.out.println(io.getMessage());
   }
 }
 static FileOutputStream createFile() throws IOException {
  File f = new File(fileName);
  FileOutputStream out = new FileOutputStream(f);
  return out;
 }
 static void writeFile(FileOutputStream out) throws
IOException {
```

```
   DataOutputStream ds = null;
   try {
    ds = new DataOutputStream(out);
    ds.writeInt(5551212);
   } finally {
    if (ds != null)
     ds.close();
    }
   }
}
```

Exercise 11-3

```
import java.io.*;

 class Gaps {
 public static void main(String[] args) throws Exception {
   File f 5 new File("Gaps.test");
  RandomAccessFile out 5 new RandomAccessFile(f, "rw");
  out.writeBytes("1 3 5");
  System.out.println("len is " 1 out.length());
   out.seek(1);
   out.writeBytes("2");
   out.seek(3);
    out.writeBytes("4");

  out.close();
 }
}
```

Review Questions

1. What are valid parameters for the FilterInputStream constructor?

a) no parameter

b) InputStream

c) File

d) RandomAccessFile

e) DataInput

f) all of the above

g) a and b

2. To create a file, you can use an instance of class

   a) `File`

   b) `RandomAccessFile`

   c) `FileOutputStream`

   d) any of these

   e) b and c

3. To create a new directory, you can use an instance of class

   a) `File`

   b) `RandomAccessFile`

   c) `FileOutputStream`

   d) any of these

   e) b and c

4. What will the result be of executing the following program?

```
import java.io.*;
class B {
 public static void main(String[] args) {
   try {
     File f = new File("B.test");
     FileOutputStream out = new FileOutputStream(f);
   } catch (IOException io) {
     System.out.println(io.getMessage());
   }
 }
}
```

   a) It will throw an IOException that will be caught.

   b) It will run fine, but no file will result since nothing is written to it.

   c) It will run fine, the file "B.test" will exist after it runs, and the file's size will be 0.

5. If file is an instance of a RandomAccessFile whose length is greater than 0, what will following line accomplish?

`file.seek(file.length()-1);`

   a) Position the file pointer at the end of the file (after the last character).

   b) Position the file pointer just before the last character.

   c) Cause seek( ) to throw an IOException.

6. You can attach a `FilterOutputStream` object to

   a) an underlying file

   b) another `FilterOutputStream` object

   c) a `FilterInputStream object`

   d) all of these

   e) a or b

7. To delete a file, you can use an instance of class

   a) `FileOutputStream`

   b) `RandomAccessFile`

   c) `File`

Answers to the Review Questions

1. b. Only objects of type InputStream are valid parameters to pass to create a new FilterInputStream object.

2. d. As of JDK 1.2, the File object can be used to create a file, as well as `FileOutputStream` and `RandomAccessFile`.

3. a. The `File` class contains a method called mkdir() that will create a new directory.

4. c. This is valid code and will run fine, creating an empty file called B.test.

5. b. You can position the file pointer at the end of the file by setting it to `file.length()`.

6. e. A `FilterOutputStream` can be attached to any OutputStream subclass. This includes other filter streams as well as file streams.

7. c. You can use the delete( ) method defined in `File` to delete a file.

CHAPTER 12

Passing Arguments to Programs

This chapter reviews how to invoke a Java program from the command line and pass parameters to the program. The exam has several questions that relate to creating a `main()` method and selecting arguments passed to `main()` from the command line. You'll also need to understand the arguments array.

Just as you can pass command-line arguments to a standalone application, you can also pass arguments to a Web-based applet. With foresight on the part of the programmer, this enables non-programmers to control the behavior of an applet. Applets are not required to have a `main()` method and no questions on the exam directly address applets. However, you may find that a basic understanding of applets is useful and coverage of applet basics is exactly what you'll find in this chapter.

Objectives for This Chapter

- Identify correctly constructed declarations for the `main()` method.
- State the correspondence between index values in the argument array passed to a main method and command-line arguments.
- Select specific command-line elements from the arguments of the `main()` method using the correct array subscript value.
- Write HTML code to embed an applet in a Web page.
- Supply parameter values to the applet within the `<applet>` tag.
- Read the values of parameters specified in an `<applet>` tag and use them in an applet.

The main( ) Method

Unlike in C/C++ where you execute a file, in Java you run a program by passing a class name to the Java interpreter. When you invoke a standalone program, the Java runtime looks for that class' `main()` method. The `main()` method must be declared as a `public`, `static`, and `void` method that does not return a value and takes an array of String objects.

Here is the template for `main()`:

```
public static void main(String[] args) {
  //add body of main here
}
```

If the Java interpreter does not find a `main()` method that follows the above format, the interpreter won't run the class.

TECHNICAL TRAP: *Some development environments, such as Metrowerks CodeWarrior, enable you to define a* `main()` *method that does not take any parameters. However, this is not the way things are done using the* Java Development Kit *(JDK), and the test is specific to the JDK.*

The JDK will complain if you run a class whose `main()` method deviates from the standard declaration. The method must be `static`, since you have not yet created any instances of your class when you run your program. You cannot return a value to the operating system or Java interpreter. You also cannot define a different argument. You can't even supply a subclass of `String`, because `String` is a `final` class and cannot be subclassed.

The exact order of the keywords `public` and `static` and the string array definition are not strictly enforced. However, the *accepted order* for the keywords is to place `public` first, `static` second, and to define the string array using `String[]`.

For example, this is also a valid `main()` method:

```
static public void main(String[] args) {
  //Not the normal way to declare main but not wrong either
}
```

However, the accepted way to write `main()` is

```
public static void main(String[] args) {
  //The normal way to declare main
}
```

Command-Line Arguments

Using the JDK, you can provide command-line arguments for a standalone Java program. To do this, place the arguments after the program name when you invoke the Java interpreter. For example, you can invoke a program called Flower, below, like this:

`java Flower rose`

This passes the String rose to the `main()` method of the `Flower` class. The runtime allocates a string array to the size of the number of command-line arguments that you supply (in this case, 1). It also allocates a string instance containing the command-line argument and places it into the array passed to `main()`.

For example, invoking the following Flower class' `main()` method using the command above

```
public class Flower {
  public static void main(String[] args) {
    System.out.println("My favorite flower is a " + args[0]);
  }
}
```

results in the following output:

`My favorite flower is a rose`

Since this is an array and since we don't know for certain that the user has supplied a command-line argument in the program, we could get into trouble. We can't just go around accessing elements from an array beyond the bounds of an array. Java will throw an exception (`ArrayIndexOutOfBoundsException`). So before using elements out of the `args` array in `main()`, it's a good idea to first check the length of the `args` array to make sure it contains what you think it contains. Here's a new version of the `Flower` class that does this in its `main()` method:

```
public class Flower {
  public static void main(String[] args) {
```

```
  if (args.length == 0)
    System.out.println("I like all flowers");
  else if (args.length == 1)
    System.out.println("My favorite flower is a " +
args[0]);
    else {
    System.out.print("My favorite flowers are " + args[0]);
    for (int i = 1; i < args.length-1; i++)
      System.out.print(", " + args[i]);
    System.out.println(" and " + args[args.length-1]);
  }
 }
}
```

When it is run with commands like this

```
java Flower
java Flower violet
java Flower violet roses daffodils
```

this prints

```
I like all flowers
My favorite flower is a violet
My favorite flowers are violets, roses, and daffodils
```

Now that you've reviewed the basics of argument passing, let's take a closer look at the args array. As you know, the args array is used to access a program's command-line arguments. In the following example, three arguments are passed to the args array:

```
java Flower tulips daisies roses
```

The arguments are read into the args array as string objects. The tulips string is accessed through args[0], the daisies string is accessed through args[1], and the roses string is accessed through args[2]. Thus, although the size of the array in this example is three, the array index goes from 0 to 2.

Exercise 12-1

Write a main() method that displays the command-line arguments you pass to a program in reverse order.

When main() Ends

When main() ends, that may or may not be the end of the program. The *Java Virtual Machine* (JVM) runs until the only remaining threads are daemon threads (meaning it runs until all of the user threads have died). If main() does not spawn any more threads, the program ends when main() ends. However, if main() creates and starts a new thread, then even when main() comes to an end, the JVM may continue executing to support these other threads.

By default, a thread is a user thread if it is created by another user thread, and it is a daemon thread if it is created by another daemon thread. This means that, by default, all threads that you create in your program will be user threads.

If you create and display a user interface element from main(), such as a frame, your program will continue to run even after main() ends. This is because user interface elements have their own user thread associated with them to handle user input. Once the user closes this frame though, the program will end (if this is the last remaining user thread).

To explicitly set whether a thread is a user thread or a daemon thread, you can use the thread method setDaemon() and pass it a boolean. To test whether a thread is a daemon thread or a user thread, you can use the thread method isDaemon(), which returns an appropriate boolean.

Embedding an Applet in an HTML Page

First, we'll look at how you embed an applet in an HTML page. You've no doubt done this already in your Java career, but let's review this process briefly. To run an applet, you need to embed a reference to the compiled applet in an HTML file. You can then view the HTML file in a Java-enabled Web browser or in a development tool such as the JDK's appletviewer. You use the `<applet>` tag to embed an applet within a Web page. Here's the simplest HTML file you can write to reference an applet (in this case, an applet with the compiled class file named `Metric.class`). It contains three keywords in the `<applet>` tag:

```
<HTML>
<HEAD>
<TITLE>Simple Applet</TITLE>
></HEAD>
<BODY>
<APPLET CODE="Metric.class" width=200 height=100>
</APPLET>
</BODY>
</HTML>
```

The `code` keyword identifies the compiled class file containing the applet. In this example, this file is relative to the IP address and directory containing the HTML file in which this reference is embedded. However, this value can also be an absolute path name, so that a Web page can contain an applet found anywhere on the Web.

TIP: *If the applet is loaded relative to the page, two aspects can change the base location. The first is if the HTML file itself contains a* `<base>` *tag; this tag specifies where to look for the applet class. The second is if the* `<applet>` *tag contains the* `codebase` *keyword, which is described in the next section.*

The two other keywords you must have inside an `<applet>` tag are `width` and `height`. These specify the size of the screen in pixels that the browser or appletviewer should use to display the applet. The browser or appletviewer sizes the applet itself to the size indicated by these keywords. Be aware that since you are specifying the height and width in pixels, different screens display the applet differently, according to their own unique resolutions.

Passing Parameters to an Applet

The conventional way to pass a parameter to an applet is to use the `<param>` tag. Each `<param>` tag can only take one parameter, so you must use one `<param>` tag per parameter. Parameter values can be retrieved by the applet as strings using methods defined in the Applet class. If you want to pass a different type of value, such as an `int` or a `boolean`, you must convert it from a string, most likely by using a wrapper class.

The `<param>` is placed between the `<applet>` and `</applet>` tags. The `<param>` tag uses two keywords: `name`, to name the parameter, and `value`, to give it a value. An example of the `<param>` tag is

```
<HTML>
<HEAD>
<TITLE>Simple Applet</TITLE>
</HEAD>
<BODY>
<APPLET CODE="Metric.class" width=200 height=100>
<PARAM NAME=state VALUE=Hawaii>
</APPLET>
</BODY>
</HTML>
```

If you'd like a parameter value to contain spaces, you should place this value within quotes. For example, to supply a parameter value that's really two words, you can write

```
<HTML>
<HEAD>
<TITLE>Simple Applet</TITLE>
</HEAD>
<BODY>
<APPLET CODE="Metric.class" width=200 height=100>
<PARAM NAME=state VALUE="North Carolina">
<PARAM NAME=state VALUE="South Carolina">
</APPLET>
</BODY>
</HTML>
```

However, it never hurts to include quotes, even for a single word, as in

```
<HTML>
<HEAD>
<TITLE>Simple Applet</TITLE>
</HEAD>
<BODY>
<APPLET CODE="Metric.class" width=200 height=100>
<PARAM NAME=state VALUE="Washington">
<PARAM NAME=state VALUE="Oregon">
<PARAM NAME=state VALUE="California">
</APPLET>
</BODY>
</HTML>
```

Retrieving Parameters

You can also retrieve the value of a parameter using the getParameter() method defined by the Applet class. This method returns a string containing the value of the parameter or null if the parameter is not defined at all. Most programmers don't realize that you can actually retrieve the parameters in the <applet> tag itself using getParameter(). Here's an example:

```
import java.applet.Applet;

public class Tag extends Applet {
  public void init() {
    System.out.println(getParameter("code"));
    System.out.println(getParameter("width"));
    System.out.println(getParameter("height"));
  }
}
```

Here's an HTML file we can use to run this applet:

```
<HTML>
<HEAD>
<TITLE>Simple Applet</TITLE>
</HEAD>
<BODY>
<APPLET CODE="Tag.class" width=200 height=100>
</APPLET>
</BODY>
</HTML>
```

The output from this program in the standard output is

```
Tag.class
200
100
```

You can even put your own parameters right into the <applet> tag, rather than the <param> tag. For the sake of convention, you shouldn't do this, but it works. For example, if you run this program

```
import java.applet.Applet;
public class Tag extends Applet {
 public void init() {
   System.out.println(getParameter("code"));
   System.out.println(getParameter("width"));
   System.out.println(getParameter("height"));
   System.out.println(getParameter("extra"));
 }
}
```

using this HTML file

```
<HTML>
<HEAD>
<TITLE>Simple Applet</TITLE>
</HEAD>
<BODY>
<APPLET CODE="Tag.class" width=200 height=100
extra=Country>
</APPLET>
</BODY>
</HTML>
```

the result in the standard output is

```
Tag.class
200
100
Country
```

However, the reverse is not true. You cannot place a width value within a <param> tag, like this:

```
<APPLET CODE="Tag.class" height=100>
<PARAM NAME=width VALUE=200>
</APPLET>
```

If you do, the appletviewer or Web browser won't run the applet and will complain that the <applet> tag was not written properly.

Exercise 12-2

Write an init() method that checks for a parameter named button and creates a button with that name as its label. If no parameter is defined, give the button any label you'd like. Clicking on the button should write the button label to the standard output.

Customizing an Applet

To put this all together, the purpose of passing parameter values to an applet is to enable an applet to be used for many slightly different purposes, yet the applet will always do the same thing. For example, it might display text that runs across the page like a stock ticker or display a sequence of images fast enough to animate them. With applet parameters, however, the specifics can change. The text an applet displays can be different text, and the images that compose the animation can be different images.

This ability to customize enables you to reuse an applet without programming. As an example, here's an applet that can convert inches to centimeters. You can see what this looks like in Figure 12-1.

Here's the code:

```java
import java.awt.*;
import java.applet.Applet;
import java.awt.event.*;
public class Metric extends Applet implements ActionListener
{
 TextField tf;
 TextField tf2;
 double convFactor;
 String toUnits;
 String fromUnits;
 public void init() {
   String factor = getParameter("factor");
   fromUnits = getParameter("from");
   toUnits = getParameter("to");
   if (fromUnits == null || toUnits == null || factor ==
null) {
     fromUnits = "inches";
     toUnits = "cm";
     convFactor = 2.56;
   } else {
     try {
       convFactor = new Double(factor).doubleValue();
     } catch (NumberFormatException e) {
       fromUnits = "inches";
       toUnits = "cm";
       convFactor = 2.56;
     }
   }
  add(new Label("Convert " + fromUnits + " to " + toUnits +
":"));
   tf = new TextField(10);
   add(tf);
   tf2 = new TextField(20);
   tf2.setEnabled(false);
   tf2.setBackground(Color.gray);
   add(tf2);
   tf.addActionListener(this);
  }
 public void actionPerformed(ActionEvent e) {
   String s = tf.getText();
   try {
     double d = new Double(s).doubleValue();
     double result = d * convFactor;
     String toEntry = new Double(result).toString();
     tf2.setText(toEntry + " " + toUnits);
   } catch (NumberFormatException x) {
```

```
    tf2.setText("Please enter a number.");
    tf.setText("");
  }
  repaint();
 }
}
```

If you run this applet using an HTML file that does not specify any parameter values, such as

```
<HTML>
<HEAD>
<TITLE>Simple Applet</TITLE>
</HEAD>
<BODY>
<APPLET CODE="Metric.class" width=266 height=72>
</APPLET>
</BODY>
</HTML>
```

then you will see an applet that enables you to convert inches to centimeters. This applet will look like Figure 12-1 once you interact with it.

However, this applet can convert from any unit to any other unit, and it's a simple matter to let users know how to embed this conversion applet into their own HTML pages. All they have to do is

Figure 12-1
The metric applet
with its default values

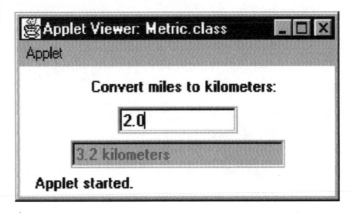

provide three <param> tags. These tags should be named `from`, `to`, and `factor`, and their values control what the applet displays (the order of these tags does not matter). For example, when run with the following HTML file

```
<HTML>
<HEAD>
<TITLE>Simple Applet</TITLE>
</HEAD>
<BODY>
<APPLET CODE="Metric.class" width=266 height=72>
<PARAM NAME=from VALUE="miles">
<PARAM NAME=to VALUE="kilometers">
<PARAM NAME=factor VALUE="1.6">
</APPLET>
</BODY>
</HTML>
```

this applet appears like Figure 12-2 once you type in a number to convert.

Now you're able to convert between miles and kilometers without any programming.

Figure 12-2
The metric applet
customized for miles
and kilometers

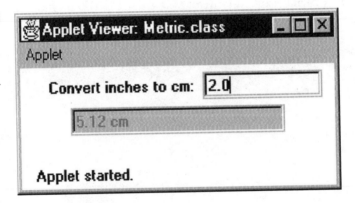

Answers to the Exercises

Exercise 12-1

```
class Reverse {
 public static void main(String[] args) {
  System.out.println("The parameters in reverse order
are:");
  for (int i = args.length-1; i >= 0; i-) {
   System.out.print(args[i] + " ");
  }
  System.out.println("");
 }
}
```

If you run this program like this

```
java Reverse My name is William
```

it will display

```
William is name My
```

Exercise 12-2

Here's the code:

```
import java.awt.*;
import java.awt.event.*;
import java.applet.*;
public class MyButtonApplet extends Applet {
 public void init() {
```

```
   String s = getParameter("button");
   if (s == null)
    s = new String("giraffe");
   add(new MyButton(s));
  }
}
class MyButton extends Button implements ActionListener {
 MyButton(String s) {
   super(s);
   addActionListener(this);
 }
 public void actionPerformed(ActionEvent e) {
   System.out.println(getLabel());
 }
}
```

When this runs with the following HTML file (where a `<param>` tag is not defined)

```
<HTML>
<HEAD>
<TITLE>Simple Applet</TITLE>
</HEAD>
<BODY>
<APPLET CODE="MyButtonApplet.class" width=230 height=100>
</APPLET>
</BODY>
</HTML>
```

this applet looks like Figure 12-3.

Figure 12-3
The Default button in
MyButtonApplet.

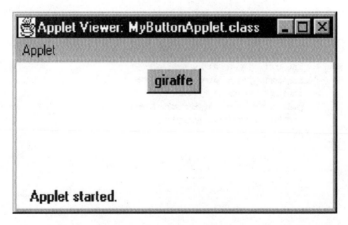

Clicking on the giraffe button writes the word "giraffe" to the standard output. When you supply the following HTML file, however (where a `<param>` tag is now defined),

```
<HTML>
<HEAD>
<TITLE>Simple Applet</TITLE>
</HEAD>
<BODY>
<APPLET CODE="MyButtonApplet.class" width=230 height=100>
<PARAM NAME=button value="elephant">
</APPLET>
</BODY>
</HTML>
```

then the giraffe button is replaced with an elephant button, and clicking on this button writes the word "elephant" to the standard output.

Review Questions

1. Which of these defines a valid main( ) method?
   - **a.** public static void main(String args[ ]) { }
   - **b.** public static void main(String[ ]) { }
   - **c.** public static void main(String[ ] args);
   - **d.** public static void main(args) { }

2. How can you access the word "kiss" from the following invocation of main():

   ```
   java lyrics a kiss is but a kiss
   ```

   - **a.** args[0]
   - **b.** args[2]
   - **c.** args[4]
   - **d.** args[5]
   - **e.** args[6]
   - **f.** b and e

3. The *Java Virtual Machine* (JVM) will run until

    a.   main( ) ends

    b.   the only threads left are user threads

    c.   the only threads left are daemon threads

    d.   a or c, whichever comes first

4. To specify a parameter in an `<applet>` tag named lastname that contains the value "Einstein," you could write:

    a.   `<param name=lastname value="Einstein">`

    b.   `<param name=lastname value=Einstein>`

    c.   either a or b

5. To retrieve a parameter named lastname, you could write code for your applet that looked like

    a.   `String s = getName("lastname");`

    b.   `String s = parameter("lastname");`

    c.   `String s = getParameter("lastname");`

6. If you try to read a parameter value and a parameter with that name is not defined in the `<applet>` tag,

    a.   the runtime throws an exception

    b.   the parameter's value is null

    c.   the parameter's value would be an empty string

Answers to the Review Questions

1. a. A string array can be defined by placing the square brackets after the variable name. The other possible main definitions are not valid.

2. d. The string array starts at 0. So, args[0] would be a, args[1] would be kiss, and so on, up to args[5], which is also kiss. (Remember, lyrics is the name of the class to run.)

3. c. The JVM will run until all user threads die and the only threads left are daemon threads.

4. c. A parameter value can have quotes, depending on your preference. If the value contains spaces, however, it must be placed within quotes.

5. c. The method getParameter( ) retrieves a parameter value given a parameter name.

6. b. The method getParameter( ) returns null if a parameter with the given name is not defined.

CHAPTER 13

Threads

One of the most powerful aspects of Java is its ability to easily perform multiple tasks concurrently. Java builds multitasking into its keywords and into its core set of classes. Such foresight not only makes multitasking easier, as an add-on class library might in C, but it also makes multitasking platform-independent, object-oriented, and part of the language itself. Multitasking also helps make Java a natural language for the Internet. For example, your program can download a file in the background while running a Java applet in the foreground.

Java enables multitasking through the use of threads. Your program can create new instances of class `Thread` or subclasses of `Thread` to represent a thread of control. A thread's life cycle helps you keep track of what a thread is doing, there are keywords to coordinate among competing threads, and there are rules about scheduling threads and assigning priorities to them.

Objectives for This Chapter

- Write code to define, instantiate, and start new threads using both `java.lang.Thread` and `java.lang.Runnable`.
- Recognize conditions that might prevent a thread from executing.
- Write code using `synchronized`, `wait`, `notify`, and `notifyAll` to protect against concurrent access problems and to communicate between threads.
- Define the interaction between threads as well as between threads and object locks when executing `synchronized`, `wait`, `notify`, or `notifyAll`.

An Overview of Threads

Java builds multitasking right into its language keywords as well as into a core set of classes. Java represents a thread of execution using an instance of class `Thread`. Threads can run independently of each other, though they can also interact with each other. To help coordinate among threads, you can use the keyword `synchronized`.

A Java program runs until the only threads left running are daemon threads. The Java runtime consists of daemon threads that run your program. A thread can be set as a daemon or user thread when it is created.

Thread States

In a standalone program, your class runs until your `main()` method exits, unless your `main()` method creates more threads. You can initiate your own thread of execution by creating a thread object, invoking its `start()` method, and providing the behavior that tells the thread what to do. The thread runs until its `run()` method exits, after which it will come to a halt, thus ending its life cycle.

When the `run()` method returns, the thread is considered to be *dead*. A dead thread cannot be restarted. If you need to run the thread's task again, you must construct and start a new thread instance. Keep in mind though that the dead thread still exists as an object (either thread or runnable), but it doesn't run as a separate thread of execution.

Threads have other states as well. These states are

- *Ready*   When you create a thread, the thread doesn't run immediately. You must call the thread's `start()` method and afterward the thread goes into a *ready* state where it waits for the scheduler to move it to the *running* state. A thread can also enter the ready state if, after previously executing, it enters the *waiting* state and is then ready to resume its execution. A call to the `yield()` method can put a thread in the ready state, provided the thread scheduler enables the thread to yield. When monitors and synchronization are used, a thread may be in a waiting because the `notify()` or `notifyall()` method is called.

- *Running*   When the thread scheduler allocates CPU time to a thread, it is in the *running* state. This means the thread is executing. The thread can be interrupted or otherwise leave this state.

■ *Waiting* Threads can enter a *waiting* state for many different reasons. The thread may be waiting in input or it may be sleeping. The thread may have been interrupted or its execution may have been blocked. When monitors and synchronization are used, a thread may be waiting because the `wait()` method was called.

Each object has a lock that can be controlled by one thread only. The lock controls access to the object's synchronized code. Before a thread can access synchronized code, the thread must attempt to acquire the lock on the object. If the lock is currently available, meaning no other thread has the lock, the thread can obtain the lock and enter the ready state. While the thread has the lock on the object, no other synchronized methods can be invoked for that object. The lock is automatically released when the method completes execution and returns. The lock can also be released when a synchronized method executes `wait()`, `yield()`, or other methods that cause the thread to change from the running state.

If another thread has the lock, the thread has to wait on the lock. The thread then enters the waiting state until it can acquire the lock. When the thread acquires the lock, it moves from the waiting state to the ready state.

Thread Life Cycles

It's often useful to think of a thread as having a life cycle. Thread life cycle stages take the descriptive names "alive" (made up of two states, "running" and "waiting") and "dead." These stages are shown in Figure 13-1. We'll look at these stages, because this progression clarifies what happens to a thread in a program.

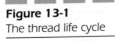
Figure 13-1
The thread life cycle

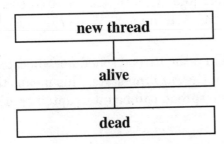

Creating a new thread instance puts the thread into the *ready* state. It's not "alive" until someone invokes the thread's `start()` method. The thread is then alive and will respond to the method `isAlive()` by returning `true`. The thread will continue to return `true` to `isAlive()` until it is "dead," no matter whether it is in the running or waiting state.

You'll often see `run()` methods that loop forever, as in

```
public void run() {
  while (true) {
   //do something continuously, like show an animation
  }
}
```

Does this mean this thread can never die? That its life cycle is different? No, because other events can transition the thread out of its current state. The two ways you can keep a thread alive and transition it between running and waiting are as follows:

- *Put the thread to sleep and then wake it up* When you put a thread to `sleep()`, you put it to sleep for a specified number of milliseconds. When this time has elapsed, the thread wakes up and continues with what it was doing. Putting a thread to sleep is a convenient way to slow down an animation. For example, rather than letting one frame move to the next in a blur, you could add a short pause to help the user keep up with the animation.

- *Pause the thread and resume it* Prior to JDK 1.2, you could use the `stop()`, `suspend()`, and `resume()` methods to control threads. The `stop()` method forcibly terminates a thread and puts it in the dead state. The `suspend()` method puts a thread in the waiting state and a subsequent call to resume enables the thread to return to the ready state where it can be scheduled to run. In JDK 1.2 and later, the `stop()`, `suspend()`, and `resume()` are deprecated.

These techniques both relate to one thread at a time; there is no communication between threads. You put one thread to sleep or wake it up; you pause one thread or resume that thread. Neither of these ways to control a thread are on the test, but, as always, the explanations for these methods are presented at the end of this chapter, because, as an expert, others will expect you to know them.

On the test is a third way of transitioning threads between running and waiting. However, unlike the two approaches listed previously, this third way enables threads to interact with each other and provides some coordination between them. This third way uses the methods `wait()`, `notify()`, and `notifyAll()`.

Thread Scheduling and Priorities

Threads have priorities. The thread with the highest priority is the one that Java runs and all the other threads have to wait. If more than one thread has the same highest priority, Java switches between them. If two threads are alive with the same highest priority, the *Java Virtual Machine* (JVM) switches between them, usually quickly enough so that you never realize they are alternating execute-sleep cycles. Java will switch between any number of threads with the same highest priority.

The priority numbers for threads fall between the range of `Thread.MIN_PRIORITY` and `Thread.MAX_PRIORITY`. The default priority, `Thread.NORM_PRIORITY`, is typically midway between these two. New threads take on the priority of the thread that spawned them.

You can use `setPriority()` to explicitly set the thread priority and you can obtain the priority of a thread using `getPriority()`. As you might expect, if a thread is currently executing and you use `setPriority()` to set a thread's priority to something less than it was before, the thread might stop executing, since there might now be another thread with a higher priority.

You can use priorities to help ensure your program responds to the user as expected. For example, let's say you are implementing a special kind of Web browser. You can set the thread to read the Web page over the Internet at a lower priority than a thread that responds to the user clicking the Stop button. This way, your browser is likely to respond immediately when the user clicks Stop, rather than waiting until a large page is downloaded because the communication thread would not yield control.

TECHNICAL TRAP: *The JVM determines when a thread can run based on its priority ranking, but that doesn't mean that a lower priority thread will* not *run. This is important, because you should not rely on priorities to predict precisely what will occur in your program and when. For example, you should not rely on priorities to determine the correctness of an algorithm.*

You don't have to rely on the JVM to switch between threads with the same priority. The currently executing thread can yield control by invoking `yield()`. If you do so, Java picks a new thread to run, but it is possible the thread that just yielded might run again immediately if it is the highest priority thread.

Creating Threads with java.lang.Thread and java.lang.Runnable

When you invoke a thread's `start()` method, the Java runtime will invoke the thread's `run()` method. However, the `Thread` class by default doesn't provide any behavior for `run()`. This thread will end mighty quickly and will not have accomplished anything useful. You have two ways of resolving this problem. You can subclass the `Thread` class and override the `run()` method, or you can implement the Runnable interface and indicate that an instance of this class will be the thread's target. Here's an example of each approach.

Subclassing Thread

You subclass threads provide their behavior. When you subclass a thread, you must override a method named `run()` to provide behavior for the thread.

Here's an example of a bouncing ball. It continuously reverses direction when it reaches the top or bottom of the screen. Figure 13-2 shows the ball somewhere in the middle of its travels up and down the applet.

Figure 13-2
A screen snapshot of
a bouncing ball

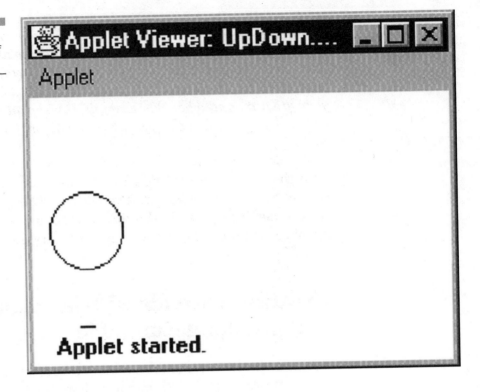

Here's the applet:

```
import java.awt.*;
import java.applet.Applet;
public class UpDown extends Applet {
  static int RADIUS = 20;
  static int X = 30;
  public int y = 30;
  public void init() {
   new BounceThread(this).start();
  }
  public void paint(Graphics g) {
   g.setColor(Color.blue);
   g.drawOval(X-RADIUS, y-RADIUS,
    2 * RADIUS, 2 * RADIUS);
  }
}
class BounceThread extends Thread {
 UpDown applet;
 int yDir = 11;
```

```
int incr = 10;
int sleepFor = 100;
BounceThread(UpDown a) {
 this.applet = a;
}
public void run() {
 while (true) {
  applet.y += (incr * yDir);
  applet.repaint();
  if (applet.y-UpDown.RADIUS < incr ||
    applet.y + UpDown.RADIUS + incr >
applet.getSize().height)
   yDir *= -1;
  try {
   sleep(sleepFor);
  } catch (InterruptedException e) {
  }
 }
 }
}
```

This applet creates a new thread and supplies a `paint()` method to draw a circle. The thread moves the circle's y value up and down, issuing a repaint and then going to sleep for $1/_{10}$ of a second. You'll learn about the `sleep()` method at the end of this chapter, but it should be fairly clear what it does: it puts a thread to sleep for a specified number of milliseconds. The thread reverses the direction and moves the ball's y value whenever the ball reaches the top or bottom of the applet's window. I've also taken the ball's (that is, the oval's) radius into account so that the ball appears to bounce off the inside edge of the applet.

TIP: *The* `drawOval()` *method used by* `paint()` *draws an oval given the left and top of the oval, so I've offset where I draw the oval to take the radius into account.*

Implementing Runnable

You can also implement the Runnable interface to provide the behavior of a thread. Here, instead of creating a `Thread` subclass, you can write the code with only one class definition. This can be accomplished by implementing the Runnable interface and specifying the Java applet as the thread's target. The Runnable interface defines one method that must be implemented: run(). A thread can look to its target, an object whose class implements Runnable, to find its run() behavior. When the thread needs to invoke its run() behavior, we can make certain the thread knows to look to its target object for the run() method.

Here's an example of the same bouncing ball, this time implemented using the Runnable interface instead of a Thread subclass:

```
import java.awt.*;
import java.applet.Applet;
public class UpDown extends Applet implements Runnable {
 static int RADIUS = 20;
 static int X = 30;
 public int y = 30;
 Thread t;
public void init() {
  t = new Thread(this);
  t.start();
 }
 public void paint(Graphics g) {
  g.setColor(Color.blue);
  g.drawOval(X-RADIUS, y-RADIUS,
   2 * RADIUS, 2 * RADIUS);
 }
 public void run() {
  int yDir = 11;
  int incr = 10;
  int sleepFor = 100;
   while (true) {
    y += (incr * yDir);
    repaint();
    if (y-UpDown.RADIUS < incr ||
      y + UpDown.RADIUS 1 incr > getSize().height)
    yDir *= -1;
    try {
     t.sleep(sleepFor);
    } catch (InterruptedException e) {
   }
  }
 }
}
```

The thread knows to look to its target because we have supplied a target object when we created the thread instance. We did this in the init() method with the line

```
t = new Thread(this);
```

In this case, we indicate that the applet object itself will be the target (that's why we used `this`). That's also why the applet implements the Runnable interface and supplies a `run()` method.

This version of `UpDown` is somewhat simpler than the first version. The `run()` method does not need to access the applet's instance or class variables through references anymore, since both `run()` and these variables are now defined in the same class definition. We do, however, have to keep track of the thread instance, so we can use this reference to invoke its `sleep()` method in run( ).

Exercise 13-1

Rewrite the following program to implement the Runnable interface, rather than using a `Thread` subclass. This applet continually displays numbers in blue, one number per second. If the number is a prime, the applet displays the number in red. Here is the code:

```
import java.awt.*;
import java.applet.Applet;
public class Ex1 extends Applet {
 Color color = Color.red;
 int candidate = 3;
 PrimeThread prime;
 public void init() {
  prime = new PrimeThread(this);
  prime.start();
 }
 public void paint(Graphics g) {
  g.setColor(color);
  g.drawString(new Integer(candidate).toString(), 30, 40);
 }
}
class PrimeThread extends Thread {
 Ex1 target;
 PrimeThread (Ex1 target) {
  this.target = target;
 }
 public void run() {
  int candidate;
  for (candidate = 3; ; candidate11) {
   if (isPrime(candidate))
    target.color = Color.red;
   else
```

```
      target.color = Color.blue;
      target.candidate = candidate;
      target.repaint();
      try {
       sleep(1000);
      } catch (InterruptedException ie) {
      }
     }
    }
   public boolean isPrime(int number) {
    boolean isPrime = true;
    for (int i = 2; i < number-1 && isPrime; i++) {
     if ( (number % i ) == 0)
       isPrime = false;
    }
    return isPrime;
   }
  }
```

Monitors and Synchronization

For the exam, you'll need to be able to write code using synchronized threads that protect against concurrent access problems. You'll also need to be able to work with wait(), notify(), and notifyAll().

Understanding Synchronization

Working with concurrent threads sounds like a great idea, but you can create a many-headed monster if you're not careful. All these threads running about doing their own thing can get confusing, and threads might start to step on each others' toes. What if multiple threads need to change the same data? What if multiple threads each want to display something to the user? Will their efforts conflict with each other?

Here's an example of what might go wrong if a program doesn't use synchronization. Imagine an airline ticketing application. A ticket agent wants to assign a passenger to a seat, so he calls up a picture of a jet and looks at a map of the open seats. He looks for a minute or two until he spots a lovely window seat, 14A, and then fills the passenger's request for a nice view and assigns the passenger to that seat.

In an application that uses only a single thread of execution, this works just fine. The ticket agent acts as the coordinator between multiple passengers who might request the same seat. In a multi-threaded application, there is the potential that two passengers will be fighting over the same seat when they board the plane. (Perhaps you've seen this happening. Do you think their tickets were issued with a Java application? I think not.) The problem is that two separate threads might try to update the same data at once.

Here's a scenario. Our ticket agent clicks a button to assign the passenger to an open seat. The thread of control used by this agent's program enters the method to update the seat. The method starts working with the data, finds the seat empty, and, having passed this test, is about to update the seat when out of the blue another ticket agent, working separately on another computer, oblivious of the first agent, does the same thing: clicks his button on his screen to assign his passenger to seat 14A. The thread of execution used by this second ticket agent interrupts the first thread (in this example) and performs its update. Then the first thread regains access to the CPU and performs its update. Now each agent has a ticket with that seat assignment. Although the computer thinks only one person is assigned to the seat, each ticket agent has a printed ticket with an identical seat assignments.

To eliminate this type of problem, where one thread is interrupted in mid-step by another thread, Java provides a way to coordinate and synchronize between multiple threads. In fact, unlike other languages, Java builds this capability right into the language.

Each object and each class has a monitor. Threads can take temporary ownership of a monitor and release it later so that another thread can take temporary ownership of the same monitor. This is important as far as synchronizing between threads, because only one thread at a time can own a particular monitor. By owning a monitor, a thread blocks all other threads from working with the other synchronized methods defined for an object or class to which the monitor belongs.

Let's take another look at the ticket reservation example and see what would have happened had the program used monitors. The first ticket agent clicks a button to assign a passenger to seat 14A. At this point, the program used by the first ticket agent would take control of the object's monitor that contained the method for updating the seat assignments, perhaps an instance of a class called SeatLayout or PassengerJet. Now the second ticket agent clicks his button, but this time there's a slight delay. His thread wants to take control of the monitor, but the thread cannot; another thread already owns it, so the second ticket agent's thread waits.

The first thread checks seat 14A, finds it open, and performs the update. Then it exits, releasing the monitor. Now the second thread can have its turn. It takes control of the monitor, but when it goes to check 14A before the update, it finds the seat is already taken, which is exactly what we want. Now the ticket agent can assign the passenger to a different seat, and all is well again. A method takes control of an object's monitor by entering a block of code or a method that's defined using the keyword `synchronized`.

Three types of code can be `synchronized`:

- Class methods
- Instance methods
- Any block of code within a method

To declare a method to be `synchronized`, you must use the keyword `synchronized` when declaring the method, as in

```
synchronized boolean reserveSeat(SeatID id) {
  //method body goes here
}
```

Declaring a class method as `synchronized` is done similarly.

To declare a block of code as `synchronized`, you use the keyword `synchronized` in front of that block. Then, in parentheses, indicate the object or the class whose monitor this code needs to acquire. Here's an example of synchronizing a block of code given an object reference:

```
boolean reserveSeat(SeatID id) {
  //method code can come before or after the synchronized
block
  synchronized (currentPlane) {
```

```
    //synchronized code goes here  . . .
  }
  //method code can come before or after the synchronized
block
  }
```

Using an object reference is appropriate in this example where we only want one ticket agent assigning seats for a single plane—the plane they're currently working on—at one time.

TIP: *Sometimes it's appropriate to list a class after the* synchronized *keyword, such as when the code will change static data.*

Using the synchronized keyword in a block of code takes the monitor from the class if it is a class method or the object if it is an instance method. The synchronized keyword guarantees that only one thread at a time will execute that object or class' code. If you have defined an instance method to be synchronized, any subclasses that override this method can be synchronized, according to their preference.

Synchronization stays in effect if you enter a synchronized method and call out to a non-synchronized method. So if a subclass overrides a non-synchronized method and declares that method to be synchronized, the thread executing the synchronized method continues to hold the monitor for an object, even if that method calls the non-synchronized superclass' method using super. The thread only gives up the monitor after the synchronized method returns.

Exercise 13-2

Variables cannot take the synchronized keyword. This means that, in the following code, even though one thread might be in the middle of updateBalance(), another thread might still come along and read the balance. You can provide accessor methods for a variable, however, and make that accessor method synchronized.

Rewrite the following class so that its variable is in effect synchronized by defining a synchronized accessor method:

```
class Account {
  double balance;
  synchronized void updateBalance(double amount) {
   balance += amount;
  }
}
```

Using wait( ), notify( ), and notifyAll( )

Synchronization stops bugs from occurring where one thread changes the state of an object that another thread had depended on to be stable. However, synchronization does nothing as far as communicating between threads. Sometimes you need a way for one thread to be informed of what another thread is doing. For example, thread number 1 might be waiting for thread number 2 to calculate some result. When thread number 2 achieves this result, it should be able to notify thread number 1 that it found the result thread number 1 was waiting for.

Java builds a wait-notify mechanism into the `Object` class. By using the methods `wait()`, `notify()`, and `notifyAll()`, any thread can wait for some condition in an object to change, and any thread can notify all threads waiting on that object's condition that the condition has changed and that they should continue. A common scenario where this is useful is where one thread produces data for an object, and another thread is using the data in the object.

Here's a simple example of using `wait()` and `notify()`. The following applet, named ClickApplet, starts by creating a couple of ClickCanvas instances in its `init()` method. Each one of these special Canvas subclasses spawns a new thread in its constructor. The thread's `run()` method (supplied by ClickCanvas) waits on a condition. It starts waiting when it invokes `wait()`. The condition it's waiting to change is the `boolean` value defined in the applet named `clicked`.

As soon as `clicked` becomes `true`, the Canvas continues. How does the Canvas' thread know when the condition becomes `true`? The `mouseDown()` method in the applet, running in the user input thread, notifies the Canvas' thread that the condition has changed. It does this by invoking `notify()`. Here's the code:

```java
import java.awt.*;
import java.applet.*;
import java.awt.event.*;
public class ClickApplet extends Applet implements
MouseListener {
 boolean clicked;
 int counter;
 public void init() {
  add(new ClickCanvas(this));
  add(new ClickCanvas(this));
  addMouseListener(this);
 }
 public void mousePressed(MouseEvent e)
 {
  synchronized (this) {
   clicked = true;
   notify();
  }
   counter++;
   Thread.currentThread().yield();
   clicked = false;
 }
 // stubbed methods from MouseListener interface
 public void mouseClicked(MouseEvent e) {}
 public void mouseReleased(MouseEvent e) {}
 public void mouseEntered(MouseEvent e) {}
 public void mouseExited(MouseEvent e) {}
}
class ClickCanvas extends Canvas implements Runnable{
 ClickApplet applet;
 ClickCanvas(ClickApplet applet) {
  this.applet = applet;
  setSize(30, 30);
  new Thread(this).start();
 }
 public void run() {
  while (true) {
   synchronized (applet) {
    while (!applet.clicked) {
     try {
      applet.wait();
     } catch (InterruptedException x) {
     }
    }
   }
  }
```

```
    repaint(250);
  }
 }
 public void paint(Graphics g) {
   g.drawString(new Integer(applet.counter).toString(), 10,
20);
  }
 }
```

This applet counts the number of clicks the user makes in the applet. Of course, we could have simply configured mouseDown() in the applet to display the clicks and update the counter variable, but we want the above code to show how to coordinate between threads. Without wait() and notify() (or without a direct method call), there is no way for the ClickCanvas objects to know when to update their displays. This applet exhibits some interesting behavior. Figure 13-3 shows what it looks like when it starts.

As the user starts clicking the applet, only one number in one ClickCanvas object updates at a time. Figures 13-4 and 13-5 display two screenshots of successive clicks.

Why aren't both ClickCanvas objects updated at the same time? Why do they seem to leapfrog each other? Because we have only invoked notify(), rather than notifyAll().

Figure 13-3
ClickApplet
when it first appears
in the Applet Viewer

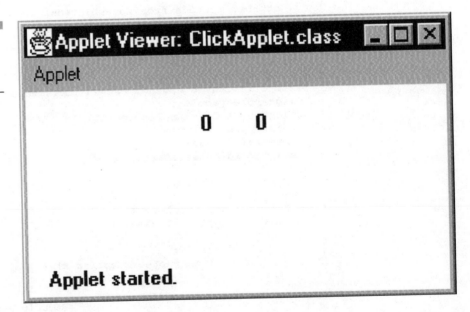

Figure 13-4
ClickApplet after
the first click

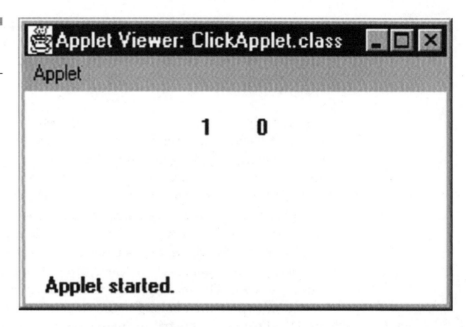

Figure 13-4
ClickApplet after
the first click

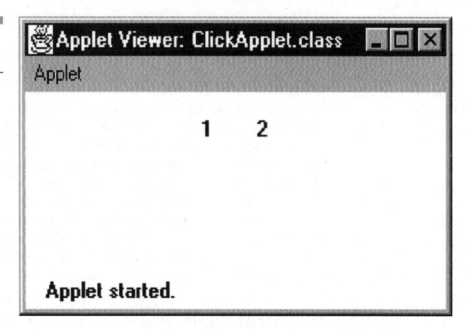

Figure 13-5
ClickApplet after
the second click

When the waiting thread pauses, it relinquishes the object's monitor and waits to be notified that it should try to reacquire it with a call to `wait()`. Notice that we indicate which object we're waiting on. In this case, we're waiting on the applet. Since we keep the applet in an instance variable named applet in the `ClickCanvas` object, we can wait on the applet object by writing:

```
applet.wait();
```

Generally, `wait()` is placed inside of a `while` clause. The idea is that just because a thread wakes up, the condition it's waiting on has not necessarily changed. Thus, this condition should be rechecked and the thread should wait again if necessary.

You'll also notice two other things about the call to `wait()`. First, it is placed inside of a `try-catch` block. The `wait()` method might throw an `InterruptedException`, so the code must be prepared to handle that. Second, `wait()` is placed inside a synchronized block. The `wait()` and `notify()` methods can only be invoked from synchronized code. The monitor that the block or method acquires for synchronization must belong to the object that the thread will wait on. In addition, if you try to invoke `wait()` on an object without owning the object's monitor, the Java runtime will throw an `IllegalMonitorStateException`.

Placing the calls to `wait()` and `notify()` within synchronized code does two things. First, it guarantees that the currently executing code owns the monitor, so that this code can give it up in the call to `wait()` or `notify()`. Second, it helps ensure that the contents of the object being used to determine the conditions are stable. For example, since a `while` loop surrounds the `wait()` call, it's important that the condition doesn't change to `false` before the code escapes the `while` loop after a `notify()` call.

The `notify()` method wakes up one thread waiting to reacquire the monitor for the object. The thread it awakens is generally the one that has been waiting the longest. If you know you only have one thread waiting on a condition, feel free to use `notify()`. Then your application's behavior is predictable.

TECHNICAL TRAP: *Just because the thread that* `notify()` *awakens is generally the one that has been waiting the longest, you should not rely on this for your algorithm to work. It is not guaranteed to awaken the longest waiting thread.*

If you have more than one thread (or if there is the potential to have more than one thread) waiting on a condition, you should use notifyAll(), instead of notify(). The notifyAll() method wakes up all threads waiting to reacquire the monitor for the object.

Exercise 13-3

Rewrite ClickApplet so that both threads are notified when the user clicks.

Managing Threads with Wait-Notify and Sleep

Prior to JDK 1.2, you could control a thread through the methods pause(), resume(), and stop(). These methods were deprecated because they could cause problems in the code. For example, if you forcibly stop a thread, you can cause data corruption or even a deadlock condition where the program freezes up. To avoid these and other pitfalls, these methods are deprecated in favor of other techniques. This doesn't mean you won't need to temporarily stop a thread from executing or that you won't need to stop thread execution altogether. You'll still need to do this, but you'll need to make use of the currently available methods to implement these behaviors safely. The new technique is to use a wait-notify-sleep mechanism.

To demonstrate the old and new methods, I have rewritten the bouncing ball program. The first version uses the deprecated pause(), resume(), and stop() methods. The second version uses wait(), notify(), and sleep(). Here's the first version using pause(), resume(), and stop():

```
import java.awt.*;
import java.applet.Applet;
public class UpDown extends Applet {
  static int RADIUS = 20;
  static int X = 30;
  public int y = 30;
  BounceThread thread;
```

```
 public void init() {
  thread = new BounceThread(this);
 }
 public void start() {
  if (thread.isAlive())
   thread.resume();
  else
   thread.start();
 }
 public void stop() {
  thread.suspend();
 }
 public void destroy() {
  thread.stop();
 }
 public void paint(Graphics g) {
  g.setColor(Color.blue);
  g.drawOval(X-RADIUS, y-RADIUS,
   2 * RADIUS, 2 * RADIUS);
 }
}
class BounceThread extends Thread {
 UpDown applet;
 int yDir = +1;
 int incr = 10;
 int sleepFor = 100;
 BounceThread(UpDown a) {
  this.applet = a;
 }
 public void run() {
  while (true) {
   applet.y += (incr * yDir);
   applet.repaint();
   if (applet.y-UpDown.RADIUS < incr ||
     applet.y + UpDown.RADIUS + incr > applet.size().height)
    yDir *= -1;
   try {
    sleep(sleepFor);
   } catch (InterruptedException e) {
   }
  }
 }
}
```

Here's the second version using wait(), notify(), and sleep():

```
import java.awt.*;
import java.applet.Applet;
public class UpDown extends Applet {
 static int RADIUS = 20;
```

```
static int X = 30;
public int y = 30;
volatile BounceThread bounceThread;
volatile boolean threadSuspended = true;
public void init() {
 bounceThread = new BounceThread(this);
 bounceThread.start();
}
public void start() {
 if (bounceThread != null)
 {
   synchronized(bounceThread)
   {
    threadSuspended = false;
    bounceThread.notify();
   }
 }
}
public void stop() {
 threadSuspended = true;
}
public void destroy() {
 synchronized(bounceThread)
 {
   Thread t = bounceThread;
   bounceThread = null;
   t.notify();
 }
}
public void paint(Graphics g) {
 g.setColor(Color.blue);
 g.drawOval(X-RADIUS, y-RADIUS,
  2 * RADIUS, 2 * RADIUS);
 }
}
class BounceThread extends Thread {
 UpDown applet;
 int yDir = +1;
 int incr = 10;
 int sleepFor = 100;
 BounceThread(UpDown a) {
  this.applet = a;
 }
 public void run() {
  Thread currThread = Thread.currentThread();
  while (applet.bounceThread == currThread) {
   try {
    currThread.sleep(sleepFor);
    synchronized (this) {
     while (applet.threadSuspended && (applet.bounceThread
== currThread))
       wait();
    }
```

```
    } catch (InterruptedException e) {
    }
    applet.y += (incr * yDir);
    applet.repaint();
    if (applet.y-UpDown.RADIUS < incr ||
     applet.y + UpDown.RADIUS + incr >
applet.getSize().height)
    yDir *= -1;
   }
 }
}
```

Compare the two examples closely. For the exam, you'll need to be able to write code that uses `wait()`, `notify()`, and `sleep()`. Note also that both versions use a thread subclass, but this would work just as well for the version that implements the Runnable interface. If the Web page containing the applet goes offscreen, the applet should stop, and that's what happens here. When the Web page comes back onscreen, the applet starts again.

Why a Thread Might Not Execute

For the exam, you'll need to be able to identify when conditions might prevent a thread from executing. Here is a list of reasons why a thread might be alive but still not run:

- The thread is not the highest priority thread and so cannot get CPU time.
- The thread has been put to sleep using the `sleep()` method.
- There is more than one thread with the same highest priority, and the JVM is switching between these threads; at the moment, the thread in question is awaiting CPU time.
- The thread is blocked. It is waiting for the I/O call or has failed to get a monitor's lock and is waiting for the monitor's lock.
- The thread is waiting on a condition because someone invoked `wait()` for the thread. The thread waits for `notify()` or `notifyAll()`.
- The thread has explicitly yielded control by invoking `yield()`.

Exercise 13-4

Write four applets, each one illustrating a different aspect from the above list of reasons why a thread might not run.

Other Useful Thread Methods

Generally, a thread created by the user is a user thread. However, you can mark a thread as a daemon thread before you start it by using `setDaemon()`. The JVM keeps running until all user threads have ended.

You can name threads using `setName()` or by supplying a name to the thread's constructor. You can retrieve a thread's name using `getName()`. Naming a thread could be useful in identifying a particular thread if you are using more than one.

A `static` method named `currentThread()` retrieves the currently executing thread. This enables you to put the current thread to sleep, for example, or to invoke some other method on it.

The `join()` method waits for a thread to die before continuing. You might use it to stop execution until a thread has completed its task.

You can treat threads as a set by using a `ThreadGroup`. The `ThreadGroup` class defines most of the methods that affect individual threads. By assigning a thread to a `ThreadGroup` when you create the thread, you can affect many threads at once.

Answers to the Exercises

Exercise 13-1

Here is one possible solution:

```
import java.awt.*;
import java.applet.Applet;
public class Ans1 extends Applet implements Runnable {
```

```
  Color color = Color.red;
  int candidate = 3;
  Thread prime;
public void init() {
  prime = new Thread(this);
  prime.start();
}
public void paint(Graphics g) {
  g.setColor(color);
  g.drawString(new Integer(candidate).toString(), 30, 40);
}
public void run() {
  for (candidate = 3; ; candidate++) {
    if (isPrime(candidate))
      color = Color.red;
    else
      color = Color.blue;
    repaint();
    try {
      prime.sleep(1000);
    } catch (InterruptedException ie) {
    }
  }
}
public boolean isPrime(int number) {
  boolean isPrime = true;
    for (int i = 2; i < number-1 && isPrime; i++) {
      if ( (number % i ) == 0)
        isPrime = false;
  }
  return isPrime;
  }
}
```

A common mistake in making this conversion is to forget to write `implements Runnable` in the class definition. If you forget this part, the compiler will complain about not finding a constructor matching the way you are trying to create the thread. The issue here is that the thread constructor that takes a target for the `run()` method takes an instance of Runnable. Remember, an object of a class that implements an interface is considered an instance of that class. You can think of it like this: `instanceof` returns `true` for a class that implements an interface. So if you forget to define your class (your applet, in this case) as implementing the Runnable interface, it won't match one of the thread's constructors.

Exercise 13-2

```
class Account {
 private double balance;
 synchronized double getBalance() {
  return balance;
 }
 synchronized void setBalance(double newBalance) {
  balance = newBalance;
 }
 synchronized void updateBalance(double amount) {
  setBalance(getBalance() + amount);
 }
}
```

With this rewrite, no other thread can access the balance field (unless it circumvents the accessor method protocol) when the updateBalance() method is in the middle of altering its value.

Exercise 13-3

Simply change the call from notify() to notifyAll(). The rest of the applet stays the same.

Exercise 13-4

Here are four programs that illustrate the first four items from this list:

■ The thread is not the highest priority thread and so cannot get CPU time.

```
class Ex1204a {
 public static void main(String[] args) {
  MyThread t1 = new MyThread(1);
  MyThread t2 = new MyThread(2);
  t1.setPriority(Thread.MAX_PRIORITY);
  t2.setPriority(Thread.MIN_PRIORITY);
  t1.start();
  t2.start();
```

```
  }
 }
class MyThread extends Thread {
 int id;
 MyThread(int id) {
  this.id = id;
 }
 public void run() {
  for (int i = 0; i < 100; i++)
   System.out.println("My id is " + id);
 }
}
```

The output from this program is 100 lines of My id is 1 and then, once that thread has completed, 100 lines of My id is 2.

■ The thread has been put to sleep using the sleep() method:

```
class Ex1204b {
 public static void main(String[] args) {
  MyThread t1 = new MyThread(1);
  MyThread t2 = new MyThread(2);
  t1.setPriority(Thread.MAX_PRIORITY);
  t2.setPriority(Thread.MIN_PRIORITY);
  t1.start();
  t2.start();
 }
}
class MyThread extends Thread {
 int id;
 MyThread(int id) {
  this.id = id;
 }
 public void run() {
  for (int i = 0; i < 100; i++) {
   if (id == 1 && i == 50) {
    try {
     sleep(1000);
    } catch (InterruptedException x) {
    }
   }
   System.out.println("My id is " + id);
  }
 }
}
```

The output from this program is 50 lines of My id is 1. Then that thread goes to sleep, long enough (on my computer, at least) for the other thread to write out all of its lines (My id is 2). Then the first thread continues. With a shorter time, the sleeping thread would wake up and, with a higher priority than the currently running thread, get immediate access to the CPU and continue on.

■ There is more than one thread with the same highest priority, and the JVM is switching between these threads; at the moment, the thread in question is awaiting CPU time:

```
class Ex1204c {
public static void main(String[] args) {
 MyThread t1 = new MyThread(1);
 MyThread t2 = new MyThread(2);
 t1.other = t2;
 t2.other = t1;
 t1.start();
 t2.start();
 }
}
class MyThread extends Thread {
 int id;
 MyThread other;
 MyThread(int id) {
  this.id = id;
 }
 public void run() {
  for (int i = 0; i < 100; i++) {
   System.out.println("My id is " + id);
  }
 }
}
```

This program unpredictably alternates between displaying a few My id is 1 messages and then a few My id is 2 in the standard output.

■ The thread has explicitly yielded control by invoking yield().

```
class Ex1204d {
 public static void main(String[] args) {
  MyThread t1 = new MyThread(1);
  MyThread t2 = new MyThread(2);
  t1.other = t2;
  t2.other = t1;
  t1.start();
```

```
    t2.start();
  }
}
class MyThread extends Thread {
  int id;
  MyThread other;
  MyThread(int id) {
    this.id = id;
  }
  public void run() {
    for (int i = 0; i < 100; i++) {
      System.out.println("My id is " + id);
    }
    yield();
  }
}
```

This program displays all of the `My id is 1` messages first, because it yields to the other thread. Once this thread's `run()` method is about to end, it runs the other thread, and it then displays all of its `My id is 2` messages.

QUESTIONS

1. If you would like to create a thread and supply a target that implements the Runnable interface, you can write:

   a. `Thread t = new Thread(target);`
   b. `Thread t = new Thread(); t.target = target;`
   c. `Thread t = new Thread(); t.start(target);`

2. Why might a thread be alive but not be the currently executing thread?

   a. It is the only thread currently running.
   b. It has been suspended.
   c. It has been resumed.
   d. It has been notified of some condition.
   e. all of the above

3. What may make this method throw an exception (other than `InterruptedException`) when it runs (if anything)?

    a. The call to `wait()` is not within a while loop.

    b. The `holdIt()` method must be synchronized.

    c. The current thread does not own the monitor it needs to invoke `wait()`.

    d. Nothing is wrong with this method definition. It will run fine and not throw an exception

4. If you have created two threads, one with a priority of `Thread.MAX_PRIORITY` and one with a normal default priority, which of these statements is true?

    a. The thread with the normal priority will definitely not run until the thread with the maximum priority ends.

    b. The thread with the normal priority will never run, even after the thread with the maximum priority ends.

    c. Neither of these statements is true.

5. The `wait()` method is defined in class

    a. `Thread`

    b. `Applet`

    c. `Object`

    d. `Runnable`

6. You can set a thread's priority

    a. when you first create the thread

    b. at any time after you create the thread

    c. both of these

ANSWERS

1. a. You must supply the target for the thread when you create it.

2. b. A suspended thread is not currently running and waits until it is resumed.

3. c. The code synchronizes on this, but then invokes `wait()` for ref, which might be a different object. If it were a different object, the call to `wait()` would cause Java to throw an `IllegalMonitorStateException`. To make this code hunky-dory, it could be written like this:

```
public void holdIt(Object ref) {
synchronized (ref) {
try {
ref.wait();
} catch (InterruptedException x) {
}
}
}
```

This time the code synchronizes on the object ref, and then uses ref to invoke wait().

4. **c.** That's right. You should not rely on thread priorities for algorithm correctness. Even a thread with a lower priority may get some time to run. It will just get less time, but simply assigning one thread to the maximum priority and another thread to the minimum priority does not guarantee that the lower priority thread will not run. These priorities would just make one thread less likely to get access to the CPU, but it wouldn't stop it completely.

5. **c.** All Objects can respond to wait().

6. **b.** You can set a priority for a thread using setPriority(). There is no constructor that takes a thread priority.

Graphics, Components, and Layout

"Graphical user interfaces" is a big topic. Entire books have been written on Java's *Abstract Windowing Toolkit* (AWT), which is the name of the package containing the classes you use to build *graphical user interfaces* (GUIs). In this chapter, we'll review the basics of the AWT package as well as the advanced aspects you'll be expected to know for the test.

Until now, this book has, for the most part, separated issues of Java programming from issues relating to the user interface. To help make Java programming clear, we have mostly used character-mode, standalone programs, as opposed to graphical programs or Web-based applets, to illustrate Java programming. In this chapter, we'll look exclusively at the classes and techniques of building graphical applications. For the exam, you'll need to know how to write code using component, container, and layout manager classes of `java.awt`. You'll need to know how create a GUI with a specific appearance and resize behavior. You'll also need to be able to distinguish the responsibilities of layout managers from those of containers.

Objectives for This Chapter

- Implement the `paint()` method for component classes.
- Describe the flow of control between the methods `repaint()` and `update()`.
- Use the following methods of the graphics class: `drawString()`, `drawLine()`, `drawRect()`, `drawImage()`, `drawPolygon()`, `drawArc()`, `fillRect()`, `fillPolygon()`, and `fillArc()`.
- Use Graphics methods in `paint()` and obtain a graphics object from an Image.
- Construct text areas, text fields, and lists.
- List the classes in the `java.awt` package that are valid arguments to the `add()` methods and those that are not valid.
- Identify AWT classes that determine layouts for components with a container.
- Change the layout scheme associated with a container instance.

- Identify the effects of layout classes.
- State strategies to achieve a dynamic resizing of a component.
- Distinguish between methods invoked by the user thread and those normally invoked by AWT.

The Abstract Windowing Toolkit (AWT)

If you want to create a GUI for your Java program, you've got to work with the `java.awt` package, referred to familiarly as AWT. This class library defines a slew of platform-independent classes that represent user interface elements.

I like to divide the classes in this package into three categories:

- Components, which the user interacts with. Subclasses of components includes `List`, `TextField`, and `TextArea`. (It also includes `Button`, `Checkbox`, `Choice`, and more, but except in a small way, these component subclasses are not on the test.)
- Containers, which are special types of components that contain and arrange other components
- Other helper classes, such as graphics, color, and classes implementing `LayoutManager`, all of which are used by components and containers to draw and place things on the screen

We'll talk about all of these types of classes and how they work in the course of this chapter. Naturally, this is not an exhaustive investigation into the AWT. Only those things that will be on the test are focused on, but with all the information discussed here, you'll still gain a very thorough understanding of the AWT.

Applets and AWT

Java's applet class is defined in the package `java.applet`, not in `java.awt`. However, the `Applet` class is a user interface component. Applet descends from Panel. This means that applets can do everything panels can do (that is, they can contain a user interface), plus a little bit more. That "little bit more" involves interacting with Web browsers. Four life cycle methods are invoked by the browser (or `appletviewer` if you're running in a development environment) at different stages of your applet's life:

■ When the applet instance is first instantiated, Java invokes the applet's `init()` method.

■ When the Web page containing the applet is about to appear, Java invokes the applet's `start()` method.

■ When the Web page is about to be replaced with another page, Java invokes the applet's `stop()` method.

TIP: *Java can alternately call an applet's* `start()` *and* `stop()` *methods as the Web page containing the applet appears and is removed from the Web browser's display.*

■ When the Web page is removed from the browser's cache and the applet instance is about to go away, Java invokes the applet's `destroy()` method.

You can override any of these methods to support your own applet's behavior. Typically, you would create a user interface in `init()`, pause and resume threads in `start()` and `stop()`, and halt threads in `destroy()`.

The paint( ) Method

The runtime environment tells every component (and, naturally, every container, because container is a subclass of component) when it is time to make something appear on the screen—that is, when to redraw. The runtime environment tells a component to redraw when it is dirty, when it has first appeared on the screen, when it is resized, when its container is resized, when something else on the screen (such as an overlapping window) that was covering the component has gone away, or when the programmer has explicitly requested a redraw.

Java tells your component to redraw by invoking its `paint()` method. The `paint()` method takes one parameter: an instance of class `Graphics`. You can use this instance to perform low-level drawing operations. We'll take a look at the `Graphics` class in just a moment. The method declaration for `paint()` is

```
public void paint(Graphics g)
```

You should put all of your drawing code into `paint()`, and no more than your drawing code. You want `paint()` to execute as quickly as possible. Don't put calculations into `paint()`, for example, or other things that will slow down the actual painting.

Repainting

If you want to explicitly repaint a component, you should not call `paint()` directly. Instead, you should invoke your component's `repaint()` method. The `repaint()` method is overloaded. The no-args version of `repaint()` does not cause your user interface to repaint right away. In fact, when `repaint()` returns, your component has not yet been repainted; you've only issued a request for a repaint, but there is another version of `repaint()` that requests the component be repainted within a certain number of milliseconds.

The `repaint()` method causes AWT to invoke a component's `update()` method. AWT passes a graphics object to `update()`, the same one it passes to `paint()`. We'll cover the `Graphics` class in a moment. (For now, we're just getting the progression of repaint calls straight.)

NOTE: *The graphics object that AWT hands to* `update()` *and* `paint()` *is different every time the component is repainted. When Java repaints on its own, such as when the user resizes an applet, the AWT does not invoke* `update()`; *it just calls* `paint()` *directly.*

The `update()` method does three things in this order:

1. Clears the background of the object by filling it with its background color.

2. Sets the current drawing color to be its foreground color.

3. Invokes paint(), passing it the graphics object it received.

The sequence you should ingrain in your memory is shown in Figure 14-1.

paint( ) and the Graphics Class

The paint() method takes an instance of the Graphics class. This object is a graphics context that is platform-specific, but with a platform-independent interface that enables you to draw on the screen.

The Graphics class defines lots of abstract methods for low-level drawing operations, such as drawing graphic primitives like lines and ovals, and setting drawing modes and colors. These abstract methods make the Graphics class an abstract class. Subclasses of Graphics implement the specific instructions that enable the graphics context to draw onto onscreen components or offscreen images. Most likely, you'll never see these Graphics subclasses, and you shouldn't care. They are platform-specific and depend on the operating environment your application is running in.

For example, running this program on Windows NT

```java
import java.applet.Applet;
import java.awt.Graphics;
public class Gr extends Applet {
 public void paint(Graphics g) {
   System.out.println(g.getClass().getName());
 }
}
```

writes this class name to the screen:

```
sun.awt.windows.Wgraphics
```

Figure 14-1
The sequence of
repaint(),
update(), and
paint()

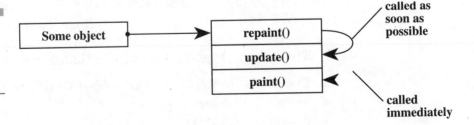

This program yields a different result when run on a Mac or under Solaris.

You can't write for this specific class, so it doesn't really matter what it is. Besides, all you care about as a Java programmer is the graphics interface. That's what Java does well: hide the implementation of the specifics to let you concentrate on your application's design.

Smoother Graphics

Because update() first clears the background, you'll sometimes find that your application flickers in an unattractive way. To avoid this poor effect, you can override the normal update() method. For example, imagine you are flipping between images in your applet and that each image is the same size. If you allow the standard update() to paint() sequence to occur each time you display a new image, the background of the image would "flash" and become the same color as the background before being replaced by the new image. In your override, you can just call paint() directly, after setting the current foreground color:

```
public void update(Graphics g) {
  g.setColor(getForeground());
  paint(g);
}
```

What this code does is eliminate the call to fill the background in the background color, preventing the flash. If you sometimes want to perform the normal behavior, you can put a test in the update() method and under normal conditions invoke your superclass' version of update(), but when you are just switching to a new image, you can branch to your flicker-free code.

You can make your painting occur faster and more smoothly in a number of ways other than by following what Java does by default. One of these ways is by overriding a method called update(). Even though all your drawing code goes into paint(), Java actually invokes update() first, due to a call to repaint(). The repaint() method invokes update() as soon as it can, which means that `repaint()` will often return before Java invokes `update()` and `paint()`.

The `update()` method does three things:

1. Clears the component of any drawing it contains (that is, it refreshes the background by redrawing the background in the background color).

2. Sets the current drawing color of the component to be the component's foreground color.

3. Invokes the component's `paint()` method.

Normally, this sequence is exactly what you want, but sometimes refreshing the background can cause your drawing to flicker. You're looking at your component, it redraws itself, you see a flash as the background is refreshed, and then it repaints itself. You can eliminate this flicker by overriding `update()`. The `update()` method is simply

```
public void update(Graphics g)
```

You can write a method that skips Step 1 above by writing an `update()` method like this:

```
public void update(Graphics g) {
 g.setColor(getForeground());
 paint(g);
}
```

Drawing Using a Graphics Object

Because `Graphics` is `abstract`, you cannot create a graphics instance directly by invoking its constructor. When you draw inside of `paint()`, the AWT gives you a graphics object to use. If you want to draw outside of `paint()`, you can get a graphics object in one of two ways:

- If you already have some other graphics object, you can create a copy of it using the `create()` method defined by `Graphics`.

- If you have a component and want a graphics object for it, you can invoke the component's `getGraphics()` method.

Graphics objects have a state that includes its drawing color, paint mode, font, and clipping region. You can receive and set any of these values. The `update()` method and the `paint()` method are handed an instance of the `Graphics` class. The graphics instance you receive in `paint()` is tied to the component responding to the `paint()` method. This means that any drawing you do using the `Graphics` class appears in the component.

The `Graphics` methods use pixels as their units of measurement. Coordinates are also relative to the component or container in which they're displayed. Horizontal (x) coordinates are measured from the left, while vertical (y) coordinates are measured from the top. If a method calls for a baseline or corner point, you should supply measurements for that point as the number of pixels from the left and top edge of the window in which it is used. Pixels are defined as `int` values. `Graphics` defines lots of methods for drawing. Most of these methods draw in the current foreground color. The following are some common `Graphics` methods you might use in `paint()`.

drawString( )

This method draws the characters in a string object into the display. This method takes three parameters: a string object (or string literal) to display and the baseline for the first character (the x and y coordinates for the first character).

Here is a classic example of using `drawString()` to create the `"Hello, world"` applet. The bottom, left of the "H" in `"Hello, world"` is at the x and y coordinates, which in this case is $x = 80, y = 30$.

```
import java.awt.*;
import java.applet.*;
public class Str extends Applet {
 public void paint(Graphics g) {
  g.drawString("Hello, world!", 80, 30);
  }
}
```

The result looks like Figure 14-2.

Figure 14-2
Using
`drawString()`

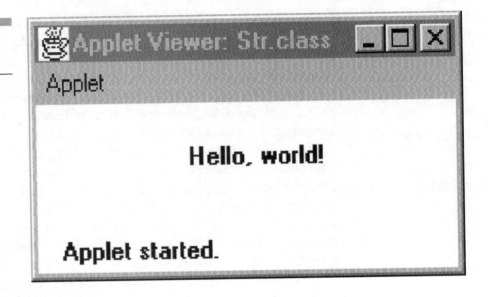

drawLine( )

This method takes four parameters: the x, y location of the starting point and the x, y location of the line's ending point. Here's an example of drawing a tic-tac-toe board.

```
import java.awt.*;
import java.applet.*;
public class Tic extends Applet {
 public void paint(Graphics g) {
   g.drawLine(60, 5, 60, 175);
   g.drawLine(120, 5, 120, 175);
   g.drawLine(5, 60, 175, 60);
   g.drawLine(5, 120, 175, 120);
  }
}
```

The display is shown in Figure 14-3.

drawRect( ) and fillRect( )

These methods draw a rectangle. The method `drawRect()` draws the outline of a rectangle, while `fillRect()` draws a solid rectangle.

Figure 143
Using drawLine()

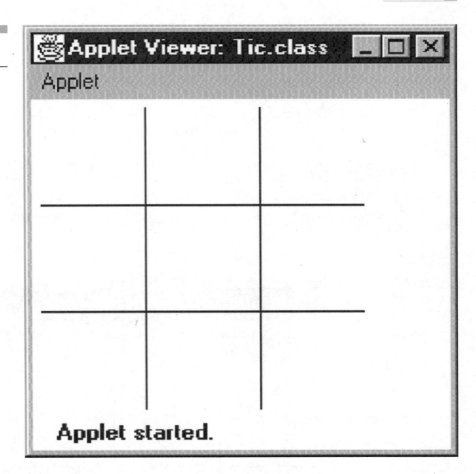

Each of these methods take three parameters: the top-left corner of the rectangle, and the width and height of the rectangle. The left and right edges of the rectangle are at x and x + width respectively. The top and bottom edges of the rectangle are at y and y + height respectively.

Here's an example of drawing a variety of rectangles:

```
import java.awt.*;
import java.applet.*;
public class Rect extends Applet {
 public void paint(Graphics g) {
   g.drawLine(60, 5, 60, 175);
   g.drawLine(120, 5, 120, 175);
```

```
  g.drawLine(5, 60, 175, 60);
  g.drawLine(5, 120, 175, 120);
  g.fillRect(80, 80, 20, 20);
 }
}
```

This code results are displayed in Figure 14-4.

TIP: *The* drawOval() *and* fillOval() *are similar to* drawRect() *and* fillRect(), *except these draw ovals inside the rectangle defined by corresponding parameters to* drawRect() *and* fillRect().

Figure 14-4
Using fillRect()

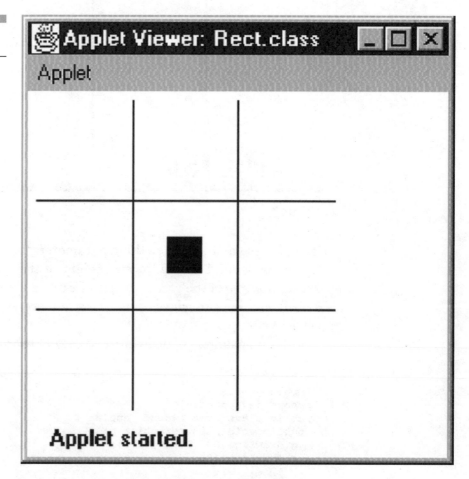

drawPolygon( ) and fillPolygon( )

You can draw a shape with any number of sides by utilizing `drawPolygon()` or `fillPolygon()`. Each of these methods is overloaded. One version takes an array of x and y coordinates (int values) and the number of elements to use in the arrays. A second version takes a Polygon instance, which defines the x and y arrays as part of its instance data.

For example, the following code draws a wacky, five-sided shape:

```
import java.awt.*;
import java.applet.*;
public class Poly extends Applet {
 public void paint(Graphics g) {
   int[] xArray = {20, 60, 90, 70, 30};
   int[] yArray = {50, 4, 45, 90, 70};
   g.fillPolygon(xArray, yArray, 5);
 }
}
```

What this code produces is shown in Figure 14-5.
Notice how the last point connects back to the first.

drawArc( ) and fillArc( )

These methods draw or fill an arc starting at a particular angle and moving counterclockwise for the number of degrees you define. The three o'clock position is 0 degrees.

To draw an arc, you supply

- The arc's top-left corner as an x, y coordinate (similar to how you define a rectangle's top-left corner)

- The width and height of the arc (again, similar to how you define the width and height of an oval)

- The start angle

- The number of degrees to move along the arc (the end angle is start angke + arc angle)

Figure 14-5
Using
`fillPolygon()`

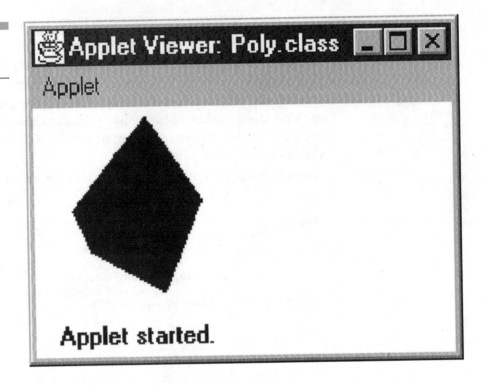

For example, to draw the arc shown in Figure 14-6, you could write code like the following:

```
import java.awt.*;
import java.applet.*;
public class Arc1 extends Applet {
 public void paint(Graphics g) {
  g.drawArc(20, 20, 150, 50, 0, 90);
 }
}
```

Notice that the x, y coordinates 20, 20 indicate the top-left of the bounding box of the arc. (Imagine continuing the arc so that it creates an oval. The left and top of the oval are at $x=20$, $y=20$.) Also notice that 0 degrees is at the three o'clock position, and that we are moving counterclockwise 90 degrees (one-quarter of the way around the oval). You can also move in the negative direction if you

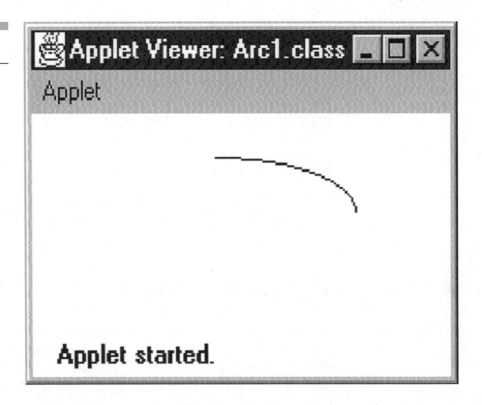

want, so that you're moving clockwise around the oval, rather than counterclockwise.

drawImage( )

This method is overloaded to enable you a great deal of control over the way an image is displayed. The minimum parameters you need to supply are

- An image to draw. This is an instance of the Image class.
- The *x* and *y* positions where the left and top corner of the image should appear.
- An image observer that communicates with the graphics system. This object helps notify the graphics system when the image is ready to be drawn, such as when it has been fully loaded over the Internet, for example.

Also, certain versions of drawImage() specify a background color in which to draw transparent pixels (for example, when using a GIF image where you can define a particular pixel color to be transparent), and that specify height and width values for squeezing or stretching an image to fit a particular region. To actually draw an image, you need to obtain an image object. We'll discuss that next.

Exercise 14-1

Write an applet to display a solid circle that fits perfectly inside the outline of a square.

The Image Class

The Image class does not provide a constructor for specifying where an image will come from. Instead of creating an image object using an image constructor, you can obtain an image typically by downloading it over the Internet by specifying a URL. (Of course, the URL can be a local URL.)

You can retrieve an image and obtain an image object by invoking an Applet method named getImage(). This method takes a URL. (There is also an overloaded version that takes a URL and another string that is a relative address to the URL in the first parameter.)

Here's the idea behind getImage(): when this method returns, you have an image object, but the data for the image is not necessarily immediately available. That is, this method returns right away, even if the image resource is located over the Internet on a Web server and must be downloaded.

When you invoke the Graphics method drawImage(), the image download will begin. The object you specify as an ImageObserver keeps the Java graphics system up-to-date on the state of the download. When the ImageObserver sees that the download is complete, it notifies the graphics system that it can draw the image in its entirety.

ImageObserver is an interface. This interface is defined in the java.awt.image package. The Component class implements this interface, so any component (such as the applet itself) can be used as an ImageObserver.

You can also create an image object, typically used as an off-screen buffer, by invoking the component method createImage(). This method creates a new image to the given width and height. If you're using this new image object as an offscreen buffer for rendering graphics that will appear in the component object you're creating it from, you'll probably want to set this image object's size to the same width and height as your component. Once you have the image object, you can obtain its graphics object to draw to it by invoking its getGraphics() method.

How Java Arranges Components within Containers

Creating a display using low-level graphics routines is fine, but at some point you'll probably want to create buttons, check boxes, and other standard user interface elements that the user can click, check, and so on. All of Java's user interface components are subclasses of the Component class.

We will look at examples of creating component objects in a moment. First, though, it's useful to know how you will arrange these component objects in your application's display. You add component objects to container objects using add(). The container object knows how to contain objects and arrange the objects it contains.

First, you will probably have a container object of some kind that will contain a component. For example, a Window is a container. Perhaps this Window object is referred to by the Object Reference window. Second, you create a component object, such as a button, text field, checkbox, and so on. Let's say you assign the object reference for a component object to a variable named component. The way you add the component to the window is to write:

```
window.add(component);
```

Keep in mind that container inherits from component. Hence, containers can contain component objects as well as other container objects. Again, we'll look at containers in more detail later in this chapter.

The Component Class, Subclasses and Methods

In this section, we will create component objects. The component objects we'll look at in this section are TextArea, List, and TextField.

TextArea

A TextArea object provides a window in which the user types. When you create a TextArea object, you specify the number of lines that the text window can contain and the number of columns of text it will contain. The number of columns that a TextArea (or TextField) object can contain is only approximate.

TextArea has five constructors. The two you'll use the most specify the number of rows and columns for the TextArea. Their format is

```
TextArea(int numRows, int numCols);
TextArea(String text, int numRows, int numCols);
```

You may also want to use the constructor introduced with Java 1.1. This constructor takes a string, a number of rows, a number of columns, and an integer describing any scrollbars desired in the TextArea. The constructor format is

```
TextArea(String text, int numRows, int numCols, int
scrollbars);
```

The other constructors are the no-args constructor and a constructor that simply takes a String parameter, the text to display in the TextArea object. Displaying a TextArea constructed without specifying the number of rows and columns will probably give you results you don't want, since the TextArea has not been sized properly.

Here's an example of a TextArea object that displays three rows of text and up to 10 columns:

```java
import java.awt.*;
import java.applet.*;
public class TA1 extends Applet {
 public void init() {
   add(new TextArea(3, 10));
  }
}
```

This applet looks like Figure 14-7 when it is first run.

Figure 14-8 shows what happens as you start typing into the TextField.

Even though the TextArea is only set to three rows and 10 columns, the user typed more text than could fit into this space. The TextArea displays little scroll bars when this happens so the

Figure 14-7
A TextArea set to three rows and ten columns

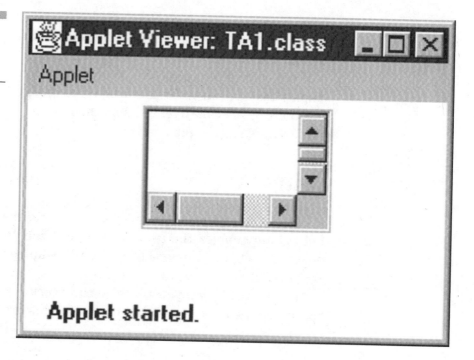

Figure 14-8
Typing into the
TextArea set to
three rows and 10
columns

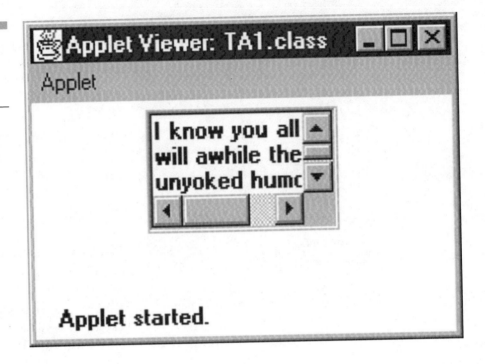

user can see the rest of the text. In this case, the user typed a speech from *Henry IV, Part 1*: "I know you all, and will awhile uphold the unyoked humor of your idleness."

If you want a TextArea (or a TextField) object to be used only to display text (if you want the user to be unable to edit the text in this object), you can invoke the method setEditable() and pass a value of false as the parameter.

TextField

A TextField object also provides a window for the user to type into, but it only enables the user to type one line. When you create a TextField object, you need to specify the number of columns in the TextField.

As with TextArea, you can also construct a TextField without specifying the number of columns. Again, this is probably not something you will want to do, because then you will not be in control of the size of the TextField.

Here is an example of creating a TextField that is 20 columns wide:

```
import java.awt.*;
import java.applet.*;
public class TF1 extends Applet {
 public void init() {
   add(new TextField(20));
 }
}
```

Figure 14-9 shows what this looks like.

Unlike a TextArea, if you type more characters than can fit within the width of the TextField, no scroll bars appear. However, you can still use the arrow keys on the keyboard to move to the front or end of the text.

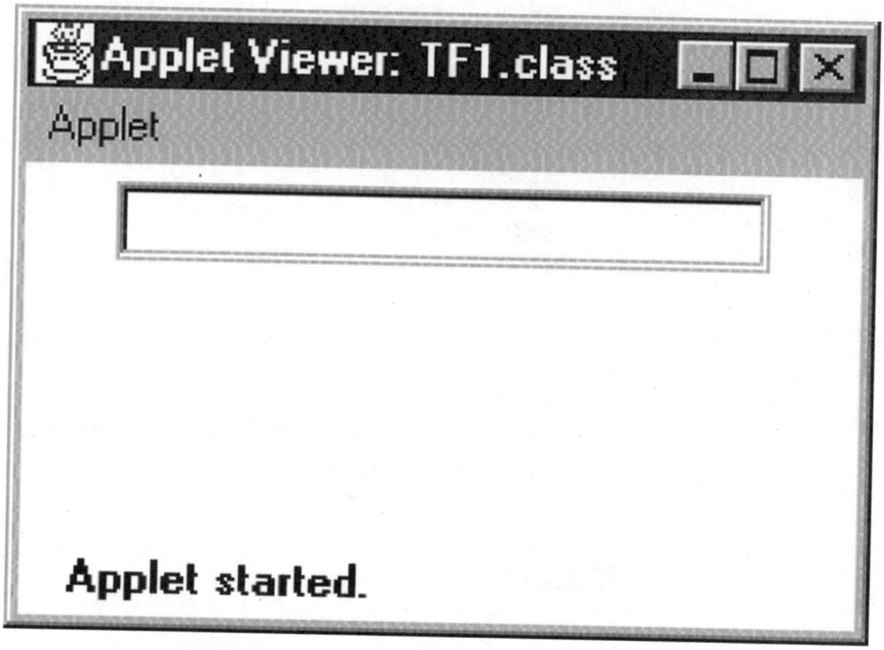

Figure 14-9
A TextField that is 20 columns wide

List

A List object presents a list of strings from which the user can select. When you create a List, you indicate the number of lines the List will show at one time. If there are more items in the List than can be displayed, scroll bars appear to the right of the List so the user can scroll through the rest of the choices. You can also indicate whether the user may make multiple selections or just a single selection.

To create a List object containing a certain number of rows, use this constructor:

```
List(int numRows, boolean multipleSelections);
```

You can populate the List by invoking add(). For example, to create a List that shows five items at a time and enables the user to select multiple types of fish, you can write

```
import java.awt.*;
import java.applet.Applet;
public class L1 extends Applet {
 public void init() {
  List l = new List(5, true);
  l.add("trout");
  l.add("salmon");
  l.add("snapper");
  l.add("bass");
  l.add("tuna");
  l.add("halibut");
  l.add("swordfish");
  add(l);
 }
}
```

This applet looks like Figure 14-10 when it first appears.

As the user interacts with it and selects multiple fish, the list might look like Figure 14-11.

Exercise 14-2

Create and display a TextArea object that contains the text "To Whom It May Concern." The TextArea should be large enough to dash off a small note to someone. (You can decide what's large enough.)

Figure 14-10
A List displayed in an applet.

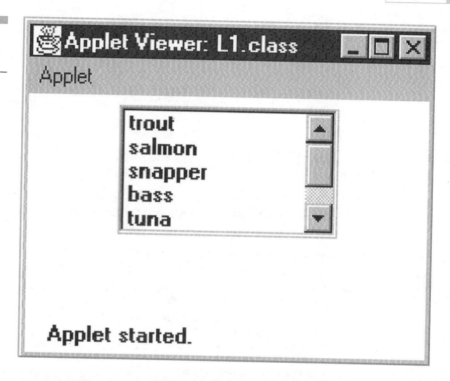

Figure 14-11
The user interacting with a list that allows multiple selections.

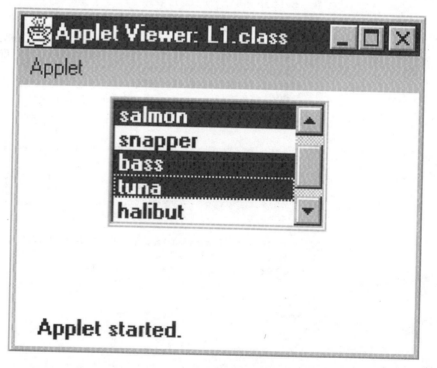

Key Component Methods

You'll find that component objects have a lot of common methods. Some of the methods are setEnabled(), setVisible(), getSize(), and setSize(). Let's look briefly at these and other key methods.

setEnabled

You can use the setEnabled() method to make a component selectable by the user. Let's say you have two buttons that you want to make mutually exclusive. You could use setEnabled(true) and setEnabled(false) so that the user can turn them on and off—to make them selectable or not selectable. Here's an example:

```java
import java.applet.Applet;
import java.awt.*;
import java.awt.event.*;
public class Toggle extends Applet {
 Button start, stop;
 public void init() {
   start = new Button("start");
   stop = new Button("stop");
   start.addMouseListener(new ButtonToggler(start, stop));
   stop.addMouseListener(new ButtonToggler(stop, start));
   start.setEnabled(true);
   stop.setEnabled(false);
   add(start);
   add(stop);
 }
}
 class ButtonToggler extends MouseAdapter {
 Button otherButton;
 Button myButton;
 public ButtonToggler(Button myButton, Button otherButton) {
   this.myButton = myButton;
   this.otherButton = otherButton;
 }
 public void mouseClicked(MouseEvent me) {
  myButton.setEnabled(false);
  otherButton.setEnabled(true);
 }
}
```

getSize/setSize

The getSize() method retrieves the size of a component. This method returns a dimension object that has two fields: width and height. The setSize() method sets the size of a component. There are two resize() methods: one takes a dimension object and the other takes the width and height directly as int values.

Components within a layout manager (discussed later in the next section), which automatically sizes the components it contains, should not call setSize() directly. Instead, the layout manager should take care of sizing the component appropriately.

setVisible

The setVisible() method makes a component visible or invisible. A boolean parameter indicates whether to show the component (if the parameter is true) or hide the component (if the parameter is false).

A common place to use setVisible() is when you create a stand-alone graphical application. Typically, your top-level container is a frame. To make the frame appear, you have got to invoke its setVisible() method. Here's an example of using both setSize() and setVisible() to make a frame take up space and appear on the screen:

```
import java.awt.*;

public class Fr extends Frame {
public static void main(String[] args) {
Fr fr = new Fr();
fr.setSize(220, 100);
fr.setVisible(true);
}
}
```

Figure 14-12 shows what this simple program looks like when you run it.

Figure 14-12
A simple frame

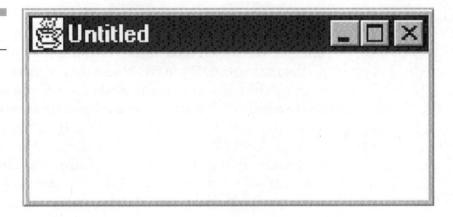

setForeground/setBackground

The setForeground() and setBackground() methods are used to set the foreground and background color of a component. These methods each take one parameter, an instance of class Color.

The Color class defines many static constants that contain instances of class Color already initialized to common colors. Each constant is named after the color. To use red, for example, you can access Color.red. To use blue, you can access Color.blue. The colors Java makes available through the Color class are black, blue, cyan, dark gray, gray, green, light gray, magenta, orange, pink, red, white, and yellow. What if you want a different color? No problem! You can mix your own color out of red, green, and blue elements by creating a new color instance and supplying the red, green, and blue values in the constructor. For example, you can use the constructor with this signature:

```
Color(int red, int green, int blue);
```

The red, green, and blue values range from 0 to 255. If all are set to 0, you get black. If all values are set to 255, you get white.

The Color class provides methods to convert between red, green, and blue, or hue, saturation, and brightness if you'd rather work with the latter system. It also provides methods for getting the red, green, and blue portions of a color. For example, to set the foreground color to green for a component referenced by the variable component, you can write

```
component.setForeground(Color.green);
```

Components and Layout Managers

That containers contain components is all well and good, but how do containers arrange the components within them? The answer is that they hand off this chore to a layout manager. Each container has exactly one layout manager. The layout manager determines how to arrange the components within a container.

Whenever the container or a component within the container changes in a way that might mean the layout needs to be updated —such as when the container first appears on the screen, if new components are added to a container, if the components within a container change size, or if the container itself is resized—the AWT invokes the container's `invalidate()` method, followed shortly later by `validate()`. The `validate()` method in turn invokes that container's `layout()` method. The container's `layout()` method, however, does not figure out what to do on its own. This method asks its container's layout manager what to do by calling the layout manager's `layoutContainer()` method. The `layoutContainer()` method takes the container as an argument.

What is a layout manager exactly? Any class that implements the `LayoutManager` interface. All Java's five layout managers will inherit directly from class `Object`, but they implement the `Layout-Manager` interface, which defines five `abstract` methods:

- `addLayoutComponent()`
- `layoutContainer()`
- `minimumLayoutSize()`
- `preferredLayoutSize()`
- `removeLayoutComponent()`

You will probably never invoke any of these methods directly, even if you implement your own layout manager instead of using one of the five that come with Java. (You'll usually find that one of Java's five layout managers works just fine.) Instead of invoking a layout manager's methods yourself, Java's default container methods invoke them for you at the appropriate times. Table 14-1 shows the connection between container and layout manager methods.

Using Layout Managers

Each type of container comes with a default layout manager. We'll discuss the different ones in this section. Later, you'll review what the default layout managers are for the different containers, and you'll review how to change the layout manager for a container. The five different layout managers consist of the classes FlowLayout, BorderLayout, GridLayout, CardLayout, and GridBagLayout.

FlowLayout

A FlowLayout object arranges components left to right and top to bottom, centering each line as it goes. As new components are added to a container with a FlowLayout, the FlowLayout positions each component on the same line as the previous one until the next component will not fit, given the width of the container. Then the FlowLayout centers that row, starts a new row, and begins adding components to the new row. A FlowLayout lets each component be its preferred size and does not change the size of a component. (The same is not true for other layout managers, as we'll review shortly.)

The FlowLayout lets the component be its preferred size even if the component cannot fit in the width or height provided. For example, if a label or button contains text that makes it too wide to display in the container, the component will be on its own row, and you'll see only the centered portion that fits in the container's width.

Table 14-1

Container and layout manager methods

Container Methods	Layout Manager Methods
add()	addLayoutComponent()
doLayout()	layoutContainer()
getMinimumSize()	minimumLayoutSize()
getPreferredSize()	preferredLayoutSize()
remove()/removeAll()	removeLayoutComponent()

Here's some code that illustrates this:

```java
import java.awt.*;
import java.applet.*;
public class Fit extends Applet {
 public void init() {
   add(new Label("Romeo, Romeo, wherefore art thou, Romeo?"));
 }
}
```

This places a long label into an applet, but if the HTML file that embeds this applet looks like this

```html
<applet code=Fit.class width=50 height=50>
</applet>
```

then the label won't be fully seen. The applet will look like Figure 14-13.

NOTE: *If a container using a* `FlowLayout` *is resized, all the components inside it might need to be rearranged. This might very well mean the components end up in a different configuration than before, depending on what now fits on each row. Although a text field, button, and choice might be on the same row at first, resizing the container to be smaller might force each component to be placed on its own row.*

Figure 14-14 shows an example of some components first arranged one way, and then when the applet is resized, Figure 14-15 shows how they look after the `FlowLayout` has rearranged them.

Here's the code for this applet:

```java
import java.awt.*;
import java.applet.*;
public class MiscComponents extends Applet {
 public void init() {
   add(new Button("launch missiles"));
   add(new Label("targets: "));
```

```
    add(new Checkbox("subs"));
    add(new Checkbox("bases"));
    add(new Checkbox("fighters"));
  }
}
```

FlowLayouts are particularly useful for arranging a series of buttons to create a kind of menu, where each button is placed after the one before it.

Figure 14-13
A label that doesn't fit in the width of the applet

Figure 14-14
An applet that uses a
`FlowLayout` to
arrange components

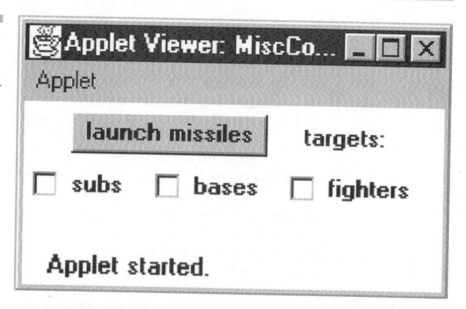

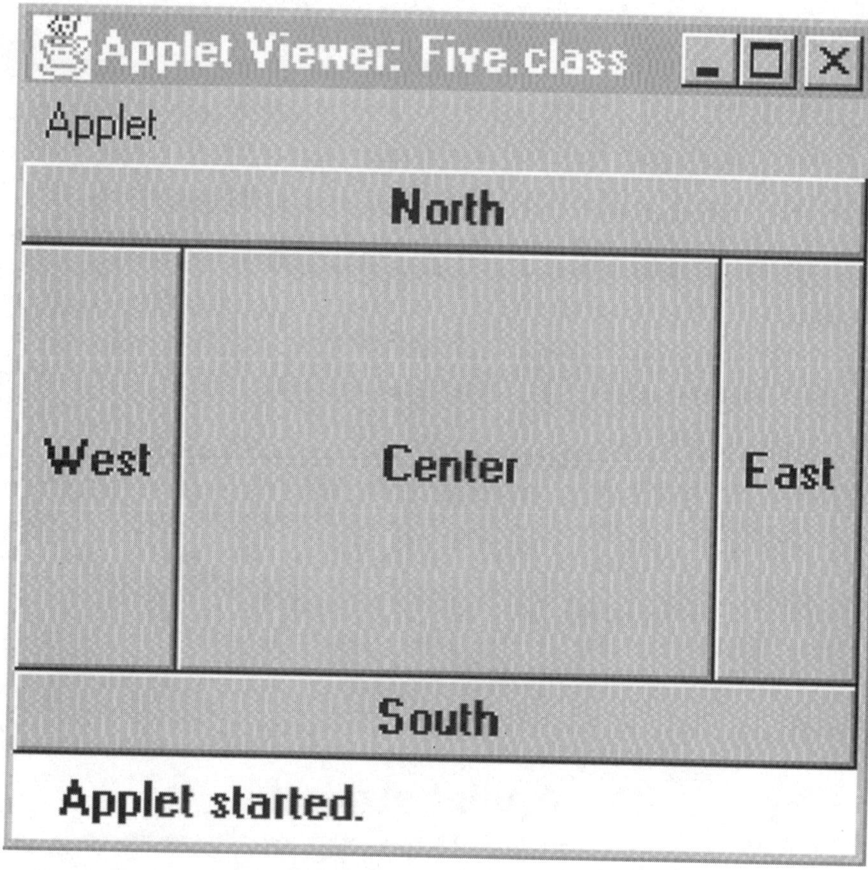

Figure 14-15
Resizing an applet
that uses a
`FlowLayout`

BorderLayout

BorderLayout objects arrange components according to the directions North, South, East, and West. There's also an area for Center, which includes any space left over from the other regions. Components are usually rarely allowed to be their preferred size in a BorderLayout. If the container is smaller than the components' preferred sizes, the components are squeezed. If the container is larger, the components are stretched. For example, Figure 14-16 shows five button objects arranged in a container that uses a BorderLayout. This figure gives a better sense of the regions of a BorderLayout than a description could. Notice that the North and South regions stretch all the way across the screen, while the East and West regions are positioned between the North and South.

Figure 14-16
Five buttons in a
BorderLayout

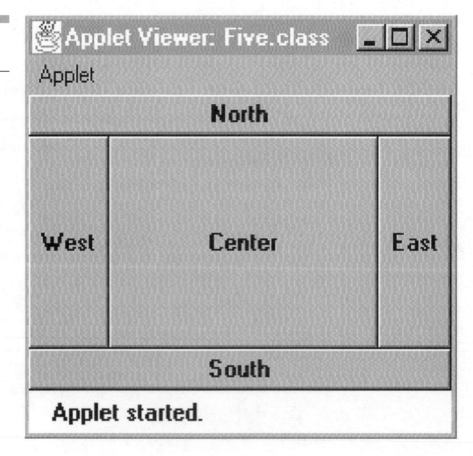

Here's the code for this picture:

```
import java.awt.*;
import java.applet.*;
public class Five extends Applet {
 public void init() {
  setLayout(new BorderLayout());
  add("North", new Button("North"));
  add("South", new Button("South"));
  add("East", new Button("East"));
  add("West", new Button("West"));
  add("Center", new Button("Center"));
 }
}
```

`BorderLayout` objects also have another limitation: you cannot display more than one component in a particular region. If you add more than one to a region, only the last component you've added will appear. For example, if you try to add three checkbox objects (though three buttons, three labels, or three of anything have the same result) to the North of a `BorderLayout`, like this:

```
import java.applet.Applet;
import java.awt.*;
public class BorderOver extends Applet {
 public void init() {
  setLayout(new BorderLayout());
  add("North", new Checkbox("mouse"));
  add("North", new Checkbox("dog"));
  add("North", new Checkbox("cat"));
 }
}
```

the result is that only the last component is displayed, as shown in Figure 14-17.

So what is a `BorderLayout` good for? Unlike a `FlowLayout`, a `BorderLayout` is useful for making certain that components keep the same relationship to each other, even if the applet is resized. They also are excellent at arranging components along the top and bottom of a container, which a `FlowLayout` cannot do.

Figure 14-17
In a BorderLayout,
only the last
component added to
a region is displayed

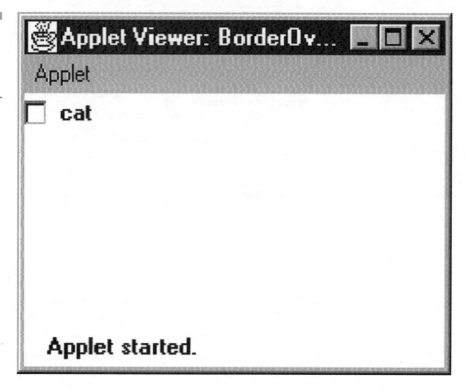

If you want to show more than one component in a particular region of a BorderLayout, you can nest another container inside the first container. For example, to place three buttons at the top of a container and three at the bottom, you can place each set of three inside their own container using a FlowLayout, and then place the two containers inside one using the BorderLayout. The code might look like this:

```
import java.applet.Applet;
import java.awt.*;
public class Border extends Applet {
 public void init() {
   Panel p;
   setLayout(new BorderLayout());
   p = new Panel();
   p.add(new Button("dog"));
   p.add(new Button("cat"));
   p.add(new Button("mouse"));
   add("North", p);
```

```
    p = new Panel();
    p.add(new Button("steak"));
    p.add(new Button("tuna"));
    p.add(new Button("cheese"));
    add("South", p);
  }
}
```

This code results in the display shown in Figure 14-18.

North and South components can be stretched horizontally; they fill up the space from the left to the right edge of the container. East and West components can be stretched vertically; they fill up the space from the top of the South area to the bottom of the North area.

Adding a component to the center of the BorderLayout will make that component take up whatever space is left over in the center (if any). A Center component can be stretched both horizontally and vertically. The Center includes regions of the BorderLayout that are not used. For example, if nothing is placed in the East or West,

Figure 14-18

Panels within a BorderLayout

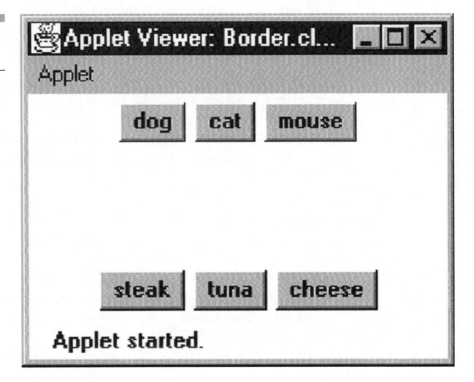

then the Center stretches all the way from the left edge of the container to the right edge.

So which components can be stretched? Well, here's a partial list of the stretchable versus the non-stretchable components:

- *Stretchable*   Buttons, label, text fields
- *Non-stretchable*   Checkboxes

Each component is placed within a different region of an applet that uses a `BorderLayout`. You can see the effect of stretching or not stretching based on the type of component.

Here's the code for this example:

```
import java.awt.*;
import java.applet.*;
public class Stretch extends Applet {
 public void init() {
   setLayout(new BorderLayout());
   add("East", new Button("East"));
   add("West", new Label("West"));
   add("North", new TextField("North"));
   add("South", new Checkbox("South"));
  }
 }
```

The result is shown in Figure 14-19. Each component fills up its region of the screen, except for the checkbox in the south.

If you don't want the components right on top of each other, one of the constructors for `BorderLayout` enables you to specify the horizontal and vertical gaps that should be placed around the regions of the layout.

GridLayout

`GridLayout` objects enable you to specify a rectangular grid in which to place the components. Each cell in the grid is the same height as the other cells, and each width is the same width as the other cells. Components are stretched both vertically and horizontally to fill the cell. The size of the cells is determined according to

Figure 14-19
In a BorderLayout,
different components
stretch or don't
stretch depending on
their type.

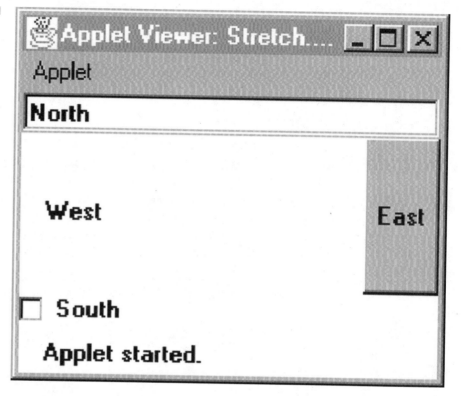

Figure 14-19
In a BorderLayout, different components stretch or don't stretch depending on their type.

how many cells are requested in the container, given the container's size.

When a GridLayout is first constructed, you must specify how many rows and how many columns the grid will have. Components are added to the GridLayout left to right and top to bottom. If more components are added than there are columns, the GridLayout keeps the same number of rows but adds the necessary number of columns.

For example, the following program causes the applet to be displayed with all six buttons on the same row:

```
import java.applet.Applet;
import java.awt.*;
public class GridOver extends Applet {
 public void init() {
  setLayout(new GridLayout(1, 2));
  add(new Button("mouse"));
```

```
    add(new Button("dog"));
    add(new Button("cat"));
    add(new Button("elephant"));
    add(new Button("monkey"));
    add(new Button("giraffe"));
  }
}
```

This results are shown in Figure 14-20.

Changing the GridLayout to be created with two rows and two columns (instead of one row and two columns) makes GridLayout arrange the button objects in two rows and three columns, like what's shown in Figure 14-21.

As with a BorderLayout, if you don't want the components right on top of each other, one of the constructors for GridLayout enables you to specify the horizontal and vertical gaps that should be placed around the cells of the layout.

Other Types of Layout Managers

CardLayout   You can use CardLayout to present different screens to a user based on a stack of cards metaphor. You can flip to

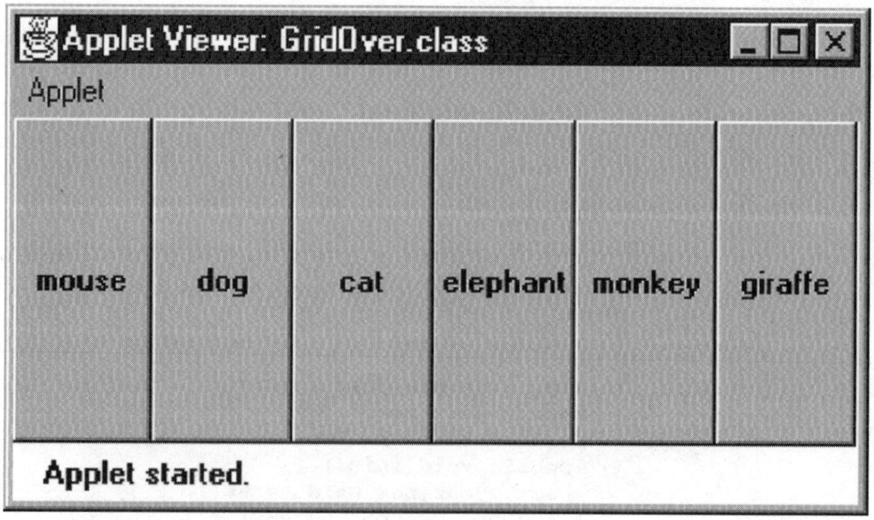

Figure 14-20
A GridLayout arranging buttons in one row

Figure 14-21
A GridLayout
arranging buttons in
two rows

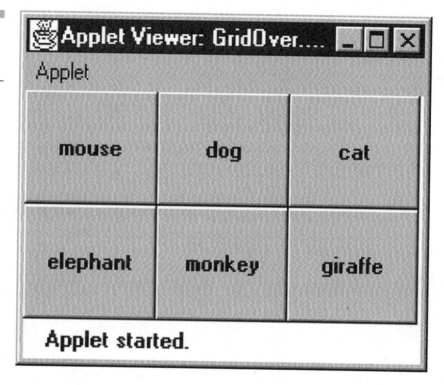

the first, second, or last card using methods defined by CardLayout. You can also go directly to a particular card, as long as you've named it, using a method named show().

GridBagLayout You saw how the GridLayout arranges components in a strict grid where each row and each column are the same size. Components can only occupy one cell.

GridBagLayout is much more complicated than that and also much more flexible. With GridBagLayout, your rows and columns don't have to all be the same size. What's more, each component can occupy more than one cell.

Default Layout Managers

Since a container class always has one layout manager associated with it, container classes are defined with a default layout manager. These defaults are shown in Table 14-2.

Table 14-2

Containers and their default layout managers

Container	Default Layout Manager
Frame	BorderLayout
Panel	FlowLayout
Dialog	BorderLayout
Window	BorderLayout

You can change a container to use a different kind of layout manager by invoking setLayout(). One common technique is to create the new layout manager and set it at the same time, as in

```
f.setLayout(new FlowLayout());
```

This creates a new FlowLayout object and assigns it as the layout manager for a container object referenced by the variable f.

Exercise 14-3

Arrange two buttons that read "yes" and "no" at the bottom of an applet. Your applet should look something like Figure 14-22.

Here's a hint: making an applet look like this involves placing the buttons within their own container, such as a panel, and then placing the panel into the applet. You'll see why if you try to place the buttons directly into the applet.

Answers to the Exercises

Exercise 14-1

```
import java.awt.*;
import java.applet.*;
public class Drawing extends Applet {
 public void paint(Graphics g) {
  g.drawRect(5, 5, 50, 50);
  g.fillOval(5, 5, 50, 50);
  }
}
```

Exercise 14-2

```
import java.awt.*;
import java.applet.*;
public class ToWhom extends Applet {
 public void init() {
  add(new TextArea("To Whom It May Concern", 10, 30));
  }
}
```

Exercise 14-3

To place components such as buttons along the bottom of an applet, you need a BorderLayout. However, to place two buttons side by side, as in this applet, you need a FlowLayout. The trick here is to place the two buttons inside a panel, and the default layout for a panel is a FlowLayout. You can then place the panel into the applet and replace the applet's layout manager to be a `BorderLayout`. That way, you can place this panel containing the two buttons at the bottom of the applet. Here's a solution:

```
import java.awt.*;
import java.applet.*;
public class TwoButtons extends Applet {
 public void init() {
   Panel p = new Panel();
   p.add(new Button("yes"));
   p.add(new Button("no"));
   setLayout(new BorderLayout());
   add("South", p);
 }
}
```

QUESTIONS

1. You should place all of your low-level graphics rendering code into
   a. `update()`
   b. `paint()`
   c. `init()`
   d. `repaint()`

2. The AWT passes your `paint()` method an instance of class
   a. `Thread`
   b. `Applet`
   c. `Graphics`
   d. `Component`

3. Given a graphics object in the variable g, the method call

   `g.DrawRect(0, 10, 30, 40);`

   a. draws the outline of a rectangle that is centered at $x = 0, y = 10$ and is 30 pixels wide and 40 pixels height.
   b. draws the outline of a rectangle whose top-left corner is at $x = 0$, $y = 10$ and whose bottom-right corner is at $x = 30, y = 40$.

    c. fills a rectangle with the foreground color where the rectangle's left edge is 0, its top is 10, its width is 30, and its height is 40.

    d. draws the outline of a rectangle where the rectangle's left edge is 0, its top is 10, its width is 30, and its height is 40.

4. Here is some partial code for a `main()` method:

```
Frame f = new Frame("My frame");
f.setSize(100, 100);
```

What line of code could you add to make this new frame object appear on the screen?

    a. `f.appear();`

    b. `f.setForeground();`

    c. `f.show();`

    d. `f.enable();`

5. To place a button at the bottom of a container, no matter how the user resized it, which type of layout manager would it be simplest to use?

    a. `BorderLayout`

    b. `GridLayout`

    c. `FlowLayout`

    d. `GridbagLayout`

6. The Graphics class has a coordinate system with an origin at

    a. the center of the space

    b. the bottom-left corner of the space

    c. the top-left corner of the space

    d. a user-configurable coordinate system

7. To add a component referenced by comp to the center of a container using a `BorderLayout` and referenced by cont, you can write:

    a. `comp.add("Center", cont);`

    b. `comp.add(cont, "Center");`

    c. `cont.add("Center", comp);`

    d. `cont.add(comp, "Center");`

8. The code

```
new List(10, true);
```

   a. creates a new list that is 10 columns wide and accepts multiple selections
   b. creates a new list that is 10 rows tall and accepts multiple selections
   c. creates a new list that can contain no more than 10 entries and accepts multiple selections
   d. creates a new list that is 10 rows tall and only enables one entry to be selected at a time

Answers to the Review Questions

1. b. All low-level drawing code should go into your `paint()` method.

2. c. You can use the graphics object to perform low-level drawing operations.

3. d. The template is `drawRect(left edge, top edge, width, height)`.

4. c. The `show()` method in Java 1.0.2 makes a component appear.

5. a. With a `BorderLayout`, you could add the component to the South and that's where it would stay.

6. a. The `Graphics` class has a coordinate system with an origin at the center of the space.

7. c. `add()` is defined as a container method. The placement of the component is the first parameter.

8. b. The first parameter is the number of rows to display without scrolling; the second parameter indicates whether or not to enable multiple selections.

CHAPTER 15

Events

Events are an important part of the Java language. When users interact with a component, the *Abstract Windowing Toolkit* (AWT) notifies the component's listeners (if any) of the events they're interested in. You can register your object as a listener interested in particular events by using methods such as `addMouseListener()` to get mouse events or `addActionListener()` to get action events. A different method corresponds to the different types of events. Objects that listen for events must conform to an interface appropriate for those events. Java defines a number of listener interfaces you can implement in your own classes.

For the exam, you'll need to be able to write code that implements listener classes and extracts information from the related events to determine the affected component, mouse position, nature, and time of the event. You'll also need to be able to state the event class for any specified event listener interface in the `java.awt.event` package.

Objectives for This Chapter

- Describe the event-handling model in Java.
- Identify important events in the `AWTEvent` hierarchy.
- Add a listener to a component's list of event listeners.
- Identify the important listener interfaces.
- Implement a listener interface.
- State the difference between low-level and semantic events.
- Extend an adapter class.

Event Classes

In Java 1.1, the Java packages define many different event classes that represent specific types of events. `EventObject`, which is at the top of the event hierarchy, is actually defined in `java.util`, not in `java.awt`. This is to make events more generic and not necessarily tied to the AWT. However, all of the events dispatched by AWT's components use event classes that are subclasses of AWTEvent, which is in `java.awt`.

The hierarchy of EventObject and AWTEvent classes that you'll work with is as follows:

```
java.util.EventObject

java.awt.AWTEvent
ActionEvent AdjustmentEvent ComponentEvent ItemEvent
TextEvent
ContainerEvent FocusEvent InputEvent PaintEvent WindowEvent
KeyEvent MouseEvent
```

What the hierarchy doesn't show are event classes that you won't use regularly. These events classes are InputMethodEvent and InvocationEvent. Both classes extend `java.awt.AWTEvent`. In addition to these event classes, some event classes are implemented in the Java Swing API. These classes are subclasses of `java.awt.AWTEvent` as well. Key `javax.swing.event` classes include

- AncestorEvent: An event generated when the ancestor of a component is added, removed, or moved

- InternalFrameEvent: An event generated when the JInternalEvent object is changed

You do *not* need to know the Swing-related events for the programmer exam.

The `java.util.EventObject` class is very basic. It only implements two methods. The key method you'll be interested in is getSource(), which returns the object that originated an event. `java.awt.AWTEvent` is a subclass of `java.util.EventObject` and the superclass of all AWT event classes. The key method that you should know about is getID(), which returns the ID of an event. The event ID is an int that specifies the type of event, such as a button or mouse click.

Subclasses of AWTEvent represent various types of events:

- ActionEvent: An event generated by the activation of components

- AdjustmentEvent: An event generated by the adjustment of adjustable components, such as moving a scrollbar

■ `ComponentEvent`:   A high-level event generated by manipulation of a component

■ `ContainerEvent`:   An event generated when components are added to or removed from containers

■ `InputEvent`:   A high-level event generated by an input device

■ `ItemEvent`:   An event generated when an item is selected form a choice, checkbox, or list

■ `KeyEvent`:   An event generated by the keyboard

■ `MouseEvent`:   An event generated by the mouse

■ `PaintEvent`:   An event generated when components are painted.

■ `TextEvent`:   An event generated when text components are modified

■ `WindowEvent`:   An event generated by window activity, such as minimizing or maximizing a window

The `AWTEvent` objects your event handlers receive are tailored to the type of event they represent. The AWT does not notify your event handler of every event that occurs over a component. Instead, AWT informs your event handler only about the events it is interested in.

Listening for Events

You must explicitly indicate which objects should handle specific events that occur in a particular component. You set up event handlers by telling a component which object will listen for the events it's interested in.

For example, let's say you have placed a button in your user interface, and you want your application to know when the user clicks this button. You need to perform the following steps in your code:

1. Define a class that implements a listener interface. There are a variety of listener interfaces, each one representing different types of events. For example, there's a `MouseMotionListener` that declares methods for handling mouse movements; there's a `FocusListener` that declares methods for reacting to a component acquiring or losing the focus.

2. Create an instance of this class.

3. Tell the component whose events you are interested in which types of events you are interested in, and which object will handle those events. You do this by invoking a method called addABCListener() and passing it the instance of your listener class. There are different addABCListener() methods, where "ABC" in the method name is replaced by the type of listener you're adding to the component's list of listeners. So, to add an instance of MouseMotionListener called myMouseMotionListener to a component's list of listeners, you would write

```
myComponent.addMouseMotionListener(myMouseMotionListener);
```

To get a flavor for this, here's a simple applet that draws scribbles by handling the MouseListener and MouseMotionListener events. This program could also use an inner class to handle the events, rather than having the applet itself implement these interfaces. It could also define a separate class that only handles the events related to scribbling. Another possibility is for it to enable certain events and handle them directly without going through this listener interface at all (we won't discuss that approach in this chapter). Let's start with this example and improve upon its design as we progress through this chapter:

```java
import java.awt.*;
import java.awt.event.*;
import java.applet.Applet;
public class Scribble extends Applet
    implements MouseMotionListener, MouseListener
{
   private int x;
   private int y;
   public void init() {
      addMouseListener(this);
      addMouseMotionListener(this);
   }
   public void mousePressed(MouseEvent e) {
      x = e.getX();
      y = e.getY();
   }
   public void mouseDragged(MouseEvent e) {
      Graphics g = getGraphics();
      int newX = e.getX();
```

```
        int newY = e.getY();
        g.drawLine(x, y, newX, newY);
        x = newX;
        y = newY;
    }
    // Left-over methods from the interfaces.
    public void mouseMoved(MouseEvent e) { }
    public void mouseClicked(MouseEvent e) { }
    public void mouseReleased(MouseEvent e) { }
    public void mouseEntered(MouseEvent e) { }
    public void mouseExited(MouseEvent e) { }
}
```

Figure 15-1 shows what this looks like after a user has inter-
acted with this applet.

NOTE: *As you can see, this applet doesn't remember the drawing
the user has performed, so if the applet is resized, the* `paint()`
operation will make the scribble vanish like shaking an Etch-a-Sketch™.

Figure 15-1
Using the scribble
applet.

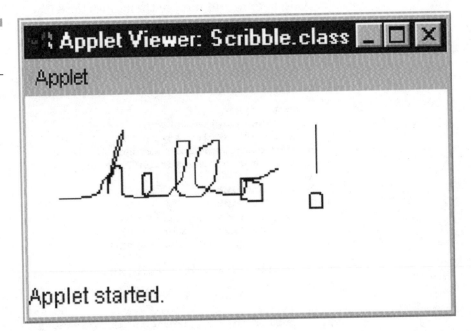

In this example, we imported `java.awt.event`, which contains all the event classes we need. Notice how we had to implement stubs for `mouseMoved()`, `mouseClicked()`, `mouseReleased()`, `mouseEntered()`, and `mouseExited()`. We do not care about these events but were forced to implement them anyway. Why? Because the `MouseListener` and `MouseMotionListener` interfaces define all of these `abstract` methods. Sure, all we care about is `mousePressed()` and `mouseDragged()`, but if we didn't implement the others, our applet subclass would be `abstract`.

Creating empty stubs seems like a waste of effort; if you are creating a class that only handles events, it is. There is a way around this problem; we'll look at that shortcut in a few pages. First, let's look at the listener interfaces in more detail.

The Listener Interfaces

The previous program showed a way to detect mouse events. What other types of listener interfaces are there? The listener interfaces are all defined in `java.awt.event`. They are presented here in alphabetical order. I've also listed the methods that you must define if you implement one of these interfaces. You can refer to this list if you would like to implement one of these interfaces and the methods you can use to add an instance of the listener.

ActionListener

`ActionListener` is implemented by objects that handle `ActionEvent` events. Its interface and add methods are

Interface Method

■ `public void actionPerformed(ActionEvent e)`

Add Method

■ `obj.addActionListener()`

AdjustmentListener

`AdjustmentListener` is implemented by objects that handle `AdjustmentEvent` events. Its interface and add methods are

Interface Method

- `public void adjustmentValueChanged(AdjustmentEvent e)`

Add Method

- `obj.addAdjustmentListener()`

ComponentListener

`ComponentListener` is implemented by objects that handle `ComponentEvent` events. Its interface and add methods are

Interface Methods

- `public void componentHidden(ComponentEvent e)`
- `public void componentMoved(ComponentEvent e)`
- `public void componentResized(ComponentEvent e)`
- `public void componentShown(ComponentEvent e)`

Add Method

- `obj.addComponentListener()`

ContainerListener

`ContainerListener` is implemented by objects that handle `ContainerEvent` events. Its interface and add methods are

Interface Methods

- `public void containerAdded(ContainerEvent e)`
- `public void containerRemoved(ContainerEvent e)`

Add Method

- `obj.addContainerListener()`

FocusListener

FocusListener is implemented by objects that handle FocusEvent events. Its interface and add methods are

Interface Methods

- public void focusGained(FocusEvent e)
- public void focusLost(FocusEvent e)

Add Method

- obj.addFocusListener()

ItemListener

ItemListener is implemented by objects that handle ItemEvent events. Its interface and add methods are

Interface Method

- public void itemStateChanged(ItemEvent e)

Add Method

- obj.addItemListener()

KeyListener

KeyListener is implemented by objects that handle KeyEvent events. Its interface and add methods are

Interface Methods

- public void keyPressed(KeyEvent e)
- public void keyReleased(KeyEvent e)
- public void keyTyped(KeyEvent e)

Add Method

- obj.addKeyListener()

MouseListener

MouseListener is implemented by objects that handle MouseEvent events. Its interface and add methods are
Interface Methods

- public void mouseClicked(MouseEvent e)
- public void mouseEntered(MouseEvent e)
- public void mouseExited(MouseEvent e)
- public void mousePressed(MouseEvent e)
- public void mouseReleased(MouseEvent e)

Add Method

- obj.addMouseListener()

MouseMotionListener

MouseMotionListener is implemented by objects that handle MouseMotionEvent events. Its interface and add methods are

Interface Methods

- public void mouseDragged(MouseEvent e)
- public void mouseMoved(MouseEvent e)

Add Method

- obj.addMouseMotionListener()

TextListener

TextListener is implemented by objects that handle TextEvent events. Its interface and add methods are:

Interface Methods

- public void textValueChanged(TextEvent e)

Add Method

- `obj.addTextListener()`

WindowListener

`WindowListener` is implemented by objects that handle `WindowEvent` events. Its interface and add methods are

Interface Methods

- `public void windowActivated(WindowEvent e)`
- `public void windowClosed(WindowEvent e)`
- `public void windowClosing(WindowEvent e)`
- `public void windowDeactivated(WindowEvent e)`
- `public void windowDeiconified(WindowEvent e)`
- `public void windowIconified(WindowEvent e)`
- `public void windowOpened(WindowEvent e)`

Add Method

- `obj.addWindowListener()`

Implementing a Listener Interface

You've already seen an example of an applet implementing a listener interface. However, you can also define a class specifically for handling an event. Here's a trivial example so that you can see the mechanics of it. You'll see fuller examples in the exercises.

In this applet, we create a button named "Click me!" We also define a class called `OurClickHandler` that implements the `MouseListener` interface. In the applet's `init()` method, we add an instance of this class to the button's list of listeners by calling `addMouseListener()`. Then when the user clicks this button, AWT routes all mouse events, including `mouseClicked()`, to our instance of `OurClickHandler`. There we write a simple message to the standard output. Here's the code:

```
import java.awt.*;
import java.awt.event.*;
import java.applet.Applet;
public class ClickApplet extends Applet {
public void init() {
Button b = new Button("Click me!");
b.addMouseListener(new OurClickHandler());
add(b);
}
}
class OurClickHandler implements MouseListener {
public void mouseClicked(MouseEvent e) {
System.out.println("button clicked");
}
// Left-over interface methods.
public void mousePressed(MouseEvent e) { }
public void mouseReleased(MouseEvent e) { }
public void mouseEntered(MouseEvent e) { }
public void mouseExited(MouseEvent e) { }
}
```

Exercise 15-1

Create an applet that contains context-sensitive help messages. Do this in an applet that places three buttons along the top of the interface. These buttons should write their names to the standard output when clicked. You can use any names you'd like for the buttons.

At the bottom of the applet, place a label. Whenever the user moves the mouse cursor over one of the buttons, display a simple message containing a few words in the label at the bottom of the applet that explains what will happen if the user clicks the button. As an example, your applet might look like Figure 15-2.

Semantic and Low-Level Events

It's convenient to separate the different types of events into two categories. You can think of these as semantic and low-level events. There are three types of semantic events: action events, item events, and adjustment events.

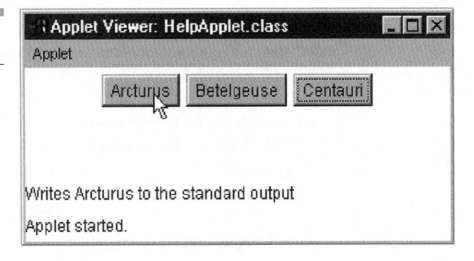

Figure 15-2
The context-sensitive
help applet.

Let's take a look at the different AWT components and see which semantic events they fire under what circumstances.

ActionEvent

AWT sends an `ActionEvent` object to any registered `ActionListener` objects when the user

- clicks a button
- hits the Enter key when typing in a text field
- selects a menu item
- double-clicks a list item

AdjustmentEvent

AWT sends an `AdjustmentEvent` object to any registered `AdjustmentListener` objects when the user

- scrolls up, down, left, or right using a scroll bar
- scrolls up, down, left, or right using a scroll pane

ItemEvent

AWT sends an ItemEvent object to any registered ItemListener objects when the user

- selects an item in a list
- selects an option from a choice box
- selects a menu item from a checkbox menu item
- clicks a checkbox

AWTEvent Subclasses

So far, we've breezed over the AWTEvent subclasses so that you could see the overall architecture of event handling. You know that you must implement a listener interface if you are interested in a particular event, and you must register an instance of the class implementing this listener interface as an event listener with the user interface component whose events you want to handle.

Now let's back up just a bit and review the AWTEvent subclasses that AWT will use to pass your event handlers. Java defines AWTEvent subclasses for different categories of events. For example, the MouseEvent class is used when the user

- clicks down on the mouse
- releases the mouse
- moves the mouse into or out of a component

If you need to identify which *particular* event occurred based on the MouseEvent object alone, you would use an int id field to determine this. You would invoke the object's getId() method and then use constants defined in MouseEvent to identify the event. In this example, the constants you would check include MOUSE_CLICKED, MOUSE_PRESSED, MOUSE_RELEASED, MOUSE_ENTERED, and MOUSE_EXITED. Different AWTEvent subclasses have their own constants. Many of these constants are presented in the section below on the AWTEvent subclasses. You can also review the APIs for a complete list, but you generally won't need to do this. You can instead simply supply the appropriate event method and let AWT invoke this method for you.

As you would expect, you will use methods in the AWTEvent sub-classes to get specific information about the event. I have listed some of the important methods and constants for each type of event.

AWTEvent

This is the root of all AWT events and is defined in java.awt. All of its subclasses are located in java.awt.event.

ActionEvent

- getModifiers() returns an int with bits that match whether the user has selected the Shift, Alt or Control keys when the user generated this event.
- The constants ALT_MASK, CTRL_MASK, META_MASK , and SHIFT_MASK can be used with the | operator with getModifiers() to determine whether any of these special modifier keys were pressed when the user generated this event.

AdjustmentEvent

- getAdjustable() retrieves the object where this event originated. This object will be an instance of a class that implements the adjustable interface.
- getValue() returns the current value in this adjustment event.

ComponentEvent

- getComponent() returns the component that triggered this event.

ContainerEvent

- `getChild()` returns a child component object.
- `getContainer` returns the container object.
- The constants COMPONENT_ADDED and COMPONENT_REMOVED are useful to help you keep track of when components have been added to or removed from a container.

FocusEvent

This class simply defines some new constants (such as FOCUS_GAINED and FOCUS_LOST).

InputEvent

- `getModifiers()` returns an int representing the bit values that determine whether the user pressed the Alt, Control, or Shift keys when the user generated this event.
- `getWhen()` returns the time stamp for this event.

ItemEvent

- `getItem()` returns the item where the event occurred.
- `getItemSelectable()` returns the object whose class implements the ItemSelectable interface where this event occurred.
- `getStateChange()` returns either SELECTED or DESELECTED, depending on whether the user just selected or deselected the item.

KeyEvent

- `getKeyCode()` returns an `int` value representing a key on the keyboard. This key may or may not generate a character; for example, the letter "a" does, but the F1 key does not.
- `getKeyChar()` returns a `char` of the character typed.

MouseEvent

- `getClickCount()` returns the number of times the user clicked the mouse to generate this event (that is, was this a double-click? A triple-click?).
- `getX()` returns the x coordinate of the mouse event.
- `getY()` returns the y coordinate of the mouse event.
- These constants identify the event type: `MOUSE_CLICKED`, `MOUSE_PRESSED`, `MOUSE_RELEASED`, `MOUSE_ENTERED`, and `MOUSE_EXITED`.

PaintEvent

Even though AWT passes this type of event to components, you should normally not listen for this type of event. Instead, you should override `paint()`.

TextEvent

- Defines the constant `TEXT_VALUE_CHANGED`.

WindowEvent

■ getWindow() returns the window that generated this event.

Exercise 15-2

Write an applet that contains three text fields. These text fields should have a white background when the user is not interacting with them. Each text field should turn red when the user is about to enter data, and each should turn yellow if the user types an exclamation point (!). Once the user has finished typing, the text field should become white again.

   Implement this by creating a special class that updates the text field's colors. This class should not be a subclass of TextField. Your application might look like what's shown in Figure 15-3.

Extending Adapter Classes

Sometimes it's not very convenient to implement a listener interface. As you saw with the scribble applet, you'll find that many methods

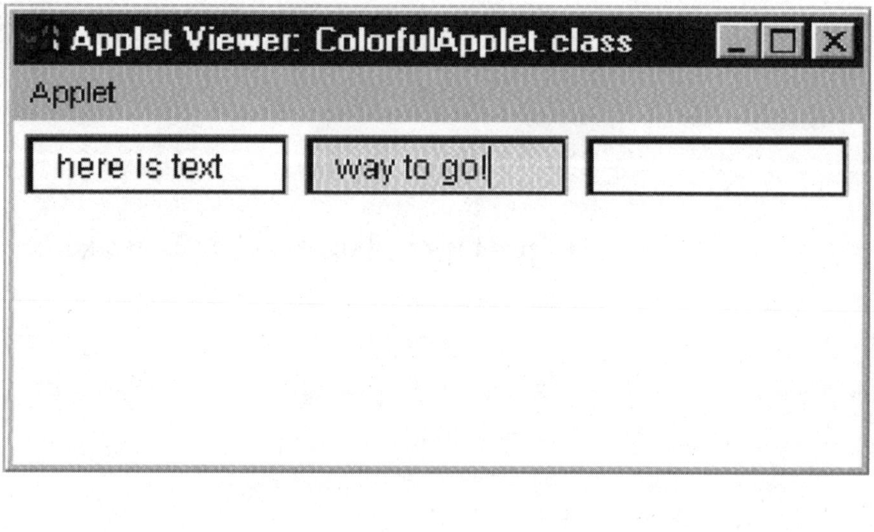

Figure 15-3
An applet with
colorful text fields.

are simply stubs and do nothing but clutter up your source code. Rather than creating a bunch of useless no-op methods, you can extend a Java class that has already taken the trouble of doing this.

There's an `Adapter` class to match most of the available interfaces. Each `Adapter` class defines no-op stubs for the methods declared in the corresponding interface. For reference, here is the complete list of the `Adapter` classes:

- `ComponentAdapter`:   Implements the `ComponentListener` interface and handles `ComponentEvent` events

- `ContainerAdapter`:   Implements the `ContainerListener` interface and handles `ContainerEvent` events

- `FocusAdapter`:   Implements the `FocusListener` interface and handles `FocusEvent` events

- `KeyAdapter`:   Implements the `KeyListener` interface and handles `KeyEvent` events

- `MouseAdapter`:   Implements the `MouseListener` interface and handles `MouseEvent` events

- `MouseMotionAdapter`:   Implements the `MouseMotionListener` interface and handles `MouseMotionEvent` events

- `WindowAdapter`:   Implements the `WindowListener` interface and handles `WindowEvent` events

The listeners in the `javax.swing.event` package also have adapters. These adapters include

- `InternalFrameAdapter`, which implements the `InternalFrameListener` interface

- `MouseInputAdapter`, which implements the `MouseInputListener` interface

The Swing adapters are not covered on the programmer exam.

Extending an `Adapter` class only makes sense when the object that will listen for and handle the event has no other responsibilities. If you want your applet to handle the event, as in the scribble example, then it must implement the appropriate listener interface, since Java does not have multiple inheritance of implementation.

Exercise 15-3

Rewrite Exercise 15-2 using an `Adapter` class, rather than implementing more than one listener interface. If possible, eliminate the need to write no-op stubs.

Answers to the Exercises

Exercise 15-1

```
import java.awt.*;
import java.awt.event.*;
import java.applet.Applet;
public class HelpApplet extends Applet {
    public void init() {
        Button b;
        Panel p = new Panel();
        setLayout(new BorderLayout());
        HelpLabel label = new HelpLabel();
        b = new Button("Arcturus");
        b.addMouseListener(label);
        p.add(b);
        b = new Button("Betelgeuse");
        b.addMouseListener(label);
        p.add(b);
        b = new Button("Centauri");
        b.addMouseListener(label);
        p.add(b);
        add("North", p);
        add("South", label);
    }
}
class HelpLabel extends Label implements MouseListener {
    public void mouseEntered(MouseEvent e) {
        Button b = (Button)(e.getComponent());
        String s = "Writes " + b.getLabel() + " to the
        standard output";
        setText(s);
    }
    public void mouseClicked(MouseEvent e) {
        Button b = (Button)(e.getComponent());
        System.out.println(b.getLabel());
```

```
        }
        // Left-over MouseListener methods.
        public void mousePressed(MouseEvent e) { }
        public void mouseReleased(MouseEvent e) { }
        public void mouseExited(MouseEvent e) { }
    }
```

Exercise 15-2

```java
import java.awt.*;
import java.awt.event.*;
import java.applet.Applet;
public class ColorfulApplet extends Applet {
    public void init() {
        for (int i = 0; i < 3; i++) {
            TFHandler tfHandler = new TFHandler();
            TextField tf = new TextField(10);
            tf.addFocusListener(tfHandler);
            tf.addKeyListener(tfHandler);
            add(tf);
        }
    }
}
class TFHandler implements FocusListener, KeyListener {
    public void focusGained(FocusEvent e) {
        e.getComponent().setBackground(Color.red);
    }
    public void focusLost(FocusEvent e) {
        e.getComponent().setBackground(Color.white);
    }
    public void keyTyped(KeyEvent e) {
        if (e.getKeyChar() == '!')
            e.getComponent().setBackground(Color.yellow);
    }
    // Left-over Listener events.
    public void keyPressed(KeyEvent e) { }
    public void keyReleased(KeyEvent e) { }
}
```

Exercise 15-3

The import statements and the `Applet` class are the same as Exercise 15–2. Here is the new event handler:

```
class TFHandler extends KeyAdapter implements FocusListener
{

   public void focusGained(FocusEvent e) {
      e.getComponent().setBackground(Color.red);
   }
   public void focusLost(FocusEvent e) {
      e.getComponent().setBackground(Color.white);
   }
   public void keyTyped(KeyEvent e) {
      if (e.getKeyChar() == '!')
         e.getComponent().setBackground(Color.yellow);
   }
}
```

QUESTIONS

1. Given an object named `myHandler` whose class implements the `FocusListener` interface, how can you tell a component named component that `myHandler` should receive all focus events?

   a) `component.add(myHandler);`

   b) `component.addListener(myHandler);`

   c) `addFocusListener(component, myHandler);`

   d) `component.addFocusListener(myHandler);`

2. Which messages appear in the standard output whenever the user clicks the button named "Click me!" given the following code?

```
import java.awt.*;
import java.awt.event.*;
import java.applet.Applet;
public class ClickExample extends Applet {
   public void init() {
      Button b = new Button("Click me!");
      b.addMouseListener(new OurClickHandler());
      add(b);
   }
}
class OurClickHandler implements MouseListener {
```

```
public void actionPerformed(ActionEvent e) {
    System.out.println("button action");
}
public void mouseClicked(MouseEvent e) {
    System.out.println("button clicked");
}
// Left-over interface methods.
public void mousePressed(MouseEvent e) { }
public void mouseReleased(MouseEvent e) { }
public void mouseEntered(MouseEvent e) { }
public void mouseExited(MouseEvent e) { }
}
```

a) button action
b) button clicked
c) both button action and button clicked
d) neither of these messages

3. If you need to create a class that will handle keystrokes as the user types, and if your new class will not need to extend any other class, you can

a) extend `KeyAdapter` to implement your new class
b) implement `KeyListener`
c) implement `ActionListener`
d) either a or b
e) either a, b, or c

4. AWT generates an action event for all of the following situations, except

a) the user clicks a list item
b) the user clicks a button
c) the user types text into a text field and hits Enter
d) the user selects a menu item

5. To identify when the user has closed a window, you can implement which listener interface?

a) `MouseListener`
b) `ActionListener`
c) `WindowListener`
d) all of these

Answers to the Review Questions

1. d. Use `component.addFocusListener()` to register the listener.

2. b. The message button action does not appear because the code never registers the instance of `MyClickHandler` as one of the button's `ActionListeners` (also, it does not declare that it implements the `ActionListener` interface).

3. d. Either extending `KeyAdapter` or implementing `KeyListener` are probably your best choices. An action event is only generated for a text field (for example) when the user hits Enter, and so is not best suited for processing keystrokes as the user types.

4. a. The user must double-click a list item to generate an action event. Single-clicking a list item causes AWT to generate an item event.

5. c. `WindowListener` interface defines methods called `windowClosing()` and `windowClosed()` that you can override to detect when the user has closed a window.

CHAPTER 16

Inner Classes

An inner class is a class defined within another class. For the exam, you'll need to know how to declare and use inner classes. We haven't covered inner classes in previous chapters, so we'll cover this now as the last item you'll need to know for the programmer exam.

Objectives for This Chapter

- Define inner classes.
- Use anonymous classes.
- Use `static` inner classes.

Inner Classes

In Java 1.1 and later, you can define classes inside other classes. If you define an inner class at the same level as the enclosing class' instance variables, the inner class can access those instance variables, no matter what their access control (even `private`), just as a method can access the variables of the class in which it is defined. If you define an inner class within a method, the inner class can access the enclosing class' instance variables and also the local variables and parameter for that method.

If you reference local variables or parameters from an inner class, those variables or parameters must be declared as final to help guarantee data integrity. (A new feature in Java 1.1 is that parameters and local variables can now be declared final.)

Creating Inner Classes

Creating inner classes enables you to better organize your classes in tune with your program. For example, if a class is really only used by one other class, that class can be placed within the class that refers to it. In a sense, the first class owns the helper class.

Here's an example (you already saw this program in Chapter 11, "Input/Output"). This applet displays a new number every second. It displayed prime numbers in red and non-primes in blue:

```java
import java.awt.*;
import java.applet.Applet;
public class Ex1 extends Applet {
    Color color = Color.red;
    int candidate = 3;
    PrimeThread prime;
    public void init() {
        prime = new PrimeThread(this);
        prime.start();
    }
    public void paint(Graphics g) {
        g.setColor(color);
        g.drawString(new Integer(candidate).toString(), 30,
        40);
    }
}
class PrimeThread extends Thread {
    Ex1 target;
    PrimeThread (Ex1 target) {
        this.target = target;
    }
    public void run() {
        int candidate;
        for (candidate = 3; ; candidate++) {
            if (isPrime(candidate))
                target.color = Color.red;
            else
                target.color = Color.blue;
            target.candidate = candidate;
            target.repaint();
            try {
                sleep(1000);
            } catch (InterruptedException ie) {
            }
        }
    }
    public boolean isPrime(int number) {
        boolean isPrime = true;
        for (int i = 2; i < number-1 && isPrime; i++) {
            if ( (number % i ) == 0)
                isPrime = false;
        }
        return isPrime;
    }
}
```

Let's take this applet and turn `PrimeThread` into an inner class. When we do this, we'll no longer have to keep tabs on the applet itself in the target variable. Now `PrimeThread`, as an inner class, can directly reference its enclosing class' variables and methods:

```
import java.awt.*;
import java.applet.Applet;
public class Ex2 extends Applet {
   Color color = Color.red;
   int candidate = 3;
   public void init() {
      new PrimeThread().start();
   }
   public void paint(Graphics g) {
      g.setColor(color);
      g.drawString(new Integer(candidate).toString(), 30,
      40);
   }
   class PrimeThread extends Thread {
      public void run() {
         for ( ; ; candidate++) {
            if (isPrime(candidate))
               color = Color.red;
            else
               color = Color.blue;
            repaint();
            try {
               sleep(1000);
            } catch (InterruptedException ie) {
            }
         }
      }
      public boolean isPrime(int number) {
         boolean isPrime = true;
         for (int i = 2; i < number-1 && isPrime; i++) {
            if ( (number % i ) == 0)
               isPrime = false;
         }
         return isPrime;
      }
   }
}
```

We can go even further and move this class definition into the applet's `init()` method so that the new class is declared right before we create an instance of it, just as we might declare a variable right before its use:

```
import java.awt.*;
import java.applet.Applet;
public class Ex3 extends Applet {
    Color color = Color.red;
    int candidate = 3;
    public void init() {
        class PrimeThread extends Thread {
            public void run() {
                for ( ; ; candidate++) {
                    if (isPrime(candidate))
                        color = Color.red;
                    else
                        color = Color.blue;
                    repaint();
                    try {
                        sleep(1000);
                    } catch (InterruptedException ie) {
                    }
                }
            }
            public boolean isPrime(int number) {
                boolean isPrime = true;
                for (int i = 2; i < number-1 && isPrime; i++) {
                    if ( (number % i ) == 0)
                        isPrime = false;
                }
                return isPrime;
            }
        }
        new PrimeThread().start();
    }
    public void paint(Graphics g) {
        g.setColor(color);
        g.drawString(new Integer(candidate).toString(), 30, 40);
    }
}
```

Where you define your class is in part a matter of style. You should define your classes where they make the most sense in your design. If you'd like to refer to the current instance of the enclosing class, you can write

`EnclosingClassName.this`

If you need to refer to the inner class using a fully qualified name, you can write

`EnclosingClassName.InnerClassName`

Anonymous Classes

You can also define an *anonymous* class, a class without a name. What does this mean? If we were to rewrite the prime number applet to define `PrimeNumber` as an anonymous thread, we could rewrite the `init()` applet like this:

```
public void init() {
    Thread t = new Thread() {
        //The old PrimeThread definition goes here  . . .
    };
    t.start();
}
```

As you can see, the `new` expression states that it is creating an instance of class `Thread`. Actually, it is creating a subclass of `Thread` that we have not named, though we have supplied a definition for this subclass. In addition, note the ending semicolon for an anonymous class, which is defined like a statement, so it needs a semicolon at the end.

Anonymous classes cannot have constructors. Java invokes their superclass constructor implicitly. Anonymous classes are great if you have a simple class that's pretty much self-documenting because of the straightforward code and familiar context. This might not necessarily be the case with the `PrimeThread` class we were working with, so in that case, an inner class with a name might be a better choice.

Static Inner Classes

If your inner class is not defined as `static`, you can only create new instances of this class from a non-`static` method. `static` inner classes don't receive an implicit `OuterClass.this` pointer and this is why they can be instantiated from a `static` method in an enclosing class. Here's an example of a `static` inner class:

```
public class Outer
{
```

```
   private StaticInner a = new StaticInner();
   private NonStaticInner b = new NonStaticInner();
   static class StaticInner
   {
      public String getName()
      {
      return "StaticInner";
      }
      public String getOuterName()
      {
         // this line will not compile since class is static
         //return Outer.this.getName();
         return "I can't do that";
      }
   }
   class NonStaticInner
   {
      public String getName()
      {
       return "NonStaticInner";
      }
      public String getOuterName()
      {
       return Outer.this.getName();
      }
   }
   public String getName()
   {
    return "Outer";
   }
   public static void main(String args[])
   {
      Outer o = new Outer();
      System.out.println(o.getName());
      System.out.println(o.a.getName());
      System.out.println(o.b.getName());
      System.out.println(o.a.getOuterName());
      System.out.println(o.b.getOuterName());
   }
}
```

Exercise 16-1

In this exercise, you'll update a program written in Chapter 15, "Events," to use inner classes. First, start with this simple applet:

```
import java.awt.*;
import java.awt.event.*;
import java.applet.Applet;
```

```
public class ClickApplet extends Applet {
   public void init() {
      Button b = new Button("Click me!");
      b.addMouseListener(new OurClickHandler());
      add(b);
   }
}
class OurClickHandler implements MouseListener {
   public void mouseClicked(MouseEvent e) {
      System.out.println("button clicked");
   }
   // Left-over interface methods.
   public void mousePressed(MouseEvent e) { }
   public void mouseReleased(MouseEvent e) { }
   public void mouseEntered(MouseEvent e) { }
   public void mouseExited(MouseEvent e) { }
}
```

Now turn `OurClickHandler` into an inner class, define it within the
`init()` method, and then make it an anonymous class. One question
you may have is, how do you implement an interface as an anonymous class? You cannot use `implements` with an anonymous class.
Try your solution, and if you have questions check out the answer.

Answers to the Exercises

Exercise 16-1

Here's the original program, now with an inner class:

```
import java.awt.*;
import java.awt.event.*;
import java.applet.Applet;
public class ClickApplet1 extends Applet {
   public void init() {
      Button b = new Button("Click me!");
      b.addMouseListener(new OurClickHandler());
      add(b);
   }
   class OurClickHandler implements MouseListener {
```

```
        public void mouseClicked(MouseEvent e) {
            System.out.println("button clicked");
        }
        // Left-over interface methods.
        public void mousePressed(MouseEvent e) { }
        public void mouseReleased(MouseEvent e) { }
        public void mouseEntered(MouseEvent e) { }
        public void mouseExited(MouseEvent e) { }
    }
}
```

Here's how we can place the class within the init() method itself, bringing it very close to where the instance is used:

```
import java.awt.*;
import java.awt.event.*;
import java.applet.Applet;
public class ClickApplet2 extends Applet {
    public void init() {
        Button b = new Button("Click me!");
        class OurClickHandler implements MouseListener {
            public void mouseClicked(MouseEvent e) {
                System.out.println("button clicked");
            }
            // Left-over interface methods.
            public void mousePressed(MouseEvent e) { }
            public void mouseReleased(MouseEvent e) { }
            public void mouseEntered(MouseEvent e) { }
            public void mouseExited(MouseEvent e) { }
        }
        b.addMouseListener(new OurClickHandler());
        add(b);
    }
}
```

As for the anonymous interface implementation, you would normally write it as if it were an instance of an interface, but here this is not possible. What's happening is that Java extends class Object and implements the interface. Here's a solution:

```
import java.awt.*;
import java.awt.event.*;
import java.applet.Applet;
public class ClickApplet3 extends Applet {
```

```
public void init() {
    Button b = new Button("Click me!");
    b.addMouseListener(myClickHandler());
    add(b);
}
private MouseListener myClickHandler() {
    return new MouseListener() {
        public void mouseClicked(MouseEvent e) {
            System.out.println("button clicked");
        }
        // Left-over interface methods.
        public void mousePressed(MouseEvent e) { }
        public void mouseReleased(MouseEvent e) { }
        public void mouseEntered(MouseEvent e) { }
        public void mouseExited(MouseEvent e) { }
    };
}
}
```

Similarly, it's easy to rewrite the first program in Chapter 15 (`Scribble.java`) so that the adapter classes are inner classes or even anonymous classes. You could also extend `MouseAdapter` here; the returned anonymous class would start out as

```
return new MouseAdapter() {  . . .  }
```

QUESTIONS ▆ ▆ ▆ ▆ ▆ ▆ ▆ ▆

1. `static` classes receive an implicit `OuterClass.this` pointer.
   a. True
   b. False

2. How can you rewrite the following two classes so that the second becomes an inner class of the first? (The resulting program should still work like the original.)

```
class First {
    public static void main(String[] args) {
        new Second().sayGoodnightGracy();
    }
```

```
   }
class Second extends First {
   void sayGoodnightGracy() {
      System.out.println("Goodnight, Gracy");
   }
}
```

a.

```
class First {
   public static void main(String[] args) {
      System.out.println("Goodnight, Gracy");
   }
}
```

b.

```
class First {
   public static void main(String[] args) {
      new First() {
         void sayGoodnightGracy() {
            System.out.println("Goodnight, Gracy");
         }
      };
   }
}
```

c.

```
class First {
   public static void main(String[] args) {
      new Second().sayGoodnightGracy();
   }
   class Second extends First {
      void sayGoodnightGracy() {
         System.out.println("Goodnight, Gracy");
      }
   }
}
```

d.

```
class First {
   public static void main(String[] args) {
      new First().test();
   }
   void test() {
      new Second().sayGoodnightGracy();
   }
   class Second extends First {
      void sayGoodnightGracy() {
         System.out.println("Goodnight, Gracy");
      }
   }
}
```

3. Java invokes the superclass constructor for anonymous classes implicitly.

   a. True

   b. False

ANSWERS

1. **b.** False. static inner classes do not receive an implicit `OuterClass.this` pointer.

2. **d.** Only this program defines an inner class that keeps the output of the original code. Answer c does not work because you cannot define an inner class within a `static` method if the inner class is not also declared as `static`.

3. **a.** True. Anonymous classes cannot have constructors. Java invokes their superclass constructor implicitly.

Studying for the Developer's Exam

CHAPTER 17

The Developer
Exam Roadmap

In this chapter, we'll introduce the topics covered in the Sun-certified developer exam for the Java 2 platform (Exam number 310–027). The developer exam consists of two parts:

1. A programming assignment
2. A short-answer essay exam

The programming assignment asks you to develop part of an application. The short-answer essay exam asks you questions about the coding assignment.

A Quick Overview

First, you take the programmer exam, Exam number 310–020. If you pass, you can proudly call yourself a Sun-certified Java programmer. You can then download a programming assignment from a Web site that you must complete as part of your developer certification. Once you complete the assignment and sign up for the developer exam, you can upload the assignment on the Web site and take the exam. Once you submit a successful programming assignment and pass the developer exam, you become a Sun-certified Java developer, which is the highest level of Java certification. Figure 17-1 shows your path to developer certification, starting with taking the Java Programmer exam.

The programming assignment consists of a complete set of specifications that you must implement. Some code is already completed for you. You can download this assignment from a Web site after you have passed the programmer exam. You can do this assignment as your schedule allows and upload it once you have finished. The developer exam consists of five to 10 short-answer questions regarding the assignment. These questions ask you to justify your design choices.

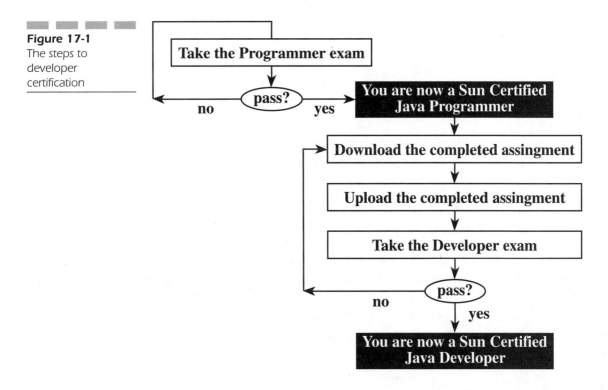

Figure 17-1
The steps to
developer
certification

Concepts You Should Know Before Getting Started

The Sun-certified developer exam is designed to test your knowledge of Java software development. You'll need to be intimately familiar with the Java language and the Java 2 API to complete and pass the assignment. The specific concepts and technologies covered by the exam include

- Client-server application design
- Interface design

- Error handling
- Event handling
- I/O streams
- Java Swing
- JDBC
- Multithreading
- Object serialization
- RMI
- TCP/IP networking
- Using Javadoc

The remaining chapters in this part of the book provide an overview of key concepts that haven't been covered previously. For specifics on multithreading, error handling, event handling, I/O streams, and object serialization, you should refer to the appropriate chapter in Part I.

The Programming Assignment

The programming assignment is the first part of the exam. Once you've paid for the exam, you'll be notified that you have permission to download the programming assignment from the Sun Educational Services Database. In the programming assignment Jar file, you'll find the following:

- A document that introduces the assignment and provides an index
- Source code that serves as a starting point for the assignment
- A flat text data file that you must convert to the required format for use in the assignment

These files contain different programs and assignments for different candidates. The idea is that multiple candidates won't be able to collaborate because of this. The instructions provided in the documentation leave gaps intentionally so that candidates must make and document design decisions. When you complete the assignment, you can upload it to Sun's Web site.

The programming assignment requires the following features:

- A *graphical user interface* (GUI) for viewing information
- Communications functionality to connect the user interface with the database
- Extensions to the database to support a more flexible search and record-locking mechanism
- Network server functionality for the database systems
- Data conversion to prepare a flat text file for use in the database

The instructions you'll see from Sun are a bit more specific, such as the following:

1. Write an application program in Java. The application requires the following:

   a. A GUI demonstrating good principles of design
   b. A network connection using a specified protocol to connect to an information server that supplies the data for display in the user interface
   c. A network server that connects to a previously specified Java database
   d. A database created by extending the functionality of a previously written piece of code, for which only limited documentation is available

2. List the main choices to be made during the implementation of the above.

3. List the main advantages and disadvantages of those choices.

4. Briefly justify the choices made in terms of the comparison of design and implementation objectives. List the advantages and disadvantages of each.

Feedback on passing the developer programming assignment and exam is not immediate, because there are no absolute right or wrong answers. The programming is graded based on a set of criteria that includes good object-oriented design, documentation, efficiency, and style. You should follow the directions that come with the programming assignment as closely as possible.

Although the examiner grades the assignment for correct operations, the actual grade you receive is based on many factors. These factors are graded on a point system with a total of 155 points possible. The factors and the possible points include

- Overall ease of use and user-friendliness of the assignment (15 points)
- Clarity and maintainability of the design and implementation. The code should be designed so that it can be easily understood and modified without requiring global changes (seven points)
- Consistent and logical approach to the design implementation in which the best algorithms are used and the solution is well thought out (20 points)
- Consistent coding style, naming conventions, and indentation (15 points)
- Documentation of obvious and non-obvious aspects of source code as well as use of the Javadoc source documentation, user documentation, and a README file (six points)
- Extensions to the database to support standard, flexible search algorithms (eight points)
- Implementing proper error-handling in the server and network interface (six points)
- Layout of the user interface with proper use of GUIs and proper implementation of event handling (20 points)
- Object-oriented design with appropriate use of standard elements and design patters (six points)
- Proper use of record locking in the database (15 points)
- Proper use of thread-safe design in the server and network interface (eight points)
- Satisfying the data conversion requirements (10 points)
- Use of standard classes and interfaces from the Java 2 API, rather than custom classes and interfaces (five points)

- Use of standard Java exception-handling facilities and the ability to communicate errors to users without the program exiting abnormally (10 points)

As you work through the assignment, you'll want to refer to this list periodically. Although the exact weighting of a specific point may change over time, the relative importance of various points should remain consistent.

The programming assignment and exam are graded by professionals outside of Sun, who are consultants in the business of providing high-level Java services. Sun Educational Services doesn't want to be accused of having a vested interest in who passes and fails, so they farm this job out. If there's a borderline case, however, the exam might go back into JavaSoft. JavaSoft engineers will then grade the test and act as a moderator. Sun will contact you to let you know the results. You should allow 30 days for the grading to be completed.

The Essay Exam

You should sign up for the essay exam once you have completed and uploaded your programming assignment. You must be sure you pass the automated tests based on the test harness, because you'll fail immediately if you submit code that fails the test harness. Instructions in the programming assignment explain how to write your code so that the test harness can interact with it and perform its tests.

The essay exam consists of five to 10 short-answer essay questions with a 90-minute time limit. These questions ask you to discuss what you did on the programming assignment and to justify your design decisions. There are no absolute right or wrong answers. The people grading your assignment and the exam will look for your understanding of the issues involved.

As with the programmer certification, the written portion of the developer certification is administered on PCs by a company called Sylvan Prometric. They have test centers all over the U.S. and the world. When you show up, you must sign in, identify yourself by showing two forms of ID (one with a picture, and both with signatures), and then you take the test at your scheduled time.

You can't bring any paper into or out of the testing room. They don't want you taking a crib sheet in with you or writing out test questions during the test. (Of course, once you leave the testing area, you can try to recall as many questions as possible. However, be aware that the tests are copyrighted, so you can't turn around and publish the questions, make copies of them, and so on.) You also can't bring in any pagers or cellular phones. After all, in this day and age, it would be a simple matter to have your local Java guru talk you through the test. Even though you can't take any paper in with you, the people at Sylvan Prometric do give you either some scratch paper or a small marker board and a marker to help you work out answers.

Your answers should be clear, concise, and well though out. You'll need to justify your answers based on the assignment, so you should thoroughly review everything you've done on the assignment before taking the essay exam. When you complete the exam, you won't know whether you've passed or not (though you might have a good feel for how things went). You'll be notified by Sun when the grading is completed.

How to Sign Up for and Take the Exams

You must call Sun and buy a voucher (or get a voucher from your company, who has in turn purchased a voucher through Sun). The idea behind the voucher system is that your company may offer vouchers for free or at a discount if they are encouraging you to become certified.

The number for Sun Educational Services in the U.S. is 1–800–422–8020. Listen to the options from the phone menu and make sure you tell them what test you want to sign up for. Outside the U.S., check out the Web site at `http://suned.sun.com/suned/` for additional phone numbers.

The good people at Sun will ask for a credit card to pay for the voucher. You must then wait for the voucher to arrive before you can sign up for the test. They send the vouchers by FedEx, so you'll receive any vouchers you purchase by the next business day. Once you get it, don't misplace it; it's like money. You can't replace them and if you drop it on the street, that's that. Some random person can pick it up and go take a Java test.

The voucher is supposed to be good for up to one year after you purchase it. However, mine came with an expiration date of seven months after the purchase that cannot be extended, but here's the loophole. After you sign up for a testing appointment, you can extend the appointment for up to one year.

You may have your voucher, but you're not done yet. You've still got to register for the test. You can do this by calling Sylvan Prometric. Their number is 1–800–795-EXAM (1–800–795–3926). You'll have to give them your social security number for identification, and they'll ask you some questions, such as which company you're with, your phone number, and your address. Then they'll schedule you for a test.

When they schedule you, they'll find a time that's convenient for you to visit one of their testing centers. You need to be there on time, because you can't stay past your stop time; the computer will shut you off. They distribute the test electronically to your test center. According to a person I spoke with at Sylvan, you need to be there when the test is ready to go. If they can fit you in the next day and that's what you want, they'll do their best to accommodate you. The only possible problem might be that a space is not available at the test center closest to you. You'll also need to bring two forms of ID, one of which must be a photo ID, just so that your friendly neighborhood Java expert doesn't show up in your place as a ringer. If you want to postpone for some reason, if you're panicking, or if you just can't make it, you can do so up until the day before the test.

How to Acquire the Programming Assignment for the Developer Test

After you've taken and passed the programmer exam, you can obtain the programming assignment that's part of developer certification. You obtain the assignment by downloading it off the Web and enter your last name and social security number (which is your Sylvan candidate ID). You should allow at least a week after passing the exam for Sylvan to let Sun know that you passed and for Sun to update their server. Until then, the server will say "user not found." Don't worry; the records will be updated as soon as they can get to them. If you've allowed a week to go by and it really looks like the server is not being updated, you can call Sun Educational Services, explain the situation, and they'll patch you through to someone who can help you.

Once your record has been updated, entering your last name and candidate ID will bring you to a screen that displays your current status in the testing cycle. If you have passed the programmer exam, you'll see a button on the bottom of the screen that says "Download assignment." Go ahead and click that for instructions on how to access the assignment.

Once you've downloaded the archive file that contains the assignment, you'll see a new button back on the page you just came from. This button reads "Upload assignment." When you're all done, you'll come back here, click this button, and upload your work to Sun. You'll get a number of files, including a postscript document, a Word for Windows document, and an *Rich Text Format* (RTF) document, all containing the same instructions. Also, some `.gif` images show some design diagrams as well as a number of source and class files that you'll use as part of your programming assignment.

The first thing you should do, before even reading over the documents, is to make backups of everything. The test is customized for you, and you need to be able to get back to what you downloaded if something goes wrong or if you want to start over again.

Only after you complete this programming assignment and sign up for the developer exam can you submit your assignment for grading. You submit the assignment by uploading it through the download Web site. All of the programming assignments are carefully marked and it takes time to ensure the quality and consistency of this process.

Strategies for Approaching the Developer Assignment

First and foremost, give yourself time—a few days, if not a week or more. The assignment is long and complicated. Think about the issues. Read the design document over two, three, or four times. Print it out and mark it up.

After you've thought about the design for a while, create the user interface. Seeing a user interface can make the assignment more tangible. This is especially true if you feel overwhelmed by what to do. You'll begin to realize which pieces have to connect with which other pieces. What's more, it's comforting to have part of it done and working.

Look over the source code that comes with the assignment. That can really help you figure out what is already done for you and what you've got to write yourself.

One of the wonderful things about this assignment is a test harness that's distributed with the assignment. You can run this test harness to see if your program is working well enough to submit. Passing the test harness can go a long way towards making you feel comfortable with your work.

Also make backups of the database files before you start testing, because, depending on your particular version of the assignment, you might start changing things.

CHAPTER 18

Developing
With Java

At this point, you've reviewed all of the basics of the Java language. If you've already taken the Sun-certified Java programmer test and passed, congratulations! If you've tried the test and failed, use the experience to focus your studying on those areas you were least certain about. Use this book's objectives to help you, and work through all the exercises. Make up your own test questions based on the samples in this book and what you can remember from the exams. Sometimes you'll come up with a question that you stump yourself with. Now is the time to do so, because you can look up the answer and write programs to verify your answers before you get into the testing room. The fun part comes after you've passed the programmer exam. After you've taken the first test, it's time become a Sun-certified Java developer.

Developer certification involves two stages: completing a programming assignment (which is really the heart of it) and then answering questions about your design. Since the programming assignment is the focus, the chapters in this section concentrate on the skills you need to complete this assignment. In this part of the book, you'll work on expanding your basic programming knowledge and learning how to implement what you know to write sophisticated programs.

The assignment is graded partly on good object-oriented programming technique, especially concerning the clarity of design. It's important to use abstract classes, interfaces, and packages correctly. The person who will grade your programming assignment gives you points based on your programming style and the comments you supply. This does not mean you should provide a page of comments for each method you write—far from it! It means you must program in the style that your grader expects. This chapter will show you what that style is.

Objectives for This Chapter

- Indent your code according to common practices
- Comment on only the non-obvious lines
- Use a consistent coding style

- Handle errors appropriately
- Use `javadoc`-style comments
- Define `abstract` classes where appropriate
- Use interfaces where appropriate
- Arrange classes into packages
- Create well-defined APIs for your classes

Styles and Conventions

Every programmer knows how to indent code so that all code in a block is easy to spot. Regardless of how many spaces you indent compared to the next programmer, your main objective, whatever your style, is to be consistent.

Beware of some *integrated development environments* (IDEs) with their own code editors. Some of these automatically indent code for you, and you're probably apt to use the tab key in these editors. That's fine, but take a look at your code using a plain ASCII editor at some point. You might find that what looks good in the editor with your IDE doesn't look so hot with another editor. If this is the case, you might want to think about changing your tabs to spaces and making sure that no matter what editor Sun engineers use to view your program, it's going to look the way you intended.

Identifiers

Again, you can use any style you would like to, but be consistent. A common practice is to make your class names start with a capital letter, and your variable and method names start with a lower-case letter. Usually, identifiers that are really multiple words, like "max value" and "the applet," start with a small letter but have a capital at the start of each word, such as `maxValue` and `theApplet`.

Another common practice is to make constants, usually defined as `public static final`, all upper-case and connect words with an underscore, as in `MAX_VALUE` and `THE_APPLET`. Names also are usually self-documenting. Unless it's a temporary variable, you might want to use descriptive names like `maxValue`, instead of `m`, for example. However, it's common to name temporary variables (such as loop indexes or nested user interface objects such as panels) with just a letter or two.

TIP: If you have a style you're comfortable with, don't change it just for this programming assignment. If you do, it might cause you to inadvertently mix styles and that's what you're trying to avoid.

Comments

Most programmers hate documentation. If you do too, this next piece of advice might not apply to you. I am one of those who likes comments; I feel the more, the better. However, be aware that you'll lose points if you put in excessive comments. In particular, you should not comment lines that essentially document themselves. You should only include comments for those lines that are tricky or not immediately obvious.

Error Handling

Sometimes it's easy to fall into a trap where you let your application take a guess at what to do, even when it encounters an unexpected situation. For example, consider the following `switch-case` statements:

```
switch (userSelection) {
  case MOVE: moveItem(); break;
  case DELETE: deleteItem(); break;
}
```

What if `userSelection` is not equal to either MOVE or DELETE? Should you do nothing? Or perhaps you should add a default case:

```
switch (userSelection) {
 case MOVE: moveItem(); break;
 case DELETE: deleteItem(); break;
 default: editItem();
}
```

In this case, what you should do really depends on whether userSelection is supposed to absolutely, positively equal either MOVE or DELETE. If it is but doesn't equal either one, then this is a serious problem. You may even want to throw an exception:

```
switch (userSelection) {
 case MOVE: moveItem(); break;
 case DELETE: deleteItem(); break;
 default: throw
   new UserSelectionException("Should be move or delete");
}
```

NOTE: We have assumed there is a class defined for this application called UserSelectionException.

It might be tempting to throw an unchecked exception, rather than make your own exception class. For example, you might think you could throw NumberFormatException or ArithmeticException if a number is not in the right format or if you are about to divide by 0. The problem is that you should never throw an unchecked exception from your own code. As we reviewed in Chapter 8, "Exceptions," you should only throw checked exceptions, which must be caught.

Another problem with throwing a generic, unchecked exception is that it does not fully identify the application-specific problem. Perhaps the problem with the number not being in the right format is a protocol error. It might make better sense to create a new class called `ProtocolException` and throw that when an error arises. By supplying a message for this object before you throw it, your exception handler can display this message to help with debugging.

When you handle the error, also give some thought about what it is you would like to do in your catch block. Should you print out a debugging message, end the application, or take a guess as to what to do? You might want to do something differently each time, but similar problems should be handled in similar ways. Remember your credo: be consistent.

Java's Documentation Problem

In C/C++, documentation is often placed into header files. This is because a header file contains the function definitions and variables shared by more than one program in an application. Since this file is shared by any program that needs it, the header file is the right place to put these comments. A great advantage of this approach is that a developer can distribute only the binary files for the actual program that keeps the implementation hidden but still distributes the header files that provide all the public documentation for these files as well as means for using them.

This approach does not even begin to work in Java. Why? Because there are no header files! There are no declarations of methods that are separate from their implementation (unless you've defined an `interface` or `abstract` method). All methods are implemented where they are declared. This might appear to mean that distributing documentation concerning how to use a Java package would run the risk of one of two extremes:

1. Distributing the source code that contains the in-line documentation for the public classes, variables, and methods, or

2. Keeping the documentation in separate files, far away from the original source, and potentially falling out of sync with the code

Happily, the JDK provides relief from both of these port choices by supplying a special utility called `javadoc`. This utility pulls out the important information concerning your classes, variables, and methods, and automatically generates great-looking documentation. The advantage of this approach is that you can run `javadoc` whenever you want and generate new documentation that reflects the current state of your code.

javadoc

When you run `javadoc` and pass it the name of a class or package, `javadoc` generates documentation in HTML format for all of your public classes, and your public and protected variables and methods.

You're no doubt familiar with the HTML format that `javadoc` generates, because this is the same format that the API files are published in. `javadoc` creates an HTML file for each class. Each HTML file lists the fields, then the constructors, and then the methods for a class. `javadoc` also places a class hierarchy at the top of the HTML file and provides an index to the fields, constructors, and methods after that. All you have to do to generate this documentation is run the command `javadoc` and place the resulting HTML files into the same directory as the API files for the JDK. Javadoc will generate four types of files:

- `packages.html`   A listing of each package that you generated documentation for and the class they contain
- `AllNames.html`   An alphabetical index of all of your method and variable names
- `tree.html`   A listing of all of the classes that you've generated documentation for and where these fit into the class hierarchy, going all the way back to `java.lang.Object`
- `classname.html`   Documentation for that class

Naturally, all of these files contain hypertext links to the classes, methods, and variables they refer to, including Java's own classes.

Helping javadoc

In addition to the two common ways of writing a comment:

```
//everything to the end of the line is a comment
```

and

```
/* everything in here is a comment */
```

Java also defines a special third way:

```
/** everything in here is a javadoc comment */
```

By default, this special `javadoc` comment only has meaning before a public class or before a public or protected variable or method. You can see `javadoc`-style comments for private variables or methods if you use the `-private` option when you run `javadoc`. With a `javadoc` comment, you can help `javadoc` to document your code. For example, here is a simple class definition:

```java
public class PrimeNumber {
  private int number;
  public int getNumber() {
   return number;
  }
  public void setNumber(int num) {
   number = num;
  }
  public boolean isPrime() { /* code to test number */ }
}
```

`javadoc` automatically generates the documentation shown in Figures 18-1 and 18-2. These show the top and bottom half of a Web browser displaying the file that `javadoc` generated.

This is fine, but what you'd really like to do is add some of your own comments to this documentation. By adding documentation to this class using special `javadoc` comments, like this

```java
/**
 * Identify a number as prime or not prime.
 */
public class PrimeNumber {
  private int number;
  /** Retrieve the number. */
  public int getNumber() {
  return number;
  }
```

```
/** Set the number. */
public void setNumber(int num) {
number = num;
}
/** Test whether the number is a prime. */
public boolean isPrime() { /* code to test number */ }
}
```

you can generate the documentation shown in Figures 18–3 and 18–4.

Figure 18-1

The javadoc-generated index

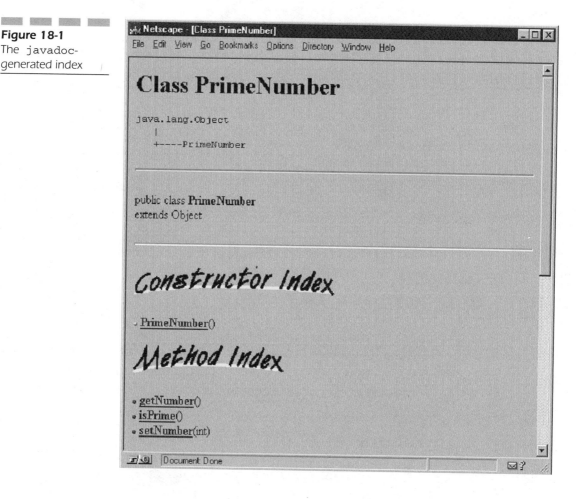

Figure 18-2
The javadoc-
generated method
documentation

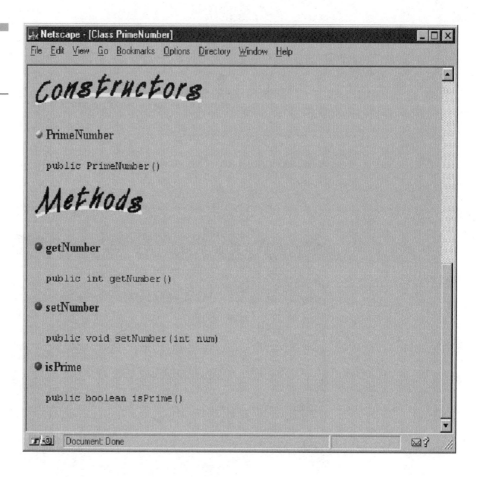

Figure 18-2
The javadoc-
generated method
documentation

javadoc Tags

You can also use special tags within your javadoc comments. javadoc seeks out these tags and creates special documentation based on them. First, let's look at the tags and then we'll look at some examples of how to use them and their resulting documentation.

Variables

When you define a variable, you can use an @see tag to reference a different object or method. There are a few versions of this tag. First, here's the format for @see to refer to a class:

Figure 18-3
The javadoc index
with comments

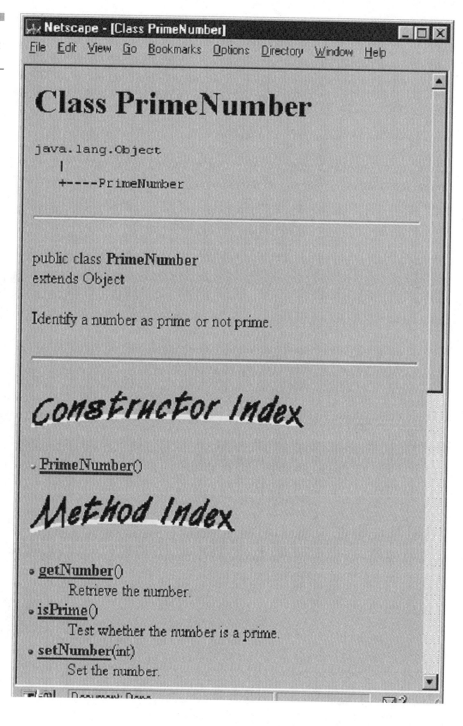

Figure 18-4
The javadoc
methods with
comments

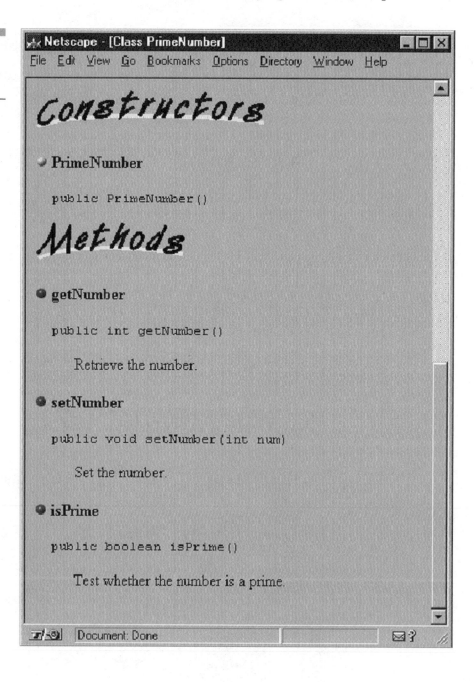

```
@see classname
```

The `classname` can simply be the class' name if the class is in the same package as the class defining the comment. The `classname` can also be fully qualified if it's in a different package. For example, if `Lightning` is the name of a class, you can write

```
@see Lightning
```

or

```
@see phenomenon.natural.Lightning
```

You can also reference a method name using the `@see` tag by writing:

```
@see classname#method
```

For example, you might write:

```
@see Lightning#flash
```

As before, you can also fully qualify the class name. The `@see` tag can refer to a package just like it can refer to a class, method or other API. Other forms of the `@see` tag use labels and hypertext links:

```
@see name label
@see <a href="linkURL">Link title</a>
```

You can also use `@link` to create inline text links:

```
@link APIName label
```

Now instead of the link appearing under the See Also heading, the link will be in the text.

Classes

You can use any of these `@see` tags with classes. There are also two other tags you can use with the class that are useful only with special keywords passed to `javadoc`. These tags are `@version` and

@author. In all cases, the text following a particular tag can go over multiple lines.

```
@version anytext
```

With @version you would typically put a version number following this tag, such as 1.0 or 2.1:

```
@version 1.0
```

```
@author anytext
```

With @author, you would normally place your name after this tag, as in:

```
@author Albert Einstein
```

To see these @version and @author values in the documentation, you must use the options:

```
-author -version
```

when you invoke javadoc, as in

```
javadoc -author -version MyClass.java
```

Methods

Methods can use any of the @see tags. In addition, there are three other tags that document the method's signature" @return, @param, @exception, and @throws. In all cases, the text following a particular tag can go over multiple lines.

```
@return anytext
```

For example, you might write

```
@return a true or false value indicating whether a number
  is prime
```

```
@param paramname anytext
```

For example, you might write

```
@param number a number to test to see if it is prime or
   not
```

```
@exception exceptionname anytext
```

For example, you might write

```
@exception ProtocolException Throws this exception when the
   client has not supplied data following the agreed-upon
   protocol
```

```
@throws exceptionname anytext
```

The `@throws` tag serves the sme purpose as `@exception`. The tag is added for convenience since `throws` is a Java keyword.

Rules for Using javadoc Comments and Tags

A typical `javadoc` comment and set of `javadoc` tags follows this format:

```
/**
* Summary comment line
* Any number of additional comment lines
* this could even include HTML
* @tag any number of lines provided text for this tag
*/
```

There's no need for row of asterisks along the left-hand side of the comments like this, but you'll see this done in most Java programs. However, it's perfectly acceptable to also write

```
/**
Summary comment line
Any number of additional comment lines
this could even include HTML
* @tag any number of lines provided text for this tag
*/
```

Notice that the first line in a `javadoc` comment is special. It is a summary line, and `javadoc` uses this in its indices. For example, the method index at the top of the class's HTML file displays this one sentence description, as does the index file `AllNames.html` for each method and variable. Following this summary line, you can include any number of lines you'd like to. `javadoc` will strip away any leading spaces (even any leading asterisk as in the first comment sample above) and will wrap the text as appropriate. Any HTML tags it finds it will use as is, so that you can format your documentation with references, links, bold or italic styles, or code snippets.

Always place all your tags at the end of your `javadoc` comments. Since tags can be spread over multiple lines, the only way for `javadoc` to identify the end of a tag is when it hits the start of a new one.

Examples of javadoc Comments and Tags

The following is an example of class documentation for a class called `Tester`:

```
/**
 * Test machine for objects.
 * This class tests objects for performance and accuracy
 * by executing standard tests.
 * @see CanBeTested
 * @version1.0
 * @author William Stanek
 */
public class Tester {  . . .  }
```

`Javadoc` will generate the display in Figure 18-5 based on this.

public class **Tester**
extends Object

Test machine for objects. This class tests objects for
performance and accuracy by executing standard tests.

Version:
    1.0
Author:
    Barry Boone
See Also:
    CanBeTested

Similarly, based on the following method documentation,

```
/**
 * Performs the standard text.
 * Invokes test() for the object to be tested and informs
 * this method how must testing should be performed.
 * @return A String that explains the results of the test
 * @param target The debug level
 * @see CanBeTested
 */
public String runTest(int debugLevel) {  . . .  }
```

javadoc will generate the HTML file shown in Figure 18-6.

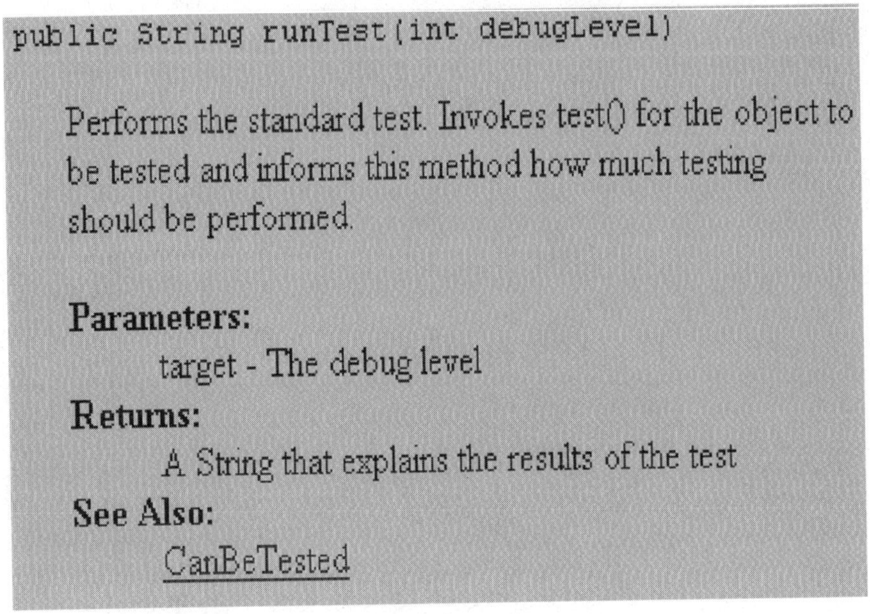

Figure 18-6
Method
documentation

```
public String runTest(int debugLevel)
```

Performs the standard test. Invokes test() for the object to be tested and informs this method how much testing should be performed.

Parameters:
> target - The debug level

Returns:
> A String that explains the results of the test

See Also:
> CanBeTested

And for this variable documentation

```
/** Debug output level.
* @see CanBeTested
*/
public int debugLevel;
```

javadoc will generate the HTML file shown in Figure 18-7.

Abstract Classes

Defining an abstract class forces you and other developers to make clear choices. We've already covered abstract classes briefly at the end of Chapter 1, "Taking the Programmer Exam," but we wanted to say a word about their role in building an API.

The big difference between an abstract class and a superclass that defines no-op stubs for its methods is that the abstract class forces you and other programmers to use your set of APIs in a particular way. Although a programmer can directly instantiate a concrete superclass, a programmer has no such option with an abstract class;

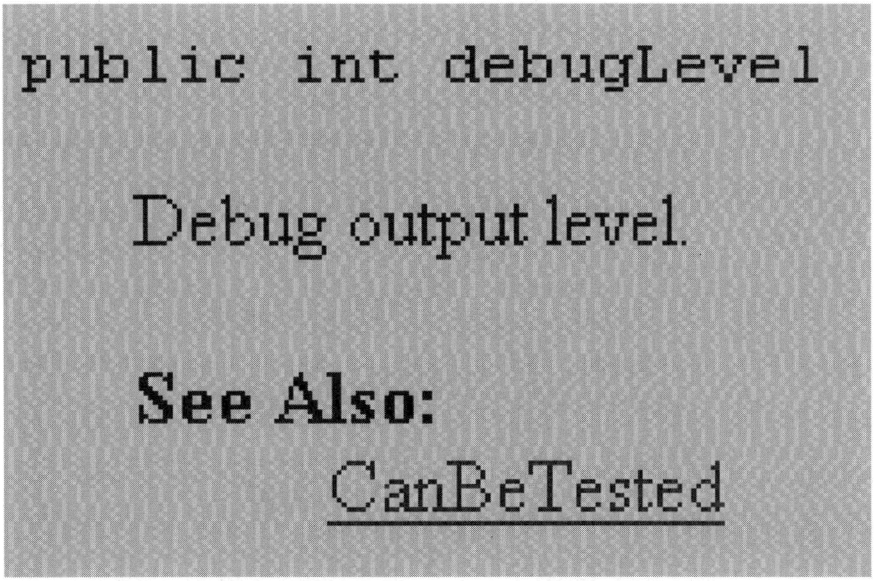

Figure 18-7
Variable
documentation

```
public int debugLevel

Debug output level.

See Also:
         CanBeTested
```

she must either instantiate a predefined subclass or create her own subclass to instantiate. This can help clarify your design.

For example, imagine a class called `Transaction` that is to be used in a home banking application. This class has two subclasses: `Deposit` and `Withdrawal`. It might not make sense to create an instance of `Transaction`; a customer doesn't generically announce to a bank teller, "I want to make a transaction," but rather, "I want to make a withdrawal," or "I want to make a deposit." (If a customer does say "I want to make a transaction," the teller will ask him to clarify his intentions.)

You can make your programmers use only a `Deposit` or `Withdrawal` class in your design by making `Transaction` abstract. By doing so, programmers using your APIs know your intention; you would like them to be specific about the type of transaction they want to perform.

TIP: You already know that if you define any `abstract` *methods, you need to make the class* `abstract`. *What if you don't have any* `abstract` *methods, but you still want to make the class* `abstract`? *Just use the* `abstract` *keyword for the class. Then any subclasses are automatically* `concrete` *classes (unless, of course, they in turn are declared as* `abstract`*)*.

Interfaces

Interfaces define constants and method signatures. Interfaces are not like `abstract` classes where all the methods are declared as `abstract`; interfaces are not classes. Instead, they define, as their name implies, an interface for you to implement.

So what good are they? Why not just define methods in a class, rather than fooling around with interfaces? The answer is that interfaces clean up your APIs. Interfaces enable you, as the developer, to clarify which sets of behavior belong together. Interfaces also help you enforce the proper use of your API.

Grouping Behavior

Identifying related behavior in one place is ideal for an interface. You can find a great example of this in Java 1.1, where interfaces identify related event methods. As one example, an interface called `FocusListener` defines `focusGained()` and `focusLost()`. It's clear that the API expects developers to supply the behavior for these two methods to be able to handle focus events.

Enforcing Your API

Since Java can identify classes that implement interfaces by using `instanceof`, interfaces can also enforce an API. Continuing with the `FocusListener` example, you must use an object whose class provides the methods `focusGained()` and `focusLost()` when you want to handle focus events. To handle focus events, you must register your object as a focus listener by using `addFocusListener()`. By declaring the parameter in this method to be an instance of type `FocusListener`, the *Java Virtual Machine* (JVM), compiler, and language, working in conjunction, will not let you pass an object whose class does not implement both methods.

Identifying Intent

Interfaces can also be used to tag a class. For example, the cloneable interface does not declare any method; there's nothing for implementers to implement. Instead, any class identified as an instance of cloneable lets the object class' `clone()` method know that this class can be cloned. The cloneable interface merely identifies the developer's intent; it does not make the developer implement any behavior.

Exercise 18-1

Image that you have developed a class named `Tester` that tests other objects. Perhaps it has a `testObject()` method that, given the name of the object to test, invokes that object's `test()` method and displays the string results in the standard output.

Naturally, you would like to use any kind of object with your `Tester` class. How can you define the API so that this will all work well and be as self-documenting as possible?

Packages

Creating packages can help you clean up your APIs in two important ways:

- You can better restrict access to methods and variables.
- You can define subsystems.

Creating Packages

Chapter 1 already covered how to create packages and place classes inside them. Here's a quick review. To tell the compiler the classes in a particular source file belong in a package, write the keyword package as the first line in your source file, followed by the package name, as in the following:

```
package MyUtils.MyPackage;
```

To import `public` classes defined in other packages, specify the packages or specific classes you want to import by writing the keyword `import` followed by the package or class names, as in

```
import MyUtils.MyPackage.Average;
import MyUtils.OtherPackage.*;
```

Java will expect your packages to be in a directory structure where each dot (.) defines a new subdirectory.

Restricting Access

Here's a quick review of restricting access to members. First of all, as we reviewed in Chapter 2, only a `public` class can be accessed outside of the packages in which it is defined. As you also know, specifying access control for a class member can be done in four ways: you can use the keyword `public`, `protected`, or `private`, or you can leave off an access control keyword and accept the default. `public` and `private` have the same effect regardless of whether or not the classes you've defined are in the same package. However, `protected` and the default are greatly affected by multiple packages.

If all of your classes are in the same package (including the default package), they can access each others' members as long as those members are declared as `protected` or have no access control specifier (or are declared as `public`). Sometimes this is what you want. For example, a small class that contains some simple utility methods only meant for other classes in its package could restrict outside classes from invoking these methods by leaving off any access control keywords. But keep in mind that a lack of access control keywords should never stem from laziness; it should be your design intent. If it is appropriate for only the class defining a member to access that member, make that member `private`.

If it is possible that some other package will define a subclass for a class you have defined, and if you would like subclasses of your class to be able to access specific members in your class, you can give those specific members the `protected` keyword.

Defining Subsystems

Packages clean up your design by allowing you to think of your application as a collection of cooperating subsystems. You can think of a subsystem as a collection of related classes that accomplish a specific design goal, accomplishing one facet of your application's architecture.

For example, imagine you are creating a database client/server application. You might have a database, a database server, a TCP/IP component that runs on the client side, and a user interface for the client. Perhaps the actual data in the database contains information on birds: their songs, migration paths, and egg colors. If you can generalize the pieces of your application, you could conceivably define four different subsystems that fit the boxes shown in Figure 18-8.

In Java, you can define each of these subsystems by creating classes and placing them into packages. Each package represents one subsystem. Packages enable you to conceive of your application as a machine constructed out of "tinkertoys." On your next project, if you need a database server and a TCP/IP client that this time accesses a database of baseball cards, you can just use these packages as-is and plug them into your new application, which might look like Figure 18-9.

You can place your applet or the class with the `main()` method in a package, as well as any other classes (rather than letting it be

Figure 18-8
The four pieces of a hypothetical database client/server application

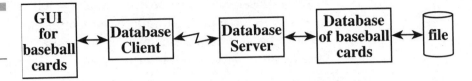

Figure 18-9
A new application
using old packages

placed in the default package). Most programmers don't do this, but this can help keep your class files organized. If you place a class defining `main()` called `MyClass` into a package named `MyPackage`, for example, you can invoke it by writing

```
java MyPackage.MyClass
```

Exercise 18-2

Consider these two class, currently defined in the same source file:

```
class Transaction {
  Amount amount;
  void process() {
  }
}
class Amount {
  int dollars;
  int cents;
}
```

Place each of these classes into a different package so that they can still access all of the same fields and methods they can access now. Call the first package banking and the second package currency.

Defining Access Methods

Rather than allowing other classes to access a class' member variables directly, you should make those members `private` and supply access methods. For example, this class enables anyone to receive and set its instance variables:

```
import java.awt.Point;

public class Circle {
 public Point position;
 public int radius;
 public boolean canDelete;
 public boolean canMove;
 }
```

This might seem okay, but perhaps you want to make sure the radius is never set to a negative number. What then? What if you want to make canMove and canDelete read-only? With the above definition, you're stuck.

The better way is to provide getter and setter methods for these values. Here's a new class definition that implements the new requirements listed in the previous paragraph. It's a little longer, but it's much more flexible. It also uses a new Exception subclass called IllegalGeometryException:

```
import java.awt.Point;

 public class Circle {
 private Point position;
 private int radius;
 private boolean canDelete;
 private boolean canMove;
 public Point getPosition() {
  return position;
 }
 public void setPosition(Point p) {
  position = p;
 }
 public int getRadius() {
  return radius;
 }
 public void setRadius(int r) throws
  IllegalGeometryException {
  if (r < 0)
   throw new IllegalGeometryException();
  radius = r;
 }
 public boolean getMove() {
  return canMove;
 }
 public boolean getDelete() {
```

```
   return canDelete;
 }
}
class IllegalGeometryException extends Exception {}
```

Defining access methods for getting and setting values for your classes is good programming practice. First, only allowing other classes to use access methods hides your class' implementation and makes these other classes much less dependent on your class' data layout.

For example, let's go back to the `Circle` class we defined above. If you decide to change `canMove` and `canDelete` into bit flags, your interface would not have to change at all. `getMove()` and `get-Delete()` would still return `boolean` values. However, rather than returning the value of a `boolean` field, your method would perform the appropriate `&` operation to mask the irrelevant bits.

Second, you can ensure an object's data integrity. Instead of enabling a class to assign arbitrary values to a field, a `setter` method can verify that the new value makes sense. If it doesn't, it can fix the problem and possibly throw an exception to inform the caller that the operation did not take place, and maybe present an indication of why. That is what we did with the radius for the `Circle` class. Similarly, a `getter` can make certain that data is in a valid and consistent state before returning this data to the caller.

Third, you have more control over the data in a multithreading environment. For example, you can make your access methods synchronized, so that one thread is not getting or setting the data while another thread manipulates it elsewhere.

TIP: *What if you have a field that contains a vector object, and some methods could change the values in the vector? If you want to ensure that no thread in a multithreaded environment accesses the vector while it's being used, you can make the methods that manipulate the vector as well as the access method synchronized.*

Fourth, you can make a value read-only or write-only if you want by only defining a `getter` or `setter`. We did this above with the canMove and canDelete fields; perhaps the value is dependent on the mode the application is in and cannot be set directly.

You can also define a method called isProperty if the property is read-only, and this approach makes sense for your code. For example, I could have defined the methods isMovable() and isDeletable(), instead of getMove() and getDelete(), but I chose not to because I'm not convinced that "deletable" is a real word (I know, details, details . . .).

Java 1.1 has introduced many getter and setter methods that used to have other inconsistent names or that used to be variables programmers could access directly. You should make sure your own APIs are as clean as Java's.

Exercise 18-3

Consider two class definitions:

```
public class Employee {
  int employeeNumber;
  Amount salary;
}
class Amount {
  int dollars;
  int cents;
}
```

Our intent is to assign an employee number for each employee when the employee object is created, and we want to number our employees sequentially. We've also created an Amount class to eliminate possible problems with rounding as far as dollars and cents goes.

These classes have three possible problems. First, anyone can set the employee number. This could lead to errors if the numbers are repeated. Second, anyone can access the employee salary and set the cents amount to something greater than 99. Third, anyone can set either the dollars or cents amount to less than 0. Modify these classes to clean up their APIs and eliminate these problems.

Answers to the Exercises

Exercise 18-1

You can define an interface, perhaps named `CanBeTested`, that declares a `test()` method, as in

```
public interface CanBeTested {
  String test();
}
```

Your `Tester` class can then require an object in its parameter list for `testObject()` that requires an instance of `CanBeTested`:

```
public class Tester {
 public void testObject(CanBeTested obj) {
   system.out.println(obj.test());
 }
}
```

Now, looking at `testObject()`, it's clear you can only use the `Tester` class if you have an instance of `CanBeTested`, which means implementing the `CanBeTested` interface for the classes you wish to test, and thus defining a `test()` method that `testObject()` will invoke.

Exercise 18-2

Here is the first source file, which we call `Transaction.java`:

```
package banking;

import currency.Amount;
public class Transaction {
 public Amount amount;
 public void process() {
 }
}
```

Here is the second source file, which we call `Amount.java`:

```
package currency;

public class Amount {
 public int dollars;
 public int cents;
}
```

There's a cleaner way to write these interfaces and that involves using `getters` and `setters`, which the next exercise explores.

Exercise 18-3

Another possible solution is to throw exceptions if the new amount values are illegal and to carry over any cents value in excess of 99 into the dollars field:

```
public class Employee {
 private static nextNumber;
 private int employeeNumber;
 private Amount salary;
 public Employee() {
  employeeNumber = nextNumber++;
 }
 int getEmployeeNumber() {
  return employeeNumber;
 }
 Amount getSalary() {
  return salary;
 }
}
class Amount {
 private int dollars;
 private int cents;
 int getDollars() {
  return dollars;
 }
 void setDollars(int d) {
  if (d >= 0)
    dollars = d;
 }
 int getCents() {
```

```
  return cents;
 }
 void setCents(int c) {
  if (c >= 0 && c <= 99)
    cents = c;
 }
}
```

Review Questions

1. Which javadoc tags are useful for documenting a class? (For this question, pick all that apply.)

    a. @see

    b. @param

    c. @version

    d. @return

    e. @author

2. If you use the @author tag

    a. you will see the author when you use javadoc, no options required

    b. you will only see the author if you use the -author option when you invoke javadoc

    c. the @author tag never displays the author; it is only used for reference within the source code

3. The proper use of the @exception tag is

    a. @exception exceptioname anytext

    b. @exception anytext

    c. @exception exceptioname

    d. There is no @exception tag.

4. If you define an interface without any method declarations,

    a. by default, all classes that implement that interface are abstract

    b. all classes that implement that interface are concrete (that is, they can be instantiated)

    c. it is illegal to define an interface without any method declarations

    d. the class is only concrete if it is not declared abstract

5. What kind of methods can be accessed by classes in the same package? (For this question, pick all the answers that apply.)
   a. `public`
   b. `protected`
   c. `private`
   d. those using the default access control

6. Which statements about the package keyword are true? (For this question, pick all the answers that apply.)
   a. It must be placed at the top of the source file.
   b. It must follow immediately after the import statements.
   c. Only public classes can be placed into a package.
   d. You can have more than one source file whose classes are put into the same package.

7. To make salary in the following class definition read-only:

```
class Employee {
 double salary;
}
```

a good approach would be to
   a. Make the Employee class `private`.
   b. Make salary `protected`.
   c. Make salary `private` and define a method called `getSalary()`.
   d. Make salary `private` and define methods named `getSalary()` and `setSalary()`.

Answers to the Review Questions

1. a, c, e. The `@param` tag and `@return` tag are only useful when documenting a method.

2. b. You must invoke `javadoc` using the `-author` keyword to see the author information.

3. a. Specify the name of the exception class, followed by your own descriptive text.

4. d. The class is only concrete if it is not declared abstract.

5. a, b, d. `private` methods can only be accessed by the same class that defines them. Other than that, any class in the same package can access the other methods.

6. a, d. The package statement must appear before the import statements. Any type of class (or interface) can be placed into a package.

7. c. First of all, there is no such thing as a private class. Also, making salary `protected` doesn't make it read-only. Making it `private` and providing a `getter` method (not a `setter` method too) does the trick.

CHAPTER 19

Accessing and Managing Databases

The programming assignment will ask you to access a database, which could be as simple as a `RandomAccessFile`. The class that accesses the database could simply read lines from the file, and each line would represent a record. Even though you might develop your own mini-database application for the exam, in real life there's a better way. You can use the *remote method invocation* (RMI) and *Java database connectivity* (JDBC). Both of these features are built into Java. We'll review them here.

No matter what method you need to implement on the exam concerning the database, you should know some concepts that will help you think through your design. These include how to query a database, how to allow your database to maintain its integrity as different clients attempt to read from and write to it at the same time, what database designers mean when they talk about two-tier and three-tier designs, and how to address concerns regarding efficiency.

The original version of the programming assignment involves accessing a database, possibly on a remote machine, using TCP/IP to communicate over the network. It also requires you to implement an application-level protocol for the client and server to communicate with each other. The client and server send Java primitives, such as opcodes, strings, and integers to each other over the network. A class on the backend accesses a `RandomAccessFile` containing database records.

The first part of this chapter reviews some concepts that can help you understand this architecture. Future versions of the programming assignment may involve JDBC and RMI. Regardless of exactly what is part of the programming assignment and exams, when you become certified in Java, others will expect you to know this advanced information. This chapter reviews these concepts and APIs.

Objectives for This Chapter

- Implement a simple database using a `RandomAccessFile` and a class to read from and write to this file.

■ Describe how to make a database server thread-safe, so that multiple clients can access it at the same time.

■ Describe an n-tiered client/server architecture.

■ Define a remote object and access it from another *Java Virtual Machine* (JVM) using RMI.

■ Use JDBC to access a database via *open database connectivity* (ODBC).

Create Your Own Databases

Performing database programming in Java can be quite easy for simple programs. At its most basic, all you need is a random access file, a method to read from the file, and a method to write to the file. Each line that you read and write can be one record.

As with any database, you first need to determine the record format. You should have a unique key for each record to search for specific records in the database. For example, let's say you want to keep a database of employees. You can track these employees by social security number. If you hire poets, you might have the following list:

432–82–3212 e e. cummings

092–55–3923 John Haines

932–11–5930 Alfred Tennyson

Such a list would represent a table. Each row in the table is a record, which is made up of fields that keep track of different data types. By reading and writing rows to a file, we can read and write records for our database.

Which field should we use as our key? It might seem that we could use either field, but only the social security field will be unique. Although we could easily have two employees named John Smith at our company, their social security numbers would still be unique.

To assist with our home-grown database, we might write a class called `EmployeeRecord` that looks like this:

```
package server;

import java.io.Serializable;
public class EmployeeRecord implements Serializable {
 private String ssn;
 private String name;
 public EmployeeRecord(String ssn, String name) {
  this.ssn = ssn;
  this.name = name;
 }
 public String getSsn() {
  return ssn;
 }
 public String getName() {
  return name;
 }
}
```

Now that we know what each record will look like, we can define a `RandomAccessFile` object to act as our database. For example, we could write the following code:

```
package server;

import java.io.*;
public class DB {
 private static final String FILE_NAME = "test.db";
 private RandomAccessFile file;
 private File test;
 private boolean open;
 public DB() throws IOException {
  try {
   test = new File(FILE_NAME);
   file = new RandomAccessFile(FILE_NAME, "rw");
   open = true;
  } catch (IOException x) {
   close();
   throw x;
  }
 }
 public void close() {
  if (open) {
  try {
   file.close();
```

```
    } catch (IOException x) {
     System.out.println(x.getMessage());
    } finally {
     open = false;
     }
    }
  }
  public void finalize() throws Throwable {
   close();
   super.finalize();
  }
  public void rewind() throws IOException {
   file.seek(0);
  }
  public boolean moreRecords() throws IOException {
   return (file.getFilePointer() < file.length());
  }
  public EmployeeRecord readRecord()
   throws IOException, EOFException
  {
   String ssn = file.readUTF();
   String name = file.readUTF();
   EmployeeRecord record = new EmployeeRecord(ssn, name);
   return record;
  }
  public void writeRecord(EmployeeRecord record)
   throws IOException
  {
   file.seek(file.length());
   file.writeUTF(record.getSsn());
   file.writeUTF(record.getName());
  }
}
```

This class lets us create an object that can access a file called test.db. This file will hold records of type EmployeeRecord. You can see that it knows how to open the file when it's created, and it closes the file if someone invokes its close() method. It also closes the file, if necessary, when the object is garbage collected, because it overrides finalize().

This class provides a way for other objects to use it in order to read all of the records. Other objects can rewind the file and then keep on checking if there are more records before reading the next one. New records are appended to the end of the file.

If we want to be able to delete records in this database file, one way to proceed would be to prefix each record with a flag that indicates whether that record is active or deleted. To delete a record, we would simply change its flag. Periodically, we could copy the database to a new file to get rid of deleted records, thereby keeping them from clogging up the database.

WARNING: *The* DB *class is not appropriate to use with multiple clients. We'll discuss how to update this class so that it is safe for multiple clients in a moment.*

Accessing Databases from Multiple Clients

We can create a `server` class that would enable any number of clients to access this database over a network using TCP/IP. Our architecture would look like Figure 19-1.

We'll look at how to implement a TCP/IP server capable of handling multiple clients in Chapter 20, "Network Programming and Communication." For now, the issue we're concerned with is what happens if multiple clients are manipulating the database at the same time. What if one client is deleting a record while another client is attempting to read from the database? How can we prevent the clients from interfering with each other?

To keep clients from working on the same record and to keep the database from becoming corrupted, it's important to make the methods that access and change records `synchronized`. Every method, except perhaps for the constructor and `finalize()`, would

Figure 19-1

A server providing multiple clients access to a database

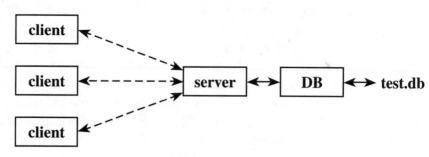

be a candidate for becoming `synchronized`. All you need to do is place the `synchronized` keyword in front of the method's return type, and voila! The class is thread-safe.

Two-Tiered and Three-Tiered Architectures

We have looked at Figure 19-1, but we have not indicated the machines that any of these objects are running on. We could assume that clients connect directly to the machine where the database resides. This is fine, but this is not always the case in the real world. Often, client/server architectures are really client/client/server, or *three-tiered*. This kind of arrangement, where one machine talks to another which talks to another, can go on indefinitely. You can have an *n-tiered architecture*, where n is essentially any number.

For example, perhaps our physical architecture looks like Figure 19-2. Here are three different groups of machines. There is a client group, which represents the first tier. There is a server, which represents a middle tier, and there are database engines, which represent the third tier or the back end. Each box in this diagram could represent a different machine, but because we think of the roles that each machine plays, we think of this as three-tiered: client, to server, which in turn is a client to the database engines.

This kind of design has a number of interesting aspects. First, it is easily extendible. Our server can act as a gateway to any number of other servers or database engines. The client never has to

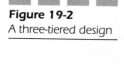

Figure 19-2
A three-tiered design

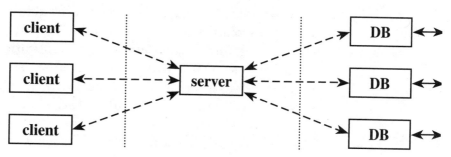

know that data is coming from two, three, or 101 different databases. This means that our server is acting as a kind of gatekeeper. It can establish security precautions, business rules, and can force clients to access data a particular way. What's more, the middle tier, where the server lives, and the back end, where the databases reside, can maintain a high-speed connection. This helps with performance. By contrast, a different architecture might involve the clients talking over a slower network, such as a dial-up network, with each individual database.

Using Java APIs

To help implement this kind of architecture, Java comes with a set of APIs that helps remove you from the low-level chore of creating your own special database and implementing your own application-level protocol used to communicate over TCP/IP networks. These new APIs provide two new features: RMI and JDBC. We'll review each of these over the remainder of this chapter.

Remote Method Invocation (RMI)

When communicating via TCP/IP, the applications themselves must define the protocol of bytes to pass back and forth. This can be difficult to work with and is definitely error-prone. Passing bytes over a network also runs counter to Java's philosophy of helping the programmer concentrate on the application code, rather than the protocol details. By providing an API to invoke methods in objects in other JVMs, Java frees you from this chore. Using RMI, you can invoke remote methods and work with remote objects as if they were defined locally in the same application.

You can use RMI to call methods in other Java applications running in different JVMs, where the JVMs are possibly running on different hosts. You can also call a method on a remote object once you have a reference to the object. Often, you can get a reference to a remote object as a return value from some other RMI call, but to get your first remote object to begin using RMI, you use a bootstrap naming service provided by RMI.

Figure 19-3 shows the basic concept behind RMI. An object in one application, perhaps on a client machine, invokes a method in another application running on a completely different machine, perhaps on a server. The client can pass parameters and even get a return value. RMI uses object serialization to pass parameters and return values between applications.

Once you establish a connection to an object in another program, you can invoke methods on that object as if it were running in the same program as your own. However, for this to work, everything must be defined and set up just right.

Defining a Remote Interface

You need to define an interface for a remote object. Here are the first steps you need to take to define a remote class:

1. Define an interface that declares the methods that objects will be able to invoke using RMI.

2. Throw RemoteException from the methods that objects will be able to invoke using RMI.

The local object will use this interface to determine what it can do with the remote object. This interface must inherit from another interface called Remote. In the example that we'll pursue here, we'll create a class called DBServer that works with our original DB class. We will define DBServer so that we can invoke methods on its objects remotely:

Figure 19-3
Invoking remote objects using RMI

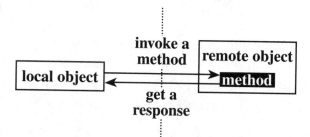

```
package server;

import java.rmi.RemoteException;
import java.rmi.Remote;
import java.io.IOException;
import java.io.EOFException;
public interface DBInterface extends Remote {
 void close()
  throws RemoteException;
 void rewind()
  throws RemoteException, IOException;
 boolean moreRecords()
  throws RemoteException, IOException;
 EmployeeRecord readRecord()
  throws RemoteException, IOException, EOFException;
 void writeRecord(EmployeeRecord er)
  throws RemoteException, IOException;
}
```

Each method must declare that it throws a RemoteException, in addition to any other application-specific exceptions you would like it to throw. RemoteException indicates that something went wrong in the communication between the local and the remote object.

Defining a Remote Class

Your remote class must extend RemoteObject and implement your remote interface. To define a remote class, you must complete the following steps:

1. Extend the RemoteObject class or one of its subclasses, such as UnicastRemoteObject.

2. Implement the remote interface you defined for your remote class' methods.

3. Define a constructor that throws RemoteException.

4. Create and install a security manager.

5. Register the first object that others will access via RMI by defining it in RMI's bootstrap-naming service.

These steps are examined in the sections that follow.

Defining the Class, Interface, and Constructor

You start defining your remote class by extending RemoteObject or a subclass of RemoteObject, such as UnicastRemoteObject. Extending UnicastRemoteObject is a common approach when you are implementing a class whose objects will not be replicated across multiple servers.

You also need to implement the interface that defines your remote methods. You might start by writing:

```
public class DBServer extends UnicastRemoteObject
 implements DBInterface
{
//source for DBServer class
}
```

Your class would go on to implement all of the methods declared in the interface. In our example, this would involve forwarding the method calls to DB, which we looked at earlier in this chapter. I did rewrite DB so it now looks like this:

```
package server;

import java.io.*;
public class DB {
 private RandomAccessFile file;
 private boolean open;
 public DB(String fileName) throws IOException {
  file = new RandomAccessFile(fileName, "rw");
  open = true;
 }
   public void close() {
   if (open) {
    try {
     file.close();
    } catch (IOException x) {
     System.out.println(x.getMessage());
    } finally {
     open = false;
    }
   }
 }
 public void finalize() throws Throwable {
```

```
  close();
  super.finalize();
}
public void rewind() throws IOException {
  file.seek(0);
}
public boolean moreRecords() throws IOException {
  return (file.getFilePointer() < file.length());
}
public EmployeeRecord readRecord()
  throws IOException, EOFException
{
  String ssn = file.readUTF();
  String name = file.readUTF();
  EmployeeRecord record = new EmployeeRecord(ssn, name);
  return record;
}
public void writeRecord(EmployeeRecord record)
  throws IOException
{
  file.seek(file.length());
  file.writeUTF(record.getSsn());
  file.writeUTF(record.getName());
  }
}
```

Here's what DBServer looks like:

```
package server;

import java.io.*;
import java.rmi.*;
import java.rmi.server.*;
public class DBServer extends UnicastRemoteObject
  implements DBInterface
{
  private static final String FILE_NAME = "test.db";
  private DB db;
  public DBServer() throws RemoteException, IOException {
    db = new DB(FILE_NAME);
  }
  public synchronized void close() throws RemoteException {
    db.close();
  }
  public synchronized void rewind()
    throws IOException, RemoteException
  {
    db.rewind();
  }
  public synchronized boolean moreRecords()
```

```
  throws IOException, RemoteException
{
 return db.moreRecords();
}
public synchronized EmployeeRecord readRecord()
  throws IOException, EOFException, RemoteException
{
 return db.readRecord();
}
public synchronized void writeRecord(EmployeeRecord record)
  throws IOException, RemoteException
{
 db.writeRecord(record);
}
public static void main(String[] args) {
 // Create and install a security manager
 System.setSecurityManager(new RMISecurityManager());
 try {
  DBServer dbServer = new DBServer();
  Naming.rebind("DBServer", dbServer);
   // located on the same machine as the client
  System.out.println("DBServer bound in registry");
 } catch (Exception e) {
  System.out.println("DBServer err: " + e.getMessage());
  e.printStackTrace();
 }
 }
}
```

Your class can define methods not declared in your remote interface, but these other methods cannot be invoked from client-side objects; the client can only invoke those methods that are defined in the interface. Also, one reason why it's necessary to create a special server class that interfaces with the DB class, rather than just interfacing directly with DB, is that interface methods cannot be synchronized.

The class you define that implements the remote interface must define its own constructor. The default no-args constructor won't do, because the object's constructor must declare that it throws a RemoteException.

Installing the Security Manager and Registering the Bootstrap-Naming Service

Your remote class must also create and install a security manager and, as with this DBServer object, register itself with the bootstrap-naming service. You can create and install a new security manager quite easily by writing:

```
System.setSecurityManager(new RMISecurityManager());
```

A security manager must be running, because RMI will be loading classes over the network. Just as with Java applets, Java takes a conservative approach and does not trust the classes that come from anywhere other than the local machine. Java insists that a security manager be up and running to make sure that the classes coming in over the network don't do anything malicious.

The security manager also requires a security policy file with the appropriate permissions. For simplicity, the following security policy file grants all permissions on a system:

```
grant {
permission java.security.AllPermission;
};
```

This security policy grants all permissions on the system to the application. You shouldn't use this in a live environment, but for testing and development, this works well. On Windows NT, the security manager looks for this file in %USERPROFILE%/.java.policy by default.

Registering an object with the bootstrap-naming service is also fairly simple. We can create the new object and register it with these two lines of code:

```
DBImplementation db = new DBImplementation();
Naming.rebind("//myhost/DB", db);
```

This says we're going to identify our DBServer object via the string that looks like a URL: //myhost/DB. This URL enables the client to identify this object later.

You also need to make sure your remote object gets exported. If you do not extend UnicastRemoteObject, you must export your object yourself. You can do this by invoking UnicastRemoteObject.exportObject(). If you extend a class such as UnicastRemoteObject, this will be done for you. This is because UnicastRemoteObject exports the object in its constructor, which is invoked with an implied call to super(). By exporting your object, you start it listening for incoming calls on an anonymous port.

To pass parameters or return values that are objects, they must be serializable. This means that we have to make `EmployeeRecord` serializable, since it is a return value for one of the methods we've defined. We don't have to register `EmployeeRecord` in the bootstrap-naming service, because it will be returned, but we must make it a remote object just like `DBImplementation` by defining a remote interface, and so on. The client also will need to import `EmployeeRecord` so that it can use it.

You can also create a *stub* and a *skeleton* for your remote object. A stub represents the remote object on the client side. The skeleton represents the remote object on the server side. Keep in mind that in a pure Java 2 environment the RMI server-side skeletons are not required. I'll review how Java uses these in just a moment. You can use the RMI compiler named `rmic` that comes with the JDK to accomplish this. Figure 19-4 shows where we are so far.

Invoking Remote Objects

Figure 19-5 shows what we've accomplished so far on the server side (we'll get to the client side next).

We've reviewed how to create an object and export it to the registry. Now we'll look at the client side. Calling a method in a remote

Figure 19-4
Creating the remote
class and skeleton

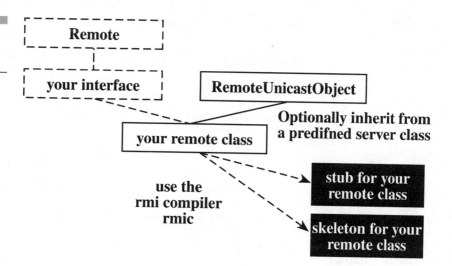

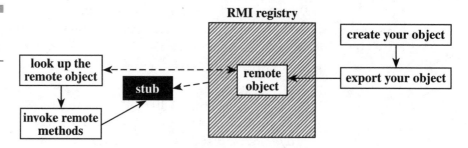

object from the client side is simple and can be performed in two steps:

1. Obtain a reference to the remote object.
2. Invoke a method in the remote object.

You can obtain a reference by using the `static` method `lookup()` in the `Naming` class and passing it the same URL you used to register your remote object. This method returns a reference to the remote object—actually, the stub representing the remote object—that you can cast to the interface type you want to use.

WARNING: *Do not cast the remote object to the object type. Remember, you can only invoke methods that are declared in the remote interface. The stub returned declares those methods in the interface. Also, don't forget to import the interface to refer to it.*

Once you acquire the stub representing the remote object, you can invoke methods for this object just as if it were a full-blown object residing locally on your machine as part of your local application. Here's an example of a client that accesses a remote object:

```
package client;

import java.rmi.*;
import java.io.*;
import java.net.MalformedURLException;
import server.DBInterface;
import server.EmployeeRecord;
```

```
public class DBClient {
 public static void main(String[] args) {
  EmployeeRecord record;
  try {
   DBInterface db =
     (DBInterface)Naming.lookup("DBServer");
   record = new EmployeeRecord("123-45-6789",
                                "William Blake");
   db.writeRecord(record);
   record = new EmployeeRecord("000-11-2222", "John Dunne");
   db.writeRecord(record);
   db.rewind();
   while (db.moreRecords()) {
    record = db.readRecord();
    System.out.println("Ssn: " + record.getSsn());
    System.out.println("Name: " + record.getName());
   }
  } catch (MalformedURLException e) {
   error(e);
  } catch (NotBoundException e) {
   error(e);
  } catch (RemoteException e) {
   error(e);
  } catch (EOFException e) {
   error(e);
  } catch (IOException e) {
   error(e);
  }
 }
 private static void error(Exception e) {
  System.out.println("DBClient exception: " +
                      e.getMessage());
  e.printStackTrace();
 }
}
```

Stubs and Skeletons

Java communicates between the local object and the remote object via a stub and a skeleton. For all appearances, the client program might believe it has actually acquired a direct reference to the remote object residing on the remote server, but Figure 19-6 shows what is really going on. In reality, the client is communicating with a stub that represents the remote object on the local machine. The stub performs the network operations to communicate with the skeleton on the remote machine; the skeleton then talks to the remote object.

Figure 19-6
Invoking a remote
method via stubs and
skeletons

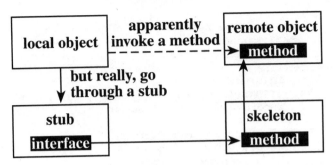

The stub is the client-side representation of the remote object. It defines an interface declaring the methods that the local object can invoke. When the server-side object responds, the flow of control goes back through the skeleton, which handles the network communication to get back to the stub, where the return values or exceptions are passed back to the local, client-side object.

Getting Things Going

To use RMI, you must start the bootstrap registry before you do anything. You must do this even before starting the server class. The RMI registry is activated by executing a command from your operating system's command line named `rmiregistry`. You can then start the server, specifying `java.rmi.registry.codebase=URL` (the URL should include a trailing `/`) and, of course, replacing `URL` with your own URL, so that clients can use the URL to find the stubs in the registry.

Finally, you can start your clients. You must have an HTTP server running on the remote machine.

Exercise 19-1

Develop a class that can be accessed remotely. This class should be named `NYSE` and should respond to a method called `dowJonesAvg()` to return a double value. This object will not be replicated across multiple servers.

Java Database Connectivity (JDBC)

JDBC provides an interface to databases and enables Java programs to access data residing in databases on servers and use that data in the client applet. Programs that use JDBC in Java can access any database that can be queried using *Structured Query Language* (SQL).

Does this mean you have to know SQL? Unfortunately, the answer is yes. JDBC does not put any restrictions on the SQL statements you can send to the database. To send SQL statements from a Java client, you need to know the APIs in the JDBC classes. These JDBC classes issue the SQL queries, passing your applet the data they retrieve.

JDBC is good at performing three important tasks as part of accessing data on a server:

1. It can establish a connection with a database.

2. It can send SQL statements.

3. It can process the results.

JDBC is a low-level API because you must issue SQL statements directly. If you want to work at a higher level, you can write an API with method names like `getEmployees()`, `setSalary()`, and so on, and have these methods make the translation into the SQL statements that you need.

The Need for Drivers

JDBC interacts with a driver that performs the database-specific connections from the general SQL and JDBC methods. Figure 19-7 shows the connections between a client applet and a backend database using JDBC.

All drivers contain a `static` initializer that creates a new instance of itself and registers itself with the `DriverManager` when it's loaded. You can force a class to be loaded by using the `static` method `forName` defined in the `class` Class. For example, your client might include this line of code:

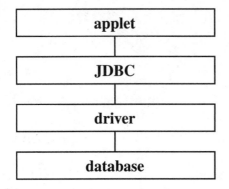

Figure 19-7
Accessing a database
from an applet using
JDBC

```
Class.forName("bluehorse.db.Driver");
```

To define a `static` initializer in the driver itself that registers the new driver object, you can write

```
static {
  Driver d = new Driver();
  DriverManager.registerDriver(d);
}
```

Using Open Database Connectivity (ODBC)

A great number of drivers for databases already exists, but since Java and JDBC are relatively new, most of these drivers conform to a protocol called *open database connectivity* (ODBC). Does JDBC start from scratch then and require a programmer to toss all of this existing work into the recycling bin of history? No! Although JDBC can interact directly with SQL databases if there's a driver written for it in Java, JDBC can also be used in conjunction with ODBC, which then goes off and interacts with SQL databases. JDBC can interact with ODBC by using what's known as a JDBC-ODBC bridge. This enables you to take two approaches to interacting with a database: you can either write a driver that takes JDBC calls and performs the SQL calls to the database, or you can use an ODBC driver that already does this and connect JDBC to ODBC using a JDBC-ODBC bridge (see Figure 19-8).

Figure 19-8
Accessing a database
using the JDBC-
ODBC bridge

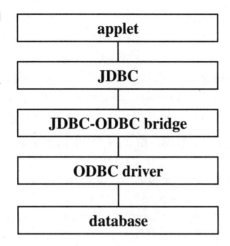

The ODBC driver will be native to the platform it's running on. Using JDBC to access ODBC, however, enables your applet to remain platform-independent while still taking advantage of ODBC. The JDBC-ODBC bridge enables a connection to be made to an ODBC *Data Source Name* (DSN). The DSN specifies either a database or a database server with multiple databases. For example, with Microsoft Access, the DSN specifies the Access database file, but with SQL Server, the DSN specifies the SQL server installation where there are multiple databases.

If the database is on a remote machine, the location of the database is specified in the DSN configuration. The Java program establishing a connection to the database is only aware of the DSN name and perhaps the username and password to access the DSN. The DSN configuration resolves the DSN to the database. It is possible to explicitly specify remote databases in JDBC, but this requires driver types other than the type-I bridge drivers. These other driver types are specific to a particular DBMS system and in some cases must be purchased from a third-party vendor.

Opening a Connection to a Database

To open a connection to a database, follow these steps:

1. Load the database driver class (which causes it to create an instance of itself and register with the `DriverManager`).

2. Invoke the `DriverManager` method `getConnection()` and identify the database driver you will use to connect to the database, the database file name, and optionally as a user ID and password.

With the JDBC-ODBC bridge, the database driver class and URL (without the DSN name) are consistent across database systems. The JDBC URL provides a way of identifying a database so that the appropriate driver will recognize it and establish a connection with it. Driver writers are the ones who actually determine what the JDBC URL looks like. You do not need to worry about how to form a JDBC URL and instead simply use the URL supplied with the drivers you are using. That said, here's how you can load the JDBC-ODBC bridge that comes with Sun's version of Java:

```
Class.forName("sun.jdbc.odbc.JdbcOdbcDriver");
```

Here is a URL you might use to access a DSN called `BaseballCards` using the JDBC-ODBC bridge:

```
String url = "jdbc:odbc:BaseballCards";
DriverManager.getConnection(url, "userID", "passwd");
```

Interacting with a Database

Once you've established a connection with the database, you can send it SQL statements and get results. Three different types of `Statement` classes exist. You can use instances of these classes to send SQL statements to a database. These classes are

- `Statement`, which sends simple SQL statements with no parameters

- `PreparedStatement` (extends `Statement`), which sends precompiled SQL statements

- `CallableStatement` (extends `PreparedStatement`), which executes a database procedure

You can also use two different types of methods to send these SQL statements: `executeQuery()` and `executeUpdate()`. Which method you use depends on what type of SQL statement you create. Table 19-1 shows you which statement you would use with which method and what that statement does.

The `SELECT` statement returns a `ResultSet` object containing the results of the search. You can use `ResultSet` methods to iterate over the results. The other SQL statements generally return a result indicating success or failure. Although statement objects are closed automatically by the garbage collector, you should close them yourself as soon as you're done using them to help Java optimize its memory management chores.

An Example of Using ODBC with Microsoft Access

The following code is one specific example of using JDBC and the JDBC-ODBC bridge. The trouble with any example is that it will be specific for the database and platform that is running. However, it still might be useful to see a working example, even if your environment is not the same as this one.

Table 19-1

Author Insert Caption

SQL Statement	Method	What This SQL Statement Does
SELECT	executeQuery()	Finds records in a database with the given criteria
INSERT	executeUpdate()	Inserts a single record into a table
UPDATE	executeUpdate()	Updates fields in a table
DELETE	executeUpdate()	Deletes records matching the criteria
CREATE TABLE	executeUpdate()	Creates a new table
DROP TABLE	executeUpdate()	Removes a table

I started by creating a simple database in Microsoft Access. This consisted of a single table and three entries. You'll see when you get to the sample programming assignment in Chapter 25, "The Sun-Certified Developer Practice Essay Exam," what this database is supposed to represent (passengers assigned to airplane seats). Figure 19-9 shows what this single table looks like.

I then acquired and installed the ODBC System Administrator from Microsoft. This is free from Microsoft's Web site. I specified my database in this system administrator software as a system data source that used the Microsoft Access ODBC driver. Then I wrote the code to access this database via JDBC:

```
import java.net.URL;
import java.sql.*;
import sun.jdbc.odbc.*;
class JdbcExample {
 public static void main(String[] args) {
   if (args.length == 0) {
     System.out.println("java JdbcExample <url>");
     System.exit(1);
   }
   try {
     Class.forName("sun.jdbc.odbc.JdbcOdbcDriver");
     Connection con = DriverManager.getConnection(args[0]);
     Statement stmt = con.createStatement();
     ResultSet rs =
       stmt.executeQuery("SELECT name, seat FROM Table1");
     while (rs.next()) {
       String name = rs.getString("name");
       int seat = rs.getInt("seat");
     System.out.println(name + " " + seat);
     }
     stmt.close();
     con.close();
   } catch (Exception x) {
     System.out.println(x.getMessage());
     x.printStackTrace();
   }
 }
}
```

The JDBC-ODBC bridge translates JDBC method calls into ODBC function calls. It enables JDBC to leverage the database

Figure 19-9
A simple table in a database

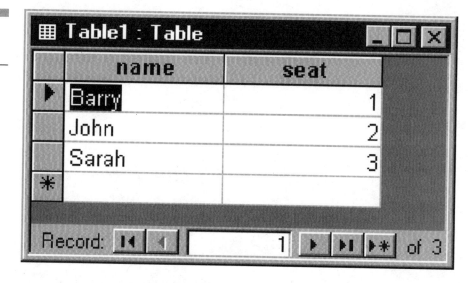

connectivity provided by the ODBC driver that already knows how to work with Microsoft Access. I ran this program by using this command:

```
java JdbcExample jdbc:odbc:mydb.mdb
```

mydb.mdb is the name of my Access file. This program ran, established the connection with the database, read the records in Table 19-1, and displayed the names and seat assignments in that database:

Barry 1

John   2

Sarah 3

Exercise 19-2

■ Establish a connection via the JDBC-ODBC bridge to an ODBC data source named thisdb, which can reference any DBMS of your choice, provided you have ODBC drivers for it.

- Execute the SQL statement `INSERT INTO Table1 (name, seat) VALUES('Greg',5)`.

- Perform any cleanup to complete this connection.

- In the final class definition, be sure to catch any errors using `try-catch` statements.

Answers to the Exercises

Exercise 19-1

First, here is the interface. Remember that it has to extend `Remote`.

```
import java.rmi.RemoteException;
import java.rmi.Remote;
public interface NYSEInterface extends Remote {
  double dowJonesAvg() throws RemoteException;
}
```

Here is the NYSE class. Notice that it has to define a constructor that throws `RemoteException`. This is true even if you only need a `no-args` default constructor.

```
import java.rmi.*;
import java.rmi.server.*;
public class NYSE extends UnicastRemoteObject
    implements NYSEInterface
{
 public NYSE() throws RemoteException {
 }
 public double dowJonesAvg() throws RemoteException {
  double avg = 0.0;
  // FIND THE AVERAGE
  return avg;
 }
}
```

Exercise 19-2

1. First, we establish a connection via the JDBC-ODBC bridge to an ODBC data source named thisdb, which can reference any DBMS of your choice, provided you have ODBC drivers for it.

```
Class.forName("sun.jdbc.odbc.JdbcOdbcDriver");
Connection con = DriverManager.getConnection
("jdbc:odbc:thisdb");
```

2. Then we execute the SQL statement INERT INTO Table1 (name, seat) VALUES('Greg', 5).

```
Statement stmt = con.createStatement();
int result = stmt.executeUpdate("INSERT INTO Table1 (name,
seat) VALUES ('Greg', '5')");
```

3. Perform any cleanup to complete this connection.

```
stmt.close();
con.close();
```

4. In the final class definition, be sure to catch any errors using try-catch statements.

```java
import java.sql.*;

public class DBInsert {

  public static void main(String[] args)
  {
    try {
    Class.forName("sun.jdbc.odbc.JdbcOdbcDriver");
    Connection con = DriverManager.getConnection
    ("jdbc:odbc:thisdb");

      Statement stmt = con.createStatement();
      int result = stmt.executeUpdate("INSERT INTO Table1
      (name, seat) VALUES ('Greg', '5')");
      stmt.close();
      con.close();
    } catch (Exception e) {
      e.printStackTrace(System.out);
    }
  }
}
```

QUESTIONS ▮ ▮ ▮ ▮ ▮ ▮ ▮

1. You can make an object that reads and writes records from a database safe for multiple clients by

   a. declaring its methods to be synchronized
   b. declaring the method as throwing a `RemoteException`
   c. implementing the remote interface
   d. closing the file on `finalize()`

2. To create an object that others can access remotely, you must implement which interface?

   a. `Clonable`
   b. `Throwable`
   c. `RemoteObject`
   d. `Remote`

3. All methods in a remote interface must

   a. not return a value
   b. throw a `RuntimeException`
   c. throw a `RemoteException`
   d. be static methods

4. When an applet obtains a reference to a remote object, that reference is

   a. a stub representing the object
   b. a copy of the object
   c. a direct reference to the object
   d. an instance of `RemoteObject`

5. You can load Sun's JDBC-ODBC bridge by invoking

   a. `Class.forName ("sun.jdbc.odbc.JdbcOdbcDriver");`
   b. `DriverManager.getConnection()`
   c. `executeQuery()`, given a statement object
   d. You don't have to do anything to load the JDBC-ODBC bridge.

ANSWERS

1. a. By synchronizing the methods that access and update a database file, multiple clients can work with the object responsible for this file at the same time.

2. d. You must implement the remote interface. Typically, you extend the remote interface by defining an interface specific to your application and then you implement this new interface. Ultimately, however, your new remote class is an instanceof remote.

3. c. All methods that you want to invoke remotely must declare that they throw a `RemoteException`.

4. a. When you find an object on a remote JVM, RMI passes back a stub representing the object.

5. a. `Class.forName()` loads a class. (Database drivers should register themselves with the `DriverManager` when they load.)

CHAPTER 20

Network Programming and Communication

With Java, network programming is, dare I say it, fun. The package java.net contains a few classes that hide what's happening at the *Transport Control Protocol / Internet Protocol* (TCP/IP) layer and make programs that communicate over the Internet relatively easy to write. However, to use these classes effectively, you've got to know how TCP/IP works, what sockets are, and the strategies for writing a client/server application. We'll review all of these topics in this chapter.

The programming assignment requires that you write a client/server application. The client and server talk to each other using TCP/IP, and data is passed between the client and server using sockets.

Objectives for This Chapter

- Describe what IP addresses are and how they work.
- State why TCP makes it possible to send streams of data over the Internet.
- Identify what a socket is and what it represents.
- Identify the classes in java.net used to communicate via TCP/IP.
- Use Java to establish network connections.
- Write a client/server application.
- Write a server that can handle more than one client.

A TCP/IP Primer

The programming assignment for the developer exam requires that you understand TCP/IP. If you're a little fuzzy on these protocols or are not quite sure what this acronym even stands for, have no fear. I'll cover these topics in this section, and you'll even write your own simple client/server programs using TCP/IP in the exercises.

TCP/IP, as stated earlier, stands for *Transport Control Protocol / Internet Protocol*. TCP and IP are really two different protocols, but together they define the way things work on the Internet. The *Internet Protocol* (IP) identifies computers on the Internet. Computers are identified by a four byte value. This four-byte value is often called a *dotted octet*, because this number—the IP address—is written in a form like this:

```
206.26.48.100
```

Given this number, one computer on the Internet can find and identify another computer. That's the IP.

Since it's not always easy to remember numbers like this, these numbers are often mapped to human names, called domain names, such as java.sun.com. Special servers on the Internet perform this mapping, called *Domain Name Servers* (DNS). If you ask your Web browser to connect to www.javasoft.com, for example, it finds a DNS, looks up its dotted octet, and connects to that machine.

Before we look at how that connection occurs, let's look at the other protocol: the *Transport Control Protocol* (TCP). TCP enables you to treat any Internet resource as a stream. It does this by guaranteeing two things:

1. Data sent to a particular machine arrives at that machine.

2. If the data sent to a particular machine had to be divided into smaller pieces and sent separately, all of these pieces are reassembled on the receiving end in the correct order.

Here's an example of why this is important and how it's used. Let's say you are about to send a memo to your boss asking for a raise. You've stated all the important reasons why you deserve one and, since you're thorough, the message is quite long. You want to make certain your boss knows each and every reason why you're worth more than his penny-pinching mind currently comprehends. You hit Send on your e-mail program. The e-mail program wants to send this over the Internet to the IP address you've specified, but it can't. Why? Because the message is too big! You were too thorough. Does the e-mail program ask you to rewrite your message and state your reasons in 50 words or less? No! It takes matters into its own hands. It divides the message you wrote into lots of smaller messages, each one small enough to travel over the Internet. This first step is shown in Figure 20-1.

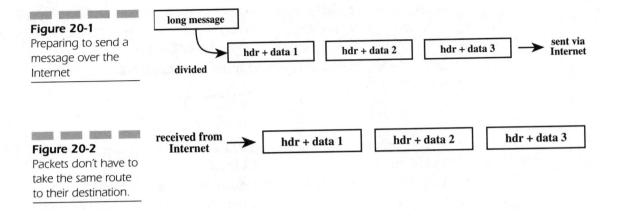

Figure 20-1
Preparing to send a message over the Internet

Figure 20-2
Packets don't have to take the same route to their destination.

Because of TCP, each piece contains a header that indicates where it's going and identifies its place in the sequence to be received. Each piece of the message, or each packet, goes out over the Internet. (For the sake of completeness, here's a simple definition of the Internet: a network of networks that relies on TCP/IP.) As each packet travels from computer to computer, or from node to node, on its way to its IP destination, not all the pieces of this monster message may go the same way. Some pieces may be rerouted. Perhaps a machine in the stepping stones across the net goes down after sending packet 16, but before sending packet 17. TCP/IP still works its magic; the pieces of your message still arrive at their correct destination, but now they start arriving in a different order from how they were sent (see Figure 20-2).

Naturally, you don't want any arguments left out, because they didn't arrive. And you don't want your e-mail in a jumbled order when your boss looks at it. You want to keep your argument cogent and focused, building to a crescendo by the time you ask for a raise at the end. This is where TCP kicks into high gear. Not only have all your message pieces arrived (guaranteed delivery), but now they are reassembled into the correct order. Once the pieces are reassembled, they're accepted by your boss' e-mail program. Your boss now has an impressive piece of e-mail to read. This is illustrated in Figure 20-3.

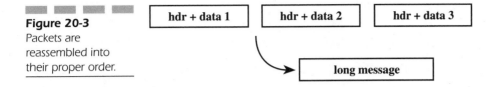

Figure 20-3
Packets are
reassembled into
their proper order.

Ports and Sockets

This is a fine TCP explanation for the most part, but I left out one
crucial step: how does the computer receiving the e-mail message
know that this message is an e-mail message? What if there is also
a Web server on your boss' machine serving up pages to the people
in your group? How can the Web server and the e-mail program
both be running at the same time and be paying attention to only
the data meant for them when they're both talking TCP/IP? After
all, both programs are running on the same machine, and that
machine has only one IP address.

The solution to this riddle is that one more piece of information
distinguishes where the data should go. That piece of information
is a *port number*. Each server program listens to a different *port*.
There are between 2^{16} different ports, or 1,024, and each is assigned
a number. By convention, these numbers are divided into two
groups:

- Port numbers below 1,024 are reserved for well-known system
  uses such as Web protocols, e-mail, ftp, and so on.
- Port numbers above 1,024, from 2^{16} minus 1 (because port
  numbers start at 0), are all yours, and you can assign your own
  programs and services to these port numbers.

Thus, the e-mail program listens to one port, and the Web server
listens to another. E-mail might arrive looking for port 25, which is
the port usually associated with *Simple Mail Transfer Protocol*
(SMTP), while requests for Web pages might arrive looking for port
80, which is the port usually associated with *HyperText Transport
Protocol* (HTTP). Each server only listens for data arriving on its
particular port. Figure 20-4 gives a sense of this.

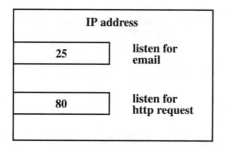

Figure 20-4
Server software
listening to specific
ports

The combination of *IP address* and *port number* uniquely identifies a service on a machine. This service could be a server program, such as a Web server. Client programs also listen to a particular port for data from the server. Just as the client uses this combination of IP address and port to send data to the server, the server also uses this combination of IP address and port to send data back to the client. Such a combination of IP address and port is known as a *socket*. A socket identifies one end of a two-way communication. When a client requests a connection with a server on a particular port, the server identifies and keeps track of the socket it will use to talk to the client. This might help explain how a server can keep track of and talk to multiple clients at once. Even though the server is communicating over the same port with many clients, it uses sockets (remember, port + IP address) to determine the destination and source of that communication. The server keeps track of each client's socket. The server knows data arriving on one socket comes from a different client than data arriving on another socket. The server also knows that it can respond to a client by passing data back to that client's socket. Figure 20-5 gives a sense of the role that sockets play in this client/server communication. We'll look at exactly what's happening on the server side regarding port numbers shortly.

Streams

With IP addressing, TCP's guaranteed data delivery, and sockets that identify the end points of two-way communications, data pass-

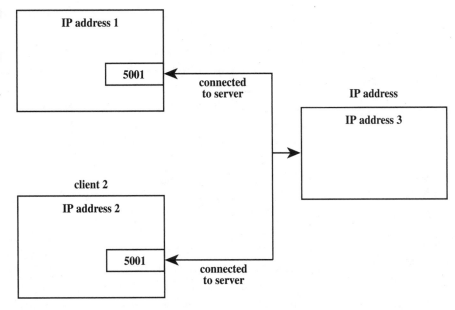

Figure 20-5
Sockets uniquely
identify the end point
of a two-way
communication.

ing over the Internet can be treated by an application as a stream. In other words, you can read from a socket just as if you were reading from a file, because TCP ensures that all the data sent from the machine on the other end of the Internet connection is received in order. TCP hides the fact that the data is arriving via the Internet and, at the level of the public interfaces declared by Java's `Stream` classes, it makes the data indistinguishable from data read from a local file. You can attach a `Stream` class to a socket and read from it or write to it just as you learned in Chapter 11, "Input/Output." We'll look at some examples in a moment.

Designing Servers and Clients

To develop an application that communicates over the Internet, you must develop a server and a client. The server listens for connections on a particular port; when it receives a connection, it obtains a socket to use for the communication and begins a dialog with the client at the other end of that socket. The client initiates the connection and communicates with the server via a socket representing that server.

A classic design for a server is one that runs forever, listening for connections with clients, and then taking part in a dialog with the client (by reading data from the client and writing data to the client, as appropriate). Figure 20-6 shows the basic steps that a client and server take in communicating with each other.

Handling Multiple Clients

As long as the server only uses a single thread, other clients attempting to communicate with the server wait in a queue until the server is through with its current client and closes its connection with that client. If you only anticipate having one client communicate with the server, then the possibility of other clients waiting in a queue is not a concern. If you have multiple clients talking to the server, you need a design that can handle this situation.

Regardless of whether the communication between the server and client is lengthy or relatively short, there's really no need to fear implementing a server that can't handle more than one client. In Java, with its ability to easily implement multithreading, synchronize between multiple threads, and work directly with sockets, it's quite straightforward to create a multithreading server. You might wish to implement a server that follows the basic flow chart shown in Figure 20-7.

Figure 20-6
The basic interaction between a server and a client

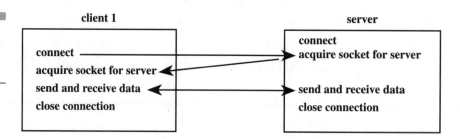

Figure 20-7
A basic flow chart for
a multithreading
server

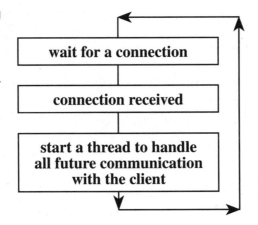

Figure 20-7
A basic flow chart for
a multithreading
server

Threads introduce new wrinkles to the server. The first wrinkle
you might want to iron out is making the server thread-safe. For
example, let's say the server is accessing a database. If one thread is
reading from the database at the same time that another thread is
writing to it, clearly this is trouble. Fortunately, it's simple to lock the
dependent methods in Java by declaring them to be `synchronized`.
You'll see an example of a working server in a few more pages.

Declaring the dependent methods as `synchronized` is great as
far as interacting with the database, but how does the server keep
track of multiple clients? How does the server know which data
read from a port goes with a particular thread? The answer is that
TCP/IP takes care of this data routing for you, and TCP is the protocol layer below the sockets, which you probably won't ever have to
deal with directly if you program in Java.

Remember that sockets encode both the port number and the IP
address. This means each client is uniquely identified. When a server
accepts a connection, it acquires the client's socket. From then on, all
data received from or sent to the client is read from or written to this
socket. The TCP protocol below the socket layer ensures the data
sent from a particular client goes to the correct socket in the correct
server thread. Because the server uses a socket to interact with the
client, the server is born ready for multithreading.

NOTE: *Assigning each socket communication with a client to its own thread also has another great benefit. If something goes terribly wrong with the communication between the server and a particular client, only the thread that's dealing with that client will be in trouble (and possibly end with an exception). The rest of the server will continue chugging along.*

Client Issues

Let's look briefly at some design issues involving the client. Here are some questions you might want to think about for your client. Your answers will depend on the needs of your particular client application. If the client sends a request to the server and the server takes some time to answer it, will the user interface freeze because it is waiting for a response from the client, or will it continue working? If the user interface continues working, what will happen if the user then issues another request? Should this second request supersede the first one?

You have a number of strategies for implementing your client, and the right approach will take into account many factors that depend on your particular situation. You've got to decide how sophisticated to make your user interface and whether that sophistication is worth the price of increased development and maintenance. Here are some possible strategies for you to contemplate:

- Block all user input until (and hopefully when) the server responds. You might want to change the cursor to a busy cursor during this communication time.

- Spawn a separate thread to communicate with the server. When the server responds, have that thread invoke a method that updates the user interface appropriately. Work at recovering gracefully if the user interface changes before the server responds.

- Spawn a separate thread that displays a modal dialog box that provides the user with the option of canceling the communication with the server. The modal dialog box should disappear when the server responds. Because it is modal, it keeps the user from altering the user interface if communication with the server is still taking place.

Two other important considerations in writing a client/server application are as follows:

1. Does the server need to save a state for each individual client, or will all clients manipulate the same data source on the server? If the server needs to save a state for each client, it will either need objects that store the relevant information or, better yet (in case the connection is dropped prematurely), a file where it can keep the information for the various clients (or perhaps the server can keep one file per client).

2. Does the server communicate with each client independently of the others or will the server broadcast information to all the clients connected to it? If the clients are operating independently of each other, the server does not need to keep track of each thread in the server. However, if the server broadcasts information to all connected clients (as in a multi-client chat program), the server needs to keep some kind of list of the threads handling communication with the various clients.

The Networking Package

Java makes working with TCP/IP easy, because it has built-in support for these protocols. Java provides this support in the form of classes. In particular, you'll find that three classes are particularly useful for this kind of low-level communication:

- `InetAddress`
- `Socket`
- `ServerSocket`

InetAddress

The InetAddress class encodes an IP address. You will obtain the InetAddress objects not by creating them with a constructor, but by calling one of three static methods defined by InetAddress. One of these is called getByName(), which takes a string object that contains the IP address either as a dotted octet or as its DNS equivalent. You can create a new InetAddress object either with this line of code:

```
InetAddress ipAddress =
InetAddress.getByName("206.26.48.100");
```

or with this one:

```
InetAddress ipAddress =
InetAddress.getByName("java.sun.com");
```

You can obtain the IP address of the machine that your code is running on by writing

```
InetAddress ipAddress = InetAddress.getByLocalHost();
```

This creates an InetAddress object that represents the local machine.

The InetAddress class defines two instance methods: getAddress(), which returns an array of four bytes, and getHostName(), which returns a string. Each returns the IP address. getAddress() returns the dotted octet, while getHostName() returns the name found in the DNS. You'll see next how you can use an InetAddress object to create a socket used to communicate with another computer over the Internet.

Socket and ServerSocket

The Socket class defines a socket, one end of a two-way communication. You'll need an IP address and a port to create a Socket object. Here's an example:

```
InetAddress ipAddress =
InetAddress.getByName("java.sun.com");


Socket s = new Socket(ipServer, 5001);
```

The first line obtains the IP address of the server. The second line creates a socket connected to that server if it's listening to port 5001 for client connections. This constructor establishes a dedicated connection between the local machine and the server. Figure 20-8 shows the first step in this process.

For this constructor to work, the server must already be waiting for clients to connect to it. The server first creates a `ServerSocket` object listening on a specified port:

```
ServerSocket serverSock = new ServerSocket(5001);
```

Then the server waits for clients to connect to it by executing

```
Socket sock = serverSock.accept();
```

The `accept()` method waits until a client connects with the server. At this point, the `accept()` method does something very interesting; it tells the client that it should use a different port to continue the communication. This is shown in Figure 20-9.

Figure 20-8
The client requests a connection with a server

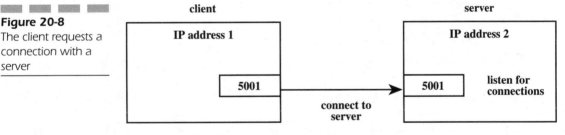

Figure 20-9
The server obtains a new local port and tells the client what it is.

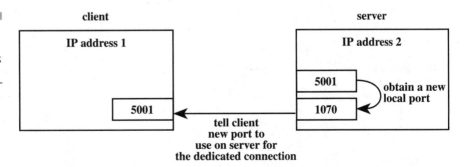

For example, the server might obtain a new, free port to use to communicate with the client whose number is 1070. The client now communicates using local port 5001 and remote port 1070 (the remote port is the server's port from the client's point of view). Similarly, the server communicates using local port 1070 and remote port 5001 (the remote port is the client's port from the server's point-of-view). The server needs to obtain a new port so that it can continue to listen for other clients trying to connect to it on port 5001. This is shown in Figure 20-10.

All you need to know as an application programmer is the original port that the server is listening to; the port that the server and client agree to use for their dedicated connection is not something you need to decide on. Java's classes will handle this detail for you. In fact, if you do not invoke `getLocalPort()` and `getPort()` on the sockets you create to identify the local and remote ports respectively, you'll never realize that ServerSocket's `accept()` method has reassigned the server's port for you.

NOTE: This is really just background information; you won't have to deal with these ports directly, other than knowing which port the server is listening to initially, but it's useful to know what's going on under the hood.

Other constructors exist as well for both `ServerSocket` and `Socket`. For example, you can specify the local port as a different number from the remote port. Perhaps you want your socket's local port to be 3333, but you still want to connect to the server listening to port 5001. You can create your socket and connect to the server by writing

```
Socket sock = new Socket(ipServer, 5001, ipLocal, 3333);
```

Figure 20-10
The server and client can now have a dedicated connection.

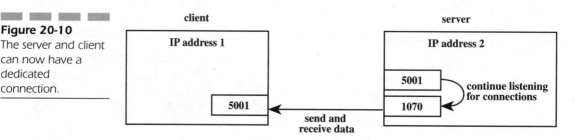

By default, the `ServerSocket` object you create will accept connections with up to 50 clients. You can also create a `ServerSocket` where you indicate this limit directly. For example, you can write

```
ServerSocket serverSock = new ServerSocket(5001, 25);
```

This server socket can only accept up to 25 simultaneous connections. If a 26th client tries to connect to it, the server socket refuses the connection.

Internet Streams

At this point, once you've established a dedicated connection between client and server, you can use everything you're familiar with from the review of streams in Chapter 11, "Input/Output." For example, you can acquire an `InputStream` object that has a socket as its source. You can then create a new filter stream object and attach it to this `InputStream`. You might create a new `DataInputStream` object and use it to read bytes from the socket.

Here's a code snippet that does this. Let's say you have a `Socket` object in the variable `sock`. You can get an `InputStream` object by writing:

```
sock.getInputStream();
```

From this, you can create a `DataInputStream` by passing this value to its constructor. You might write this all in one line of code:

```
DataInputStream remoteIn = new
DataInputStream(sock.getInputStream());
```

You can then use `remoteIn` to read from the socket and receive data from the machine to which you're connected. For example, to read an integer, you can write

```
int myInt = remoteIn.readInt();
```

To send data, you need to acquire an output stream for the client by using the method `getOutputStream()`:

```
DataOutputStream remoteOut = new
DataOutputStream(sock.getOutputStream());
```

You can then use `remoteOut` to write to the socket and send data to the machine you're connected to. For example, to write the number 5, you might write

```
remoteOut.writeInt(5);
```

You've got to be sure to handle all of the exceptions appropriately. In particular when reading and writing using streams, you need to wrap your `read()` and `write()` calls in `try-catch` blocks and be prepared to catch `IOException`.

Of course, you need to read and write according to a protocol that both the server and client know how to speak. When your client reads, the server better send you something. Similarly, when your client writes, the server better try to read it. Some `read()` methods will time out if nothing appears, but if you don't use these, `read()` will block forever until data finally arrives.

When your protocol is clearly established and you're reading and writing in the right sequence, you'll find that you're communicating over the Internet with just a few lines of code. Once you have completed your connection, you should close any streams you've created. After this, you should close the socket connection. You can invoke `close()` for both a stream and a socket to accomplish this.

Client-Server Examples

You've learned the basics of TCP/IP, seen the design issues and approaches for servers and clients, and learned about the networking classes available in Java to help you work with TCP/IP. Now let's look at how to write a client/server application in Java by writing two types of chat programs. In the first program, we'll write a simple chat program that connects one computer with another and passes messages back and forth. In the next program, we'll write a server that enables any number of clients to connect to it. In this second version, the server will broadcast each message it receives from a client to all other connected clients. These servers do not require synchronization.

To see how to synchronize between multiple clients, work through the practice programming assignment for the developer exam. You'll find that you've seen some of the code in the snippets presented in this chapter so far. Now you'll see these snippets as part of a working program.

Writing a Single-Client Server in Java

Let's take a look at how the single-client chat program works. You can launch this program from the command line; it runs as a standalone graphical application, not as an applet. If you specify no command-line arguments, it's launched as a server, waiting for a connection from a client. You can also launch it as a client by specifying the name of the host to connect to. If you are running both the client and the server on the same machine, you can pass it the name `local`. In other words, this program can act as either the client or the server, depending on whether or not you have supplied a command-line parameter.

When you first launch the program as a server (without a command-line parameter), by typing

```
java SingleChat
```

it will appear as in Figure 20-11.

Then when you launch the program as a client (by specifying the host where the server is already running) by typing

```
java SingleChat local
```

the new program runs and displays the user interface shown in Figure 20-12.

These two *graphical user interfaces* (GUIs) look mighty similar; the difference is in the title of the frame (and what went on behind the scenes, which we'll look at in a moment). Notice the title of the client states that it has connected to the server named `localhost`. In the meantime, the title of the server application has changed to indicate it has `Accepted connection from localhost`.

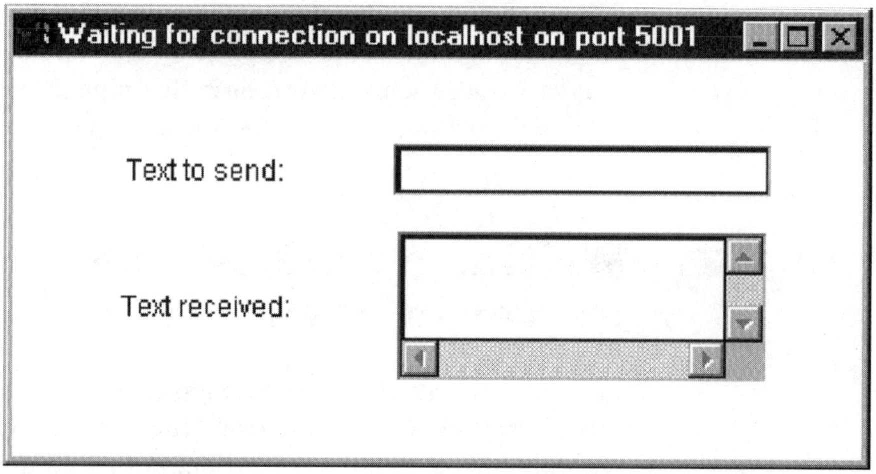

Figure 20-11
The SingleChat application launched as a server

Figure 20-12
The SingleChat application launched as a client with a server already running

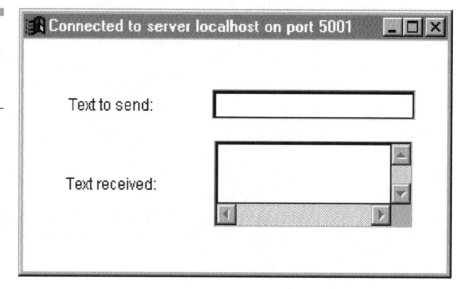

Now whenever one person types text into the field labeled Text to Send and hits Enter, the text is sent over the network connection using TCP/IP to the other version of SingleChat with which it is connected. This is shown in Figure 20-13 and Figure 20-14. The first figure shows text being typed into the Text to send text field. Then, after the user hits Enter, the text is sent to the other SingleChat application. The text is received and displayed in the Text Received text area shown in the second figure.

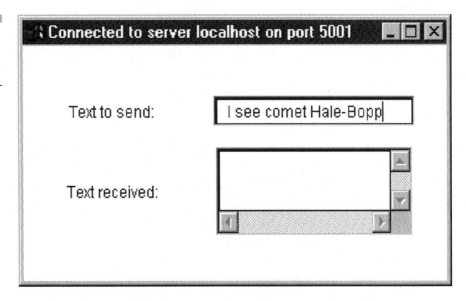

Figure 20-13
Text typed into the
Text to Send text
field

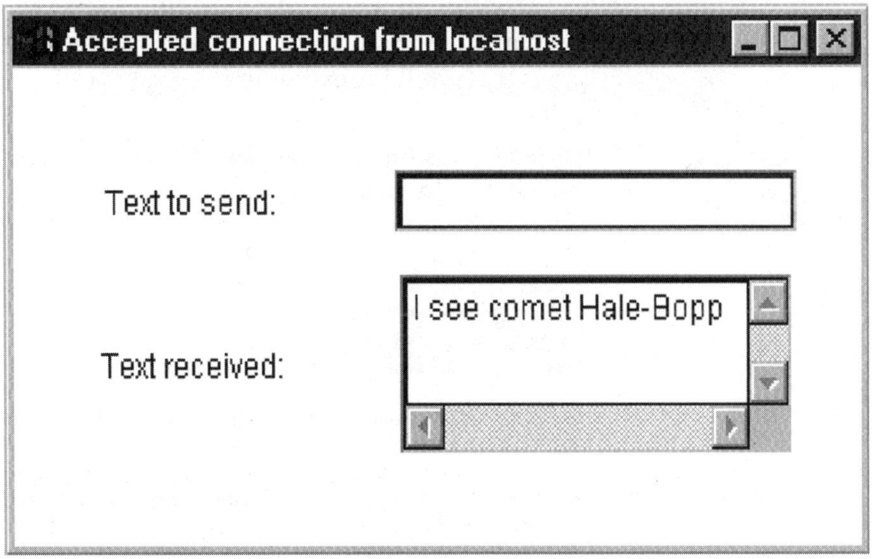

Figure 20-14
Text received and
displayed in the
Text Received
text area

So how does this work? Let's look at the basic architecture first. Then I'll present the entire source code and then we'll examine the lines of code specific to TCP/IP.

The `SingleChat` class is a panel. It creates a frame in `main()` so that it can appear on the screen. It lays out its user interface using a `GridBagLayout`. `SingleChat` invokes one of two methods, `client()` or `server()`, depending on whether or not the user has supplied a command-line parameter. Without a parameter, it runs as a server. With a parameter, it runs as a client, and the server's name is passed to `client()`.

The `server()` method waits for a connection. When a client connects to it, it obtains a socket for the client and spawns a thread that loops forever. This thread listens to this socket for data sent by the client.

The `client()` method tries to establish a connection with the server, given the name of the machine the server is running on. Once it establishes this connection, it obtains a socket for the server and spawns a thread that loops forever. This thread listens to this socket for data sent by the server.

When the user hits the Enter key in the text field labeled Text to Send, the application gets the text in this field and writes it to the socket it obtained when the two applications connected. When data arrives on the socket, as monitored in the thread that's continually looping, the application takes this text and displays it in the text area labeled `Received Text`.

Here is the complete code listing. It weighs in at under 200 lines of code, including comments:

```
import java.io.*;
import java.net.*;
import java.awt.*;
import java.awt.event.*;
/**
 }* SingleChat - A chat program between a server and one  client.
 *
 * To run as a server, do not supply any command line arguments.
 * SingleChat will start listening on the default port, waiting
 * for a connection:
 *   java SingleChat
 *
 * To run as a client, name the server as the first command
 * line argument:
 * java SingleChat bluehorse.com
 * or
 * java SingleChat local // to run locally
 */
```

```java
public class SingleChat extends Panel {
 Socket sock;
 TextArea receivedText;
 private GridBagConstraints c;
 private GridBagLayout gridBag;
 private Frame frame;
 private Label label;
 private int port = 5001; // The default port.
 private TextField sendText;
 private DataOutputStream remoteOut;
 public static void main(String args[]) {
  Frame f = new Frame("Waiting for connection . . . ");
  String s = null;
  if (args.length > 0)
   s = args[0];
  SingleChat chat = new SingleChat(f);
  f.add("Center", chat);
  f.setSize(350, 200);
  f.show();
   // Make the connection happen.
   if (s == null)
    chat.server();
   else
    chat.client(s);
 }
 public SingleChat(Frame f) {
  frame = f;
  frame.addWindowListener(new WindowExitHandler());
  // Build the user interface.
  Insets insets = new Insets(10, 20, 5, 10); // bot, lf, rt,
top
  gridBag = new GridBagLayout();
  setLayout(gridBag);
  c = new GridBagConstraints();
  c.insets = insets;
  c.gridy = 0;
  c.gridx = 0;
  label = new Label("Text to send:");
  gridBag.setConstraints(label, c);
  add(label);
  c.gridx = 1;
  sendText = new TextField(20);
  sendText.addActionListener(new TextActionHandler());
  gridBag.setConstraints(sendText, c);
  add(sendText);
  c.gridy = 1;
  c.gridx = 0;
  label = new Label("Text received:");
  gridBag.setConstraints(label, c);
  add(label);
  c.gridx = 1;
  receivedText = new TextArea(3, 20);
  gridBag.setConstraints(receivedText, c);
```

```
    add(receivedText);
  }
  // As a server, we create a server socket bound to the
specified
  // port, wait for a connection, and then spawn a thread to
  // read data coming in over the network via the socket.
  private void server() {
   ServerSocket serverSock = null;
   try {
    InetAddress serverAddr = InetAddress.getByName(null);
    displayMsg("Waiting for connection on " +
      serverAddr.getHostName() +
      " on port " + port);
    // We'll only accept one connection for this server.
    serverSock = new ServerSocket(port, 1);
    sock = serverSock.accept();
    displayMsg("Accepted connection from " +
      sock.getInetAddress().getHostName());
      remoteOut = new DataOutputStream(sock.getOutputStream());
      new SingleChatReceive(this).start();
   } catch (IOException e) {
    displayMsg(e.getMessage() +
    ": Failed to connect to client.");
   } finally {
    // At this point, since we only establish one connection
    // per run, we don't need the ServerSocket anymore.
    if (serverSock != null) {
     try {
      serverSock.close();
     } catch (IOException x) {
     }
    }
   }
  }
  // As a client, we create a socket bound to the specified
port,
  // connect to the specified host, and then spawn a thread to
  // read data coming coming in over the network via the
socket.
  private void client(String serverName) {
   try {
    if (serverName.equals("local"))
     serverName = null;
   InetAddress serverAddr = InetAddress.getByName(serverName);
    sock = new Socket(serverAddr.getHostName(), port);
    remoteOut = new DataOutputStream(sock.getOutputStream());
    displayMsg("Connected to server " +
      serverAddr.getHostName() +
      " on port " + sock.getPort());
      new SingleChatReceive(this).start();
   } catch (IOException e) {
    displayMsg(e.getMessage() +
     ": Failed to connect to server.");
```

```
   }
  }
  void displayMsg(String s) {
   frame.setTitle(s);
  }
  protected void finalize() throws Throwable {
   try {
    if (remoteOut != null)
     remoteOut.close();
    if (sock != null)
     sock.close();
   } catch (IOException x) {
   }
   super.finalize();
  }
  class WindowExitHandler extends WindowAdapter {
   public void windowClosing(WindowEvent e) {
    Window w = e.getWindow();
    w.setVisible(false);
    w.dispose();
    System.exit(0);
   }
  }
  class TextActionHandler implements ActionListener {
  public void actionPerformed(ActionEvent e) {
   try {
    // Send it.
    remoteOut.writeUTF(sendText.getText());
    // Clear it.
    sendText.setText("");
    } catch (IOException x) {
     displayMsg(x.getMessage() +
     ": Connection to peer lost.");
    }
   }
  }
 }
 /*
 * SingleChatReceive takes data sent on a socket and
   displays it in
 * a text area. This receives it from the network.
 */
 class SingleChatReceive extends Thread {
  private SingleChat chat;
  private DataInputStream remoteIn;
  private boolean listening = true;
  public SingleChatReceive(SingleChat chat) {
   this.chat = chat;
  }
  public synchronized void run() {
   String s;
   try {
   remoteIn = new
```

```
DataInputStream(chat.sock.getInputStream());
   while (listening) {
    s = remoteIn.readUTF();
    chat.receivedText.setText(s);
   }
  } catch (IOException e) {
   chat.displayMsg(e.getMessage() +
    ": Connection to peer lost.");
  } finally {
   try {
    if (remoteIn != null)
     remoteIn.close();
    } catch (IOException x) {
   }
  }
 }
}
```

Here are the key lines of code as far as TCP/IP is concerned.

server( )

First, here is how the `server()` method works. The two lines that actually wait for a client to connect to it and then accept this connection are

```
serverSock = new ServerSocket(port, 1);
sock = serverSock.accept();
```

The constructor for `ServerSocket` takes a port number and, optionally, the number of connections to allow at one time. The default is 50; in this version of the chat program, we only allow one connection from one client. In the next version, we'll allow multiple clients to be connected to the server simultaneously.

The `ServerSocket`'s `accept()` method waits for a connection from a client. When it accepts a connection and returns, it passes back a `Socket` object that represents the client. Previous to these two lines, this method simply acquires the machine name that this server is running on so that it can display this to the user. After these two lines, it formats and displays a message containing the client's name. It then acquires a stream to use to write to the socket and starts a thread that waits for data coming in on this socket.

client( )

The two lines that connect with the server are

```
InetAddress serverAddr = InetAddress.getByName(serverName);
sock = new Socket(serverAddr.getHostName(), port);
```

serverName is a string that represents the IP address (either the dotted octet or the DNS name) where the server is running. If this name is null, then getByName() returns the name of the local machine. When the constructor for the socket returns, you will have obtained a socket you can use to communicate with the server. Before these two lines, this method sets the serverName string to null if the name is local, so that the Java methods will work with the local host. After these two lines, it formats and displays a message containing the server's name. It then acquires a stream to use to write to the socket and starts a thread that waits to process data arriving on this socket.

NOTE: *As we explained already, the actual remote port number that this socket contains will be a port the server has decided it will use to establish the dedicated connection with the client. As I indicated earlier, this is a detail that is handled by Java classes, though it is useful to keep this in mind while trying to understand what is going on.*

action( )

When the user types some text into the Text to Send field and hits Enter, the application finds out about it in action(). Since we have already acquired a DataOutputStream object, we can use any DataOutputStream method and write the data to the socket. From there, Java handles the TCP/IP and makes sure the data goes out over the network and finds its destination.

run( ) for SingleChatReceive

The first thing this method does is acquire a `DataInputStream` object with the line

```
remoteIn = new DataInputStream(chat.sock.getInputStream());
```

We reference this socket via the `SingleChat` object, since `SingleChatReceive` is a different class than `SingleChat`. This thread loops forever, reading text from the socket and displaying it in the text area.

Cleaning Up

You'll notice that this application is careful to clean up after itself. If we fall out of the listening loops, or if this object is finalized, it first closes the streams and then closes the sockets.

Writing a Multi-Client Server in Java

The `SingleChat` server is a little unusual in that it only communicates with one client during its life. Let's write a server that accepts connections from multiple clients. When one client sends the server a message, the server will broadcast this message to all clients attached to it. As with the `SingleChat` application, we'll look first at how it works. Then we'll look at the basic architecture, view the source code, and examine the lines of code that make this a good multi-client, multithreaded server.

For this application, it is easier to write two different programs. One program is the server, which runs as a standalone character-mode program. (It doesn't really have much of an interface at all.) The other program is a client program that looks and acts very similar to the client program we looked at already. When you launch the server (called `MultiChatServer`) by typing

```
java MultiChatServer
```

at the command line, the program writes the following messages to the screen:

```
Hit control-c to exit the server.
Waiting for first connection on localhost on port 5001.
```

At this point, it's ready for clients to connect to it. There is a hard limit in the code of 50 clients, which is set somewhat arbitrarily with the intent of ensuring the server doesn't get swamped with requests. Otherwise, the server might get bogged down with keeping track of lots of network connections and performance could become slow. The server will run forever, until the user hits Control-C to actually break out of the program with this interrupt.

Once the server is running, the user can launch clients—any number theoretically, but up to 50 in this case—that connect to the server. To launch a client for this multi-chat application, specify two command line parameters: the name of the person taking part in the chat session and the name of the host where the server is running. As before, you can type local to run locally with the server and the client on the same machines. The name of this program is MultiChat. For example, you might type

```
java MultiChat Shakespeare local
```

This launches the client, this time putting the user's name in the title of the frame. Other clients can also connect to the same server. Now, when the user types in Text to Send and hits Enter, all other clients connected to the server will receive that message, with the client's name also displayed as a prefix, as in

```
Shakespeare: If music be the food of love, play on.
```

This identifies who this message came from.

Now here's the architecture. The server loops forever, waiting to accept connections from clients. When a client connects with the server, the server acquires a stream to use to write to the socket and saves this stream in a list. It then creates a new thread that will handle all future communication with the client. It passes the client's socket to the thread and this output stream, since the thread will use this socket to communicate with the client. The server also passes the server instance to the thread, because the thread will later need to invoke some server methods.

NOTE: *Even if multiple clients can connect with the server, there might not be a need to keep track of all the currently connected clients in a list in the server. If the clients do not need to interact with each other, the server can just spawn a new thread that handles the connection with the client independently of the other client-handling threads. It is only because each client's message is broadcast to all the other clients that the server must keep track of all of the clients in this application.*

The thread that interacts with the client also loops forever, waiting to receive data from the client. When it receives a message from the client, it invokes a method called `broadcast()`. This method loops through the different client output streams and sends the message to each of them.

After setting up the user interface, the client establishes a connection with the server and starts a thread that will listen for messages from the server. This thread listening for server messages loops forever. When it receives a message, it displays it in the `Received Text` field. Whenever the user types into the `Text to Send` field and hits Enter, the `action()` method sends this text to the server (where it gets broadcast to all other clients connected to the server).

Now that you've gotten an overview of the architecture for both the client and the server, let's look at the source code. This application has two separate source files, one representing the server and one representing the client. After each listing, I'll go over the lines of code you need special attention. First, here's the server:

```java
import java.io.*;
import java.net.*;
import java.util.Vector;
import java.util.Enumeration;
/**
 * MultiChatServer — A chat program between any number of
 * clients.
 *
 * The server acts as the central clearing house of all
 * messages.
 * To run as a server, do not supply any command-line
 * arguments.
 * MultiChat will start listening on the default port,
 * waiting
 * for a connection:
 *
 * java MultiChatServer
 */
public class MultiChatServer {
  private int port = 5001; // The default port.
  private boolean listening = true;
  private Vector clients = new Vector();
  public static void main(String args[]) {
    System.out.println("Hit control-c to exit the server.");
    new MultiChatServer().server();
  }
  // As a server, we create a server socket bound to the
  specified
  // port, wait for a connection, and then spawn a thread
  // to read data coming in over the network via the socket.
  private void server() {
   ServerSocket serverSock = null;
   try {
    InetAddress serverAddr = InetAddress.getByName(null);
    System.out.println("Waiting for first connection on " +
      serverAddr.getHostName() +
      " on port " + port);
    // Accept up to 50 connection at a time.
    // (This limit is just for the sake of performance.)
    serverSock = new ServerSocket(port, 50);
   } catch (IOException e) {
    System.out.println(e.getMessage() +
     ": Failed to create server socket.");
    return;
   }
   while (listening) {
    try {
     Socket socket = serverSock.accept();
     System.out.println("Accepted connection from " +
       socket.getInetAddress().getHostName());
```

```
        DataOutputStream remoteOut =
          new DataOutputStream(socket.getOutputStream());
        clients.addElement(remoteOut);
        new ServerHelper(socket, remoteOut, this).start();
      } catch (IOException e) {
        System.out.println(e.getMessage() +
        ": Failed to connect to client.");
      }
    }
    if (serverSock != null) {
     try {
      serverSock.close();
     } catch (IOException x) {
     }
    }
  }
  synchronized Vector getClients() {
   return clients;
  }
  synchronized void removeFromClients(DataOutputStream
  remoteOut) {
   clients.removeElement(remoteOut);
  }
}
/*
 * ServerHelper handles one client. The server creates one
   new ServerHelper thread for each client that connects
 * to it.
 */
class ServerHelper extends Thread {
  private Socket sock;
  private DataOutputStream remoteOut;
  private MultiChatServer server;
  private boolean listening = true;
  private DataInputStream remoteIn;
  ServerHelper(Socket sock, DataOutputStream remoteOut,
   MultiChatServer server) throws IOException
   {
    this.sock = sock;
    this.remoteOut = remoteOut;
    this.server = server;
    remoteIn = new DataInputStream(sock.getInputStream());
   }
  public synchronized void run() {
    String s;
    try {
     while (listening) {
      s = remoteIn.readUTF();
      broadcast(s);
     }
    } catch (IOException e) {
     System.out.println(e.getMessage() +
      ": Connection to peer lost.");
```

```
  } finally {
   try {
    cleanUp();
   } catch (IOException x) {
   }
  }
 }
// Send the message to all the sockets connected to the
server.
 private void broadcast(String s) {
  Vector clients = server.getClients();
  DataOutputStream dataOut = null;
  for (Enumeration e = clients.elements();
  e.hasMoreElements(); ) {
   dataOut = (DataOutputStream)(e.nextElement());
   if (!dataOut.equals(remoteOut)) {
    try {
     dataOut.writeUTF(s);
    } catch (IOException x) {
     System.out.println(x.getMessage() +
      ": Failed to broadcast to client.");
     server.removeFromClients(dataOut);
    }
   }
  }
 }
 private void cleanUp() throws IOException {
  if (remoteOut != null) {
   server.removeFromClients(remoteOut);
   remoteOut.close();
   remoteOut = null;
  }
  if (remoteIn != null) {
   remoteIn.close();
   remoteIn = null;
  }
  if (sock != null) {
   sock.close();
   sock = null;
  }
 }
 protected void finalize() throws Throwable {
  try {
   cleanUp();
  } catch (IOException x) {
   }
   super.finalize();
  }
 }
```

server( )

This time we allow up to 50 clients to connect to the server. We accomplish this with the following line of code:

```
serverSock = new ServerSocket(port, 50);
```

Then the server loops forever (until the user hits Control-C). At each iteration in the loop, the server waits to accept a connection with a client:

```
Socket socket = serverSock.accept();
```

If the clients are operating independently of each other (such as in a database server), the server can simply create a new thread to handle all future communication with that client. In this program, however, we need to keep track of all of the clients connected to the server; that's how we'll know to whom to broadcast the message. Thus, we create a DataOutputStream object, save this object in a list of all the other client DataOutputStreams, and then start our new thread, which we've called ServerHelper. Now ServerHelper will handle all future communication with the client, but it will turn to this list of output streams to broadcast any messages it receives from the client it's handling:

```
DataOutputStream remoteOut = new
  DataOutputStream(socket.getOutputStream());
clients.addElement(remoteOut);
new ServerHelper(socket, remoteOut, this).start();
```

run( )

The run() method in ServerHandler loops forever, simply reading data from the socket and broadcasting it to other clients also connected to the server.

```
while (listening) {
  s = remoteIn.readUTF();
  broadcast(s);
}
```

broadcast( )

This method simply enumerates the list of clients connected to the server, and as long as the DataOutputStream object in this list is not from the client that sent the message, it writes the message to that client.

cleanUp( )

As always, we're very careful to close all the streams and sockets when we're through with them.

The Client

Here's the client (it's very similar to the SingleChat program in many ways):

```java
import java.io.*;
import java.net.*;
import java.awt.*;
import java.awt.event.*;
/**
 * MultiChat — A chat program between any number of clients.
 *
 * To run as a client, supply two parameters:
 *   1. The name of the person to identify this user
 *   2. the name the server:
 *   java MultiChat Spielberg bluehorse.com
 * or
 *   java MultiChat Spielberg local // to run locally
 */
public class MultiChat extends Panel {
  TextArea receivedText;
  Socket sock; // The communication socket.
  private GridBagConstraints c;
  private GridBagLayout gridBag;
  private Frame frame;
  private Label label;
  private int port = 5001; // The default port.
  private TextField sendText;
  private String hostname;
  private String username;
  private DataOutputStream remoteOut;
  public static void main(String args[]) {
```

```
    if (args.length != 2) {
     System.out.println("format is: java MultiChat <username>
     <hostname>");
     return;
    }
    Frame f = new Frame(args[0]);
    MultiChat chat = new MultiChat(f, args[0], args[1]);
    f.add("Center", chat);
    f.setSize(350, 200);
    f.show();
    // Make the connection happen.
    chat.client();
   }
   public MultiChat(Frame f, String user, String host) {
    frame = f;
    frame.addWindowListener(new WindowExitHandler());
    username = user;
    hostname = host;
    // Build the user interface.
    Insets insets = new Insets(10, 20, 5, 10); // bot, lf,
    rt, top
    gridBag = new GridBagLayout();
    setLayout(gridBag);
    c = new GridBagConstraints();
    c.insets = insets;
    c.gridy = 0;
    c.gridx = 0;
    label = new Label("Text to send:");
    gridBag.setConstraints(label, c);
    add(label);
    c.gridx = 1;
    sendText = new TextField(20);
    sendText.addActionListener(new TextActionHandler());
    gridBag.setConstraints(sendText, c);
    add(sendText);
    c.gridy = 1;
    c.gridx = 0;
    label = new Label("Text received:");
    gridBag.setConstraints(label, c);
    add(label);
    c.gridx = 1;
    receivedText = new TextArea(3, 20);
   gridBag.setConstraints(receivedText, c);
    add(receivedText);
   }
   // As a client, we create a socket bound to the specified
   port,
   // connect to the specified host, and then spawn a thread to
   // read data coming coming in over the network via the
   socket.
   private void client() {
    try {
     if (hostname.equals("local"))
```

```
      hostname = null;
    InetAddress serverAddr = InetAddress.getByName(hostname);
     sock = new Socket(serverAddr.getHostName(), port);
     remoteOut = new
DataOutputStream(sock.getOutputStream());
    System.out.println("Connected to server " +
      serverAddr.getHostName() +
      " on port " + sock.getPort());
    new MultiChatReceive(this).start();
  } catch (IOException e) {
    System.out.println(e.getMessage() +
     ": Failed to connect to server.");
  }
}
protected void finalize() throws Throwable {
  try {
   if (remoteOut != null)
   remoteOut.close();
   if (sock != null)
   sock.close();
  } catch (IOException x) {
  }
  super.finalize();
}
class WindowExitHandler extends WindowAdapter {
 public void windowClosing(WindowEvent e) {
  Window w = e.getWindow();
  w.setVisible(false);
  w.dispose();
 System.exit(0);
 }
}
// Send data out to the socket we're communicating with
// when the user hits enter in the text field.
class TextActionHandler implements ActionListener {
 public void actionPerformed(ActionEvent e) {
  try {
   // Send it.
   remoteOut.writeUTF(sendText.getText());
   // Clear it.
   sendText.setText("");
  } catch (IOException x) {
   System.out.println(x.getMessage() +
    ": Connection to peer lost.");
  }
 }
}
}
/*
 * MultiChatReceive takes data sent on a socket and
   displays it in a text area. This receives it
 * from the network.
 */
```

```
class MultiChatReceive extends Thread {
 private MultiChat chat;
 MultiChatReceive(MultiChat chat) {
  this.chat = chat;
 }
 public synchronized void run() {
   String s;
   DataInputStream remoteIn = null;
   try {
     remoteIn = new
DataInputStream(chat.sock.getInputStream());
    while (true) {
     s = remoteIn.readUTF();
     chat.receivedText.setText(s);
    }
   } catch (IOException e) {
    System.out.println(e.getMessage() +
     ": Connection to peer lost.");
   } finally {
    try {
     if (remoteIn != null)
       remoteIn.close();
    } catch (IOException x) {
    }
   }
 }
}
```

The only real difference between the client version of `MultiChat` and the client portion of `SingleChat` is that one of the command-line parameters is the user's name. This name is placed in front of the user's message to identify the speaker when the message is broadcast.

Cleaning Up

You'll also notice that, once again, we're careful about closing the streams and sockets after we're through with them.

Exercise 20-1

Write a standalone character-mode client/server chat application using sockets. The server should accept only one connection from the client. Each peer should write what the user types via the keyboard to its communication socket. The peer should also read what comes in over this communication socket and display it in the standard output.

Exercise 20-2

Write a standalone character-mode client/server application where the client guesses a number between 0 and 9 chosen by the server. The client should send messages that follow this protocol: If the client wants to know whether the number chosen by the server is greater than some number, it should send a string in the format

```
>#
```

For example, to guess if the number is greater than 5, the client can send

```
>5
```

To ask whether the number is less than a value, the client can send

```
<#
```

To guess if the number is equal to a particular value, the client can send

```
=#
```

The server should send true or false, depending on the number it has chosen and on the client's guess. When the client has guessed the number correctly, the server should send a congratulatory message and then end the connection to the client.

Uniform Resource Locator (URL)

Here's a quick word about URLs (you won't really have to program using URLs on the programming assignment). Java defines a class called URL. When you use this class, you don't have to concern yourself with what's really going on with TCP/IP. All you have to do is point to the Internet address you are interested in and use the java.io classes to read from (and write to) that location. The basic format of a URL address is

```
access-method://server-nameport]/dir/file
```

As you can see from this, a URL indicates the access method, server name, and file name of an Internet resource. Typically, the access method is something like http or ftp. The server name for a Web address might be `www.tvpress.com`. The server name for an ftp address might be `ftp.tvpress.com`. The directory and file name refer to the directory structure of the server.

You can create a URL object using a variety of constructors. The easiest way is to create a new URL like this:

```
URL myHome = new URL("www.tvpress.com");
```

You can then use an `openConnection()` to begin reading from this URL, using the same I/O classes and methods you've already learned about. The `openConnect()` method returns a `URLConnection` object. With this, you can obtain an input stream or an output stream by calling `getInputStream()` or `getOutputStream()`. As you might suspect, you can then use this stream to access the resource.

Answer to the Exercises

Exercise 20-1

The only important change in this particular solution, compared to the example programs in the text, is that I used two threads: one to continually monitor what the user types and one to read from the socket.

```
import java.io.*;
import java.net.*;
import java.awt.*;
/**
 * CharChat - A chat program between a server and one client.
 *
 * To run as a client, name the server as the first command
   line
 * argument:
 *  java CharChat bluehorse.com
```

```java
 * or
 *   java CharChat local // to run locally
 */
public class CharChat {
 private int port = 5001; // The default port.
 public static void main(String args[]) {
  String s = null;
  if (args.length > 0)
   s = args[0];
  CharChat chat = new CharChat();
  if (s == null)
   chat.server();
  else
   chat.client(s);
 }
 // As a server, we create a server socket bound to the
specified
 // port, wait for a connection, and then spawn a thread
 // to read data coming in over the network via the socket.
 private void server() {
  Socket sock = null;
  ServerSocket serverSock = null;
  try {
   serverSock = new ServerSocket(port, 1);
   //We'll only accept one connection for this server.
   sock = serverSock.accept();
   new CharChatSend(sock).start();
   new CharChatReceive(sock).start();
  } catch (IOException x) {
   System.out.println(x.getMessage() +
   ": Failed to connect to client.");
   System.exit(1);
  } finally {
   // At this point, we don't need the ServerSocket anymore.
   if (serverSock != null) {
    try {
     serverSock.close();
    } catch (IOException x) {
    }
   }
  }
 }
 // As a client, we create a socket bound to the specified
ort,
 // connect to the specified host, and then spawn a thread
 // to read data coming in over the network via the socket.
 private void client(String serverName) {
  try {
   if (serverName.equals("local"))
    serverName = null;
   InetAddress serverAddr = InetAddress.getByName(serverName);
   Socket sock = new Socket(serverAddr.getHostName(), port);
```

```
    new CharChatSend(sock).start();
    new CharChatReceive(sock).start();
  } catch (IOException e) {
   System.out.println(e.getMessage() +
     ": Failed to connect to server.");
   }
 }
}
/*
 * CharChatReceive takes data sent on a socket and displays it
 * in the standard output.
 */
class CharChatReceive extends Thread {
 private Socket sock;
 private DataInputStream remoteIn;
 private boolean listening = true;
 public CharChatReceive(Socket sock) throws IOException {
  this.sock = sock;
  remoteIn = new DataInputStream(sock.getInputStream());
 }
 public synchronized void run() {
  String s;
  try {
   while (listening) {
    s = remoteIn.readUTF();
    System.out.println(s);
   }
  } catch (IOException e) {
   System.out.println(e.getMessage() +
     ": Connection to peer lost.");
  } finally {
   try {
    if (remoteIn != null) {
     remoteIn.close();
     remoteIn = null;
    }
    if (sock != null) {
     sock.close();
     sock = null;
    }
   } catch (IOException x) {
   }
  }
 }
 protected void finalize() throws Throwable {
  try {
   if (remoteIn != null)
    remoteIn.close();
   if (sock != null)
    sock.close();
  } catch (IOException x) {
  }
  super.finalize();
```

```
      }
    }
    /*
     * CharChatSend takes data entered on the standard input and
     * sends it out over a socket.
     */
    class CharChatSend extends Thread {
     private Socket sock;
     private DataOutputStream remoteOut;
     private boolean listening = true;
     public CharChatSend(Socket sock) throws IOException {
       this.sock = sock;
       remoteOut = new DataOutputStream(sock.getOutputStream());
     }
     public synchronized void run() {
      BufferedReader in = null;
      String s;
      try {
       in = new BufferedReader(new
    InputStreamReader(System.in));
       while (listening) {
        s = in.readLine();
        if (s.equals(""))
         break;
        remoteOut.writeUTF(s);
       }
      } catch (IOException e) {
        System.out.println(e.getMessage() +
        ": Connection to peer lost.");
      } finally {
        try {
         if (in != null)
          in.close();
         if (remoteOut != null) {
          remoteOut.close();
          remoteOut = null;
         }
        // Socket closed in receive thread
        } catch (IOException x) {
        }
      }
    }
    protected void finalize() throws Throwable {
     try {
      if (remoteOut != null)
       remoteOut.close();
       // Socket closed in Receive thread
      } catch (IOException x) {
      }
      super.finalize();
     }
    }
```

Exercise 20-2

Here is the client:

```java
import java.io.*;
import java.net.*;
import java.awt.*;
/**
* NumberClient — The client program for the guessing game.
*
* To run as a client, name the server as the first command-
* line argument:
*    java NumberClient bluehorse.com
* or
*    java NumberClient local // to run locally
*/
public class NumberClient {
 private int port = 5001; // The default port.
 private Socket sock;
 private DataInputStream remoteIn;
 private DataOutputStream remoteOut;
 private boolean listening = true;
 public static void main(String args[]) {
  if (args.length != 1) {
   System.out.println("format is: java NumberClient
<hostname>");
   return;
  }
  new NumberClient().client(args[0]);
 }
 // As a client, we create a socket bound to the specified
port,
 // connect to the specified host, and then start
communicating
 // over the network via the socket.
 private void client(String serverName) {
  BufferedReader in = new BufferedReader(new
InputStreamReader(System.in));
  try {
   if (serverName.equals("local"))
    serverName = null;
   InetAddress serverAddr =
InetAddress.getByName(serverName);
   sock = new Socket(serverAddr.getHostName(), port);
   remoteIn = new DataInputStream(sock.getInputStream());
   remoteOut = new DataOutputStream(sock.getOutputStream());
   while (listening) {
    String s = in.readLine();
    if (s.equals(""))
     listening = false;
```

```
      else
       remoteOut.writeUTF(s);
      String response = remoteIn.readUTF();
      System.out.println(response);
     }
   } catch (IOException e) {
     System.out.println(e.getMessage() +
       ": Connection with server closed.");
   } finally {
    try {
      if (remoteIn != null) {
       remoteIn.close();
       remoteIn = null;
      }
      if (remoteOut != null) {
       remoteOut.close();
       remoteOut = null;
      }
      if (sock != null) {
       sock.close();
       sock = null;
      }
    } catch (IOException x) {
    }
   }
  }
  protected void finalize() throws Throwable {
   try {
     if (remoteIn != null)
      remoteIn.close();
     if (remoteOut != null)
      remoteOut.close();
     if (sock != null)
       sock.close();
   } catch (IOException x) {
   }
   super.finalize();
  }
 }
```

Here is the server:

```
import java.io.*;
import java.net.*;
import java.awt.*;
/**
 * NumberServer — The server for a number-guessing
 * application.
 * To run as a server, name the server as the first command-
 * line argument
```

```
 *   java NumberServer bluehorse.com
 * or
 *   java NumberServer local // to run locally
 */
public class NumberServer {
 private int port = 5001; // The default port.
 private boolean listening = true;
 public static void main(String args[]) {
  new NumberServer().server();
 }
 // As a server, we create a server socket bound to the
specified
 // port, wait for a connection, and then spawn a thread to
 // read data coming in over the network via the socket.
 private void server() {
  ServerSocket serverSock = null;
  try {
   serverSock = new ServerSocket(port, 50);
  } catch (IOException x) {
   System.out.println(x.getMessage() +
    ": Failed to create server socket.");
   System.exit(1);
  }
  while (listening) {
   try {
    Socket sock = serverSock.accept();
    new HandleGuesses(sock).start();
   } catch (IOException x) {
    System.out.println(x.getMessage() +
     ": Failed to connect to client.");
    System.exit(1);
   }
  }
  // At this point, we don't need the ServerSocket anymore.
  if (serverSock != null) {
   try {
    serverSock.close();
   } catch (IOException x) {
   }
  }
 }
}
/*
 * HandleGuesses communicates with the client.
 */
class HandleGuesses extends Thread {
 private Socket sock;
 private DataInputStream remoteIn;
 private DataOutputStream remoteOut;
 private boolean listening = true;
 private int num = (int)(Math.random() * 10);
 public HandleGuesses(Socket sock) throws IOException {
  this.sock = sock;
```

```
    remoteIn = new DataInputStream(sock.getInputStream());
    remoteOut = new DataOutputStream(sock.getOutputStream());
  }
 public synchronized void run() {
  String s;
  String op;
  String guessString;
  int guessInt;
  try {
   while (listening) {
    s = remoteIn.readUTF();
    op = s.substring(0, 1);
    guessString = s.substring(1, 2);
    guessInt = new Integer(guessString).intValue();
    if (op.equals(">"))
     handleGreaterThan(guessInt);
    else if (op.equals("<"))
     handleLessThan(guessInt);
    else
     handleEquals(guessInt);
   }
  } catch (NumberFormatException x) {
   System.out.println(x.getMessage() +
    ": Protocol problem: expected a number.");
  } catch (IOException x) {
   System.out.println(x.getMessage() +
    ": Connection to peer lost.");
  } finally {
   try {
    if (remoteIn != null) {
    remoteIn.close();
    remoteIn = null;
   }
    if (remoteOut != null) {
     remoteOut.close();
     remoteOut = null;
    }
    if (sock != null) {
     sock.close();
     sock = null;
    }
   } catch (IOException x) {
  }
 }
}
private void handleGreaterThan(int i) throws IOException {
 if (num > i)
  remoteOut.writeUTF("true");
 else
  remoteOut.writeUTF("false");
}
private void handleLessThan(int i) throws IOException{
 if (num < i)
```

```
    remoteOut.writeUTF("true");
  else
    remoteOut.writeUTF("false");
}
private void handleEquals(int i) throws IOException {
  if (i == num) {
    remoteOut.writeUTF("You guessed it!");
    listening = false;
  }
  else
    remoteOut.writeUTF("false");
  }
  protected void finalize() throws Throwable {
    try {
      if (remoteIn != null)
        remoteIn.close();
      if (remoteOut != null)
        remoteOut.close();
      if (sock != null)
      sock.close();
    } catch (IOException x) {
    }
    super.finalize();
  }
}
```

QUESTIONS

1. To wait for a client to request a connection, your server can use the class

   a. Socket

   b. ServerSocket

   c. Server

   d. URL

2. The ServerSocket's accept() method returns an object of type

   a. Socket

   b. ServerSocket

   c. Server

   d. URL

3. When you create a new socket instance using a constructor that takes a host address,

   a. Java attempts to establish a connection over the Internet with the host

   b. Java starts a server running on the host

   c. nothing special happens until you invoke the socket's `accept()` method

4. To acquire an output stream to use to communicate via a socket given a socket instance named sock, you can write

   a. `sock.accept();`

   b. `sock.getDataOutputStream();`

   c. `sock.getOutputStream();`

   d. `new DataOutputStream(sock);`

5. TCP is used to

   a. identify a machine on the Internet based on a dotted octet or domain name

   b. ensure packets arrive in the same order they are sent

   c. Both a and b

   d. Neither of these

6. A socket encodes

   a. a port number

   b. an IP address

   c. both a port number and an IP address

   d. none of these

Answers to the Review Questions

1. b. Invoke the ServerSocket's `accept()` method to wait for an incoming request.

2. a. The ServerSocket's `accept()` method returns an instance of class `Socket`, which the server can use to communicate with the client.

3. a. Creating a socket using a constructor that specifies a host causes Java to attempt to establish a connection with that host.

4. c. Use `getOutputStream()` to acquire a stream. You can then create a `DataOutputStream` by passing this stream to its constructor.

5. b. TCP guarantees packets arrive in the same order they are sent. IP identifies machines on the Internet.

6. c. A socket encodes both a port number and an IP address.

Designing
Application
Interfaces

If you have been reading this book straight through, you have already read Chapters 14 and 15, where we discussed the basics of creating a *Graphical User Interface* (GUI). With that knowledge, you can probably fish around in the APIs for the methods you need, piece together more complicated user interfaces, and add the little flourishes that will make your interface behave exactly as you would like. There is no need to waste your time through trial and error, however. This chapter helps point you in the right direction when building advanced GUIs.

Imitating a typical real-world situation, the programming assignment requires you to create a GUI that exactly matches a set of specifications. The assignment provides diagrams that show you how the user interface should look when it first appears and how it should look if the user enlarges the enclosing frame.

To meet the specifications, you have to create a hierarchy of containers within other containers using a combination of different layout managers. You should also know how to change components after they have been displayed on the screen.

The programming assignment is a stand-alone graphical application, which means that there is no appletviewer or Web browser to create an enclosing frame for you. You need to know how to write your own enclosing frame.

Objectives for This Chapter

- Use layout managers to size and space components as desired.
- Embed layout managers within other layout managers to achieve sophisticated effects.
- Set fonts and colors for your components.
- Change a component after it has been displayed.
- Place user-interface elements within top-level frames.

Mix and Match

In Chapter 14, we briefly examined how components are sized. Our objective then was to understand enough information to pass the programmer's test; however, our objective now is a little broader. We want to use the proper layout manager in the proper way to achieve a specific look. You can create arbitrarily complex arrangements in your user interface by nesting layout managers. Here are some scenarios.

Let's say that you want to arrange five buttons along the top of an applet. You might want these five buttons to have any number of appearances:

- All with a width equal to the widest button
- Each only as large as necessary to contain its label
- Centered, left aligned, or right aligned
- Centered but equal in width

Achieving the look you want involves two tasks:

1. Using the right layout manager to stretch or not stretch the buttons as appropriate
2. Using the right combination of layout managers so that the buttons are aligned and are arranged correctly in relation to each other

Using One Layout Manager

Let's look at the simplest situation first: using one layout manager to achieve the button layouts. A `BorderLayout` is not the best choice to use directly for laying out five buttons, because each region ("North," "South," and so on) can only contain one component. Therefore, the look of all five regions being used by five buttons is unusual. This arrangement is shown in Figure 21-1.

Figure 21-1
Five buttons
arranged in a
`BorderLayout`

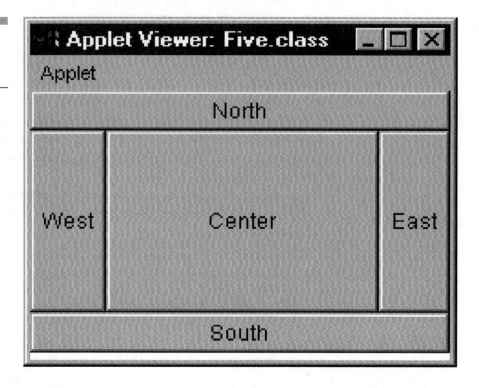

Each button expands to fill its region. In particular, the "North" and "South" buttons expand horizontally, while the "East" and "West" buttons expand vertically. The "Center" button takes up the remaining space.

The code for this arrangement, which you saw in Chapter 14, is as follows:

```java
import java.awt.*;
import java.applet.*;

public class Five extends Applet {
    public void init() {
        setLayout(new BorderLayout());
        add("North", new Button("North"));
        add("South", new Button("South"));
        add("East", new Button("East"));
        add("West", new Button("West"));
        add("Center", new Button("Center"));
    }
}
```

Usually, a GridLayout is not what you want (if a GridLayout is the only layout manager you are using). For example, arranging five buttons in a grid that is one row by five columns will produce a display similar to the one in Figure 21-2.

As you can see, the buttons are all equally sized and take up the full region of the grid cell. The code is as follows:

```
import java.awt.*;
import java.applet.*;

public class GridFive extends Applet {
    public void init() {
        setLayout(new GridLayout(1, 5));
        add(new Button("First"));
        add(new Button("Second"));
        add(new Button("Third"));
        add(new Button("Fourth"));
        add(new Button("Fifth"));
    }
}
```

Figure 21-2
Five buttons in a
GridLayout

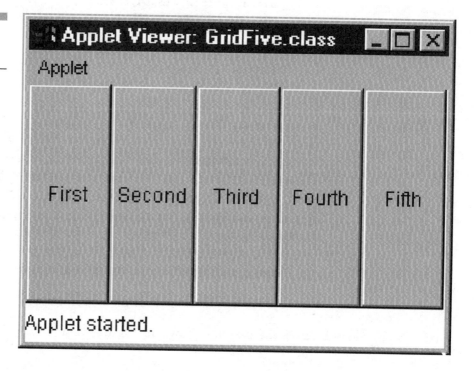

You can also create the GridLayout using a constructor, where you define space around the cells. For example, using this line of code creates the GridLayout,

```
setLayout(new GridLayout(1, 5, 10, 0));
```

which creates the display in Figure 21-3.

If there were multiple rows, we could also specify a vertical gap. In the previous snippet, we passed zero to the constructor for GridLayout for the vertical gap, because we only had one row.

First, a FlowLayout will arrange the buttons left to right, and as it runs out of room on each row, it will then arrange the buttons top to bottom. The buttons take on their natural size. By default, each row is centered, as in Figure 21-4.

Here is the code that produced Figure 21-4:

```
import java.awt.*;
import java.applet.*;

public class FlowFiveA extends Applet {
    public void init() {
        setLayout(new FlowLayout());
        add(new Button("First"));
        add(new Button("Second"));
        add(new Button("Third"));
        add(new Button("Fourth"));
        add(new Button("Fifth"));
    }
}
```

You do not have to accept that each row is centered, however. You can use the constants FlowLayout.LEFT, FlowLayout.CENTER, and FlowLayout.RIGHT to set the alignment. One of the constructors enables you to pass in this alignment value.

You can also specify horizontal and vertical gaps between components and rows by invoking the constructor that takes three parameters: the alignment, the horizontal gaps, and the vertical gaps. For example, creating the FlowLayout with this line of code,

```
setLayout(new FlowLayout(FlowLayout.LEFT));
```

creates the display shown in Figure 21-5.

Figure 21-3
A GridLayout with space around each cell

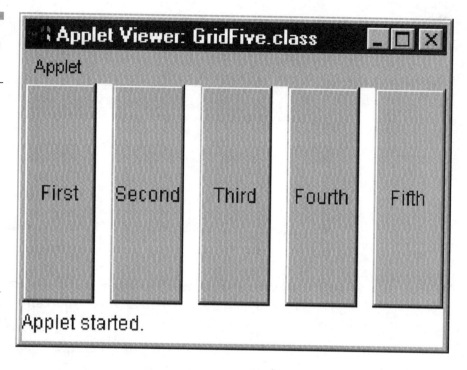

Figure 21-4
A FlowLayout arranging five buttons

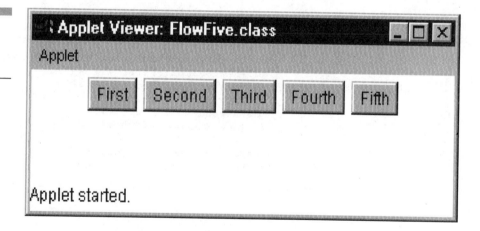

As you can see, there is only so much you can achieve when you use layout managers one at a time. The power comes when you use them in combination.

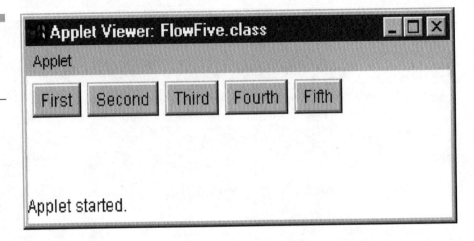

Figure 21-5
A `FlowLayout`
arrangement where
the components are
left aligned

For example, to arrange the five buttons along the bottom of an applet and make them left aligned, you can write the following code:

```java
import java.awt.*;
import java.applet.*;

public class FlowFiveB extends Applet {
    public void init() {
        Panel p = new Panel();
        p.setLayout(new FlowLayout(FlowLayout.LEFT));
        p.add(new Button("First"));
        p.add(new Button("Second"));
        p.add(new Button("Third"));
        p.add(new Button("Fourth"));
        p.add(new Button("Fifth"));

        setLayout(new BorderLayout());
        add("South", p);
    }
}
```

In this code, we first place the buttons into a `Panel` object that uses a `FlowLayout` to left-align them. Then, we add the `Panel` object to the applet, which uses a `BorderLayout`. This program produces the display shown in Figure 21-6.

Figure 21-6
Using
BorderLayout *and*
FlowLayout
together

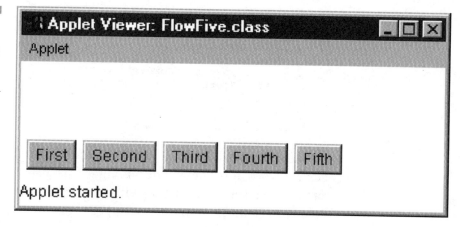

What if you wanted to make each button the same size, but still align them on the left at the bottom of the applet? Then, you would have to use three layout managers in combination. That is no problem at all; just think through your design carefully so that it all comes together in the end.

First, you want to size all of the buttons to be the size of the largest one (you can use a GridLayout to achieve this effect). Then, you want to align this group of buttons on the left (you can use a FlowLayout to accomplish this task). Finally, you want the left-aligned buttons on the bottom of the applet (naturally, you use a BorderLayout to achieve this result).

Figure 21-7 shows the layout that you ultimately want.

Here is the code that produced Figure 21-7:

```java
import java.awt.*;
import java.applet.*;

public class FlowFiveC extends Applet {
    public void init() {
        Panel p1 = new Panel();
        p1.setLayout(new GridLayout(1, 5));
        p1.add(new Button("First"));
        p1.add(new Button("Second"));
        p1.add(new Button("Third"));
        p1.add(new Button("Fourth"));
        p1.add(new Button("Fifth"));
```

```
        Panel p2 = new Panel();
        p2.setLayout(new FlowLayout(FlowLayout.LEFT));
        p2.add(p1);

        setLayout(new BorderLayout());
        add("South", p2);
    }
}
```

The examples so far have involved buttons, because you can clearly see where the layout managers are placing each button. You can achieve the same effects with other components, however. `Button`, `Label`, `TextField`, `TextArea`, `Choice`, and `List` will all stretch in `GridLayout` and `BorderLayout` regions. `Checkbox` will not.

Exercise 21-1

Create a user interface that looks similar to the display shown in Figure 21-8.

This figure shows the interface for a word-processing application. There are two rows of options on the bottom of the applet. The first row contains checkboxes indicating possible text colors: black, blue, and red. Notice that these are evenly spaced in their row. Naturally, they should be mutually exclusive. The second row offers a

Figure 21-7
A layout involving three layout managers

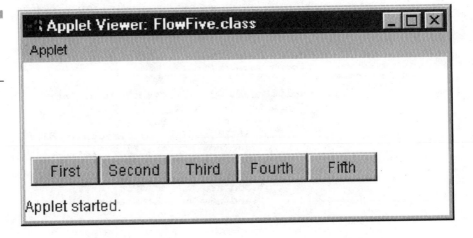

Figure 21-8
An interface with a
text area and two
rows of options

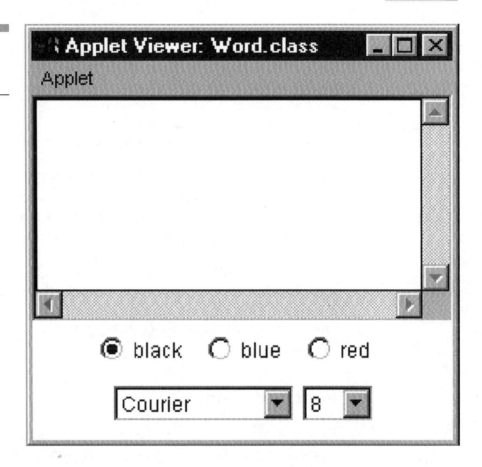

list of font types (Courier, Helvetica, and Times Roman) and point sizes (8, 10, and 12). Notice that these font types are centered.

The text area should take up the rest of the applet and should be 60 columns wide and 10 rows high. (You do not need to make this applet functional now.)

Changing Your Look

Just because you have displayed a component does not mean that component is out of your hands entirely. As long as you can find the component through an object reference, you can continue to change its appearance.

Text

One common task is to change the text in a label. For example, you might have a label that displays a status message. You can use the method `setText()` to change what a Label object displays and pass this method a new string to use.

Updating a label or a button can be tricky in certain situations. If the label is in a `BorderLayout` in the "North" or "South" region, it will already be stretched to its maximum width, and you will not have to concern yourself with the label's size. If the label is in a flow layout, however, the label will not change its size if the new text is longer than the old text. This situation can cause your new text to be clipped.

If your label will not stretch because the label is in a flow layout (but the label will not display any text initially), you might want to create the label with some blank spaces. That way, when you do place text into the label, it is already sized large enough to contain the text.

Font and Color

Here are some important classes and methods to keep in mind when changing the appearance of a component:

- *The Font class defines a font*   To define a new Font object, you supply the font name, font style (from a set of constants defined by the Font class), and the size of the font. You can then set the font used by a component by invoking `setFont()` and passing your new Font object.

- Courier is a proportional font, which means that each letter's width is the same. You will find it convenient to use a proportional font when you want your text to line up with text in other lines (such as in a text area or list).

- You can use `setForeground()` to set the text color for components. You can also use `setBackground()` to set the component's background color. Pass both of these methods a

Color object. Almost always, you will use a predefined Color object referenced from the Color class, such as Color.blue, Color.red, or Color.gray, to name three colors. Many common colors are represented as static variables (such as these) in the Color class.

Replacing a Component

If you would like to remove a component from a container, all you have to do is invoke `remove()` and pass this method the object reference of the component that you want to remove.

You can even add a component by invoking `add()` at any time—not just when you initially build your user interface. Invoking `remove()` and `add()` back to back can replace a component. There are a number of gotchas, however. First, you might have to force the user interface to lay itself out again after you have tinkered with it. You can do this task by invoking `validate()`. Second, and perhaps most importantly, you have to be aware of the order in which you added components to your container. If you are attempting to replace the third button in a grid that is two rows by three columns, you cannot just remove the third button and replace it by invoking `add()`. That action would cause the new button to be added to the end of the grid. Instead of using `add()` and only passing the component to add, you can use an overloaded version of `add()` that also takes a position index, indicating where it should be added to the container. So, to replace the third button in this scenario, you can write the following code:

```
remove(oldButton);
add(newbutton, 2); // 0 based
```

Sometimes, if you want to replace components in a panel or replace the text in a choice or list, the best way to achieve a smooth look is to create a new component or set of components and then replace the ones on-screen, rather than changing the on-screen components as you go. That action can cause the display to look messy while the change is taking place.

Exercise 21-2

Extend the applet you wrote in Exercise 21-1 so that the text in the text area matches the selections in the options on the bottom-two rows.

Working with Frames

If you climb the container hierarchy to the top, you will always find a frame. All components must ultimately be contained inside a frame. You can either create this enclosing frame yourself, or in the case of an applet, you might use the frame that the appletviewer or Web browser provided for you.

You should know that you need a top-level frame for a number of reasons:

- If you want to display a window separately from your applet, perhaps outside of the Web browser, you will need to create a frame to contain this separate window.

- If you do not create an applet, you must create a frame for any stand-alone GUIs that you create.

- You need a frame to show dialogs.

Let's start our work with frames by looking at a snippet (which we will improve upon) to display a stand-alone GUI contained in an object reference called panel:

```
Frame f = new Frame();
f.add("Center", panel); // BorderLayout is the default for
frame
f.pack();
f.show();
```

Let's nit-pick this snippet for a moment. First of all, the frame's title will say "Unknown," because we have not explicitly supplied our own title. Second, the application will not close or exit when the user clicks the Close button in this frame. In fact, in Windows and

Solaris, the user has to use Control-C in the window from which the user launched this program to end the program. That user interface is not exactly graceful.

Closing the Frame

We can fix the lack of a title in the frame by passing a title to the frame's overloaded constructor. The inability to exit when the user clicks the Close button can best be fixed by providing a WindowListener for the frame and by handling the WindowClosing() event as follows:

```
import java.awt.Window;
import java.awt.event.WindowAdapter;
import java.awt.event.WindowEvent;

/**
 * This handler helps a window (such as a top-level Frame)
 * exit gracefully.
 */
public class WindowCloser extends WindowAdapter {
    public void windowClosing(WindowEvent e) {
        Window w = e.getWindow();
        w.setVisible(false);
        w.dispose();
        System.exit(0);
    }
}
```

Then, add an instance of this class to the window listeners for the window or frame that you want to be able to close. For example, if your frame is in a reference called topFrame, and WindowCloser is in a reference called closer, you can write the following line:

```
topFrame.addWindowListener(closer);
```

Making an Applet a Stand-Alone Application

If you would like to turn an applet into a stand-alone application so you can run the applet outside a Web browser (free of many security requirements related to accessing servers and the file system), you can write a `main()` method for your applet. That way, you can invoke the applet from the command line.

To make this feature work, you have to handle the chores that the Web browser used to handle. As far as Java is concerned, a Web browser's chores include the following:

1. Creating an instance of your applet

2. Making sure your applet progresses through its life-cycle—especially so that it creates and arranges its user-interface components. (If your applet creates a user interface in `init()`, make sure that any frame you write that replaces the applet also invokes `init()`.)

3. Creating a top-level frame for your applet and placing your applet in this frame

4. Setting this frame to its appropriate size. (You can either set the frame's size directly by using `setSize()`, or you can invoke `pack()` to shrink-wrap the frame around your user interface.)

5. Making this frame appear on the screen. (You can accomplish this task by invoking your frame's `setVisible(true)` method.)

Exercise 21-3

Take the word-processing applet you wrote in Exercises 21-1 and 21-2 and add a `main()` method to this applet so that it can run as a stand-alone application.

Answers to the Exercises

Exercise 21-1

This code contains a few instance variables in preparation for making this interface operative:

Chapter 21: Designing Application Interfaces

549

```
import java.awt.*;
import java.applet.Applet;

public class Word extends Applet {
    private TextArea area;
    private Choice fonts;
    private Choice sizes;

    private String currentFont = "Courier";
    private int currentSize = 8;
    private int style = Font.PLAIN;
    private Color currentColor = Color.black;

    public void init() {
        setLayout(new BorderLayout());

        area = new TextArea(10, 60);
        area.setFont(new Font(currentFont, style,
currentSize));
        area.setForeground(currentColor);
        add("Center", area);

        Panel p = new Panel();
        p.setLayout(new GridLayout(2,1));

        Panel firstRow = new Panel();
        CheckboxGroup group = new CheckboxGroup();
        firstRow.add(new Checkbox("black", group, true));
        firstRow.add(new Checkbox("blue", group, false));
        firstRow.add(new Checkbox("red", group, false));
        p.add(firstRow);

        Panel secondRow = new Panel();
        fonts = new Choice();
        fonts.addItem("Courier");
        fonts.addItem("Helvetica");
        fonts.addItem("Times Roman");
        secondRow.add(fonts);

        sizes = new Choice();
        sizes.addItem("8");
        sizes.addItem("12");
        sizes.addItem("16");
        secondRow.add(sizes);

        p.add(secondRow);

        add("South", p);
    }

}
```

Exercise 21-2

```
import java.awt.*;
import java.awt.event.*;
import java.applet.Applet;

public class Word extends Applet {
    private TextArea area;
    private Choice fonts;
    private Choice sizes;

    private String currentFont = "Courier";
    private int currentSize = 8;
    private int style = Font.PLAIN;
    private Color currentColor = Color.black;

    public void init() {
        setLayout(new BorderLayout());

        area = new TextArea(10, 60);
        area.setFont(new Font(currentFont, style,
currentSize));
        area.setForeground(currentColor);
        add("Center", area);

        Panel p = new Panel();
        p.setLayout(new GridLayout(2,1));

        Panel firstRow = new Panel();
        CheckboxGroup group = new CheckboxGroup();
        Checkbox[] checkBoxes = {new Checkbox("black", group,
                                 true),
                                  new Checkbox("blue", group,
                                 false),
                                  new Checkbox("red", group,
                                 false)};
        for (int i = 0; i<checkBoxes.length; i++) {
          checkBoxes[i].addItemListener(new
ChooseColorHandler());
          firstRow.add(checkBoxes[i]);
        }
        p.add(firstRow);

        Panel secondRow = new Panel();
        fonts = new Choice();
        fonts.addItem("Courier");
        fonts.addItem("Helvetica");
        fonts.addItem("Times Roman");
        fonts.addItemListener(new ChooseFontStyleHandler());
```

```
      secondRow.add(fonts);

      sizes = new Choice();
      sizes.addItem("8");
      sizes.addItem("12");
      sizes.addItem("16");
      sizes.addItemListener(new ChooseFontSizeHandler());
      secondRow.add(sizes);

      p.add(secondRow);

      add("South", p);
   }


   class ChooseFontSizeHandler implements ItemListener {

     public void itemStateChanged(ItemEvent ie) {
       Choice c = (Choice)ie.getSource();
       currentSize =
Integer.valueOf(c.getSelectedItem()).intValue();
       area.setFont(new Font(currentFont, style,
currentSize));
     }
   }

   class ChooseFontStyleHandler implements ItemListener {

     public void itemStateChanged(ItemEvent ie) {
       Choice c = (Choice)ie.getSource();
       currentFont = c.getSelectedItem();
       area.setFont(new Font(currentFont, style,
currentSize));
     }
   }

   class ChooseColorHandler implements ItemListener {

     public void itemStateChanged(ItemEvent ie) {
       Checkbox c = (Checkbox)ie.getSource();
       String s = c.getLabel();
       if (s.equals("black"))
         currentColor = Color.black;
       else if (s.equals("blue"))
         currentColor = Color.blue;
       else
         currentColor = Color.red;

       area.setForeground(currentColor);
     }
   }
}
```

Exercise 21-3

You can use the `WindowCloser` class provided in the text. Here is how you can write a `main()` method for the Word applet:

```
public static void main(String[] args) {
    Word w = new Word();
    w.init();
    Frame frame = new Frame("Word processor");
    frame.add("Center", w);
    frame.addWindowListener(new WindowCloser());
    frame.pack();
    frame.show();
}
```

QUESTIONS ▬ ▬ ▬ ▬ ▬ ▬ ▬ ▬

1. To force a layout manager to re-layout the components in a container, you can invoke the container method called
   a. `validate()`
   b. `repaint()`
   c. `layout()`
   d. `update()`

2. To set the text color for a component, you can use the component method
   a. `setColor()`
   b. `setFont()`
   c. `setForeground()`
   d. `setBackground()`

3. What is the cleanest way to make a window vanish permanently?
   a. Invoke `dispose()`
   b. Invoke `setVisible(false)`
   c. Invoke `dispose()` and then `setVisible(false)`
   d. Invoke `setVisible(false)` and then `dispose()`

4. What method can you invoke for a frame enclosing a user interface so that it fits perfectly around that interface?

   a. `resize()`
   b. `size()`
   c. `pack()`
   d. `show()`

5. How can you display three labels that line up top to bottom along the right-hand side of an interface and are sized equally?

   a. Place the labels into a `GridLayout`.
   b. Place the labels into a `BorderLayout`.
   c. Place the labels into a container that uses a `BorderLayout`, and then place this container into another container which uses a `GridLayout`.
   d. Place the labels in a container which uses a `GridLayout`, and then place this container into another container which uses a `BorderLayout`.

Answers to the Review Questions

1. a. The `validate()` method forces a layout manager to lay out the components again.

2. c. `setColor()` sets the drawing color; `setFont()` changes the font type; and `setBackground()` sets the background color. `setForeground()` changes the text color.

3. d. You should always hide the window before disposing of it to make sure that the interface looks clean.

4. c. The `pack()` method makes the frame shrink or expand as necessary to contain the interface.

5. d. First, you can place the components into a container using a `GridLayout` that is three rows by one column. Then, you can place this container into another container using a `BorderLayout` on the "East" side.

Practice
Exam

CHAPTER 22

Sun Certified Programmer Practice Exam

Practice Exam Number 1

Here are the rules:

Allow 90 minutes to complete this exam. You should turn off the telephone, go someplace where you will not be disturbed, check the time on your watch, and begin. Do not bring any books with you, because you will not have them during the test. You can take breaks, but do not look up any information. You can have a piece of scratch paper and a pen or pencil, but you cannot have any crib sheets.

If you get 42 questions right, you have hit the 70 percent mark, and you have passed. Good luck.

Questions

1. Given the following class definition,

```
class A {
   public int x;
   private int y;
   class B {
      protected void method1() {
      }
      class C {
         private void method2() {
         }
      }
   }
}
class D extends A {
   public float z;
}
```

what can `method2()` access directly, without a reference to another instance? Select all valid answers.

a. the variable x defined in A
b. the variable y defined in A
c. method1 defined in B
d. the variable z defined in D

2. You have an eight-bit file using the character set defined by ISO 8859-8. You are writing an application to display this file in a TextArea. The local encoding is already set to 8859-8. How can you write a chunk of code to read the first line from this file? You have three variables that are accessible to you:

   `myfile` is the name of the file you want to read

   `stream` is an `InputStream` object associated with this file

   `s` is a `String object`

   Select all valid answers.

   a.

   ```
   InputStreamReader reader = new InputStreamReader(stream,
   "8859-8");
   BufferedReader buffer = new BufferedReader(reader);
   s = buffer.readLine();
   ```

   b.

   ```
   InputStreamReader reader = new InputStreamReader(stream);
   BufferedReader buffer = new BufferedReader(reader);
   s = buffer.readLine();
   ```

   c.

   ```
   InputStreamReader reader = new InputStreamReader(myfile,
   "8859-8");
   BufferedReader buffer = new BufferedReader(reader);
   s = buffer.readLine();
   ```

   d.

   ```
   InputStreamReader reader = new InputStreamReader(myfile);
   BufferedReader buffer = new BufferedReader(reader);
   s = buffer.readLine();
   ```

   e.

   ```
   FileReader reader = new FileReader(myfile);
   BufferedReader buffer = new BufferedReader(reader);
   s = buffer.readLine();
   ```

3. How can you write a line of code for an applet's `init()` method that determines how wide the applet is? Select all valid answers.

   a. `int width = this.getY();`
   b. `int width = this.getSize().w;`
   c. `int width = getSize();`
   d. `int width = getSize().w;`
   e. `int width = getWidth();`

4. For a variable-width font, how wide is a `TextField` created using the following expression?

   ```
   new TextField(20)
   ```

   a. 20 times the average of all the characters in the font used for this `TextField` object
   b. 20 times the width of the letter M
   c. 20 times the width of the letter A
   d. 20 inches
   e. 20 picas

5. Given this interface definition,

   ```
   interface A {
       int method1(int i);
       int method2(int j);
   }
   ```

   which of the following classes implements this interface and is not abstract? Select all valid answers.

   a.

   ```
   class B implements A {
       int method1() { }
       int method2() { }
   }
   ```

   b.

   ```
   class B {
       int method1(int i) { }
       int method2(int j) { }
   }
   ```

c.

```
class B implements A {
    int method1(int i) { }
    int method2(int j) { }
}
```

d.

```
class B extends A {
    int method1(int i) { }
    int method2(int j) { }
}
```

e.

```
class B implements A {
    int method2(int j) { }
    int method1(int i) { }
}
```

6. Given the following code,

```
import java.awt.*;
import java.awt.event.*;
public class MyApplet extends java.applet.Applet {
    public void init() {
        Button b = new Button("Button1");
        b.addMouseListener(new ClickHandler());
        add(b);
    }
    class ClickHandler extends MouseAdapter {
        public void mouseClicked(MouseEvent evt) {
            // A
        }
    }
}
```

what line of code at A writes the mouse's horizontal location to the standard output at the time of the event? Note that the value output should be with respect to the component that handled the event. Fill in the blank.

7. Given the same code as in Question 11, how can you write a line of code at A that will place the Button object into a variable called mybutton that is already defined as a reference to a Button object? Fill in the blank.

8. Which Listener interface can you implement to respond to the user hitting the Enter key after typing in a `TextField` object? Fill in the blank.

9. What is written to the standard output as the result of executing the following statements?

```
Boolean b1 = new Boolean(true);
Boolean b2 = new Boolean(true);
if (b1 == b2)
    if (b1.equals(b2))
        System.out.println("a");
    else
        System.out.println("b");
else
    if (b1.equals(b2))
        System.out.println("c");
    else
        System.out.println("d");
```

   a. a
   b. b
   c. c
   d. d

10. Which Listener interfaces can you add to a `TextArea` object?
   a. `TextListener`
   b. `ActionListener`
   c. `MouseMotionListener`
   d. `MouseListener`
   e. `ComponentListener`

11. What appears in the standard output if the method called `problem()` in the following code throws an instance of class exception when the method called `trythis()` is invoked?

```
public void trythis() {
    try {
        System.out.println("1");
        problem();
    } catch (RuntimeException x) {
        System.out.println("2");
        return;
    } catch (Exception x) {
```

```
        System.out.println("3");
        return;
    } finally {
        System.out.println("4");
    }
    System.out.println("5");
}
```

Select all valid answers.

a. "1"
b. "2"
c. "3"
d. "4"
e. "5"

12. What is the type of the Event object passed to the `mouseDragged()` method defined in a class that implements `java.awt.event.MouseMotionListener` (that is, what is the class name for the argument)? Fill in the blank.

13. Examine the following switch block:

```
char mychar = 'c';
switch (mychar) {
    default:
    case 'a': System.out.println("a"); break;
    case 'b': System.out.println("b"); break;
}
```

Which of the following questions are definitely true? Select all valid answers.

a. This switch block is illegal, because only integers can be used in the switch statement.
b. This switch block is fine.
c. This switch block is illegal, because the default statement must come last.
d. When this code runs, nothing is written to the standard output.
e. When this code runs, the letter a is written to the standard output.

14. Which keyword must appear in a method declaration (followed by the name of the exception) when that method might cause an exception to be thrown and that method does not handle the exception? Fill in the blank.

15. Which statements accurately describe the following line of code?

```
String[][] s = new String[10][];
```

Select all valid answers.

a. This line of code is illegal.

b. s is a two-dimensional array containing 10 rows and 10 columns.

c. s is an array of 10 arrays.

d. Each element in s is set to "".

e. Each element in s is uninitialized and must be initialized before it is referenced.

16. What will happen if you try to compile and run the following class?

```
class Test {
    static int myArg = 1;
    public static void main(String[] args) {
        int myArg;
        System.out.println(myArg);
    }
}
```

a. This code compiles and displays 0 in the standard output when run.

b. This code compiles and displays 1 in the standard output when run.

c. This code does not compile, because you cannot define a local variable with the same name as a static variable.

d. This code does not compile, because the local variable is used before it is initialized.

17: Which declarations for the `main()` method in a stand-alone program are NOT valid? Select all valid answers.

a. `public static void main()`

b. `public static void main(String[] string)`

c. `public static void main(String args)`

d. `static public int main(String[] args)`

e. `static void main(String[] args)`

18. Which of the following identifiers are ILLEGAL? Select all valid answers.

  a. `#_pound`
  b. `_underscore`
  c. `5Interstate`
  d. `Interstate5`
  e. `_5_`

19. If the user invokes a stand-alone application by typing the following line,

    `java YourApp 1 2 3`

    and the `main()` method defines its `String[]` parameter as `args`, how can you access the number two using `args`? Fill in the blank.

20. Which interface implementations can you add as listeners for a `TextField` object? Select all valid answers.

    a. `ActionListener`
    b. `FocusListener`
    c. `MouseMotionListener`
    d. `WindowListener`
    e. `ContainerListener`

21. What must be true for the `RunHandler` class so that instances of `RunHandler` can be used as written in the following code?

```
class Test {
    public static void main(String[] args) {
        Thread t = new Thread(new RunHandler());
        t.start();
    }
}
```

    Select all valid answers.

    a. `RunHandler` must implement the `java.lang.Runnable` interface.
    b. `RunHandler` must extend the `Thread` class.
    c. `RunHandler` must provide a `run()` method declared as public and returning void.
    d. `RunHandler` must provide an `init()` method.

22. To determine whether you can invoke
`addContainerListener()` for a component referenced using a
variable called *c*, which expression(s) can you evaluate that will
give you a true or false answer to this question? Select all valid
answers.

a. `c == Container`
b. `c.equals(Class.Container)`
c. `c instanceof Container`
d. `c instanceof Component`
e. `c implements Container`

23. Write a statement for a constructor that invokes the no-`args`
default constructor in its superclass. Fill in the blank.

24. What is written to the standard output given the following
statement?

```
System.out.println(4 & 7);
```

a. 4
b. 5
c. 6
d. 7
e. 0

25. What will the following block of code write to the standard
output when it is executed?

```
int i = 3;
int j = 0;
double k = 3.2;
if (i < k)
    if (i == j)
        System.out.println(i);
    else
        System.out.println(j);
else
    System.out.println(k);
```

a. 3
b. 0
c. 3.2
d. None of these

26. How can you use the String method `indexOf()` to determine which position the letter C is in (when given the following string)?

```
String s = "ABCDE";
```

You should write a complete statement in your answer, but you do not have to assign the value you retrieve to another variable. Fill in the blank.

27. Given that the variable *g* references a valid Graphics object, what does the following statement do?

```
g.fillRect(2, 3, 10, 20);
```

Select all valid answers.
   a. Draws the outline of a rectangle in the current background color
   b. Draws the outline of a rectangle in the current foreground color
   c. Fills in a rectangle using the current background color
   d. Fills in a rectangle using the current foreground color
   e. Fills in a rectangle in black

28. Describe the following applet:

```
import java.applet.Applet;
import java.awt.event.*;
import java.awt.*;
public class MyApplet extends Applet {
   Button b1, b2;
   public void init() {
      ActionListener a = new ActionListener() {
         public void actionPerformed(ActionEvent evt) {
            if (evt.getSource() == b1) {
               b1.setEnabled(false);
               b2.setEnabled(true);
            } else {
               b1.setEnabled(true);
               b2.setEnabled(false);
            }
         }
      };
      b1 = new Button("1");
      b1.addActionListener(a);
      add(b1);
      b2 = new Button("2");
      b2.addActionListener(a);
```

```
        add(b2);
    }
}
```

Select all valid answers.

a. Nothing appears in the applet.
b. One button appears in the applet, but the button does nothing.
c. Two buttons appear in the applet.
d. When the user clicks a button, nothing happens.
e. When the user clicks a button, it becomes disabled.
f. When a user clicks a button, the other button becomes enabled.

29. Select all possible answers: The method setBackground() defined for the Graphics class

a. takes an integer value
b. takes an instance of class Color
c. takes an instance of a Component subclass
d. sets the drawing mode for the associated Component object
e. sets the drawing color for the associated Component object
f. changes the background color for the associated Component object

30. What does the following program do when it is run with the following command?

```
java Mystery Mighty Mouse
class Mystery {
    public static void main(String[] args) {
        Changer c = new Changer();
        c.method(args);
        System.out.println(args[0] + " " + args[1]);
    }
    static class Changer {
        void method(String[] s) {
            String temp = s[0];
            s[0] = s[1];
            s[1] = temp;
        }
    }
}
```

a. This program causes an ArrayIndexOutOfBoundsException to be thrown.
b. This program runs but does not write anything to the standard output.

    c. This program writes "Mighty Mouse" to the standard output.

    d. This program writes "Mouse Mighty" to the standard output.

31. What happens when you try to compile and run the following program?

```
class Mystery {
   String s;
   public static void main(String[] args) {
      Mystery m = new Mystery();
      m.go();
   }
   void Mystery() {
      s = "constructor";
   }
   void go() {
      System.out.println(s);
   }
}
```

    a. This code will not compile.

    b. This code compiles but throws an exception at run time.

    c. This code runs, but nothing appears in the standard output.

    d. This code runs, and "constructor" appears in the standard output.

    e. This code runs and writes "null" in the standard output.

32. What can you write at the comment //A in the following code so that this program writes the word *running* to the standard output?

```
class RunTest implements Runnable {
   public static void main(String[] args) {
      RunTest rt = new RunTest();
      Thread t =new Thread(rt);
      //A
   }
   public void run() {
      System.out.println("running");
   }
   void go() {
      start(1);
   }
   void start(int i) {
   }
}
```

Select all valid answers.

a. `System.out.println("running");`
b. `rt.start();`
c. `rt.go();`
d. `rt.start(1);`

33. In which order can you place the following pieces of a source file so that the source file will compile without errors or warnings?

```
//A
import java.applet.*;
//B
class Helper {
}
//C
package myclasses;
//D
public class MyApplet extends java.applet.Applet {
}
```

Select all valid answers.

a. A, B, C, D
b. A, C, B, D
c. C, A, B, D
d. C, A, D, B
e. C, B, A, D

34. Analyze these two consecutive lines of code:

```
float f = 3.2;
int i = f;
```

Select all valid answers.

a. This code would not compile.
b. This code would compile, and i would be set to three.
c. The second line could compile if it were written instead as follows:

```
int i = (byte)f;
```

d. The first line could compile if it were written instead as follows:

```
float f = 3.2F;
```

35. Construct an array of three String objects containing the strings a, b, and c using the { } notation. Call the String by the variable name *s*.

36. What is the final value of temp in this sequence?

```
long temp = (int)3.9;
temp %= 2;
```

  a. 0
  b. 1
  c. 2
  d. 3
  e. 4

37. Analyze this line of code:

```
if (5 & 7 > 0 && 5 | 2) System.out.println("true");
```

  a. This line of code will not compile.
  b. This code will compile, but nothing will appear in the standard output.
  c. This code will compile and will write the word *true* in the standard output.

38. Create a List object that enables multiple selections and displays five rows at a time. Start by writing

```
List l =
```

in your answer.

39. What will the user interface look like in an applet, given the following init() method?

```
public void init() {
   setLayout(new BorderLayout());
   add("East", new Button("hello"));
}
```

  a. Nothing will appear in the applet.
  b. A button will appear in the applet and will be set in the exact center.
  c. A button will appear on the left side of the applet.
  d. A button will appear on the right side of the applet.
  e. A button will fill the entire applet.

40. Choose all true statements about the `paint()` method defined in the Component class.

   a. It is protected.
   b. It takes an instance of class Graphics.
   c. It is static.
   d. It is invoked automatically whenever you minimize and then maximize a component, such as a window.
   e. There is also a version that takes an int.

41. Given the following `ActionListener`,

```
class HandleClick implements ActionListener {
   public void actionPerformed(ActionEvent evt) {
      // A
   }
}
```

what line of code can you write at A that will make a component referenced by *c* disappear from the display? Fill in the blank.

42. Analyze the following code:

```
class WhatHappens implements Runnable {
   public static void main(String[] args) {
      Thread t = new Thread(this);
      t.start();
   }
   public void run() {
      System.out.println("hi");
   }
}
```

   a. This program does not compile.
   b. This program compiles, but nothing appears in the standard output.
   c. This program compiles, and the word *hi* appears in the standard output (once).
   d. This program compiles, and the word *hi* appears continuously in the standard output until the user hits Control-C to stop the program.

43. What is wrong with the following code?

```
final class First {
   private int a = 1;
   int b = 2;
}
class Second extends First {
   public void method() {
      System.out.println(a + b);
   }
}
```

Select all valid answers.

a. You cannot invoke `println()` without passing it a `String`.

b. Because a is private, no classes other than `First` can access it.

c. `Second` cannot extend `First`.

d. `Final` is not a valid keyword for a class.

44. Analyze the following two classes:

```
class First {
   static int a = 3;
}
final class Second extends First {
   void method() {
      System.out.println(a);
   }
}
```

a. Class `First` compiles, but class `Second` does not.

b. Class `Second` compiles, but class `First` does not.

c. Neither class compiles.

d. Both classes compile, and if `method()` is invoked, it writes 3 to the standard output.

e. Both classes compile, but if `method()` is invoked, it throws an exception.

45. Why won't the following class compile?

```
class A {
   private int x;
   public static void main(String[] args) {
```

```
    new B();
  }
  class B {
    B() {
      System.out.println(x);
    }
  }
}
```

a. Class B tries to access a private variable defined in its outer class.
b. Class A attempts to create an instance of B when there is no current instance of class A.
c. Class B's constructor must be public.

46. Analyze the following code:

```
void looper() {
  int x = 0;
one:
  while (x < 10) {
two:
    System.out.println(++x);
    if (x > 3)
      break two;
  }
}
```

Select all valid answers.

a. This code compiles.
b. This code does not compile.
c. This method writes the number 0 to the standard output.
d. This method writes numbers 1 and 2 to the standard output.
e. This method writes the number 3 to the standard output.
f. This method writes the number 4 to the standard output.
g. This method writes numbers 5 through 9 to the standard output.
h. This method writes the number 10 to the standard output.

47. What appears in the standard output when the method called `testing` is invoked?

```
void testing() {
one:
two:
    for (int i = 0; i < 3; i++) {
three:
        for (int j = 10; j < 30; j+=10) {
            System.out.println(i + j);
            if (i > 2)
                continue one;
        }
    }
}
```

Select all valid answers.

a. 10 and 20
b. 11 and 21
c. 12 and 22
d. 13 and 23
e. 30, 31, 32, 33

48. What will the result be for the following block of code when it is executed?

```
int i = 3;
int j = 0;
float k = 3.2F;
long m = -3;
if (Math.ceil(i) < Math.floor(k))
    if (Math.abs(i) == m)
        System.out.println(i);
    else
        System.out.println(j);
else
    System.out.println(Math.abs(m) + 1);
```

a. 3
b. 0
c. −3
d. 4
e. None of these

49. The ISO code for the language you are interested in is 8859-5. Assume that you have a stream in a variable called mystream that is associated with a file generated in this eight-bit character set. If the default conversion to Unicode in your environment is for the encoding 8859-1, how can you create a new instance of InputStreamReader that will automatically perform the conversion from ISO 8859-5 to Unicode? (Start by writing the keyword new, and do not add a semicolon at the end.)

50. What is written to the standard output as the result of executing the following statements?

```
Boolean b1 = new Boolean(true);
Boolean b2 = new Boolean(true);
Object obj1 = (Object)b1;
Object obj2 = (Object)b2;
if (obj1 == obj2)
    if (obj1.equals(obj2))
        System.out.println("a");
    else
        System.out.println("b");
else
    if (obj1.equals(obj2))
        System.out.println("c");
    else
        System.out.println("d");
```

a. a
b. b
c. c
d. d

51. What will the user interface look like in an applet, given the following init() method?

```
public void init() {
    setLayout(new BorderLayout());
    add(new Button("hello"));
}
```

a. Nothing will appear in the applet.
b. A button will appear in the applet and will be set in the exact center.

    c. A button will appear in the applet along the top and will be centered horizontally.

    d. A button will appear in the top left corner.

52. What expressions are true concerning the following lines of code?

```
int[] arr = {1, 2, 3};
for (int i=0; i < 2; i++)
   arr[i] = 0;
```

Select all valid answers.

    a. `arr[0] == 0`

    b. `arr[0] == 1`

    c. `arr[1] == 1`

    d. `arr[2] == 0`

    e. `arr[3] == 0`

53. What will happen if you try to compile and execute B's `main()` method?

```
class A {
   int i;
   A(int i) {
      this.i = i * 2;
   }
}
class B extends A {
   public static void main(String[] args) {
      B b = new B(2);
   }
   B(int i) {
      System.out.println(i);
   }
}
```

    a. The instance variable i is set to 4.

    b. The instance variable i is set to 2.

    c. The instance variable i is set to 0.

    d. This code will not compile.

54. Which best describes the user interface of an applet, given the following `init()` method?

```
public void init() {
    setLayout(new BorderLayout());
    add("North", new TextField(10));
    add("Center", new Button("help"));
}
```

Select all valid answers.

a. The `TextField` object will be placed at the top of the applet and will be 10 columns wide.

b. The `Button` object will be centered in the applet and will be just large enough to contain the text *help*.

c. The `Button` object will be centered in the applet and will start at the left edge of the applet, fitting just under the `TextField` object above it, and will extend to the right and bottom edge of the applet.

d. The `TextField` object will be placed along the top of the applet and will stretch from the left edge to the right edge.

e. The placement of the `Button` object and the `TextField` object depends on the overall size of the applet.

55. Which of the following statements about try, catch, and finally are true? Select all valid answers.

a. A try block must always be followed by a catch block.

b. A try block can be followed either by a catch block, a finally block, or both.

c. A catch block must always be associated with a try block.

d. A finally can never stand on its own (that is, without being associated with a try block).

e. None of these statements is true.

56. Given the following class definition,

```
class A {
    protected int i;
    A(int i) {
        this.i = i;
    }
}
```

which of the following would be a valid inner class for this class? Select all valid answers.

a.

```
class B {
}
```

b.

```
class B extends A {
}
```

c.

```
class B {
    B() {
        System.out.println("i = " + i);
    }
}
```

d.

```
class B {
    class A {
    }
}
```

e.

```
class A {
}
```

57. Which statements are true concerning the method `notify()` that is used in conjunction with `wait()`? Select all valid answers.

    a. If there is more than one thread waiting on a condition, only the thread that has been waiting the longest is notified.

    b. If there is more than one thread waiting on a condition, there is no way to predict which thread will be notified.

    c. `notify()` is defined in the `Thread` class.

    d. It is not strictly necessary to own the lock for the object for which you invoke `notify()`.

    e. `notify()` should only be invoked from within a while loop.

58. Given the following class,

```
class Counter {
   public int startHere = 1;
   public int endHere = 100;
   public static void main(String[] args) {
      new Counter().go();
   }
   void go() {
      // A
      Thread t = new Thread(a);
      t.start();
   }
}
```

what block of code can you replace at line A so that this program will count from startHere to endHere? Select all valid answers.

a.

```
Runnable a = new Runnable() {
   public void run() {
      for (int i = startHere; i <= endHere; i++) {
         System.out.println(i);
      }
   }
};
```

b.

```
a implements Runnable {
   public void run() {
      for (int i = startHere; i <= endHere; i++) {
         System.out.println(i);
      }
   }
};
```

c.

```
Thread a = new Thread() {
   public void run() {
      for (int i = startHere; i <= endHere; i++) {
         System.out.println(i);
      }
   }
};
```

59. What is written to the standard output given the following statement:

```
System.out.println(4 | 7);
```

a. 4
b. 5
c. 6
d. 7
e. 0

60. Given the following class,

```
class Counter {
    public static void main(String[] args) {
        Thread t = new Thread(new CounterBehavior());
        t.start();
    }
}
```

which of the following is a valid definition of CounterBehavior that would make Counter's main() method count from 1 to 100, counting once per second?

a. This class is an inner class to Counter:

```
class CounterBehavior {
    for (int i = 1; i <= 100; i++);
        try {
            System.out.println(i);
            Thread.sleep(1000);
        } catch (InterruptedException x) {}
    }
}
```

b. This class is an inner class to Counter:

```
class CounterBehavior implements Runnable {
    public void run() {
        for (int i = 1; i <= 100; i++);
            try {
                System.out.println(i);
                Thread.sleep(1000);
            } catch (InterruptedException x) {}
        }
    }
}
```

c.   This class is a static inner class to Counter:

```
static class CounterBehavior implements Runnable {
    public void run() {
        try {
            for (int i = 1; i <= 100; i++) {
                System.out.println(i);
                Thread.sleep(1000);
            }
        } catch (InterruptedException x) {}
    }
}
```

Answers to Exam Questions

1. a, b, and c. An inner class cannot access a variable in a subclass of an enclosing class without a reference to it, so *d* is not correct.

2. a, b, and e. The other answers will not compile.

3. e. The other answers are either partial answers or will not compile.

4. a. Variable-width fonts are based on the average of the letters when specifying the width.

5. c and e. c and e are the only correct answers. b is a concrete class, but it does not implement the interface.

6. `System.out.println(evt.getX());`

7. `mybutton = (Button)evt.getComponent();`

8. `ActionListener`

9. c. b1 and b2 are different objects, but the Boolean class overrides the `equals()` test to return true if the two objects being compared have the same Boolean value.

10. a, c, d, and e. b is not correct, because you cannot add an `ActionListener` to a `TextArea`. (You can add an `ActionListener` to a `TextField`, however.)

11. a, c, and d. Note that even with a return statement at the end of the catch block, the finally block is still executed.

12. `MouseEvent`

13. b and e are both correct. Putting the default case first is perfectly valid. Because there is no break statement at the end of the default, the *a* case is always run if there is no match for *a* or *b*.

14. throws

15. c. c is the only correct answer. The entries in an array of objects all are set to null if no explicit value is given.

16. d. Although there is a static variable called `myArg`, the local variable takes precedence.

17. b. a, c, d, and e are not valid. b is the only valid declaration (although we have used the parameter name string, rather than the usual args).

18. a and c. a and c are illegal. Note that e is legal because a variable can start with an underscore. Therefore, a variable does not have to contain any letters at all.

19. `args[1]`

20. a, b, and c. The answers d and e are not valid for TextField objects.

21. a and c. a and c are the correct answers. The answer b is an option, but it does not have to be. `RunHandler` could extend `Thread`, which would then indicate that it implements the `Runnable interface`—but it does not need to extend `Thread` to implement `Runnable`.

22. c. c is the only correct answer.

23. `super();`

24. a. The values of four and seven can clearly be seen as binary digits:

```
100 &
111
—
100
or 4
```

25. b.

26. `s.indexOf('C');`

27. d. d is the only correct answer. There is a method called `drawRect()` that draws the outline of a rectangle.

28. c, e, and f. c, e, and f all describe this applet accurately.

29. b and f.

30. d. The method in the inner class changes the entries in the array, because objects are passed by reference (non-objects are passed by value).

31. e. Note that there is no real constructor. What appears to be a constructor is really a method, because it specifies a return type (void). A real constructor does not have a return type. Hence, s is never initialized, and therefore null appears in the standard output.

32. a.

33. c and d. The package statement must come first, and import must come second. After that, classes can be declared in any order. (There can only be one public class per source file.)

34. a, c, and d. The default value for a floating-point number is a double. Because a double has greater precision than a float, a floating-point constant assigned to a float data type must be cast or specified as a float by appending the number with an F.

35. `String s = {"a", "b", "c"};`

36. b. `temp` is truncated to 3. The result of 3 % 2 is 1.

37. a. The problem is in 5 | 2. An `if()` expression must resolve to true or false.

38. `List l = new List(5, true);`

39. d.

40. b.

41. c. `setVisible(false);`

42. a. This code does not compile, because there is no `this` variable in the static `main()` method to pass to the `Thread`'s constructor.

43. b and c.

44. d. This code is perfectly fine, and Second can access the static variable in its superclass.

45. b. This code could be made to compile by making class B static or by creating class B from an instance method.

46. b. This code does not compile because the label two: is not associated with a loop.

47. a, b, and c.

48. d. Math.floor(3.2) is 3, so the first if() expression yields false, taking us to the final else clause.

49. new InputStreamReader(mystream, "8859-5");

50. c. Why? Although we have cast the Boolean objects to be of type Object, the method invoked still goes to the actual object type, which is Boolean. So, as is the case here, equals() will return true in the case of Boolean objects assigned to the same Boolean value.

51. b. The button appears centered in the Applet.

52. a.

53. d. Because B's constructor implicitly calls A's no-args constructor, and such a constructor is not defined.

54. c and d.

55. b, c, and d. A try block does not need to be followed by a catch block as long as it is followed by a finally block. Therefore, answer a is not correct.

56. a and c. Instantiating an inner class does not imply anything about constructors of the outer class, unless the inner class is derived from the outer class. Thus, both a and c are valid options.

57. b. a, c, and d are definitely false. For e, one common construct is to invoke wait() in a while loop, but it is not necessary to invoke notify() or wait() in a while loop.

58. a and c. b is definitely not correct. a and c are anonymous inner classes that implement Runnable.

59. d. The value of 4 | 7 can clearly be seen as binary digits:

```
100 |
111
─
111
or 7
```

60. c. A static inner class can be instantiated from static methods of the enclosing class. b is not correct because the inner class is needed in `main()`, where there is no instance of the enclosing class (Counter).

CHAPTER 23

Sun Certified Programmer Practice Exam Number 2

As before, here are the rules:

Allow 90 minutes to complete this exam. You should turn off the telephone, go someplace where you will not be disturbed, check the time on your watch, and begin. Do not bring any books with you, because you will not have them during the test. You can take breaks, but do not look up any information. You can have a piece of scratch paper and a pen or pencil, but you cannot have any crib sheets.

If you get 42 questions right, you have hit the 70 percent mark, and you have passed. Good luck.

Questions

1. In the following example, you create an instance of the `StringBuffer` class, then you call the `append()` method of the `StringBuffer`:

```
StringBuffer strBuf = new StringBuffer("ABC");
strBuf.append("DEF");
```

After executing line two, does `strBuf` still reference the same object instance (true or false)?

2. If you want to associate keys with values and you are using JDK Version 1.2, which one of the following classes is preferred?
   a. `Dictionary`
   b. `HashTable`
   c. `Properties`
   d. `HashMap`
   e. `TreeMap`

3. Which of the following classes can store duplicate elements?
   a. `List`
   b. `Set`
   c. `Map`
   d. `Collection`

4. If you need to store multiple data elements that must not appear more than once in the data store, which class/interface would you use if searching is not a priority?

   a. List
   b. Set
   c. Map
   d. Vector
   e. Collection

5. Which of the following class definitions defines a legal abstract class? Select all right answers.

   a.

   ```
   class Animal {
     abstract void growl();
   }
   ```

   b.

   ```
   abstract Animal {
     abstract void growl();
   }
   ```

   c.

   ```
   class abstract Animal {
     abstract void growl();
   }
   ```

   d.

   ```
   abstract class Animal {
     abstract void growl();
   }
   ```

   e.

   ```
   abstract class Animal {
     abstract void growl() {
       System.out.println("growl");
     }
   }
   ```

6. For an object to be a target for a Thread, that object must be of which type?

7. What is the proper way to define a class called `Key` so that it cannot be subclassed?

    a.

```
class Key { }
```

    b.

```
abstract final class Key {   }
```

    c.

```
native class Key { }
```

    d.

```
class Key {
  final;
}
```

    e.

```
final class Key { }
```

8. Which modes are legal for creating a new `RandomAccessFile` object? Select all valid answers.

    a. "w"
    b. "r"
    c. "x"
    d. "rw"
    e. "xrw"

9. Given the following code,

```
class Tester {
  public static void main(String[] args) {
    CellPhone cell = new CellPhone();
    cell.emergency();
  }
}

class Phone {
  final void dial911() {
    //code to dial 911 here
```

```
    }
}

class CellPhone extends Phone {
  void emergency() {
    dial911();
  }
}
```

what will happen when you try to compile and run the `Tester` class?

a. The code will not compile, because `Phone` is not also declared as final.

b. The code will not compile, because you cannot invoke a final method from a subclass.

c. The code will compile and run fine.

d. The code will compile but will throw a `NoSuchMethodException` when `Tester` is run.

e. `Phone` and `CellPhone` are fine, but `Tester` will not compile because it cannot create an instance of a class that derives from a class that defines a final method.

10. Which assignments are legal? Select all valid answers.

  a. `long test = 012;`
  b. `float f = -412;`
  c. `int other = (int)true;`
  d. `double d = 0x12345678;`
  e. `short s = 10;`

11. Given this class definition,

```
abstract class Transaction implements Runnable { }
class Deposit extends Transaction {
  protected void process() {
    addAmount();
  }
  void undo(int I) {
    System.out.println("Undo");
  }
}
```

what will happen if we attempted to compile the code?

a. This code will not compile, because the parameter i is not used in undo().

b. This code will not compile, because there is no main() method.

c. This code will not compile, because Deposit must be an abstract class.

d. This code will not compile, because Deposit is not declared public.

e. Everything will compile fine.

12. Which exception might wait() throw?

13. Which of the following represents an octal number? Select all that apply.

a. 0x12

b. 320

c. 032

d. (octal)2

e. 12

14. What will appear in the standard output when you run the Tester class?

```
class Tester {
  int var;
  Tester(double var) {
    this.var = (int)var;
  }
  Tester(int var) {
    this("hello");
  }
  Tester(String s) {
    this();
    System.out.println(s);
  }
  Tester() {
    System.out.println("good-bye");
  }
  public static void main(String[] args) {
    Tester t = new Tester(5);
  }
}
```

a. nothing

b. "hello"

c. 5

d. "hello" followed by "good-bye"

e. "good-bye" followed by "hello"

15. Write a line of code to use the String's substring() method to obtain the substring "lip" from a String instance called s that is set to "tulip."

16. What are the range of values for a variable of type short?

a. -2^7 to 2^7-1

b. 0 to 2^8

c. 2^16 to 2^15-1

d. 2^15 to 2^15-1

e. 2^15-1 to 2^15

17. What will happen when you try to compile and run the following program?

```
class Car {
  int milesPerGallon;
  int index;
  Car(int mpg) {
    milesPerGallon = mpg;
    index = 0;
  }

  Car() {
  }

  public static void main(String[] args) {
    int index;
    Car c = new Car(25);
    if (args.length > 0)
      if (args[index].equals("Hiway"))
        c.milesPerGallon *= 2;
    System.out.println("c.milesPerGallon:  " +
c.milesPerGallon);
  }
}
```

a. The code compiles and displays "mpg: 50" if the command-line argument is "Hiway." If the command-line argument is not "Hiway," then the code displays "mpg: 25."

b. The code compiles and displays "mpg: 50" if the command-line argument is "Hiway." If the command-line argument is not "Hiway," the code throws an ArrayIndexOutOfBoundsException.

c. The code does not compile, because the automatic variable called index has not been initialized.

d. The code does not compile, because milesPerGallon has not been initialized.

e. The code does not compile, because the no-args constructor is not written correctly.

18. What will happen when you compile and run this program?

```
class Array {
  public static void main(String[] args) {
    int length = 100;
    int[] d = new int[length];
    for (int index = 0;index < length; index++)
      System.out.println(d[index]);
  }
}
```

a. The code will not compile, because the int[] array is not declared correctly.

b. The code will will throw an IndexArrayOutOfBoundsException when it compiles and runs, and nothing will appear in the standard output.

c. The code will display the numbers 0 through 99 in the standard output and will then throw an IndexOutOfBoundsException.

d. The code will compile, but the println() method will throw a NoSuchMethodException.

e. This code will work fine and will display the number zero 100 times in the standard output.

19. What is the result of attempting to compile and run the following class?

```
class Ar {
  public static void main(String[] args) {
    int[] seeds = new int[3];
    for (int i = 0; i < seeds.length; i++)
      System.out.println(I);
    }
  }
}
```

Select all valid answers.

a. 0

b. 1

c. 2

d. 3

e. The program does not compile, because the seeds array is not initialized.

20. What method name can you use from the applet to read a String passed to an applet via the <param> tag? (Supply the method name only, without parameters.) Fill in the blank.

21. Given these class definitions

```
class Superclass { }
class Subclass1 extends Superclass { }
```

and these objects

```
Superclass a = new Superclass();
Subclass1 b = new Subclass1();
```

which of the following explains the result of the statement a = b?

a. Illegal at compile time

b. Legal at compile time, but possibly illegal at run time

c. Definitely legal at run time

22. Given these class definitions

```
class Superclass { }
class Subclass1 extends Superclass { }
class Subclass2 extends Superclass { }
```

and these objects

```
Superclass a = new Superclass();
Subclass1 b = new Subclass1();
Subclass2 c = new Subclass2();
```

which of the following explains the result of the statement:

```
b = (Subclass1)c;
```

   a. Illegal at compile time
   b. Legal at compile time, but possibly illegal at run time
   c. Definitely legal at run time

23. How can you use the escape notation \u to set the variable c, declared as a char, to the Unicode character whose value is hex 0x30A0?

24. Which operators are overloaded for `String` objects? Select all valid answers.

   a. −
   b. +=
   c. >>
   d. &
   e. none of these

25. How can you change the following break statement so that it breaks out of both the inner and middle loops and continues with the next iteration of the outer loop?

```
outer: for (int x = 0; x < 3; x++) {
  middle: for (init y = 0; y < 3; y++) {
    inner: for (init z = 0; z < 3; z++) {
      if (arr(x, y, x) == targetValue)
        break;
    }
  }
}
```

   a. `break inner;`
   b. `break middle;`
   c. `break outer;`
   d. `continue;`
   e. `continue middle;`

26. Given this code snippet,

```
try {
  tryThis();
  return;
} catch (IOException x1) {
  System.out.println("exception 1");
  return;
} catch (IOException x2) {
  System.out.println("exception 2");
  return;
} finally {
  System.out.println("finally");
}
```

what will appear in the standard output if `tryThis()` throws a `NumberFormatException`?

   a. Nothing
   b. "`exception 1`" followed by "`finally`"
   c. "`exception 2`" followed by "`finally`"
   d. "`exception 1`"
   e. "`exception 2`"

27. Given these class definitions

```
class Superclass { }
class Subclass1 extends Superclass { }
```

and these objects

```
Superclass a = new Superclass();
Subclass1 b = new Subclass1();
```

which of the following explains the result of the statement b = a?

   a. Illegal at compile time
   b. Legal at compile time, but possibly illegal at run time
   c. Definitely legal at run time

28. Given these class definitions

```
class Superclass { }
class Subclass1 extends Superclass { }
```

and these objects

```
Superclass a = new Superclass();
Subclass1 b = new Subclass1();
```

which of the following explains the result of the statement b = (Subclass1)a?

    a. Illegal at compile time

    b. Legal at compile time, but possibly illegal at run time

    c. Definitely legal at run time

29. To invoke `read()` from an `InputStream` subclass, you must handle which type of exception?

30. Imagine that there are two exception classes called `Exception1` and `Exception2` that descend from the `Exception` class. Given these two class definitions,

```
class First {
  void test() throws Exception1, Exception2 { . . . }
}
class Second extends First {
  void test() { . . . }
}
```

create a class called Third that extends Second and defines a `test()` method. What exceptions can Third's `test()` method throw? Select all valid answers.

    a. `Exception1`

    b. `Exception2`

    c. no checked exceptions

    d. any exceptions declared in the throws clause of the Third's `test()` method

31. Given this code snippet,

```
double a = 90.7
double b = method(a);
System.out.println(b);
```

if this snippet displays 90 in the standard output, what Math method did `method()` invoke? Select all valid answers.

   a. abs

   b. min

   c. floor

   d. round

   e. ceil

32. Given this code snippet,

```
double a = 14.9
double b = method(a);
System.out.println(b);
```

if this snippet displays 15 in the standard output, what Math method(s) could `method()` have invoked?

   a. `ceil()` and round

   b. `floor()` and round

   c. `ceil()` only

   d. `floor()` only

   e. `round()` only

33. What methods does Java define in the Math class specifically for trigonometric calculations? Select all valid answers.

   a. cos

   b. asin

   c. tan

   d. sin

   e. angle

34. What `String` instance method would return true when invoked as follows?

```
a.method(b);
```

where a equals "GROUNDhog" and b equals "groundHOG"?

a. equals
b. toLowerCase
c. toUpperCase
d. equalsIgnoreCase
e. none of the above

35. What access control keyword should you use to enable other classes to access a method freely within its package, but to restrict classes outside of the package from accessing that method? Select all valid answers.

a. public
b. protected
c. private
d. Do not supply an access control keyword.

36. What does the following code do?

```
File f = new File("hello.test");
FileOutputStream out = new FileOutputStream(f);
```

a. Creates a new file called `hello.test` (if the file does not yet exist); also opens the file so that you can write to it and can read from it
b. Creates a new file called `hello.test` (if the file does not yet exist). The file is not opened.
c. Opens a file called `hello.test` so that you can write to the file and read from it, but does not create the file if it does not yet exist
d. Opens a file called `hello.test` so that you can write to it but cannot read from it.
e. Creates an object that you can use to create and open the file called `hello.test`, and you can write to and read from the file

37. Which expressions are illegal? Select all valid answers.

a. `(true & true)`
b. `(4 & 5)`
c. `(int myInt = 0 > 3)`
d. `float myFloat = 40.0;`
e. `boolean b = (boolean)99;`

38. Which label name(s) are illegal? Select all valid answers.

- **a.** `here:`
- **b.** `]_there:`
- **c.** `this:`
- **d.** `that:`
- **e.** `2to1odds:`

39. Which keyword, when used in front of a method, must also appear in front of the class?

40. Which letters are written to the standard output with the following code?

```
class Unchecked {
  public static void main(String[] args) {
   try {
     method();
   } catch (Exception e) {
   }
  }

  static void method() {
    try {
      wrench();

      System.out.println("a");
    } catch (ArithmeticException e) {
      System.out.println("b");
    } finally {
      System.out.println("c");
    }
      System.out.println("d");
  }

  static void wrench() {
    throw new NullPointerException();
  }
}
```

Select all valid answers.

- **a.** `"a"`
- **b.** `"b"`
- **c.** `"c"`
- **d.** `"d"`
- **e.** none of these

41. What happens if the file `Ran.test` does not yet exist, and you attempt to compile and run the following code?

```
import java.io.*;

class Ran {
  public static void main(String[] args) throws IOException
{
    RandomAccessFile out = new RandomAccessFile("Ran.test",
"rw");
    out.writeBytes("Ninotchka");
  }
}
```

   a. The code does not compile, because `RandomAccessFile` is not created correctly.
   b. The code does not compile, because `RandomAccessFile` does not implement the `writeBytes()` method.
   c. The code compiles and runs but throws an IOException, because `Ran.test` does not yet exist.
   d. The code compiles and runs, but nothing appears in the file `Ran.test`.
   e. The code compiles and runs, and "Ninotchka" appears in the file `Ran.test`.

42. If you supply a target object when you create a new `Thread`, as in the following line,

   `Thread t = new Thread(targetObject);`

   what test of instanceof does `targetObject` have to pass for this action to be legal?
   a. `targetObject instanceof Thread`
   b. `targetObject instanceof Object`
   c. `targetObject instanceof Applet`
   d. `targetObject instanceof Runnable`
   e. `targetObject instanceof String`

43. What appears in the standard output when you run the `Dots` class?

```
import java.io.*;

class Dots {
  Thread t;
  public static void main(String[] args) throws Exception {
    Dots d = new Dots();
    d.t = new DotThread();
  }

  public void init() {
    t.start();
    t = new DashThread();
    t.start();
  }
}

class DotThread extends Thread {
  public void run() {
    for (int index = 0; index < 100; index++)
      System.out.println(".");
  }
}

class DashThread extends Thread {
  public void run() {
    for (int index = 0; index < 100; index++)
      System.out.println("-");
  }
}
```

a. nothing
b. 100 dots
c. 200 dots
d. 100 dashes (-)
e. 100 dots (.) and 100 dashes (-)

44. When you invoke `repaint()` for a component, the AWT package calls which component method?

a. repaint
b. update
c. paint
d. draw
e. show

45. How can you test whether an object referenced by `ref` implements an interface called `MyInterface`? Replace your test with the following test:

```
if (your test here) {
   System.out.println("ref implements MyInterface");
```

46. What does the following line of code do?

```
TextField tf = new TextField(30);
```

   a. This code is illegal. There is no such constructor for `TextField`.
   b. This code creates a `TextField` object that can hold 30 rows, but because it is not initialized to anything, it will always be empty.
   c. This code creates a `TextField` object that can hold 30 columns, but because it is not initialized to anything, it will always be empty.
   d. This code creates a `TextField` object that can hold 30 rows of text.
   e. This code creates a new `TextField` object that contains 30 columns of text.

47. Given these code snippets,

```
Boolean b1 = new Boolean(true);
Boolean b2 = new Boolean(true);
```

which expressions are legal Java expressions that return true? Select all valid answers.

   a. `b1 == b2`
   b. `b1.equals(b2)`
   c. `b1 & b2`
   d. `b1 | b2`
   e. `b1 && b2`
   f. `b1 || b2`

48. Which `LayoutManager` arranges components left to right and then top to bottom, centering each row as it moves to the next row?

   a. `BorderLayout`
   b. `FlowLayout`
   c. `GridLayout`
   d. `CardLayout`
   e. `GridBagLayout`

49. A component will automatically be resized horizontally, but not vertically, when it is placed in which region of a `BorderLayout`?

    a. North or South

    b. East or West

    c. Center

    d. North, South, or Center

    e. any region

50. How can you place three components along the bottom of a Container?

    a. Set the Container's `LayoutManager` to be a `BorderLayout`, and add each Component to the "South" of the Container.

    b. Set the Container's `LayoutManager` to be a `FlowLayout`, and add each Component to the Container.

    c. Set the Container's `LayoutManager` to be a `BorderLayout`, add each Component to a different Container that uses a `FlowLayout`, and then add that Container to the "South" of the first Container.

    d. Use a `GridLayout` for the Container; add each Component to the Container.

    e. Do not use a `LayoutManager` at all; add each Component to the Container.

51. What will happen when you attempt to compile and run the following program by passing the test class to the Java interpreter?

```
class test {
  public static void main() {
    System.out.println("hello");
  }
}
```

    a. The program does not compile, because `main()` is not defined correctly.

    b. The program compiles, but when you try to run the interpreter, the program complains that it cannot find the `main()` method necessary to run.

    c. The program compiles, but you cannot run the program because the class is not declared public.

    d. The program compiles and runs without an error but does not display anything in the standard output.

    e. The program compiles and displays "hello" in the standard output when you run the program.

52. How would you make the background color red for a Panel referenced by the variable *p*?

53. What is the result of invoking `main()` for classes D and E (see the following code)?

```
class D {
  public static void main(String[] args) {
    String s1 = new String("hello");
    String s2 = new String("hello");
    if (s1.equals(s2))
      System.out.println("equal");
    else
      System.out.println("not equal");
  }
}

class E {
  public static void main(String[] args) {
    StringBuffer sb1 = new StringBuffer("hello");
    StringBuffer sb2 = new StringBuffer("hello");
    if (sb1.equals(sb2))
      System.out.println("equal");
    else
      System.out.println("not equal");
  }
}
```

a. D: equal; E: equal
b. D: not equal; E: not equal
c. D: equal; E: not equal
d. D: not equal; E: not equal
e. Nothing appears in the standard output for either class.

54. Which method from Java can you use to remove a Component from a user interface display? Select all valid answers.

a. disable
b. setVisible(false)
c. remove
d. delete
e. unhook

55. Which statements about garbage collection are true? Select all valid answers.

    a. You can directly free the memory allocated by an object.

    b. You can directly run the garbage collector whenever you want.

    c. The garbage collector informs your object when it is about to be garbage collected.

    d. The garbage collector reclaims an object's memory as soon as it becomes a candidate for garbage collection.

    e. The garbage collector runs in low-memory situations.

56. If you would like to change the size of a Component, you can use the following method:

    a. `size`

    b. `resize`

    c. `area`

    d. `setSize`

    e. `dimension`

57. The `setForeground()` and `setBackground()` methods are defined in the following class:

    a. `Graphics`

    b. `Container`

    c. `Component`

    d. `Object`

    e. `Applet`

58. How many bits are used to maintain a `char` data type?

59. The `&&` operator works with which data types? Select all valid answers.

    a. `int`

    b. `long`

    c. `double`

    d. `boolean`

    e. `float`

60. To place a "1" in the high-bit of an int called ref that is set to 0x00000001, you can write the following line:

a. ref >> 31;

b. ref >>= 31;

c. ref << 31;

d. ref <<= 31;

Answers and Explanations

1. True. The StringBuffer class is read-write only. For this reason, the example modifies the existing StringBuffer object.

2. d and e. Maps are replacing dictionaries as the preferred way to associate keys with values. Both HashMap and TreeMap are maps.

3. a and d. Only lists and collections can have duplicate elements.

4. b. A set rejects duplicate entries, so if you want to ensure that data elements only appear once, this choice is the best. We could also have used a map; however, because searching is not a priority, the best choice is b.

5. d. An abstract class is defined using the keyword abstract in front of the class keyword and almost always defines at least one abstract method. An abstract class does not have to define an abstract method. If there are no abstract methods in an abstract class, then any subclasses of the abstract class can be instantiated (as long as they are not (in turn) defined using the abstract keyword.

6. "Runnable." Only classes that implement the Runnable interface (and therefore are of type Runnable) can be targets of threads.

7. e. Use the final keyword in front of the class to make the class unable to be subclassed.

8. b, d. Only "r" and "rw" are legal modes for a RandomAccessFile.

9. c. This code is perfectly fine.

10. a, b, d, and e. The other tries to cast a `Boolean` to an 0, which is illegal.

11. c. Because the superclass is abstract and implements `Runnable` but does not supply a `run()` method, the subclass must supply `run()` or also be declared abstract.

12. "`InterruptedException`" or "`IllegalMonitorException`"

13. c. An octal number in Java is preceded by a 0.

14. e. There are three constructors that come into play. First, the constructor that takes an int is invoked. This constructor invokes the constructor that takes a String, which in turn invokes the no-args constructor, which displays "good-bye." Then, the constructor that takes a String displays "hello."

15. "s.substring(2, 5)" or "s.substring(2)"

16. d. A short is a signed 16-bit number, so the correct answer is (-2^{15} to 2^{15}-1). The range of integer types goes from minus 2(number of bits - 1) to 2(number of bits - 1) minus 1.

17. c. Although there is an instance variable called index that is defined in the Car class, the local or automatic variable called index takes precedence. Because automatic variables do not have a default value, this code will not compile, because it is uninitialized when we attempt to access the element in the args array.

18. e. There is nothing wrong with this code. One hundred zeros will appear in the standard output.

19. a, b, c. The elements in arrays are initialized to their default values: 0, 0.0, null, false, or \u0000, depending on the data type.

20. "getParameter"

21. c. Assigning a subclass type to a superclass type is perfectly legal and will cause the program to run just fine at run time.

22. a. You cannot assign an object to a sibling object reference, even with casting.

23. "c = '\u30A0';". You can set a char to a Unicode sequence by matching the template \udddd, where dddd is four hexadecimal digits that represent the Unicode character you want.

24. b. Only + and += are overloaded for String objects.

25. b. Changing the break statement to break middle will break out of the loop named using the label middle and will continue with the next iteration of the outer loop. The statement continue outer would also have this effect.

26. c. NumberFormatException will be handled in the catch clause for Exception. Then, regardless of the return statements, the finally clause will be executed before control returns to the calling method.

27. a. An explicit cast is needed to assign a superclass type to a subclass type.

28. b. If the object contained in *a* is not actually a Subclass1 object, the assignment will cause Java to throw a CastClassException.

29. "IOException" or "java.io.IOException"

30. c. A method in a subclass cannot add new exception types that it might throw. Because its superclass, Second, does not define any exceptions in its test() method, Third cannot either.

31. c. The Math method floor() finds the integer closest to but less than the parameter to floor(). The methods round() and ceil() would both result in 91, and min() and max() both require two parameters.

32. a. Both ceil() and round() will produce 15 from 14.9. The floor() method yields 14.

33. a, b, c, and d. The methods Java defines for trig operations include sin(), asin(), cos(), and tan().

34. d. The method equalsIgnoreCase() would return true for the two Strings a and b in the question.

35. d. This answer is the default access control for methods and member variables.

36. a. The first line creates a File object that represents the file. By creating a FileOutputStream, you create the file (if it does not yet exist) and open that file for reading and writing.

37. c, d, e. You cannot assign an integer to a boolean—not even with casting. Also, the default type for a floating-point literal is double, and you cannot assign a double to a float without casting.

38. c, e. `this` is a reserved word, so it cannot be used as an identifier (such as a label). `2to1odds` starts with a number, so it is also invalid as an identifier.

39. "abstract"

40. c. Only the "c" from `finally` gets written out. The exception thrown does not match the exception caught, so the `catch` block is not executed. Control returns to the caller after `finally` to see whether there is a `catch` block there to handle this unchecked exception. If there is not (as is the case here), execution comes to an end.

41. e. This code compiles and runs fine. RandomAccessFile implements the DataOutput interface, so it does implement `writeBytes()`, among others. RandomAccessFile creates the file if it does not yet exist.

42. d. The target object for a Thread must implement Runnable, which means that it will pass the following test:

```
targetObject instanceof Runnable
```

43. a. The thread with `start()` method is never invoked. (This method is not an applet, so `init()` is not automatically invoked.)

44. b. The AWT invokes `update()` for the Component, which invokes `paint()` in its default behavior.

45. "ref instanceof MyInterface"

46. e. TextField defines a constructor that takes the number of columns, as shown in the example. TextField objects can have their text updated at any time, including long after they are created.

47. b. The first yields `false`, and the others are not legal Java expressions (we are using a wrapper type here).

48. b. A FlowLayout arranges components in this way.

49. a. North and South only can resize a component horizontally, to the width of the Container.

50. c. Complicated as it might seem, this method is the best way to accomplish this goal. First, you set the Container's

LayoutManager to be a BorderLayout. Then, you create an intermediate Container and add each Component to this new Container that uses a FlowLayout. Finally, you add that Container to the "South" of the original Container.

51. b. The program will compile fine; however, the Java interpreter specifically looks for a `main()` method that is declared as `public` and `static`, that returns no value, and that takes an array of String objects as its parameter.

52. "p.setBackground(Color.red);"

53. c. The StringBuffer class does not override `equals()`. Hence, this class returns `false` when passed two different objects.

54. b. The `setVisible(false)` removes a Component from the display.

55. b and c. e is not a correct answer, because you can explicitly run the gc regardless of the amount of memory your system has available.

56. d. `setSize()` is the correct method.

57. c. These are Component methods. (The `setColor()` method is defined in the Graphics class.)

58. "16"

59. d. The `&&` operator combines two `boolean` expressions.

60. d. The `<<` operator shifts the bits the given number of places to the left.

CHAPTER 24

Sun Certified Developer Practice Exam

Developer certification takes place in stages. First, you complete a programming assignment that you download from the Web. Then you take a test that asks you to justify decisions you made in completing the programming assignment. The assignment consists of implementing a client/server application, where the client and server talk to each other using TCP/IP. Although the actual assignment is, of course, different from this one, the two are similar in scope and the topics they cover. Read over the scenario and instructions for this assignment, and then go to it.

The Scenario

"Aunt Edna's Airlines" started as a one-woman operation. Edna rented a small two-seater and flew passengers to the San Juan Islands from Seattle, a short hop of less than an hour. No one thought her business would make it, but her flying was flawless and her service professional. She now owns two planes, capable of carrying five passengers each. She hired her niece as the other pilot and set up regular flight schedules.

Edna has been taking reservations over the phone, but with business booming, that has became too cumbersome. She has allowed travel agents to mail in reservations, but this is not a very efficient system. What's more, they keep on booking passengers in the same seats (numbered 1 through 5) because there is no coordination between them. (Remember the discussion of this scenario back in Chapter 13, "Threads," when we talked about threads?)

Edna talked things over with her niece, and they came up with a plan. They have an idea that travel agents should tap directly into their reservation computer over the Internet. They could maintain a simple database that travel agents could use to make reservations and assign passengers seats.

Her niece worked on this program for a few days when it was rainy and no one wanted to visit the San Juans. Being a Mac person, she bought *Learn Java on the Macintosh*. She got as far as defining what the prototype database should look like and providing a few simple methods to access the database. However, business soon picked up, and she headed back into the skies (where she preferred to be anyway).

Edna has looked around for a qualified Java programmer, and since you are Sun certified as a Java programmer, she thought you would be ideal for the task. She would like you to write a prototype system so that she can begin to get a sense of what this might look like. The prototype is only proof of a concept that she hopes will do the following things:

- Offer a simple user interface that displays the date, flight number, and passenger list
- Enable the user to make a new reservation, type in the passenger's name, and assign the passenger a seat from a list of those available
- Let the user delete a reservation
- Provide access to the database over the Internet, possibly by multiple travel agents at a time

She wants this done in a very particular way, because she wants to make sure that if you decide to move on to other projects after implementing the prototype, her niece can understand how the program works and maintain it. This means that you should favor code that is easy to understand, instead of code that might be slightly more efficient. You should also provide all the necessary `javadoc`-style comments so that the code is well-documented, without being filled with unnecessary, trivial comments.

The Prototype Specifications

The rest of this document describes

- The design completed so far
- The protocol you will use to communicate between the client and server
- The code completed so far
- What you will add to the code
- What the user interface will look like

The Design Completed So Far

The current design identifies the class names for the prototype, but the only completed classes are those for the record layout for the database (the classes `PassengerRecord` and `FileHeader`) and some support methods to manipulate the database file (in the class `DB`). The database file is simply an ASCII file that we'll read from and write to using the `java.io` classes, especially `RandomAccessFile`. Also, an interface called `CanUpdate` and two new `Exception` classes are complete, but their definitions are simple. You can implement the other classes as you think best, but you should try to follow the designs presented here.

Figure 24-1 shows the user interface classes for the prototype. The only one of these currently written is an interface called `CanUpdate`. This interface defines a single method that other classes can call to force the user interface to be updated to reflect the current state of the database.

Figure 24-1 shows the intended flow of control between these classes. A user can launch the client by invoking the Java inter-

Figure 24-1
The current design

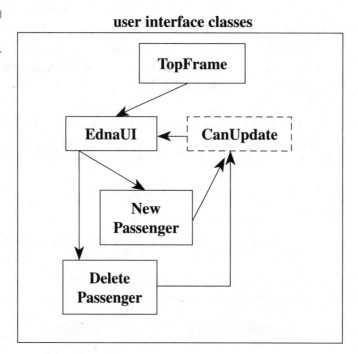

user interface classes

preter and passing it a top-level frame. The main() method of this new Frame subclass creates an instance of a Panel subclass called EdnaUI. EdnaUI implements the CanUpdate interface.

When the user wants to add a new passenger to the passenger list, the user interface brings up a new window, a Frame subclass called NewPassenger. (I'll discuss the exact look and feel of the user interface later in this chapter.) When the user wants to delete a passenger from the passenger list, the user interface brings up a new window, a Frame subclass called DeletePassenger.

Once the user has added or deleted a passenger, these Frame subclasses invoke updateUI() for the EdnaUI object. The updateUI() method is the method defined by the CanUpdate interface and is implemented by EdnaUI, so that the user interface reflects the new state of the database. If this is not to a client/server application, NewPassenger and DeletePassenger could access the database directly, as shown in Figure 24-2.

The DB class reads from and writes to a Reservations.db. It uses the FileHeader and PassengerRecord classes to keep track of the data in each record. The DB class can also use two exceptions if

Figure 24-2
Directly accessing the
database

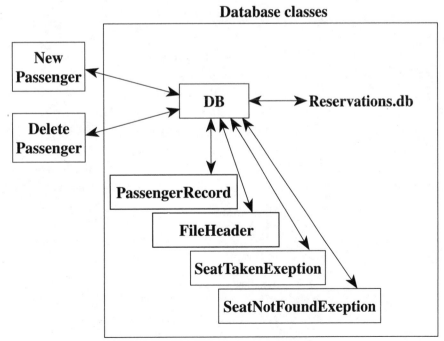

Database classes

it encounters any trouble assigning seats. All of the classes are currently part of the same default package.

The New Design

To complete this assignment, you should place the classes into one of two packages: `client` or `server`. Any new classes you create should go into one of these packages. You can import classes from one package to another, as required. However, you may only need to import a class called `server.Server` (which I'll discuss shortly) in the class called `client.Client`. You can probably find ways around this, if you would like to.

Figure 24-3 shows the new design on the client side. This is the final design that you should achieve in your solution.

`NewPassenger` and `DeletePassenger` don't communicate directly with the database. Instead, they create a new instance of a class called `Client`. `Client` defines methods that establish a TCP/IP connection with a server and communicate with the server to perform database operations. On the server side, there are two new classes, shown in Figure 24-4.

Figure 24-3
The design on the client side

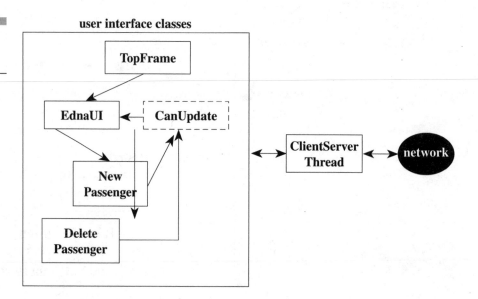

Figure 24-4
The design on the
server side

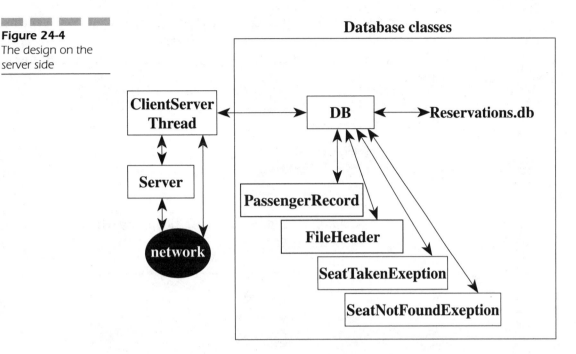

The first server class is called Server. This class simply loops forever, waiting for a client to connect to it. When it establishes a connection, Server creates a new instance of a Thread subclass called ClientServerThread and starts this thread. This thread reads data from the network, interacts with the database, and passes the appropriate data back out over the network.

The Code Completed So Far

You must use the following code as part of your solution. This code defines the database entries and specifies how you will access the database. Optimizations such as compressing the database by squeezing out deleted records will be a future consideration, implemented at some point after the prototype is completed, so don't concern yourself with this now.

Here are two classes that define the record layout. Each record consists of a header and passenger information. The FileHeader class can be placed in the file DB.java (which I'll discuss in just a second):

```
class FileHeader {

    int totalRecords;
    int numPassengers;
}
```

The class PassengerRecord must be placed in its own file, PassengerRecord.java:

```
package server;

public class PassengerRecord {
    private long ptr;
    private String name;
    private int seat;

    public String getName() {
        return name;
    }

    public void setName(String n) {
        name = n;
    }

    public int getSeat() {
        return seat;
    }

    public void setSeat(int s) {
        seat = s;
    }

    public long getPtr() {
        return ptr;
    }

    public void setPtr(long p) {
        ptr = p;
    }
}
```

As far as the code to manipulate a database, here is the start of the class called DB that does this (there are three methods still to implement). This class is defined in DB.java:

```java
package server;

import java.io.*;

/**
 * Record format is:
 * <num records>
 * <name> <seat #>
 * repeat as necessary
 */
public class DB {
    public static final String FILE_NAME = "Reservations.db";
    public static final int MAX_SEATS = 5;

    private static final int ACTIVE_REC = 0;
    private static final int DELETED_REC = 1;

    private boolean open;
    private RandomAccessFile file;

    public DB() throws IOException {
        try {
            File test = new File(FILE_NAME);
            boolean alreadyExisted = test.exists();
            file = new RandomAccessFile(FILE_NAME, "rw");
            open = true;

            if (!alreadyExisted) {
                FileHeader header = new FileHeader();
                writeHeader(header);
            }

        } catch (IOException x) {
            close();
            throw x;
        }
    }

    public synchronized String[] getPassengerList() throws
IOException {
        String[] reservations = null;

        // PLACE YOUR CODE HERE.

        return reservations;
```

```
   }

   public synchronized int getSeat(String passenger)
      throws IOException, SeatNotFoundException
   {
      int seat = 0;

      // PLACE YOUR CODE HERE.

      return seat;
   }

   public synchronized void reservePassenger(String
passenger, int seat)
      throws IOException, SeatTakenException
   {

      // PLACE YOUR CODE HERE.

   }

   public synchronized int[] getOpenSeats() throws
IOException {
      PassengerRecord record;

      FileHeader header = readHeader();
      // Do the case where there are no seats:
      if (header.numPassengers == MAX_SEATS)
         return new int[0];

      // Do the case where all seats are still available.
      if (header.numPassengers == 0) {
         int[] open = {1, 2, 3, 4, 5};
         return open;
      }

      // Determine the open seats from the reserved seats.
      boolean[] reserved = new boolean[MAX_SEATS];
      String passenger;
      for (int i = 0; i < header.numPassengers; i++) {
         record = readNextRecord();
         reserved[record.getSeat() - 1] = true;
      }

      // Make the int array only as large as it needs to be.
      int[] open = new int[MAX_SEATS -
header.numPassengers];
      int next = 0;
      for (int i = 0; i < MAX_SEATS; i++) {
         if (reserved[i] == false)
            open[next++] = i + 1;
```

```
      }

      return open;
   }

   public synchronized void deletePassenger(String name)
      throws IOException
   {
      FileHeader header = readHeader();

      boolean found = false;
      PassengerRecord record = null; // make the compiler
happy
      for (int i = 0; i < header.numPassengers && !found;
i++) {
         record = readNextRecord();
         if (name.equals(record.getName()))
            found = true;
      }

      // Delete at the position before we read the record to
      // be deleted.
      if (found) {
         file.seek(record.getPtr());
         file.write(DELETED_REC);

         header.numPassengers-;
         writeHeader(header);
      }
   }

   public synchronized void close() {
      if (open) {
         try {
            file.close();
         } catch (IOException x) {
            System.out.println(x.getMessage());
         } finally {
            open = false;
         }
      }
   }

   public void finalize() throws Throwable {
      close();
      super.finalize();
   }

   private synchronized PassengerRecord readNextRecord()
      throws IOException
   {
```

```
        boolean looking = true;
        PassengerRecord record = new PassengerRecord();

        try {
           while (looking) {
              record.setPtr(file.getFilePointer());
              int type = file.readInt();
              record.setName(file.readUTF());
              record.setSeat(file.readInt());
              if (type == ACTIVE_REC)
                 looking = false;
           }
        } catch (EOFException x) {
           System.out.println("read past the end of the file");
        }

        return record;
     }

   private synchronized void writeRecord(PassengerRecord
record)
        throws IOException
     {
        FileHeader header = readHeader();
        header.totalRecords++;
        header.numPassengers++;
        writeHeader(header);

        file.seek(file.length());
        file.writeInt(ACTIVE_REC);
        file.writeUTF(record.getName());
        file.writeInt(record.getSeat());
     }

   private synchronized FileHeader readHeader() throws
IOException {
        FileHeader header = new FileHeader();
        file.seek(0);
        header.totalRecords = file.readInt();
        header.numPassengers = file.readInt();
        return header;
     }

   private synchronized void writeHeader(FileHeader header)
        throws IOException
     {
        file.seek(0);
        file.writeInt(header.totalRecords);
        file.writeInt(header.numPassengers);
     }

}
```

The three methods that you will need to implement are getPassengerList(), getSeat(), and reservePassenger(). You will invoke these methods from ClientServerThread when appropriate. The two other methods that you will invoke from ClientServerThread are deletePassenger() and getOpenSeats(), which are already implemented for you.

A new exception called SeatNotFoundException is defined in SeatNotFoundException.java like this:

```
package server;
public class SeatNotFoundException extends Exception { }
```

Also, a new exception called SeatTakenException is defined in SeatTakenException.java like this:

```
package server;
public class SeatTakenException extends Exception { }
```

On the client side, the interface CanUpdate looks like this:

```
package client;

public interface CanUpdate {
    void updateUI();
}
```

You will find all of this code on the CD-ROM included with this book.

What You Will Add to the Code

You need to complete the DB class, create the user interface for accessing the database, and turn this into a client/server application by defining client and server classes.

The Database

The basic structure of the database has already been implemented for you. However, here's what's going on, if it helps you to write your software. The database consists of a header followed by any number of records. Only five records will be active at a time; if there are more, it is only because the others have been deleted. The database's header consists of two numbers: the total number of records in the database and the total number of passengers. Nothing is currently done with the integer for the total number of records.

Each record in the database consists of an integer indicating whether it is active or deleted, a string indicating the passenger's name, and an integer specifying the passenger's seat assignment. The DB class already implements methods to append a new record to the database, delete a record, and retrieve the open seats.

The Server

The server should be able to handle multiple clients. Each transaction with a client should be one complete connect-process-close cycle. For example, if the client wants to add a new passenger to the database, it should connect with the server and pass the server the new passenger name and seat assignment. The server should add this passenger to the database if it can and tell the client whether or not it was successful. Then the connection ends.

The server and the client can both run on the local machine by default for the purposes of this exercise. However, all of the proper TCP/IPs should be in place so that they can reside on different machines if necessary. (You can pick a port you think is appropriate for the client and server to use to communicate. The port number 5001 is one candidate.)

The server consists of the Server class and the ClientServer-Thread class. The server handles connections arriving over the network and interacts with the DB class to work with the database.

The Client

The client consists of the user interface and a class called Client that knows how to establish a connection with the server, communicate with the server, and close the connection. The `Client` class can define different methods to perform different transactions, such as adding a new passenger to the list, deleting a passenger, and so on.

The User Interface

The user interface is discussed below, after the discussion of protocol. Your user interface should match the figures in this chapter as closely as possible. The user interface can create a new `Client` instance when it needs to talk to the server and invoke the proper method in the `Client` instance to make the client communicate with the server.

The Protocol

In order for the client and the server to talk to each other, they have to speak the same language. In other words, they need to agree on a protocol. Each transaction represents a new connection between the client and the server.

Making a New Reservation

The client sends an integer opcode that means "make a new reservation," followed by a string representing the passenger name, followed by an integer for the seat number. The server returns a 0 if the reservation is successful or a 1 if it is not.

Delete a Passenger's Reservation

The client sends an integer opcode that means "delete this reservation," followed by a string representing the passenger name. The server returns a 0 if the reservation is deleted or a 1 if it is not.

Finding a Passenger's Seat

The client sends an integer opcode that means "get this passenger's seat," followed by a string representing the passenger name. The server returns an integer representing the passenger's seat number.

Finding All Open Seats

The client sends an integer opcode that means "find all open seats." The server returns an integer that indicates how many open seats there are, followed by integers that specify the open seat numbers. If there are no open seats, the first integer is 0, followed, of course, by no other numbers.

Retrieving the List of Passengers

The client sends an integer opcode that means "return the passenger list." The server returns an integer that indicates how many passengers there are, followed by strings that contain the passenger names. If there are no passengers, the first integer is 0, followed by no other strings.

What the User Interface Should Look Like When You're Done

Figure 24-5 shows what will first appear on the screen when the user launches the client. (The client is a standalone graphical program. It does not run within a Web browser.)

There are three regions to this user interface:

1. At the top are the date and flight number. These can be labels purely for aesthetic purposes that don't have to reflect any real data.

Figure 24-5
The initial client
interface

2. In the center is the list of passengers. This list reflects the
   current state of the database.

3. At the bottom is a button that enables the user to make new
   reservations

When the user first launches the client, it should connect with
the server. Once it establishes a connection, it should update the
passenger list if there is already data in the database, so that the
user interface displays any passenger data when it first appears.

As the user enters data into the database, the center portion of
the user interface will show this data. Figure 24-6 shows the list of
passengers after the user has made two new reservations.

The database method `getPassengerList()` returns an array of
strings that you can use to display in this list, one string per list
item. To make this clearer, Figure 24-7 shows the generic arrangement of the user interface components you need to implement.

Two other features of this user interface should be implemented:

1. The new reservation button becomes disabled when the flight
   is full (that is, when there are five passengers).

Figure 24-6
The list of
passengers.

Figure 24-6
The list of
passengers.

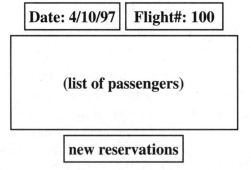

Figure 24-7
The user interface
components

2. The client program ends when the user clicks the close button in the frame enclosing this interface.

In addition to these, clicking the new reservation button and double-clicking a list entry both cause the user interface to bring up other windows. The new reservation button brings up a window that enables you to add passengers to the database. Double-clicking a list entry brings up a window that enables you to delete that passenger.

Updating the Passenger List

When the user clicks the new reservation button, a new window appears that floats separately from the main user interface (see Figure 24-8).

The only entries in the choice box should be those for the open seats, which are numbered 1 through 5. You can use the database method getOpenSeats() to determine which entries to place in the choice box. The user types the passenger name into the text field and clicks the Reserve Seat button to make the reservation. To make this work, you'll have to implement the database method reservePassenger(). If the seat the user is trying to reserve is already taken (because another thread has beaten the user to it), then no reservation should be made. If the text field is all spaces or blank, the Reserve Seat button should not change the database. The window will then vanish. If the user clicks the Close button for this enclosing frame, the floating window disappears without the user having made a reservation. When the window vanishes, the main user interface's list of passengers should be updated to reflect the new passenger in the database. To do this, the window can invoke EdnaUI's implementation of updateUI().

When the user double-clicks an entry in the list, a new window appears that floats separately from the main user interface (see Figure 24-9).

This window shows the passenger's name and seat assignment. To show the seat assignment, you'll have to implement the database method getSeat(). The two buttons on the bottom of this

Figure 24-8
The New Passenger window

Figure 24-9
The Delete
Passenger window

floating window enable the user to either keep or delete this reservation. If the user clicks Delete, the passenger is removed from the database. (To do this, you should implement the database's `deletePassenger()` method.) Then the window vanishes. If the user clicks Keep or clicks the Close button in the enclosing frame, the floating window will disappear. Again, when the window vanishes, the main user interface's list of passengers should be updated to reflect the change to the database.

Final Words of Advice

Implement this as you think best. Keep in mind the chapters we've covered in the previous section, especially regarding TCP/IP and building user interfaces by placing layout managers inside other layout managers. I have provided a few lines of working code on purpose. The more you work through the issues yourself, the easier you'll find the actual developer programming assignment. Don't worry if it takes some time. You can always look at the answer at the end of this chapter if you get stuck, but try to get as far as you can on your own and really think about what's happening.

One Possible Answer for the Client Side

Client.java

```java
package client;

import java.io.*;
import java.net.*;
import server.Server;

/**
 * Communicates with the database server.
 * @see server.Server
 * @version 1.1
 * @author Barry Boone / William Stanek
 */
public class Client {

    /* Data stream to read from server. */
    DataInputStream remoteIn;

    /* Data stream to write to server. */
    DataOutputStream remoteOut;

    private int port = 5001;
    private Socket sock;
    private String server = null;
        // name of the remote server (null if on same machine)

    /**
     * Establish a connection with the database server.
     * @exception IOException  Thrown if there's trouble
     *    connecting to the server
     */
    void establishConnection() throws IOException {
        try {
            InetAddress serverAddr =
InetAddress.getByName(server);
            sock = new Socket(serverAddr.getHostName(), port);

            remoteIn = new
DataInputStream(sock.getInputStream());
            remoteOut = new
DataOutputStream(sock.getOutputStream());
```

```
        } catch (IOException e) {
           System.out.println(e.getMessage() +
              ": Failed to connect to server.");
           throw e;
        }

    }

    /*
     * Close the connection with the database server.
     */
    void closeConnection() {
        try {
            if (remoteOut != null) {
                remoteOut.close();
                remoteOut = null;
            }

            if (remoteIn != null) {
                remoteIn.close();
                remoteIn = null;
            }

        } catch (IOException x) {
           System.out.println(x.getMessage());
        } finally {
           try {
              if (sock != null) {
                 sock.close();
                 sock = null;
              }
           } catch (IOException x) {
              System.out.println(x.getMessage());
           }
        }
    }

    int[] getOpenSeats() throws IOException {
        establishConnection();
        remoteOut.writeInt(Server.OP_GET_OPEN_SEATS);
        int numSeats = remoteIn.readInt();
        int[] seats = new int[numSeats];
        for (int i = 0; i < numSeats; i++)
           seats[i] = remoteIn.readInt();

        closeConnection();
        return seats;
    }
```

```java
    String[] getPassengerList() throws IOException {
        establishConnection();
        remoteOut.writeInt(Server.OP_GET_PASSENGER_LIST);
        int numPassengers = remoteIn.readInt();
        String[] passengers = new String[numPassengers];
        for (int i = 0; i < numPassengers; i++)
            passengers[i] = remoteIn.readUTF();

        closeConnection();
        return passengers;
    }

    int reservePassenger(String name, int seat) throws
IOException{
        establishConnection();
        remoteOut.writeInt(Server.OP_MAKE_RESERVATION);
        remoteOut.writeUTF(name);
        remoteOut.writeInt(seat);
        int rv = remoteIn.readInt();
        closeConnection();
        return rv;
    }

    int deletePassenger(String name) throws IOException {
        establishConnection();
        remoteOut.writeInt(Server.OP_DELETE);
        remoteOut.writeUTF(name);
        int rv = remoteIn.readInt();
        closeConnection();
        return rv;
    }

    int getSeat(String name) throws IOException {
        establishConnection();
        remoteOut.writeInt(Server.OP_GET_SEAT);
        remoteOut.writeUTF(name);
        int seat = remoteIn.readInt();
        closeConnection();
        return seat;
    }

    protected void finalize() throws Throwable {
        super.finalize();
        closeConnection();
    }

}
```

TopFrame.java

```java
package client;

import java.awt.*;
import java.awt.event.*;

public class TopFrame extends Frame {
    public TopFrame(String s) {
        super(s);

        WindowAdapter closeHandler = new WindowAdapter() {
            public void windowClosing(WindowEvent e) {
                Window w = e.getWindow();
                w.setVisible(false);
                dispose();
                System.exit(0);
            }
        };
        addWindowListener(closeHandler);
    }

    public static void main(String[] args) {
        TopFrame frame = new TopFrame("Aunt Edna's Airlines");
        EdnaUI ui = new EdnaUI();
        frame.add("Center", ui);
        frame.pack();
        frame.show();

        ui.updateUI();
    }
}
```

EdnaUI.java

```java
package client;

import java.awt.*;
import java.awt.event.*;
import java.util.Date;
import java.util.StringTokenizer;
import java.io.IOException;
```

```
public class EdnaUI extends Panel implements CanUpdate {
    private static final int MAX_SEATS = 5;

    private List      passengerList;
    private Button    reserve;

    public EdnaUI() {
        setLayout(new BorderLayout());

        Panel p;
        p = new Panel();

        p.add(new Label("Date: 4/10/97"));
        p.add(new Label("Flight #: 100"));

        add("North", p);

        passengerList = new List(5, false);
        add("Center", passengerList);

        p = new Panel();
        reserve = new Button("new reservation");
        p.add(reserve);

        add("South", p);

    /*
     * Show frame to make a new reservation when the user
clicks
     * the "new reservation" button.
     * Show frame to delete a reservation when the user
double-clicks
     * the list.
     */
    ActionListener actionHandler = new ActionListener() {
        public void actionPerformed(ActionEvent e) {
            try {
                if (e.getSource() == reserve)
                    showNewWindow();
                else if (e.getSource() == passengerList)
                    showDeleteWindow();
            } catch (IOException x) {
                System.out.println("could not edit passenger
list");
            }
        }
    };
    reserve.addActionListener(actionHandler);
    passengerList.addActionListener(actionHandler);

    }
```

```java
    private void showDeleteWindow() throws IOException {
       Frame pass;

       // Get the selected entry in the list, if there is
one.
       String name = passengerList.getSelectedItem();
       if (name != null) {
          pass = new DeletePassenger(name, this);
          pass.pack();
          pass.show();
       }
    }

    private void showNewWindow() throws IOException {
       Frame pass;

       pass = new NewPassenger(this);
       pass.pack();
       pass.show();
    }


    public void updateUI() {
       String[] reservations;
       try {
          reservations = new Client().getPassengerList();
       } catch (IOException x) {
          System.out.println("Unable to show list");
          System.out.println(x.getMessage());
          return;
       }
       passengerList.removeAll();

       int total = reservations.length;
       for (int i = 0; i < total; i++)
          passengerList.add(reservations[i]);

       // Update the "make reservation" button as
appropriate.
       if (reservations.length == MAX_SEATS)
          reserve.setEnabled(false);
       else
          reserve.setEnabled(true);

       validate();
    }

}
```

NewPassenger.java

```
package client;

import java.awt.*;
import java.awt.event.*;
import java.io.IOException;

public class NewPassenger extends Frame {
    String     thePassenger;
    TextField  passengerField;
    Choice     seatNumber;
    Button     makeRes;
    CanUpdate  ui;
    int[]      openSeats;

    public NewPassenger(CanUpdate edna) throws IOException {
        super("Make New Reservation");

        ui = edna;

        setLayout(new GridLayout(3, 1));
        Panel p;

        p = new Panel();
        p.add(new Label("passenger: "));

        passengerField = new TextField(30);
        p.add(passengerField);
        add(p);

        p = new Panel();
        openSeats = new Client().getOpenSeats();

        seatNumber = new Choice();
        for (int i = 0; i < openSeats.length; i++) {
            String s = new Integer(openSeats[i]).toString();
            seatNumber.addItem(s);
        }
        p.add(seatNumber);

        add(p);

        p = new Panel();
        makeRes = new Button("make reservation");
        p.add(makeRes);
        add(p);

        WindowAdapter closeHandler = new WindowAdapter() {
```

```
         public void windowClosing(WindowEvent e) {
           Window w = e.getWindow();
           w.setVisible(false);
         }
      };
      addWindowListener(closeHandler);

      ActionListener actionHandler = new ActionListener() {
         public void actionPerformed(ActionEvent e) {

           String passenger = passengerField.getText();
           passenger = passenger.trim();
           if (passenger.length() > 0) {
             int seatIndex = seatNumber.getSelectedIndex();
             int seatNum = openSeats[seatIndex];
             try {
                new Client().reservePassenger(passenger,
seatNum);
             } catch (IOException x) {
                System.out.println("Unable to reserve " +
passenger +
                   "for seat number " + seatNum);
             }
           }

           hide();
           ui.updateUI();
         }
      };
      makeRes.addActionListener(actionHandler);
   }
}
```

DeletePassenger.java

```
package client;

import java.awt.*;
import java.awt.event.*;
import java.io.IOException;

public class DeletePassenger extends Frame {
   String    thePassenger;
   Button    keepRes;
   Button    deleteRes;
```

```
    CanUpdate ui;

  public DeletePassenger(String s, CanUpdate edna) throws
IOException {
      super("Delete Reservation");

      thePassenger = s;
      ui = edna;

      setLayout(new GridLayout(2, 1));
      Panel p;

      p = new Panel();
      p.add(new Label("passenger: " + thePassenger));

      int seat = new Client().getSeat(thePassenger);

      p.add(new Label("seat #: " + seat));

      add(p);

      p = new Panel();
      keepRes = new Button("keep");
      p.add(keepRes);
      deleteRes = new Button("delete");
      p.add(deleteRes);

      add(p);

      WindowAdapter closeHandler = new WindowAdapter() {
        public void windowClosing(WindowEvent e) {
          Window w = e.getWindow();
          w.setVisible(false);
        }
      };
      addWindowListener(closeHandler);

      ActionListener actionHandler = new ActionListener() {
        public void actionPerformed(ActionEvent e) {

          if (e.getSource() == keepRes)
            setVisible(false);
          else if (e.getSource() == deleteRes) {
            try {
              new Client().deletePassenger(thePassenger);
            } catch (IOException x) {
              System.out.println(x.getMessage());
            }
            setVisible(false);
            ui.updateUI();
          }
        }
```

```
        };
        keepRes.addActionListener(actionHandler);
        deleteRes.addActionListener(actionHandler);
    }
}
```

One Possible Answer
for the Server Side

Server.java (Including ClientServerThread)

```java
package server;

import java.io.*;
import java.net.*;

/**
 * The DataServer processes requests from clients to access
the
 * database.
 * The DataServer runs until you hit Control-c. It is a
multithreaded
 *   server and spins off threads to process each connection
 *   from a client.
 * @see server.DB
 * @version 1.1
 * @author Barry Boone / William Stanek
 */
public class Server {

    /** opcode for making a reservation. */
    public static final int OP_MAKE_RESERVATION = 1;

    /** opcode for deleting a reservation. */
    public static final int OP_DELETE = 2;

    /** opcode for getting a passenger's seat. */
    public static final int OP_GET_SEAT = 3;

    /** opcode for getting all open seats. */
```

```
      public static final int OP_GET_OPEN_SEATS = 4;

      /** opcode for getting all passengers. */
      public static final int OP_GET_PASSENGER_LIST = 5;

      private int port = 5001;
      private boolean listening = true;
      private DB db;
      private ServerSocket serverSock;

      /** Start the database server spinning. */
      public static void main(String args[]) {
         int portnum = 5001;

         System.out.println("The server runs until you hit
Control-c");

         try {
            Server server = new Server();
            server.start();
         } catch (IOException x) {
            System.out.println("Could not create server socket:
" +
               x.getMessage());
            System.exit(1);
         }
      }

   /**
    * Put the Server object into action.
    * @exception IOException thrown if we cannot create a
ServerSocket
    *        bound to the specified port
    */
   public void start() throws IOException {

      serverSock = null;
      Socket sock;

      db = new DB();

      try {
         serverSock = new ServerSocket(port, 50);

         while (listening) {

            // Wait for a client to connect with server
               socket.
            // Then spin off a thread to handle the
               connection
            // with the client, repeat.
            try {
```

```
                            // Wait here until contacted by a client.
                            sock = serverSock.accept();

                            new ClientServerThread(sock, db).start();
                        } catch (IOException e) {
                            System.out.println("Connection dropped?: " +
                                e.getMessage());
                        }
                    }

                } finally {
                    serverSock.close();
                    serverSock = null;
                }
            }

        protected void finalize() throws Throwable {
            super.finalize();
            if (serverSock != null) {
                serverSock.close();
                serverSock = null;
            }
        }
    }

    // Handles one transaction with a client.
    class ClientServerThread extends Thread {

        private static final int SUCCESS = 0;
        private static final int FAILURE = 1;

        private static final int PAUSE_FOR = 50;

        private DB db;
        private Socket sock;
        private DataInputStream remoteIn;
        private DataOutputStream remoteOut;

        ClientServerThread(Socket sock, DB db) {
            this.sock = sock;
            this.db = db;
        }

        // This run() method processes just one request from a
client // and then ends.
        public void run() {
            try {
                remoteIn = new
DataInputStream(sock.getInputStream());
                remoteOut = new
DataOutputStream(sock.getOutputStream());
```

```
        // Get the opcode so we know how to handle this
        // transaction.
        int opcode = remoteIn.readInt();

        switch (opcode) {
            case (Server.OP_MAKE_RESERVATION):
                makeReservation();
                break;
            case (Server.OP_DELETE):
                delete();
                break;
            case (Server.OP_GET_SEAT):
                getSeat();
                break;
            case (Server.OP_GET_OPEN_SEATS):
                getOpenSeats();
                break;
            case (Server.OP_GET_PASSENGER_LIST):
                getPassengerList();
                break;
            default:
                done();
                return;
        }

    } catch (IOException e) {
        error(e);
    }
}

// Make a reservation.
// in:  <opcode> <passenger name> <seat number>
// out: <0 OR 1 (success or failure)>
private void makeReservation() {
    try {
        String name = remoteIn.readUTF();
        int seat = remoteIn.readInt();
        db.reservePassenger(name, seat);
        sendToClient(SUCCESS);
    } catch (SeatTakenException x) {
        sendToClient(FAILURE);
    } catch (IOException x) {
        System.out.println(x.getMessage());
        sendToClient(FAILURE);
    } finally {
        done();
    }
}

// Delete a reservation.
// in:  <opcode> <passenger name>
// out: <0 OR 1 (success or failure)>
```

```
private void delete() {
   try {
      String name = remoteIn.readUTF();
      db.deletePassenger(name);
      sendToClient(SUCCESS);
   } catch (IOException e) {
      error(e);
      sendToClient(FAILURE);
   } finally {
      done();
   }
}

// Get a seat given a passenger.
// in:   <opcode> <passenger name>
// out: <seat number> (-1 if no seat found)
private void getSeat()
{
   try {
      String name = remoteIn.readUTF();
      int seat = db.getSeat(name);
      sendToClient(seat);
   } catch (Exception x) {
      sendToClient(FAILURE);
   } finally {
      done();
   }
}

// Get all open seats.
// in:   <opcode>
// out: <number of open seats> { <seat number> }
private void getOpenSeats()
{
   try {
      int[] seats = db.getOpenSeats();
      sendToClient(seats.length);
      for (int i = 0; i < seats.length; i++)
         sendToClient(seats[i]);
   } catch (Exception x) {
   } finally {
      done();
   }
}

// Get passenger list.
// in:   <opcode>
// out: <number of passengers> { <passenger name> }
private void getPassengerList()
{
   try {
      String[] passengers = db.getPassengerList();
```

```
                sendToClient(passengers.length);
                for (int i = 0; i < passengers.length; i++)
                    sendToClient(passengers[i]);
        } catch (Exception x) {
        } finally {
            done();
        }
    }

    // Close the connection with the client.
    private void done() {
        try {
            if (remoteOut != null) {
                remoteOut.close();
                remoteOut = null;
            }

            if (remoteIn != null) {
                remoteIn.close();
                remoteIn = null;
            }
        } catch (IOException x) {
            error(x);
        } finally {
            try {
                if (sock != null) {
                    sock.close();
                    sock = null;
                }
            } catch (IOException x) {
                error(x);
            }
        }
    }

    private void sendToClient(int i) {
        try {
            remoteOut.writeInt(i);
        } catch (IOException x) {
            error(x);
        }

        pause();
    }

    private void sendToClient(String s) {
        try {
            remoteOut.writeUTF(s);
        } catch (IOException x) {
            error(x);
        }
```

```
        }

        // On Windows 95/98, at least when the client and server are
        // running on the same machine, we have to pause for the
        // client to read the data when the server writes it to the
        // socket. Otherwise, the client hangs.
        private void pause() {
            try {
                sleep(PAUSE_FOR);
            } catch (InterruptedException x) {
                error(x);
            }
        }

        private void error(Exception x) {
            System.out.println("Connection dropped?: " +
x.getMessage());
        }

        protected void finalize() throws Throwable {
            super.finalize();
            done();
        }

}
```

The Three Missing Methods from DB.java

```
public synchronized String[] getPassengerList() throws
IOException {
        String[] reservations = null;
        PassengerRecord record;

        FileHeader header = readHeader();

        reservations = new String[header.numPassengers];

        for (int i = 0; i < header.numPassengers; i++) {
            reservations[i] = readNextRecord().getName();
        }
        return reservations;
}

public synchronized int getSeat(String passenger)
        throws IOException, SeatNotFoundException
    {
```

```
        boolean found = false;
        PassengerRecord record;

        int seat = 0; // satisfy the compiler
        FileHeader header = readHeader();

        for (int i = 0; i < header.numPassengers && !found;
    i++) {
            record = readNextRecord();
            if (passenger.equals(record.getName())) {
                found = true;
                seat = record.getSeat();
            }
        }

        if (!found)
            throw new SeatNotFoundException();

        return seat;
    }

    public synchronized void reservePassenger(String
    passenger, int seat)
        throws IOException, SeatTakenException
    {
        // Make sure the seat is still available
        boolean taken = true; // prove it false
        int[] open = getOpenSeats();
        for (int i = 0; i < open.length && taken; i++) {
            if (seat == open[i])
                taken = false;
        }

        if (taken)
            throw new SeatTakenException();

        PassengerRecord record = new PassengerRecord();
        record.setName(passenger);
        record.setSeat(seat);
        writeRecord(record);
    }
```

CHAPTER 25

The Sun-Certified Developer Practice Essay Exam

On the essay exam, there are no absolute right or wrong answers. It includes five to 10 essay questions. Each of these questions asks you to justify your design decisions, comment on your approach to designing applications in Java, and, to some extent, explain how an aspect of Java works in the first place.

You have 90 minutes to answer these questions. On the test, you'll read the question (which often has multiple parts) and then, by clicking a Comment button, you bring up a window to type in your response. You can bring up the Comment window as many times as you like so you can keep on adding to your answer. At the end, you can easily go back over your answers and change them again before submitting them.

Once you do submit them, you'll have to wait until Sun Microsystems has a chance to look over your answers, which can take up to four weeks. So relax until then; you have no choice, anyway. You'll generally know if you did okay. Remember, there are no right or wrong answers. If you justified your design decisions in a way that makes sense, you'll do fine.

To prevent you from worrying about whether you've written too much or not enough, the question instructions state very clearly the maximum number of sentences or words you should stay within as you're typing away.

These practice questions relate to the sample programming assignment from Chapter 24, "The Sun-Certified Developer Practice Programming Assignment." Of course, the questions on the real exam relate to the programming assignment you're asked to complete after you pass the programmer certification exam.

QUESTIONS ■ ■ ■ ■ ■ ■ ■ ■ ■

1. In order for the client and server to talk to each other, they need to agree on a protocol involving opcodes.

   a. Where did you define the opcodes? Did you define these in one place or in more than one? If you only defined the opcodes in one place, how did you use the opcode numbers in other classes? (If you did not need to use opcodes in more than one class, explain why.)

   b. How did you define the opcodes? For example, what did the opcode for making a reservation look like (its value is equal to 1)? Did you create a constant or did you use these numbers inline, written directly in the code? In either case, describe your design decisions that led to your choice.

2. What types of layout managers did you use in `EdnaUI`?

   a. What did you use for the overall layout manager for `EdnaUI`? In no more than two sentences, describe what led to your choice.

   b. How did you make the New Reservation button centered in the bottom of `EdnaUI` without stretching from side to side? If your button has stretched from side to side, how might you use a combination of layout managers so that this does not occur?

3. Many of the methods of the `DB` class are `synchronized`.

   a. In a paragraph, explain why you think this is. What might happen if they were not `synchronized`?

   b. The `reservePassenger()` method in `DB` is one of the three methods in that class that you were asked to implement. Did you throw a `SeatTakenException` (the method declares this method might throw such an exception)? Why or why not? In no more than two paragraphs, describe how it might be possible for this situation to arise (that is, for a seat to be already taken when you call this method) even though most of the `DB` methods are `synchronized`.

4. The following questions relate to how you might extend the client's design.

   a. When your client communicates with the server, does your client wait for the server to respond before it continues? If so, provide an overview in no more than 100 words on how you might redesign your client so the user has the ability to cancel the client's wait for a response and the client does not hang indefinitely if the server is no longer running. If your client already does this, describe your design.

   b. Does your client provide some kind of feedback when it is attempting to communicate with the server? Describe at least two ways to provide feedback and name one advantage for each of them.

5. Describe how TCP/IP works in relation to this program by answering the following questions.

    a. In no more than three paragraphs, describe how the client and server establish a dedicated connection with each other.

    b. In an additional one or two paragraphs, explain how it is possible for there to be two clients and one server all with dedicated connections on the same machine. (In your answer, mention how sockets are used in Java.)

ANSWERS

1. a. The opcodes are defined in the `Server` class and is the only place they are defined. When the `Client` class in the client package needs them, it must import the `Server` class, like this:

```
import server.Server;
```

b. The `Server` class creates constants to define each of the opcodes. The opcode for making a reservation looks like the following:

```
public static final int OP_MAKE_RESERVATION = 1;
```

2. a. The `EdnaUI` object uses a `BorderLayout` overall. The specifications indicate it should arrange objects within it in three sections, which happen to fall naturally into North, Center, and South arrangements.

b. Since `EdnaUI` uses a `BorderLayout`, if the New Reservation button is added directly in the South region, it would stretch from the left edge of `EdnaUI` to the right. To stop this from happening, we can place the button into a panel. This keeps the button centered and at its natural size. We can then place the panel South in `EdnaUI`'s `BorderLayout`.

3. a. The methods in `DB` that are `synchronized` are those that access and change the database. If they are not `synchronized`, then multiple threads can act on different parts of the database at once. This could easily result in the database becoming corrupted. For example, imagine one thread that deleted records as another added records. This could throw off the record count or cause records to be overwritten.

b. Even though the methods in DB are synchronized, that does not mean you don't have to guard against data becoming corrupted by some other mechanism. synchronized methods cannot be executed at the same time by multiple threads. However, in a client/server application such as this one, a client can acquire data, disconnect, and then connect again to act on that data.

That's exactly what happens when a client gets the open seats and then enables a user to pick one. If more than one client is active, both clients will obtain the open seats (one at a time) and try to reserve a seat (again one at a time). This means that there's nothing stopping one client from booking a passenger in the same seat as another client; that's why you must check if the seat is still available and inform the client if it is not.

4. a. The client could spawn a separate thread to perform the communication with the server. In addition, the client could display a window that contains a Stop button. If the user clicks Stop, it halts the communication thread. Otherwise, this window would disappear when the server responds. Note that with Java 1.1, we could make this even better and make the cursor a busy cursor over all parts of the application, except for the Stop button.

b. Two ways to provide feedback to the user are to change the cursor and provide a window containing an informative message. With a cursor, the user knows that any click he makes will be ineffective until the cursor changes back to a normal cursor. With a message, the user can read exactly what the application is doing because the message can explain it to him in detail. A combination of these two approaches might also work well.

5. a. An instance of class ServerSocket waits for a connection by invoking accept(). At this point, the ServerSocket is listening on a particular port for a client to try to connect with it. A client will try to establish a connection by creating a `Socket` instance, specifying the server and the port the server is listening to.

The ServerSocket passes a new port number to the client that he should use for all further communication with the server. This port number gets encoded into the Socket object the client creates and it is also encoded into the Socket object returned by `accept()`.

b. Once the client has a port to use for the dedicated connection, the server continues to listen for more connections on the original port. Each new client, even if it's on the same machine, uses a different port to communicate with the server (even though each client originally connects to the server through the server's one known port).

Java uses `Socket` objects to communicate via TCP/IP. A Java socket object encodes an IP address and a port to use for communication. `ServerSocket` ensures each port is different, so each socket is different, and multiple clients can communicate with the same server; each uses a different port.

Appendices

APPENDIX A

The CD-ROM

The accompanying CD-ROM contains resources to help you use this book more effectively. We've included all the source code in the chapter and exercises, links to key Web sites, Sun's latest JDK, and the javadoc-style API files for the Java packages in HTML format. You'll also find a Java certification application called JCertify.

How the CD-ROM Is Organized

On the CD-ROM, you'll find that the source files and Web links are organized like a Web site. At the top level of the CD-ROM, you'll find a directory named "Web Links and Code." Within this there's a file called index.html. You can view this HTML file with any standard Web browser.

We have included links to these categories:

- Code listings for the chapter text
- Code listings for the exercises
- Answers to the exercises
- Code listings for the review questions
- Code for the programming assignment
- Where to find more about Java and Java certification

Source Code

The code listings are organized by chapter. Just follow the links until you're looking at Java code.

Sun's JDK

The reason this book includes the JDK is that the exam assumes you are using the JDK to develop your code. You can always grab newer versions of the JDK off the JavaSoft Web site, but for your convenience it's included on the CD-ROM as well. To find installation notes and troubleshooting ideas for the JDK, you can visit `http://java.sun.com/products/OV_jdkProduct.html`.

Web Links

For all the latest and greatest information concerning this book and Java certification, we've included links to places on the Web. You'll find this on the CD-ROM in the HTML files by following the link titled "Where to Find More About Java and Java Certification."

What Is JCertify?

JCertify is a training tool for the Sun-certified Programmer Exam on the Java 2 platform (Exam number 310-025). The program provides an interactive training environment and an exam simulator. You'll also find extensive on-line help and you can even create your own personalized practice exams.

APPENDIX B

The Java Development Kit (JDK)

The programmer test assumes you are using Sun's *Java Development Kit* (JDK). The JDK often insists on certain configurations, and it has its own commands and characteristics not shared by all development environments. Let's take a quick look at how to use the JDK. I'll also touch some aspects of the JDK that might appear on the test.

The Pieces of the JDK

First, in case you're using a different development environment, you might find it useful to get an overall picture of the JDK. This environment is not graphical; instead, you issue commands from the command line. For example, to compile a program, you type `javac`, list any options, and then type the name of the file or files you wish to compile.

The JDK comes with the following:

- A compiler
- *A Java Virtual Machine* (JVM) runtime environment for standalone programs
- An applet viewer to run applets without the need for starting a full-blown Web browser
- A debugger
- Documentation

The debugger is not mentioned on the exam, and we've already covered `javadoc`-style comments in Chapter 24, "The Sun-Certified Developer Practice Programming Assignment," which is the format for the JDK's documentation. That leaves the compiler, the runtime environment for standalone programs, and the `appletviewer`.

The Compiler

Execute the compiler using the command `javac`. Invoking `javac` can be as simple as naming the Java source file you want to compile:

```
javac Bagel.java
```

Here are three compiler options you might find useful:

- You can specify the `-classpath` path option to tell the compiler where your class files exist. Without this option, the compiler relies on the CLASSPATH environment variable to find the class files you want to include.

- The `-d` directory option tells the compiler to place the classes it generates into a particular directory. You can use this option when creating classes that belong in packages. For example, if you have defined a source file named `CertClass.java` that contains code like this

```
package cert.util;
class CertClass { }
```

you can compile this class and generate the directory structure Java expects to be in place with packages by issuing the command

```
javac -d . Certclass.java
```

`javac` creates a new directory at the same node as your source file, `cert`. Below that, it creates a directory called `util` and it places `CertClass.class` within `util`.

Also, the compiler option `-O` enables the compiler to generate inline code for `static`, `final`, and `private` methods. This option stands for "optimize."

The JDK enforces the rule that `public` classes must be placed in a file named after the class. If `CertClass` is declared as `public`, it would have to be placed in a file named `CertClass.java`. Although you can place as many classes in the same source file as you want, you can only have one `public` class per file.

The Runtime Environment for Standalone Programs

You can invoke the Java interpreter using the command `java`. You pass the interpreter the name of the class you want to run, not the file name. For example, you can run the `Bagel` class by typing

```
java Bagel
```

The interpreter will seek out this class's `public`, `static main()` method. This method must not return a value, and it must take an array of string objects. If the `main()` method is declared in any other way, the interpreter will complain that it cannot find the `main()` method it was looking for and it will not run your class.

You might be interested in the `-classpath`, `-noasyncgc`, and `-verbosegc` options:

■ As with the compiler, you can specify the `-classpath path` option to tell the compiler where your class files are. Without this option, the compiler relies on the CLASSPATH environment variable to find the class files you want to include.

■ The `-noasyncgc` option turns off garbage collection.

■ The `-verbosegc` option asks the interpreter to tell you when it has performed the garbage collection.

appletviewer

You can use the `appletviewer` command to test an applet without starting a full-fledged Web browser. You pass the `appletviewer` command the name of an HTML file that references your applet class. For example, if you have an HTML file named `Bagel.html` that includes an `<applet>` tag referencing an `Applet` subclass, you can type

```
appletviewer Bagel.html
```

You don't have to only provide the name of a local HTML file. You can supply any URL as the parameter to `appletviewer`. Another useful feature is the `-debug` option, which writes debugging messages to the standard error.

INDEX

Symbols

"" (quotes), spaces in applet parameter values, 284

& operator, 149

&& (short-circuit) operator, 145, 172, 607

() separators, expression evaluation precedence, 155

<< operator, 148

@author tag, 436

@exception tag, 436

@param tag, 436

@return tag, 436

@see tag, 432, 435

@throws tag, 436

@version tag, 436

A

Abs() method, Math class, 227

abstract classes
   comments, javadoc tags, 440
   defining legal, 589

Abstract keyword, 46, 83

Abstract method, 46–47, 51, 73

Accept() method, 497, 508

access control, 39
   between classes, 59
   exam objectives, 17
   keywords, 54–59, 600
   overriding methods, 210

access methods, writing code, 446–448

access restrictions, writing code, 444

Access, *see* Microsoft Access

accessor methods, variables, 311

Action() method, SingleChat application, 509

ActionEvent subclass, 375, 385–387

ActionListener interface, 379

Adapter class, 391

Add() method, 545
   adding components to containers, 345
   populating lists, 350

AddABCListener() method, 377

AddContainerListener() method, 566

adding components to containers, 545

AddMouseListener() method, 383

addresses, IP, 487, 496

AdjustmentEvent subclass, 375, 385–387

AdjustmentListener interface, 380

administering exam, 21–27

alive threads, 300

allocating memory, JVM, 106

AncestorEvent class, 375

anonymous classes, 402

APIs (Application Programming Interfaces)
   Collection, 239
   multi-tiered architectures, 462
   writing code, interfaces, 442

Append() method, StringBuffer class, 237, 248

appending files, 267–268

Applet class, getParameter() method, 285, 331

applets
   bouncing ball, 305
      Runnable interface, 306
      thread management, 317–320
      Thread subclass, 303
   chase tags, 283
   Click Me
      inner classes, 403
      listener interface, 383–384
   ClickApplet, 312
   coverting to applications, 547–548
   customizing, 287
   embedding in HTML pages, 282
   measurement conversion, 287–290
   number display, inner classes, 399–401

L

M

P